MATHEMATICS RESEARCH DEVELOPMENTS

MODELING OF CORRUPTION IN HIERARCHICAL ORGANIZATIONS

MATHEMATICS RESEARCH DEVELOPMENTS

Additional books in this series can be found on Nova's website
under the Series tab.

Additional e-books in this series can be found on Nova's website
under the e-book tab.

MATHEMATICS RESEARCH DEVELOPMENTS

MODELING OF CORRUPTION IN HIERARCHICAL ORGANIZATIONS

OLGA I. GORBANEVA
GUENNADY A. OUGOLNITSKY
AND
ANATOLY B. USOV

nova publishers
New York

Library of Congress Cataloging-in-Publication Data

Names: Gorbaneva, Olga I., author. | Ougolnitsky, Guennady, author. | Usov, Anatoly B., author.
Title: Modeling of corruption in hierarchical organizations / Olga I. Gorbaneva, Guennady A. Ougolnitsky, and Anatoly B. Usov (Southern Federal University, Russian Federation).
Description: Hauppauge, New York : Nova Science Publishers, Inc., [2016] | Series: Mathematics research developments | Includes bibliographical references and index.
Identifiers: LCCN 2015050165 (print) | LCCN 2016005043 (ebook) | ISBN 9781634843980 (hardcover) | ISBN 9781634845212 ()
Subjects: LCSH: Corruption--Mathematical models. | Bribery--Mathematical models. | Ethics--Mathematical models. | Management--Moral and ethical aspects.
Classification: LCC HV6768 .G664 2016 (print) | LCC HV6768 (ebook) | DDC 658.4/7--dc23
LC record available at http://lccn.loc.gov/2015050165

Published by Nova Science Publishers, Inc. † New York

CONTENTS

INTRODUCTION

Describing corruption as a complex socioeconomic phenomenon, endeavoring to reveal the regularities of corruption behavior based on its mathematical modeling and to suggest a system of restrictive measures for the negative impact of this phenomenon on a society and a national economy represents a very ambitious intention whose comprehensive coverage goes beyond the scope of a monograph. Therefore, let us formulate a series of propositions outlining the specifics of this book and its place against the background of other research works in the field.

First, our study focuses on hierarchical organizational structures. On the one hand, this specifies the class of models to-be-used, as the "Principal – supervisor – agent – object" structure becomes the main object of modeling. This structure is considered fully (with explicit description of the object's dynamics) in the dynamic case and partially (with implicit description of the object, i.e., confined to the agent's impact on the object) in the static case. On the other hand, such an approach does not cause appreciable loss of generality, since a hierarchical structure is inherent to an overwhelming majority of social organizations of any scale, level, form and field of activity.

Second, we perform modeling in the context of solving control problems. Control-related analysis covers the activity of an agent as a potential or real briber, a supervisor as a government official inclined to bribery and a Principal as a subject of anti-corruption struggle (note that wider interpretations are also possible). In the elementary setting (from the agent's viewpoint), this leads to a static optimization problem or a dynamic optimal control problem. In the general case, the noncoinciding interests of all participants make the hierarchical game-theoretic (static and dynamic) settings of conflict control problems more adequate. Here a leader (a Principal or supervisor, depending on the level of analysis) applies administrative (compulsion) and economic (impulsion) control method. The basic idea lies in treating corruption as additional feedback in the control loop by bribe amount. And we share the following opinion expressed in the monograph (Russian corruption, 2013) which will be repeatedly mentioned throughout this book: "To the degree corruption induces management inefficiency, it is a key to identify this inefficiency. Therefore, by studying corruption, we discover tools to improve management efficiency." (p. 77).

Third, in the conditions of corruption a major task of control consists in ensuring sustainable development of modeled hierarchical organizations. Here we proceed from the original concept of sustainable management (Ougolnitsky, 2002, 2005, 2010, 2011; Ougolnitsky and Usov, 2010-2014). In contrast to the classical approach of Gary Becker and

Susan Rose-Ackerman (which states that the efficiency of anti-corruption struggle is defined via comparing losses due to corruption and the costs of such measures), the above concept applies certain requirements of sustainable development of a modeled system with proper consideration of economic restrictions.

Fourth, a prominent role belongs to a complex issue on the empirical base of investigations and identification of mathematical models used. No doubt, it is necessary to solve the measurement problem with regard to any object of scientific research, as measurements form an integral part of science. Another well-known fact is that data acquisition in socioeconomic studies causes much more difficulties than in natural science studies, although considerable methodological problems in the latter do exist. Georgy Satarov noted the existence of two major approaches to corruption measurement, namely, the sociological approach (surveys with results processing) and the empirical approach (international indices assessing corruption in different countries), see (Levin et al., 2011, p. 251). Actually, the second approach is inapplicable within our research, since international indices do not serve for identification of hierarchical control models in the conditions of corruption. The sociological approach is more flexible and universal by far. Its detailed description and practical interpretation in the context of corruption analysis can be found in the fundamental monograph edited by Satarov (Russian Corruption, 2013). Moreover, the cited book adopted the model of Principal-agent relations as the theoretical base of public administration analysis in Russia, which agrees with our concept. Nevertheless, direct usage of the available data (to say nothing of other sociological studies data) for model identification in our research seems impossible. The underlying reasons are obvious: the authors of other studies posed different problems and answered different questions. Therefore, to use the data acquired by other investigators, we have to construct a certain "transition module"; in the sense of labor intensiveness, this task is comparable with organization of a separate sociological study. Even more the aforesaid concerns any attempts to employ existing statistical data on corruption as a delicate problem (e.g., the results of BEEPS surveys).

Hence, a way of principle to solve the problem is conducting special sociological studies focused on identification of sustainable management models of hierarchical organizations in the conditions of corruption (i.e., according to a client's order). Here we inevitably face systematic, organizational and financial problems whose solution appreciably exceeds the capabilities of the current research project.

And so, we have recourse to the following methodology. Model relationships proceed from general beliefs about the nature of corruption, which allow establishing basic qualitative properties of corresponding functions (e.g., monotone increase or decrease, convexity or concavity, optimum points, etc.). Then it is possible to choose classes of functions enjoying required properties. The primary aim of our research is revelation of qualitative regularities in corruption behavior and, on the one hand, numerical identification of functions from chosen classes seems not important in many cases. Roughly speaking, in the class of linear functions $y = ax + b$, not the absolute value of the coefficient a but its sign is crucial for qualitative analysis. On the other hand, if the inclination of a line and its intersection points with coordinate axes do matter, one can perform (a) simulation experiments for different values of the coefficients and (b) the practical interpretation of the derived results. This identification methodology will be described in detail in the course of further exposition.

Despite the stated arguments, the chiefly mental and somewhat conditional character of the models is to all appearance the most susceptible attribute of this work often subjected to criticism. Nevertheless, we believe that constructing a logically consistent system of models for the complex socioeconomic phenomenon of corruption based on plausible assumptions reflecting real experience (some assumptions can be refined to become axioms), as well as on preceding studies is well justified and can yield practically sound conclusions, interpretations and recommendations.

Therefore, the main idea of our research consists in designing a system of universal theoretical models describing basic regularities of corruption behavior in hierarchical control systems, regardless of their industrial, territorial, cultural, historical or other specifics. The capabilities gained by additional consideration of such specifics are illustrated by some applications of the theoretical models.

The formulated assertions define the structure and content of the monograph (their complete set underlying the authors' concept of corruption modeling in hierarchical control systems is discussed in detail in Section 1.2).

Chapter 1 is dedicated to existing mathematical models of corruption. Section 1.1 overviews and classifies the mathematical models of corruption in hierarchical control systems. As classification bases, we choose the domains of corruption (microeconomics, macroeconomics, politics), the type of models (static, dynamic ones) and mathematical apparatus employed (optimization and optimal control theory, game theory, simulation modeling). And Section 1.2 introduces the authors' concept of corruption modeling based on sustainable management theory.

Chapter 2 considers the theoretical models of corruption in hierarchical control systems. The logic of exposition is defined by the matrix "statics – dynamics" and "administrative corruption – economic corruption." Under administrative (economic) corruption, a briber relaxes administrative (economic, respectively) requirements of an upper-level control subject. In the sense of modeling, administrative corruption means compulsion (an impact on the admissible control domain) of an agent by a supervisor with bribe feedback, whereas economic corruption represents impulsion (an impact on the payoff function) of an agent by a supervisor with unique or additional bribe feedback. In all cases, we construct a sequence of gradually complicated models providing more and more accurate description of real corruption phenomena in hierarchical control systems. The main logical scheme of such a complication is "optimization models – hierarchical two-player games – hierarchical three-player games" (in statics) and "optimal control problems – hierarchical dynamic two-player games – hierarchical dynamic three-player games" (in dynamics). In addition, Chapter 2 describes a simulation complex for static models of corruption. We characterize the regularities of corruption behavior depending on the model parameters, as well as formulate appropriate recommendations on anti-corruption measures. The definitions of compulsion and impulsion equilibria are given for dynamic models considering sustainable development requirements in the conditions of corruption, including some algorithms of their evaluation.

Chapter 3 presents the applied models of corruption in hierarchical control systems. A hierarchical system of control models of investment and construction projects in the conditions of corruption is characterized. A sequence of gradually complicated quality control models in production systems with corruption is described, which realizes the idea of quality management compliance with sustainable development in organizational control. Next, we study a hierarchical system of electricity stealing prevention models. Analysis models for (im)proper resource utilization in hierarchical control systems are suggested. And finally, we design and explore quality control models of water resources in hierarchical ecological-economic systems, which involve the definitions of compulsion and impulsion equilibria with due consideration of sustainable development requirements in the conditions of corruption (including some algorithms of their evaluation). The created software tools and the results of numerical experiments are demonstrated.

The monograph summarizes the outcomes of decennial investigations performed by the authors, with the most active phase in the recent four years (2012-2015) owing to the deeply appreciated support from the Russian Foundation for Basic Research (projects 12-01-00017-a, 15-01-00432-a). The authors are also grateful to Andrei Antonenko, Konstantin Denin, Sergei Kornienko and Evgeny Rybasov for their materials used in compilation of the book. Sincere gratitude belongs to the reviewers for careful reading of the monograph, support and helpful remarks.

And finally, a deep appreciation is addressed to A. Mazurov for his careful translation, permanent feedback and contribution to the English version of the book.

Chapter 1

Corruption Problem and Its Mathematical Modeling

Section 1.1 overviews and examines mathematical models of corruption. The fundamental models of anti-corruption struggle (S. Rose-Ackerman) and rent-seeking behavior (G. Tullock) are considered. For convenience of general survey, this monograph adopts a somewhat conditional "matrix" classification of corruption models. On the one hand, classification bases are the common domains of corruption (microeconomics, macroeconomics, politics); on the other hand, they are the type of models (static, dynamic ones) and mathematical apparatus employed (optimization and optimal control theory, game theory, simulation modeling). A special emphasis is placed on the models of corruption in hierarchical structures. A brief discussion touches upon identification of corruption models, with certain conclusions drawn using performed analysis.

Section 1.2 introduces the authors' concept of corruption modeling in hierarchical systems based on sustainable management theory. We formulate the basic assertions of this theory, *viz*., give a characterization of compulsion, impulsion and cooperation as hierarchical control methods; describe sustainable development requirements (homeostasis, compromise, time consistency); substantiate transition from the framework of a controlled dynamic system to the framework of a hierarchically controlled dynamic system which is more adequate to the sustainable management problem. The authors' early sustainable management models of ecological-economic systems in the conditions of corruption are considered. And finally, the major theses forming the concept of corruption modeling are stated and discussed.

1.1. Mathematical Models of Corruption: A Survey and Analysis

Basic models. As a matter of fact, there are hundreds of publications on mathematical modeling of corruption and their comprehensive overview seems unreal. We pay almost no attention to the practical aspects of corruption, particularly, the debates whether this phenomenon is purely negative (G. Myrdal) or possesses a fruitful effect under some conditions (S. Huntington), referring an interested reader to (Klyamkin and Timofeev, 2000; Luneev, 2000; Timofeev, 2000; Myslovsky, 2007; Levin and Satarov, 2012; Russian

Corruption, 2013; Aidt, 2003; International Handbook, 2006; Lambsdorff, 2007; Rose-Ackerman, 2010). Instead, this section endeavors to provide a general idea of corruption modeling, stressing on corruption relations in hierarchical control systems.

The main methodological premise of most research works on anti-corruption modeling is Gary Becker's general economic rule of crime, see (Becker, 1968): it is necessary to compare losses caused by corruption with the costs of anti-corruption measures. According to Becker, fight against crime (particularly, corruption) appears reasonable and efficient if benefits from prevented losses exceed the costs of anti-corruption measures. A similar approach is employed by Russian researchers M. Levin and G. Satarov (2012) to analyze economic behavior strategies of entrepreneurs: by assumption, the latter choose between the legal strategy (honesty) and the corruption strategy (bribery). Each strategy incurs certain costs including direct costs, risk assessment, moral losses and so on. The strategy associated with the minimum total costs is the solution.

Becker's approach was refined with regard to mathematical modeling of corruption by Susan Rose-Ackerman in the seminal paper (Rose-Ackerman, 1975) and further developed in her monographs (Rose-Ackerman, 1978, 1999). The paper (Rose-Ackerman, 1975) presented a series of models describing the corruption behavior of economic subjects under the following conditions.

Government plans to acquire some product on a competitive market and delegates the monopoly right for signing a purchase contract to a bureaucrat (executor). The product is manufactured and sold by several firms (clients) at different price and quality. Each client tries to bribe the executor for concluding the purchase contract. Both the executor and clients can be penalized for bribery, thereby having material and moral losses. Government precisely formulates its preferences regarding the product, and several firms compete for the purchase contract. Different modifications of the model assume that either all firms provide a homogeneous product, or the products of firms differ.

Analysis focuses on the conditions guaranteeing illegal bargaining (i.e., contract conclusion "for bribery") and bribe evaluation under certain assumptions on the behavior of participants and contract conclusion conditions.

While exploring the model with precisely formulated preferences and homogeneous product, Rose-Ackerman made the following conclusion. The bureaucrat defines the winning firm according to the bribe it suggests. Suppose that all firms have identical expected penalties; then the winner is the firm described by the largest difference between the income and the sum of production costs and moral losses under a fixed bribe. Since production costs and moral losses are treated similarly, the maximum bribe a firm is willing to pay decreases due to higher production costs or positive changes in the civil conscience of its top managers.

While exploring the model with imprecisely formulated preferences and homogeneous product, Rose-Ackerman suggested the following three-step procedure of winner choice without cooperation among firms. First, for each firm define a function as a combination of product price and bribe leading to zero profit of the firm. Second, find the price-quality combinations maximizing the payoff function of the bureaucrat under zero profit of the firm (as the difference between its income from product sales, bribe and losses). And third, choose the firm maximizing the bureaucrat's profit.

The cited paper considered several types of the firm's penalty functions:

F1. Penalty is a function of bribe amount, while the probability of bribery detection is a convex function of firm income. By assumption, penalty (a concave function) increases simultaneously with unit product price.
F2. Penalty is a monotone increasing concave function of firm income, while the probability of bribery detection and conviction does not explicitly depend on firm income or depends on possible penalty by a court order.

It was demonstrated that penalization using functions F1 may lead to situations when a corruption equilibrium is potentially infinite (this testifies to low efficiency of such strategies). Corruption equilibria do not possess similar properties in the case of penalization using functions F2.

Rose-Ackerman studied two penalty strategies of bureaucrats, namely:

- penalty is independent from bribe amount, while the probability of conviction depends on the amount of contract;
- penalty imposed on a bribetaker is comparable with bribe amount.

By analyzing the combinations of penalty strategies of both players, the author concluded that, in some cases, bribery prosecution can be inefficient due to potentially infinite corruption equilibria. She also noted that the existence conditions of such equilibria are asymmetrical for the players: the penalty of a firm does not depend explicitly on its income, while the penalty of a bureaucrat does not depend on bribe amount. Adherence to the inverse conditions allows eliminating corruption via reasonable (yet, finite) penalties. However, such conditions are not sufficient. As a sufficient condition, the author mentioned a direct functional relationship between penalty and the probability of bribery detection.

Concerning general recommendations on anti-corruption struggle in the case of government purchases, it was counseled to provide an accurate description of product characteristics and the existence of a product market (as far as possible). If market creation seems impossible, it was counseled not to purchase products from private firms, but to organize production at government-owned enterprises owing to higher control of top management activity and wider impact capabilities, as well as smaller costs of crime detection and penalization (Rose-Ackerman, 1975).

Another fundamental direction in the field concerns the models of rent-seeking behavior developed by George Tullock and its followers (Tullock, 1967; Toward a Theory, 1980). Note that rent-seeking behavior (opportunism) is more general in comparison with corruption; Williamson (1981) defined opportunism as "self-interest seeking with guile."

In the principal paper, Tullock mentioned that appreciable resources of a society can be simply wasted trying to gain economic rent (Tullock, 1967). Later the researcher introduced a game-theoretic approach for rent-seeking behavior modeling. Within the framework of his basic model, n competing groups struggle for rent by consuming some resource x_i, where i denotes the number of a group. The probability p_i that group i achieves a favorable result is defined by $p_i = \frac{\alpha_i x_i}{\sum_{j=1}^{n} \alpha_j x_j}$, where α_i means the relative weight of resources available to group i, $0 < \alpha_i \leq 1, \sum_{j=1}^{n} \alpha_j = 1$. The coefficients α_i show that different groups may have different return from struggle for rent (Toward a Theory, 1980). For a detailed treatment of rent-seeking behavior models, we refer to (Levin et al., 2011). A recent research work in this direction is the paper (Kahana and Qijun, 2010); using the example of China, the authors considered corruption as a tool for accumulating financial resources necessary for career development.

There exist various approaches to separate out types and forms of corruption and classify corresponding models. For instance, a possible classification of corruption types is the following:

1. government (bureaucratic) corruption when an official disposes of a government resource committed to it for personal mercenary ends, and private corruption when an employee of a private firm disposes of a firm resource committed to it for personal mercenary ends;
2. external corruption when an act of corruption occurs between representatives of different economic structures (private firms or government authorities) using a monopolized resource (in most cases, by a government authority), and internal corruption when an act of corruption occurs within a same economic structure (a firm or government authority);
3. economic corruption when a deal yields a direct positive economic effect to a corruptor, e.g., establishing higher quotas or partial immunity from taxation in exchange for an illegal payment by a client (a bribe) unobservable or observable with some delay by superior authorities, and non-economic corruption a deal yields an indirect positive economic effect to a corruptor. For instance, non-economic corruption covers political corruption in the context of bribery of voters: a corruptor obtains greater power than in the case of honest elections, thereby gaining higher economic effect (Denin and Ougolnitsky, 2010).

Within the scope of government corruption, M. Levin and G. Satarov identified social corruption arising in everyday interaction of citizens and authorities in the fields of public health, education, legal proceedings, etc., and business corruption arising in the mutual relations of business structures and authorities. Furthermore, the authors distinguished among Western, Eastern, Latin American, African and Socialistic corruption based on sociocultural attributes (Levin and Satarov, 2012).

According to the Russian tradition, corruption was classified as payments for legal actions (bribery) or illegal decisions (extortion), only the latter was treated as a crime.

The general survey in this monograph adopts the “matrix” classification of corruption models, which appears somewhat conditional. On the one hand, classification bases include the general domains of corruption (microeconomics, macroeconomics, politics); on the other hand, they are the type of models (static, dynamic ones) and mathematical apparatus employed (optimization and optimal control theory, game theory, simulation modeling). Corruption models in hierarchical structures are studied separately.

Static models of corruption in microeconomics. This group mostly includes optimization and game-theoretic models describing corruption relations of firms and separate entrepreneurs with government officials, both in social and business fields (the so-called petty corruption). Consider several typical examples.

The paper (Cadot, 1987) studied a game-theoretic model of corruption in permit issuance. Let us discuss possible results of such interaction in detail, as it admits numerous applications (similar situations arise in licensing of a particular activity including issuance of driver's licenses and health certificates, product quality assessment or certification according to certain standards, paper review, financial projects expertise, and so on).

Suppose that an official tests all candidates for permit issuance according to some procedure. The procedure is objective, but the ultimate decision regarding the results of testing belongs to the official. There exist two types of candidates, namely, "good" (qualified) ones, i.e., meeting the procedural requirements and objectively deserving the permit, and "bad" (non-qualified) ones, i.e., not meeting the above requirements. On the other hand, officials are also of two types, *viz.*, "honest" ones assessing all candidates objectively and "corrupt" ones neglecting the objective picture in exchange for a bribe. The expected utility of corrupt officials comprises their legal income (wage) and bribes. In this case, four outcomes are possible, as illustrated by Table1.1.1.

Table 1.1.1. Possible outcomes in permit issuance

Candidate Official	Good	Bad
Honest	Permit issuance	Refusal of permit issuance
Corrupt	Possibly, illegal bribe exacting in exchange for permit issuance (extortion)	Possibly, illegal permit issuance in exchange for a bribe (collusion, capture)

Table 1.1.1 shows that the strategies of an honest official have no connection to corruption. A good candidate surely receives a permit, whereas a bad one surely does not. A corrupt official adheres to strategies of two types. First, a bad candidate may receive an illegal permit in exchange for a bribe. This form of corruption is called collusion or capture (i.e., an official gives in to a briber). Second, a corrupt official may exact a bribe even from a good candidate by threatening with refusal of permit issuance. This form of corruption is called extortion.

The framework of the model (Cadot, 1987) proceeded from the following assumption. If a corrupted official exacts a bribe, a candidate either agrees and receives the permit or submits a complaint; in the latter case, the official suffers from the lifelong ban on employment and deprivation of any income, while the candidate takes no risk.

According to the methodology of contract theory, a key role in the model belongs to the assumptions imposed on the information sets of players. First, Cadot examined the case of perfect awareness, where all candidates know their own types and the result of the testing procedure (accept or reject). This determines construction of a simple separating equilibrium. Recall that, in contract theory, a separating equilibrium in a game is when different-type players choose different actions, in contrast to a uniting equilibrium when all players act identically (Yudkevich et al., 2002). Second, the author analyzed the case of asymmetrical awareness, where the official knows the result of the testing procedure but a candidate does not (this leads to possible manipulation). However, a candidate possesses an a priori belief about its type, which is correct in the following sense. A good candidate has a higher a priori probability of test passing than a bad one. The official also possesses some a priori beliefs. In this case, a separating or uniting equilibrium occurs depending on players' characteristics. And third, the assumption on the imperfect awareness of both sides was made. Here a candidate does not know its type, but has an a priori belief about it (which is not available to the official). And so, the official cannot predict the response of a candidate to bribe exacting.

The mentioned paper also explored the comparative statics and the impact of the risk function. It was demonstrated that: 1) increasing the discount factor of the official causes corruption growth; 2) officials with higher risk aversion exact smaller bribes; 3) higher wages of officials reduce corruption; 4) in the linear case, the impact of the risk function reflecting how an official correlates the critical bribe amount with corruption level becomes ambiguous (Cadot, 1987).

The publication (Bliss and Di Tella, 1997) considered the competition-corruption model, where bribery is caused by a group of corrupted bureaucrats confiscate some income of firms under their control. The number of firms and corruption level were treated as the internal variables of the model. The authors investigated three approaches to describe competition level, namely: 1) as a variable characterizing the object of tough competition among the firms; 2) as a tendency towards close costs structures; 3) as a tendency towards costs decrease against profit.

The conducted analysis of the model demonstrated that, generally, higher competition does not imply smaller corruption. Even in the simplest model, the key role belongs to the agent's awareness about the costs structure of a firm.

The impact of competition among officials on corruption was also investigated in (Drugov, 2010). The author considered the set of outcomes shown by Table 1.1.1. Actually, two testing modes were assumed, namely, the monopoly mode (a permit can be issued by a unique a priori known official) and the competition mode (a permit can be issued by any official from some set). Striking examples are the driver's licensing procedures established in Russia and India, respectively. Drugov's model took into account that each candidate may invest in its professional development.

The cited research yielded the following primary result. The monopoly mode leads to a better ex post distribution of licenses from the social viewpoint when the investments of candidates are known. On the contrary, in the competition mode candidates have more relevant ex ante motives for investments. Really, competition stimulates more candidates to invest in their professional development reckoning on an honest official. However, non-investing candidates can receive a permit with higher probability by facing a corrupt official. In this case, the total impact on public welfare becomes ambiguous and depends, among other factors, on the distribution of investment costs. If they are small for most firms, then ex ante motives are strong and competition becomes more beneficial. If they are high and candidates do not invest anyway, monopoly has higher preference. The first situation corresponds to driver's license issuance, whereas the second one characterizes acquiring the citizenship of some country (Drugov, 2010).

One of the pioneering Russian works in this direction (Polterovich, 1998) was focused on a game-theoretic model incorporating a certain number of firms and a bureaucrat. Each firm possesses some circulating capital and is characterized by a production function reflecting investment costs and the amount of produced goods. The bureaucrat levies a tax, and its share is transformed into public goods. However, the bureaucrat offers any firm a share of collected incomes (as subsidies or tax privileges) in exchange for a bribe. The author proved the existence of two equilibria:

1. corruption equilibrium; in such an equilibrium, each firm distributes capital between production and bribes in some ratio. The bureaucrat distributes the levied taxes to public goods production or subsidies. The amount of subsidies is chosen via comparing the income from taken bribes and the expected losses due to bribery detection.
2. non-corruption equilibrium: a firm utilizes capital only for goods production. The bureaucrat is absolutely honest.

V. Polterovich examined the conditions making a non-corruption equilibrium Pareto improving in comparison with its corruption counterpart:

A. Tax burden is not "very high";
B. Production is "efficient enough."

In addition, the above paper considered a game-theoretic model with a fixed finite number of bureaucrats serving a homogeneous flow of visitors. Each bureaucrat defines a share of visitors to-be-exacted a fixed bribe. If a bureaucrat takes no bribes, its payoff equals its wage only. Owing to a successful corruption deal, a bureaucrat receives the bribe also. Otherwise (a superior official discovers the fact of the deal), the bureaucrat has zero payoff. The probability of successful deal depends on the "mean rate" of corruption in the system. The author found two Nash equilibria in the game, *viz.*, (1) a non-corruption equilibrium corresponding to the absolute honesty of all bureaucrats and (2) an absolute corruption equilibrium, where all bureaucrats adhere to bribery (the so-called corruption trap). Model modification by replacing the deprivation of wage for a fixed penalty for bribery leads to the following result. The model still admits two Nash equilibria similar to the above ones. It was noted that higher penalties reduce the attraction domain of the absolute corruption equilibrium; starting from a certain threshold, the non-corruption domain becomes more beneficial.

On the basis of the suggested models, the author explained the growing corruption phenomenon for countries in transition: the difference between the basic wage of a bureaucrat and the expected bribe acceptable for clients increases appreciably. At the same time, penalties for bribery remain invariable, which extends the attraction domain of the absolute corruption equilibrium. Consequently, economy walks into the corruption trap (Polterovich, 1998).

A close approach was adopted in the papers (Cule and Fulton, 2005, 2009) dedicated to the tax evasion problem. The authors considered a group of firms having taxable profits and deciding whether to pay taxes honestly or avoid and a group of tax officers deciding whether to penalize law-breakers (in the case of fraud detection) or allow their escape by bribes.

For tax officials, the costs are described by a random variable α with a density function $g(\alpha)$ and a cumulative distribution function $G(\alpha)$; for firms, the costs are characterized by a random variable β with a density function $h(\beta)$ and a cumulative distribution function $H(\beta)$. The functions $g(\alpha), h(\beta)$ are strictly positive, unimodal and defined on certain segments of the positive semiaxis. To incorporate a more practical structure into the model, the corruption costs of tax officers with a characteristic α and the fraud costs of firms with a characteristic β were assumed to be $\lambda\alpha$ and $\mu\beta$, respectively.

The nonnegative parameters λ and μ have two possible interpretations. First, they may reflect attitude to government and its laws including moral losses caused by illegal activity. Second, these parameters may describe transaction costs of agents' activity. In the earlier paper, Cule and Fulton treated λ and μ as constants; later, $\lambda = \lambda(x)$ and $\mu = \mu(y)$ were functions of the shares x and y of tax officials and firms, respectively, involved in corruption activity. The performed analysis of the game-theoretic model resulted in the following conclusions.

1. If there exist multiple equilibria, then some of them are "good" (tax evasion of firms and corruption of tax officials appear relatively small) and "bad" (both indicators have relatively large values). The existence of a certain-type equilibrium is determined by coordination among the players. Good equilibria occur when most firms and tax officials prefer honesty, whereas bad equilibria take place in the opposite case.

2. Under the introduced assumptions on the model functions, increasing the frequency of tax audits and penalties reduces tax evasion in stable good equilibria (under relatively small x, y). The opposite result when increasing the frequency of tax audits and penalties enhances tax evasion is more probable in bad equilibria (under relatively small x, y); in addition, here the mode $g(\alpha)$ is achieved for relatively large α and the distribution on the right from the mode is rather flat.

3. Under the introduced assumptions on the model functions, increasing the frequency of tax audits and penalties reduces corruption in stable good equilibria (under relatively small x, y). The opposite result when increasing the frequency of tax audits and penalties enhances corruption is more probable in bad equilibria (under relatively small x, y); in addition, here the function $\mu(y)$ is nonelastic, the mode $h(\beta)$ is achieved for relatively small large β and the distribution on the left from the mode is rather flat.

Therefore, business culture and tax audit culture can lead to different-type equilibria. In bad equilibria (characterized by high levels of fraud and corruption), increasing penalties and the frequency of tax audits merely deteriorate the things. As tax evasion and corruption become widespread, they intensify each other and their costs go down (Cule and Fulton, 2009).

Dynamic models of corruption in microeconomics. This class of models describes same phenomena as static models, but in terms of multistep (generally, hierarchical) games (some publications also employ optimal control models and differential games). For instance, Biccieri and Rovelli (1995) demonstrated that corruption evolution in an economy may spontaneously cause an explosion, i.e., "the honesty revolution" passing the control vector to a new state. Within the framework of the model (Lui, 1996), the author showed the existence of situations, where economies with identical evolution parameters have different levels of corruption. The paper (Feichtinger and Wirl, 1994) was dedicated to cyclicity modeling in political corruption: the phases of anti-corruption campaigns often change into the phases of its tacit approval at the macroeconomic level.

Yang (2005) developed the permit issuance scheme of Table 1.1.1 in the following way. Consider a multistep extensive-form game with asymmetrical awareness between two players, i.e., an official and a candidate. The official knows its type and the type of the candidate; yet, the candidate knows neither the former nor the latter, but assesses their probabilities.

At step 1 the official issues the permit or refuses. If the permit is issued, the game ends; otherwise, the candidate makes necessary corrections in its application or offers a bribe (but the candidate does not know its position in the game tree for sure). In the first case, the candidate incurs additional costs C and the game ends. In the second case, the official takes the bribe and issues the permit or refuses. Actually, only a corrupt official prefers bribery; and its profit makes up the difference between bribe amount and expected sanctions. If the bribe is "good," the candidate is not penalized even in the case of bribery. If not, the candidate then pays a penalty B.

Suppose that the bribe is rejected. Again, the candidate makes corrections in the application or offers another bribe. In the first case, the game ends. The official obtains the same payoff at each step, whereas the candidate incurs the costs $C+\Delta(t)$ due to delay, where $\Delta(t)$ is a strictly increasing function of $t \in [1,\infty)$ such that $\Delta(1)=0, \Delta(t) \to \infty$ as $t \to \infty$ (t is the index of an attempt to offer a bribe). If the official appears honest, the candidate incurs additional costs A. If the candidate offers a new bribe, the official again decides whether to take it or reject. Thus, bargaining is potentially infinite, at each step the candidate incurs additional costs. The game ends when the official takes the bribe or the candidate appropriately modifies the application. Clearly, the candidate is interested to end the game as soon as possible.

The study of the above game indicated that bureaucratic monopoly is a key factor of corruption dominance in the modeled situation (the Chinese licensing system). According to the comparative statics analysis, toughening of sanctions seems to gain little effect, and alternative anti-corruption measures should be found (Yang, 2005).

A series of research works (Chaudhuri and Gupta, 1996; Gupta and Chaudhuri, 1997; Chaudhuri and Dastidar, 2011) considered the agricultural credit problem in India taking into account corruption. By assumption, there exist credits of two types. Formal credits are issued by government officials at a fixed interest rate, but government officials possibly exact bribes. Informal credits are issued by private money lenders, but at arbitrary interest rates. The early publications of the series were focused on the horizontal interaction between officials and money lenders in the form of a noncooperative game, with Nash equilibrium search. The investigators derived several interesting results: 1) in an equilibrium, the interest rate of an informal credit equals the effective interest rate of a formal credit (including bribes); 2) active regulation measures can stimulate higher interest rates of informal credits and cause corruption growth if formal and informal credits are supplementary; 3) these measures do not increase corruption if the probability of bribery detection depends on its amount.

The paper (Chaudhuri and Dastidar, 2011) modeled sequential vertical interaction among an active major money lender, other potential money lenders and a bank officer issuing formal credits. The active money lender is a leader in the Stackelberg sense. At step 1 of the game, it defines the interest rate of an informal credit. At step 2, the bank officer establishes the bribe "rate" and the number of other money lenders (formal credit recipients). At step 3, each potential money lender announces the amount of formal credit it pretends. It was illustrated that the vertical interaction between the two credit markets accentuates the presence of corruption in formal credits distribution. If corruption takes place, then increasing the amounts of formal crediting by new money lenders may cause (against all expectations!) higher interest rates of informal credits.

Static models of corruption in macroeconomics. This group of models studies corruption relations at the government level (the so-called grand corruption). The paper (Acemoglu and Verdier, 2000) analyzed the consequences of government interference into economy in the presence of corruption. The model is organized as follows. By assumption, an economy consists of the continuum of risk-neutral agents. They are homogeneous and choose between entrepreneurship and government service. Entrepreneurs select one of production technologies (good or bad). Each technology yields some income, but the good technology causes positive costs less than income. The authors considered three settings of the model:

1. Equilibrium in decentralized economy. In this case, there exists no government and all agents are entrepreneurs. In the absolutely optimal (first-best) outcome, all agents prefer the good technology. However, such an income is nonimplementable, since (similarly to the well-known prisoner dilemma) the dominant strategy of each agent lies in choosing the bad technology.
2. Optimal regulation without corruption. Here government solves a simple linear maximization problem of the total surplus subject to some constraints. It was demonstrated that, under certain conditions, the optimal distribution is when a share of agents prefers the good technology (otherwise, setting 1 arises immediately).
3. Optimal regulation with corruption: a) under homogeneous bureaucrats; b) under heterogeneous bureaucrats (if an agent becomes a bureaucrat, it surely knows whether to take bribes or not).

A series of interesting results was established within the scope of the above hypotheses. The main result can be formulated as follows. Under well-defined conditions, government regulation aiming at correction of market failures unexpectedly causes government failure. These conditions are: (1) government interference requires that bureaucrats collect information, make decisions and realize government policy; (2) at least, some bureaucrats are corrupt, i.e., misrepresent real information for bribes; (3) bureaucrats are heterogeneous. The suggested model indicates that, in the conditions of corruption, government interference is reasonable only if corruption appears relatively small and market dips are sufficiently serious. As a matter of fact, many developing countries have high corruption and government regulation should be very careful (Acemoglu and Verdier, 2000).

Next, the research work (Choi and Thum, 2005) concentrated on the connection between corruption and shadow economy. According to the basic model, economy comprises the continuum of entrepreneurs differing in their money-earning skills. Denote by v the gross income of an entrepreneur, reflecting its skills. The distribution of v is defined by the inverse cumulative distribution function $F(v)$ which describes the share of entrepreneurs being able to earn more than v. To start a business, an entrepreneur has to pay a bribe m determined by an official. Furthermore, to start a business an entrepreneur needs a seed capital k .

In the absence of shadow economy, the market is entered by entrepreneurs yielding nonnegative profit: $\pi_{OE} = v - k - m \geq 0$. The official solves the optimization problem

$\max_m R(m) = \max_m [mF(k+m)]$, which can be rewritten as $\max_v R(v) = \max_v [(v-k)F(v)]$. Its potential solution v^* follows from the first-order optimality conditions $F(v^*) + (v^* - k)F'(v^*) = 0$; under natural assumptions, this is the maximum point. Hence, the number of entrepreneurs entering the market makes up $F(v^*)$, while the bribe amount for licensing equals $m^* = v^* - k$.

Compare this value with the Pareto optimal one–the solution of the public welfare maximization problem $\max_v W(v) = \max_v \int_v^{\infty} (x-k)dF(x)$. The solution is $v^{\max} = k$, i.e., any entrepreneur obtaining an income higher than its seed capital actually enters the market. As far as $F(v^{\max}) + (v^{\max} - k)F'(v^{\max}) = F(k) > 0$, then $v^* > v^{\max}$. Therefore, corruption reduces the number of entrepreneurs entering the market (in comparison with the optimal value). The pure losses due to corruption constitute $-\int_k^{v^*} (x-k)dF(x)$.

Then Choi and Thum supposed that entrepreneurs can run their business in the shadow sector without any license. On the one hand, such a choice allows avoiding costs associated with bribery. On the other hand, additional costs appear due to possible detection of shadow entrepreneurship and further penalization. Let μ be the probability of illegal entrepreneurship detection. If this happens, government confiscates all the capital of its firm. The profit of a risk-neutral entrepreneur in the shadow sector is $\pi_{SE} = (1-\mu)v - k$. By assumption, $v^* > \frac{k}{1-\mu}$, i.e., the probability of illegal entrepreneurship detection is rather small. For a given bribe amount m, the following situations occur:

1) if $\frac{m}{\mu} \le v$, the entrepreneur prefers legal business;

2) if $\frac{k}{1-\mu} \le v < \frac{m}{\mu}$, the entrepreneur chooses the shadow sector;

3) if $v < \frac{k}{1-\mu}$, the entrepreneur does not start business at all.

For the corrupt official, the optimization problem acquires the form $\max_v \widetilde{R}(m) = \max_v [mF(m/\mu)]$. The "limit" type of entrepreneur meets the equality $v = m/\mu$, and the above problem can be rewritten as $\max_v \widetilde{R}(v) = \max_v [\mu v F(v)]$. The first-order optimality conditions $F(v) + vF'(v) = 0$ describe the "limit" entrepreneur $\widetilde{v}$ preferring legal business (under $v \ge \widetilde{v}$).

The following assertion is valid: in the presence of corruption, the legal sector of an economy exceeds its shadow counterpart if $\widetilde{v} < v^*$ (i.e., it is impossible to choose the shadow sector). Therefore, production activity in shadow economy is complementary to the activity in legal sector.

Actually, this draws an unexpected conclusion. In the presence of shadow sector, public welfare becomes higher. First, an economy directly benefits by shadow sector, as it allows entrepreneurs to start a business even if they disagree to do it legally. The corresponding payoff makes up $\int_{\frac{k}{1-\mu}}^{\tilde{v}}(x-k)dF(x)$. Second, shadow sector compels officials to reduce bribes; this benefit is defined by $\int_{\tilde{v}}^{v*}(x-k)dF(x)$.

The authors also studied several modifications of the basic model, *viz.*, possible endogenous investments, the dependence of the probability of illegal business detection on the level of investment, and useful public welfare creation by officials. However, in these cases the major conclusion remains in force: shadow sector facilitates economic activity in legal sector, thereby complementing (not replacing) legal economy. Hence, struggling with shadow sector seems pointless in the presence of corruption (Choi and Thum, 2005).

Dynamic models of corruption in macroeconomics. The paper (Chakrabarti, 2001) described a general equilibrium model in the conditions of corruption. Due to the complexity of this model, its preliminary analytical treatment was followed by simulation experiments. Here the central place is occupied by generations of agents having risk-aversion degrees b_i and human capital k_i. Risk-aversion degree obeys uniform distribution with mean $\bar{b}$ and variance b_{range}. The human capital of the first generation is distributed with mean $\bar{k}$ and variance 1. From generation to generation, human capital evolves according to

$$k_i = [k_{\min} + \frac{y_i - y_{\min}}{y_{\max} - y_{\min}}(k_{\max} - k_{\min})](1-\tau) + \tau Z,$$

where $Z \approx U(k_{\min}, k_{\max})$, τ is an efficiency measure of governmental and political institutions, y_i means corruption income. Each generation consists of 1000 agents, and 100 generations observe social corruption q and national income Y. The level of social corruption is defined by $q = \frac{1}{K}\sum_i p_i k_i$, where $p_i \in [0,1]$ specifies the agent's dishonesty index (a share of rent appropriated via corruption); K designates the total human capital as a production factor. National income is evaluated by $Y = SK$, where S indicates the institutional production factor. In the presence of corruption, $Y = (1-q)SK$.

The model contains six parameters $\bar{b}, b_{range}, \bar{k}, \tau, \gamma, q_{start}$ as described above; in addition, γ is a share of national income assigned to anti-corruption measures; q_{start} answers to the initial level of corruption. Each parameter was given three possible values. And so, the numerical experiment covered $3^6 = 729$ points.

The simulation results showed that there exist locally stable equilibrium levels of corruption, which depend on a few socioeconomic parameters. Under their certain values, hypercorruption may occur: a society is so corrupt that its economy fails. An equilibrium level of corruption mostly depends on risk-aversion degree, the share of national income assigned to anti-corruption measures and human capital (Chakrabarti, 2001).

The paper (Kessing et al., 2006) continued a line of intensive investigations and considered a repeated game associated with the hold-up problem under direct foreign investments. The analysis was focused on the vertical disintegration problem of state power in a federative system, with emphasis placed on two related issues: 1) is there a collusion between an investor and different-level governments in the game with repeated interaction?; 2) how much does higher decentralization (comprehended as increasing the number of levels in a vertical federative hierarchy) relax the hold-up problem? For a certain class of implicit collusion equilibria, the authors demonstrated that decentralization growth reduces cooperation capabilities.

Moreover, Kessing, Konrad and Kotsogiannis claimed that an adequate and reliable income distribution system gradually diminishes the problems caused by the absence of stable cooperation in a multilevel government system. In contrast to a common opinion, lower competition between state power levels owing to income distribution promotes foreign investments.

Therefore, decentralization *per se* exerts neither positive nor negative impact on investments: the key role is played by proper organization of internal fiscal interaction between state power levels. Such a result elucidates the achievements of China and the abortive attempts of Russia in attraction of direct foreign investments (Kessing et al., 2006).

The paper (Blackburn and Forgues-Puccio, 2010) posed the problem of a relationship between economic development, corruption in social sector and international financial integration within a dynamic general equilibrium. First, using numerous scientific publications, the authors analyzed the pairwise interactions between development, corruption and integration. Then they introduced a discrete-time dynamic model of general equilibrium, which incorporates government, farms, entrepreneurs and bureaucrats. The cases of closed and open economy (in the sense of financial flows) were treated independently. Here are the major conclusions of the paper: 1) corruption is always pernicious for economic development, but it inflicts more damage at open financial markets rather than closed ones; 2) high corruption is likely to appear in open economies and poor countries; 3) financial liberalization facilitates economic development under good government control and impairs (or even interferes with) economic development under bad government control; 4) corruption and poverty form inherent features of an economy prior to fundamental reformation (Blackburn and Forgues-Puccio, 2010). This approach was further developed by Blackburn and colleagues in (Blackburn et al., 2006; Blackburn and Powell, 2011).

The paper (Cerqueti and Coppier, 2011) considered a dynamic model of the Ramsey-Solow economy with corruption, which is actually an extension of the static model suggested in (Cerqueti and Coppier, 2009). The framework of this model involves controllers, tax officers and entrepreneurs. By assumption, entrepreneurs can avoid taxation and tax officers shut their eyes to it in exchange for bribes. An interesting feature of the model is taking into account the moral factors. Particularly, each entrepreneur j compares an objective penalty c for tax evasion with its subjective losses c_j ("disgrace costs") defined by its individual moral standards. Based on this attribute, the authors distinguished among countries with uniform, low and high disgrace costs. In the uniform case, the numbers of honest and corrupt entrepreneurs are almost same; corrupt entrepreneurs dominate honest ones in countries with low disgrace costs, and the opposite situation takes place in countries with high disgrace costs. Such separation is rigorously defined via the two-parameter Kumaraswamy distribution of c_j; different parameter values cover the three cases above. Moreover, several instructions on model identification using available empirical data were given.

According to Cerqueti and Coppier, in long term analysis corruption has a mixed impact on economic growth. On the one hand, tax evasion increases the capital of entrepreneurs and promotes investments, accumulation and economic growth. On the other hand, reduced tax proceeds impede public welfare production and decelerate economic growth. More precisely put, in all the three cases of disgrace costs distribution, economic growth rate increases simultaneously with tax rate until the latter reaches a certain threshold; and further tax increment cuts economic growth.

Hence, if political administration strives for economic growth maximization, it should adjust economic growth rate in accordance with tax rate. The corresponding thresholds vary depending on the level of corruption monitoring and the "internal honesty" of a country. For a given internal honesty, the higher is the maximizing tax rate, the lower is the level of corruption monitoring. At the same time, for a given level of corruption monitoring, the higher is the internal honesty of a country, the greater is the maximizing tax rate (Cerqueti and Coppier, 2011).

The fundamental monograph (Schelling, 1978) proposed a static model, where each member of society chooses between honesty and corruption. This forms an aggregated picture of corruption in the society, characterized by different-type equilibria (high or low corruption). In the paper (Caulkins et al., 2013), Schelling's idea was transformed into the optimal control model

$$\max_u \int_0^\infty e^{-rt}[\alpha u x(t) + \beta u(t) - \frac{1}{2}u^2(t) - Cx(t) - \frac{G}{2}x^2(t)]dt$$

$$\dot{x} = u(t) - \delta x(t), \quad 0 \le u(t) \le 1.$$

The decision-maker is the leader of society (e.g., the head of government): its decisions affect the behavior of bureaucracy. In contrast to the binary model introduced by Schelling, here the leader's level of corruption is its continuous control variable $u \in [0,1]$. The state variable x characterizes the corruption culture of bureaucracy. The first two summands in the objective function describe the leader's corruption income, i.e., the direct income (the second summand) and assignments from interaction with bureaucracy (the first summand). More specifically, the coefficient α reflects the leader's income potential from bribes taken by ordinary bureaucrats (petty corruption), whereas the coefficient β is the difference between the sum of all bribes directly taken by the leader (grand corruption) and risk losses associated with corruption. The rest summands answer to the leader's losses caused by corruption. All coefficients are assumed positive (perhaps, except β in the case of society with strong anti-corruption institutions). To avoid remainder description, the problem is considered on the infinite horizon with the discount factor r.

Interestingly, model exploration accentuates on equilibria search for the dynamic equation and their stability analysis rather than on optimal control design. This methodology was stated in detail in (Optimal Control, 2008). Actually, the described model admits four types of equilibria, namely: 1) no corruption; 2) maximum-level corruption; 3) middle-level corruption; 4) path dependency including the Skiba threshold (Skiba, 1978), which resembles Schelling's model.

Path dependency arises only in the presence of synergetic interaction between the corruption levels of the leader and bureaucracy. Path dependency (if any) takes the following form. Suppose that the corruption level of bureaucracy is initially lower than the Skiba threshold. Then the leader benefits from being rather "pure," and its level of corruption vanishes. In this case, the leader is not obliged to be perfectly honest: it can take bribes while the general culture of corruption is relatively high. However, with the course of time the leader and bureaucracy become less corrupt and the former reduces its corruption activity earlier than the latter. Assume that the initial corruption level of bureaucracy exceeds the Skiba threshold. Then the leader is interested in making use of this circumstance and taking bribes independently. And the corruption levels of the leader and bureaucracy both demonstrate growth with the course of time. Thus and so, if society is initially in an equilibrium with high corruption, it stays there until an appreciable impact drives the system away from this equilibrium.

And finally, the model reflects the public role of individual reformers. If a non-corrupt leader (with small values of α and β) remains in power long enough so that the corruption level of bureaucracy dips below the threshold, then subsequent administrations can be free of corruption (even though their heads possess medium ethical attitude). Conversely, a mercenary-minded leader staying on for a long term can deprave even almost non-corrupt bureaucracy (Caulkins et al., 2013).

Models of political corruption. This group unites models describing the impact of corruption on political processes (including voting system, the activity of legislative bodies, ideology, etc.). Actually, they are related to macroeconomic models via the term "grand corruption." Models of political corruption are considered in static and dynamic settings.

The survey (Levin and Levina, 2001) studied 60 sources dedicated to the lobby problem. The notion of lobbying covers different attempts to effect decision-making in government structures and commercial organizations: provision of actual information and expert appraisals, public opinion formation, contributions to election campaigns, and bribes. Lobbying models can be divided into statistic and game-theoretic ones. Most research works on statistic modeling of lobbying belongs to investigators from the United States: this phenomenon plays an essential role in political life of Americans and there exist much empirical data available. Generally, statistic models represent regressions used to verify certain hypotheses. Game-theoretic models operate normal-form games, cooperative games, multistep games, and differential games. Modeling focuses on various problems such as competition among lobbyists, lobbying costs estimation, the impact of lobbying on public welfare, collective struggle for rent and payoff distribution within a group, tarrification and international trade, the behavior of organized groups during elections, the impact of contributions to election campaigns on the behavior of politicians, lobbying within organizations, etc. The results of modeling demonstrated that lobbying has a negative (inefficient resource distribution) or positive effect (provision of information) (Levin and Levina, 2001).

Acemoglu and the colleagues (Acemoglu et al., 2004) employed game-theoretic modeling to show that kleptocratic modes (personal power used for profit-making) may have long-period stable existence by bribery of potential opponents. According to Mauro's viewpoint (Mauro, 2004), the stability of corruption as a socioeconomic institution is explained by the absence of individual stimuli for anti-corruption struggle (even though the whole society benefits from this). In other words, corruption forms "an institutional trap," i.e., an inefficient equilibrium, where none of players is motivated to change its behavior.

The paper (Lazarev, 2011) introduced a simple game-theoretic model of government-opposition interaction, which describes political processes in "weak" countries. This notion concerns countries, where: 1) holding power is the highest value; 2) facing opposition, government has to form a "winning coalition" not necessarily reflecting the interests of majority population in order to remain in power; 3) corruption is beneficial to all its participants and burdensome for the rest; insurrection is burdensome for everybody; 4) government can apply two strategies to opposition (bribery or suppression) and work towards corruption market formation or conduct policy in the interests of majority via economic growth stimulation. The payoff matrix of the game is defined by Table 1.1.2.

Government possesses political power of value P. Opposition consists of the continuum S and disposes of political capital W. If government prefers corruption (bribery), it gives a certain share C of its capital to the opposition. In the case of suppression, government spends some share R of its capital on repressive measures (R > C). A successful insurrection passes political power to the opposition and insurrection losses make up r. The overthrow probabilities are X (corrupt government) and Y (repressive government), where X > Y.

Table 1.1.2. The game-theoretic model of corruption in "weak" country

	Loyalty	Insurrection
Bribery	P–C (W+C)/S	(1-X)(P-C) X(P-r)/S
Suppression	P-R (W-R)/S	(1-Y)(P-R) Y(P-r)/S

The choice of government depends on the proportion between the payoffs from corruption P-C+(1-X)(P-C) and repressions (P-R)+(1-Y)(P-R). Despite that the overthrow probability is higher in the case of corruption than repressions, government rather chooses the first strategy: repressions cause higher losses (R > C and R/C > X/Y).

The choice of opposition is defined by the proportion between the payoffs from insurrection [(X+Y)(P-r)]/S and loyalty retention (2W+C-R)/S; by-turn, this proportion depends on the model parameters. Here the major role belongs to the amount of financial resources government is willing to spend on bribery of opposition. Naturally enough, a rich government (in the sense of natural resources) can easier guarantee the loyalty of opposition. Generally, different values of the parameters correspond to either stable or instable corrupt mode (Lazarev, 2011).

The authors of the paper (Wilson and Damania, 2005) considered environmental protection and proposed a "stratified" model of corruption with bribery at the upper (grand corruption) and lower (petty corruption) levels of government control. The former is intended for legislature changes, while the latter allows avoiding real application of active legislature. Thereby, the model combines two directions of research, *viz.*, corruption models at the upper level during environmental policy formation and administrative corruption models of Principal-agent relations. Most attention was paid to the impact of political competition on corruption.

It was found that this impact is ambiguous. On the one hand, political competition brings to tougher environmental policy and reduction of environmental degradation. On the other hand, under weak right-supporting institutions, competition increases corruption and law-breaking at the lower level.

The authors arrived at the following conclusion. While assessing corruption, it is necessary to consider the negative impact on economy rather than the degree of bribery. If grand corruption is defined in terms of government policy distortion, then grand corruption and petty corruption can be either mutually complementary or interchangeable depending on the efficiency of the right-supporting system. This has obvious consequences in environmental and anti-corruption policy-making (Wilson and Damania, 2005).

The interconnection of natural resources, democracy and corruption was also explored by Bhattacharyya and Hodler (2010). The model includes a sitting president, a presidential candidate and population. The both politicians have "good" type θ_g with probability α and "bad" type θ_b with probability $1-\alpha$. Each politician knows its own type, the value α is known to all participants. During step $t=1$, the sitting president chooses a corruption level $c_1 \in [0,1]$. At the end of step 1, population observes c_1 and selects between the sitting president and the candidate. During step $t=2$, the elected politician again chooses a corruption level $c_2 \in [0,1]$.

National economy consists of production sector with output $A_t = A(c_t)$, where $A' \le 0, A'' < 0, A'(0)=0, A'(1)=-\infty$, and natural resource sector with rent $\Omega_t = \Omega \ge 0$. At step t, public welfare is defined by $W_t = W(c_t) = (1-c_t)[A(c_t)+\Omega]$. And the politician's profit takes the form

$$u_t = u(c_t,\theta) = \Pi(c_t) + \theta W(c_t) = [c_t + \theta(1-c_t)][A(c_t)+\Omega].$$

Here $\Pi(c_t) = c_t[A(c_t)+\Omega]$ denotes its corruption income (the Laffer curve) and θW_t gives its profit determined by public welfare, $0<\theta_b<1<\theta_g$.

This framework is remarkable for taking into account the maturity of democratic institutions. Let p and q be the probabilities of power retainment by the incumbent when population supports it and the candidate, respectively. Then the quantity $D = p - q$ characterizes the quality of democratic institutions.

The model represents a two-step game with incomplete information and backward induction serves for evaluating a perfect Bayesian equilibrium (PBE). The authors established the following results:

1) there exists a PBE, where good (bad) incumbent chooses $c_1(\theta_g)=0$ ($c_1(\theta_b)=0$, respectively) if $D \geq D'$ and $c_1(\theta_b)=\hat{c}$ otherwise; moreover, population supports the sitting president iff $c_1=0$. Other PBE with $c_1(\theta_g)=0$ take no place;
2) the limit increment of the natural resource rent Ω increases corruption $c_1(\theta_b)$ iff $D < D'$, where $\hat{c}, D'$ are some threshold values of the parameters.

Consequently, high natural resource rent increases corruption iff democratic institutions are weak. The model was tested using panel data over 124 countries and the period from 1980 to 2004 (Bhattacharyya and Hodler, 2010).

The paper (Evrenk, 2011) studied the motives of honest and corrupt politicians for implementing a full-fledged efficient anti-corruption reform. The model represents a multistep game with Nash equilibria in pure strategies. The analysis showed that, under high corruption, none of politicians chooses anti-corruption strategy in an equilibrium.

Schumacher (2013) examined a dynamic model, where a politician prefers bribery and tax evasion under the endogenous dynamics of trust. The income of a politician comprises its wage, bribes and tax hold-up; in addition, a politician has personal motives for tax redistribution. However, the higher is corruption and tax hold-up, the lower is population trust in such a politician, *ergo* the probability of its re-election. Trust evolution was substantiated by econometric studies.

By scrutinizing the necessary and sufficient conditions, the author demonstrated that tax evasion and bribery can be either interchangeable strategies (substitutes) or mutually complementary strategies (complements) for a politician, depending on the motives for tax redistribution. In the absence of such motives, the mentioned strategies are substitutes; under strong motives, they are complements. The latter means that a politician, at least in part, takes more bribes: this increases tax redistribution, thereby creating additional motives for redistribution. Comparative statics analysis of stable equilibria also elucidated that, the higher is officials' wage, the lower is corruption and the higher is trust (Schumacher, 2013).

An interesting publication (Balafoutas, 2011) studied how corruption depends on guilt aversion in a repeated psychological game. In addition to purely economic factors, payoff functions in such games incorporate higher-order values. The game engages a bureaucrat, a lobby and the public. The bureaucrat has moral losses due to corruption, as it strives for meeting public expectations. Public expectations can be constant or variable. In the latter case, corruption appears with higher probability if game horizon is sufficiently large and public expectations are relatively small and vary fast (Balafoutas, 2011). The influence of cultural factors on corruption was also investigated in (Kingston, 2008).

Models of corruption in hierarchies. Insofar as corruption is the manifestation of rational economic thinking by officials possessing power and arbitrary rule of its application, adequate anti-corruption strategies can be designed using appropriate motivation schemes based on the carrot-and-stick approach (stimulation of honest and penalization of corrupt officials). But these schemes require successful detection of corruption and correct implementation of incentives. If officials responsible for such detection and implementation are corrupt, we inevitably face the original problem. It is necessary to discover how and to what extent corruption can be eliminated in these situations. Actually, models of corruption in hierarchies pursue exactly this aim. Further exposition follows the survey (Mishra, 2006b).

Corruption often includes two intersecting types of relations. First, the matter concerns relations between government and its clients. For instance, consider relations between government and taxpayers, a regulation authority and firms, police and potential criminals, public service providers and potential clients within the Principal-agent interaction scheme. Identification of a Principal and agent, as well as the nature of their relations may vary appreciably. In this context, potential criminals hoping to avoid capture after law-breaking differ a lot from those who strive for government privileges. However, all these cases are characterized by the noncoinciding interests of a Principal and clients and the absence of complete information for the former. Second, a Principal can use an agent (a mediator) for implementing public programs. As an example, take a regulation authority which controls pollution and monitors satisfaction of appropriate environmental requirements by firms. To realize such a policy, the authority employs an inspector auditing firms. But the agent's goal not necessarily matches the Principal's one. An agent can be corrupt, and the Principal has to design certain mechanisms to suppress corruption. These mechanisms (anti-corruption strategies) include agents' monitoring and substantiation of penalties and incentives.

To consider agent relations in detail, take an example of a regulation authority striving for satisfaction of environmental standards via inspectors auditing polluting firms. The early paper by Rose-Ackerman (1978) was mostly dedicated to agent relations between a regulation authority and an inspector. Corruption arises when a third party which can benefit from the agent's actions tries to affect its decision by suggesting an amount of money to transferred to Principal (Rose-Ackerman 1978:6). In our example, the role of such a third party belongs to the polluting firm. Klitgaard (1988) applied a similar model, where a Principal is a regulation authority, an agent is an inspector and a client is a firm. The early work by Tirole (1986) studied collusion in organizations using the Principal–supervisor–agent scheme. Actually, it entailed numerous publications on the collusion problem, some of them also considered corruption.

It is fruitful to classify agent–client relations based on the agent's authority and responsibility. Asymmetrical awareness and incomplete contracts form the basic sources of such an authority. First, the agent's role can be restricted to information acquisition. In this case, authority is generated by possible manipulation of this information. Most problems in decision execution (regulating orders, levying of taxes, policy realization) refer to this category. Second, a Principal can set large-scale goals to an agent, but the latter has authority of choosing an appropriate motivation mechanism for clients. A Principal retains some control, but delegates motivation mechanism realization and, moreover, its design to an agent. Upper-level bureaucratic corruption in policy-making and rendering of public services follow this scenario. A bureaucrat can have a strict goal, but enjoy full freedom *au reste*. And third, a Principal can simply delegate all authorities to an agent. In this case, the latter acts as a private monopolist. Such a monopoly exists in license and permit issuance procedures, where well-defined rules are absent or almost inapplicable. Depending on the nature of agent relations and a corresponding awareness structure, investigators discriminate between two major types of corruption, namely, collusion and extortion, see Table 1.1.1.

Although the impact of corruption on resource allocation and design of different anti-corruption measures attracted much attention in research works, the role of organizational structures was insufficiently explored. In her early paper Rose-Ackerman (1978) performed the comparative analysis of different-type bureaucratic structures and stimulated further research in the field. A series of authors including Basu et al. (1992), Bac (1996a,b), Carrillo (2000), Mishra (2002) examined various aspects of corruption in hierarchies.

Consider a group of individuals (clients) engaged in illegal activity. The private benefit from it equals x , where the variable x obeys the uniform distribution on the interval $[0, x]$. Take a typical client Z with partial benefit x . Being captured for illegal activity, client Z pays a penalty $F, F > x$. Denote by p the probability of capture/penalization; then client Z commits a crime iff

$$x - pF > 0. \tag{1.1.1}$$

For any p and F , it is possible to find the share of individuals preferring illegal activity. These individuals (clients) form the objects of monitoring by officials (agents). By assumption, the latter submit a corresponding report to a Principal. Actually, we have described the basic hierarchy $H0$, see Figure 1.1.1. Heavy-line arrow (down) reflects monitoring, whereas dashed-line arrow indicates reporting. For instance, in the hierarchy $H0$ an agent monitors a client and submits a report to a Principal. As far as officials are corrupt, they practice bribery and do not report on illegal activity. Therefore, a Principal faces the dual motivation problem: construct motivation mechanisms for individuals and monitoring agents.

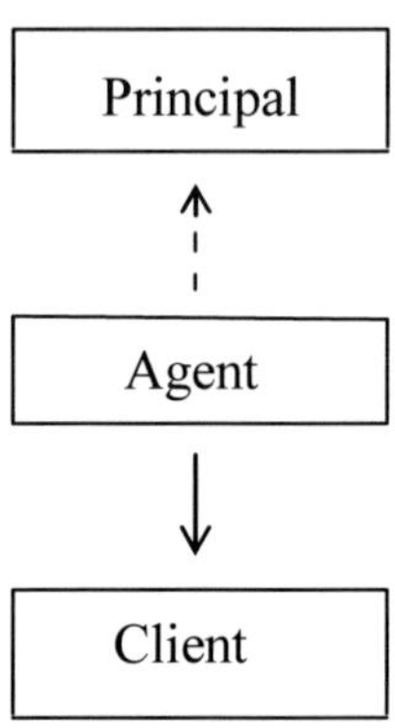

Figure 1.1.1. The basic hierarchy $H0$.

This model admits different interpretations. For instance, a group of clients includes entrepreneurs striving for a license or permit for certain activities. They provide a benefit x depending on the profitability of their projects. In this case, agents are bureaucrats exacting bribes in exchange for permit issuance. Pure extortion is also possible when all projects increase public good and deserve permit issuance. However, some projects can incur higher public costs and should be rejected. As a result, a bureaucrat captures entrepreneurs with undesired projects, approving their projects in exchange for bribes. Obviously, compliance with legislature is reduced to the degree of official's corruption. If the negotiation authority completely belongs to an official, it exacts bribe F. In this extreme case, loss of income is possible, but the suppression effect is maximized.

On the other hand, if negotiation authority completely belongs to a client, then it can avoid bribery and suppression vanishes. Many authors consider the intermediate case when bribe amount is defined by a Nash bargaining solution with equal negotiation authorities. Using such bribe amount evaluation, it is possible to show that individual Z has to bribe $F/2$. Then Z commits a crime iff

$$x - pF/2 > 0. \tag{1.1.2}$$

Suppose that penalties might not be increased arbitrarily: $x/p < F < 2x/p$. Then the only way to guarantee the law-abiding behavior of Z lies in stimulation of truth-telling (objective reporting) by an official. For this, the official has to-be-paid an incentive R. Anyway, the official can obtain an incentive by crime reporting after negotiations on bribery with individual Z have failed. Hence, R can be called the payment for official's refusal of agreement. Then the bribe individual Z has to pay to the official makes up $(F+R)/2$. Higher incentive causes higher bribe. Therefore, even if incentive does not guarantee the official's honesty, negotiations on bribery become costly. Let $R < F$; in this case, it is easy to show that the official never prefers truth-telling, but individual Z commits a crime iff

$$x - p(R+F)/2 > 0. \tag{1.1.3}$$

Even under $F > x/p$, the above inequality remains in force for R appreciably smaller than x/p; and so, individual Z benefits from execution of a crime. Nevertheless, direct comparison of formulas (1.1.1) – (1.1.3) indicates that some suppression takes place.

Clearly, objective reporting disappears if $R < F$. And it is possible to employ another official to watch over the first one, see the hierarchy $H1$ in Figure 1.1.2.

Agent 2 (A2) detects the bribery of agent 1 (A1) with some probability q. Now, A1 can incur a penalty G with possible confiscation of the received bribe. After bribery detection, client Z can be penalized by a same amount and, moreover, a certain amount for the act of bribing. For simplicity, suppose that Z is not penalized (A1 possibly destroys evidence) and the Principal does not confiscate the bribe received by A1. In such a hierarchical setting, the threat of punishment to some degree prevents corruption of A1. At the same time, there exists no guarantee that A2 prefers truth-telling. Official 2 can take a bribe from official 1 and withhold the crime. The Nash bargaining solution for the negotiations between A1 and A2 is simply $G/2$ under the assumption that official 2 has no incentive. But this produces an appreciable effect on the bribery negotiations between A1 and Z.

The bribe individual Z has to pay constitutes

$$b = (F+R)/2 + qG/4. \tag{1.1.4}$$

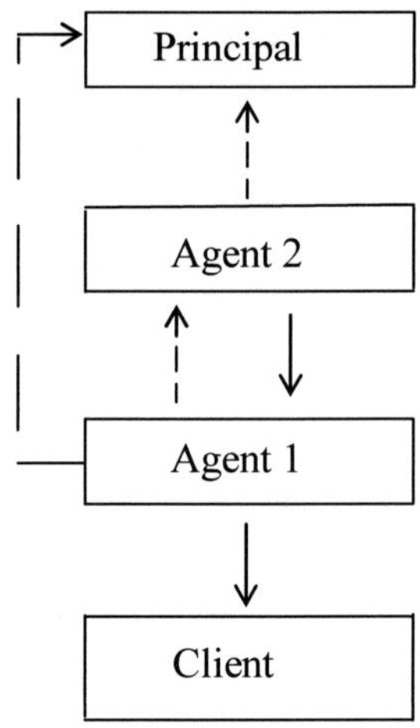

Figure 1.1.2. The hierarchy $H1$.

Hence, the pure expected payoff of A1 owing to corruption is $(F+R)/2-qG/4$. Then under $R<F$ the official prefers truth-telling if $R>F-qG/2$. Therefore, additional-level monitoring makes corruption less attractive, even if official 2 is also corrupt. In the case of $F>x/p$, objective reporting forces individual Z to refuse from crime commitment.

Another consequence of introducing the hierarchy $H1$ is that the penalty F guaranteeing the honesty of A1 can be moderate. Assign the superscript *max* to the maximum values of the quantities. If there exist upper bounds on R (or budget constraints on high incentives) and G such that $R^{\max}<F^{\max}-qG^{\max}/2$, then F must be decreased for corruption elimination. However, maximum suppression dictates maximality of the optimal penalty. It follows from (1.1.1) that the optimal penalty necessarily equals the maximum value $F^{\max}$, since increasing the probability of corruption detection p costs more. This statement applies to the current case, too. And so, generally maximum suppression does not mean zero corruption level in the hierarchy.

Analysis of $H1$ naturally leads to the following question. Is it required to introduce another hierarchical level A3 for proper supervising of A2? Suppose that A2 is promised an incentive S for reporting on the act of bribing by A1. Clearly, if $S<G$, agent A2 never gives an objective report without an additional level of monitoring. The honesty of A2 makes bribery less beneficial to A1; even if corruption takes place, the real bribe for Z becomes higher. Considerations are similar to the ones in the previous subsections. In general, unless explicit constraints are imposed on the control parameters (F,G,R,S), embedding new hierarchical levels is not an optimal solution. In principle, corruption of A1 can be eliminated via proper monitoring by A2. If an existing hierarchy includes A3 or even higher levels, the question where corruption can be uprooted easier ("top" or "bottom") appears nontrivial and, unfortunately, admits no direct answer. The preceding research works studied heterogeneous corruption rates (cake sizes) at different levels, which complicates comparative analysis.

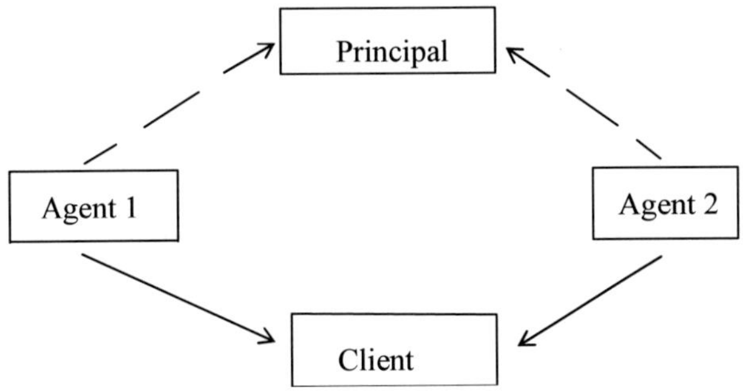

Figure 1.1.3. The hierarchy $H2$.

Instead of introducing a higher level of monitoring in the basic hierarchy $H0$, it is possible to add another horizontal level (see Figure 1.1.3).

Many organizations have such an intersection of jurisdictions. For instance, a license or permit can be issued by different bureaucrats in different ministries. By assumption, both bureaucrats possibly detect the illegal activity of individual Z. If a bureaucrat catches Z out and honestly reports this fact, then Z pays a penalty and the actions of other bureaucrat are not considered. However, if official 1 (A1) takes a bribe of Z and sets the individual free, then official 2 (A2) can catch Z out and exact a bribe or report on crime commitment. In contrast to the previous case when A2 catches Z out and the latter is penalized, nothing happens to A1 which has taken a bribe earlier. Official 2 does not supervise official 1.

On the other hand, official 2 can take a bribe if the bribery of Z has yet not been reported. Supposing same incentive for honesty, official 2 takes the bribe $b_2 = (R+F)/2$ whenever $R<F$. In other words, the bribe of official 1 is smaller. During negotiations with official 1, individual Z knows that this is not the last chance. Let p be the probability of catching Z out by official A2 provided that it has been caught out by official A1. Then the bribe of A1 has the form

$$b_1 = (F+R)(2-p)/4. \tag{1.1.5}$$

This quantity is smaller than $(F+R)/2$ under $p>0$. The bribe received by A1 appears even smaller if we know about the honesty of A2. Similarly to the hierarchy $H1$, bribery is less beneficial to the official. Honesty can be ensured even if $R<F$. Mishra (2002) demonstrated that, for some parameter values, honesty can be guaranteed within the hierarchy $H2$ even if this is impossible within the hierarchy $H1$.

Analogous properties can be introduced in $H1$. Following Basu et al. (1992), consider a situation when corruption detection at some hierarchical level causes penalization of all lower levels. If A2 is caught up, then A2, A1 and Z pay penalties. Therefore, A3 can exact bribes from all the three. In this case, it is easier to eliminate corruption and guarantee the law-abiding behavior of Z.

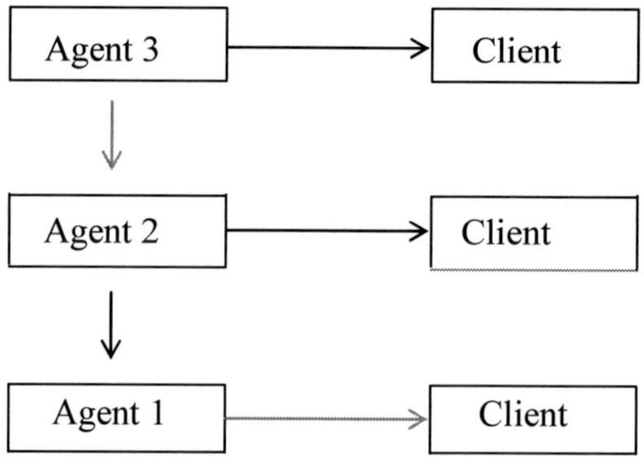

Figure 1.1.4. The hierarchy $H3$.

A common feature of all hierarchies above is that only lower-level officials interact with a client: A1 within the hierarchies $H0$ and $H1$, both A1 and A2 within the hierarchy $H2$. In certain organizations, upper-level officials also communicate with clients. For instance, consider Income Tax Department in India; here upper-level officials supervise and assess tax incomes personally. And so, agents at different levels combine client servicing with supervising functions. In the context of $H1$, this means that A2 deals with clients and also supervises A1. Such an organizational structure opens another source of corruption for upper-level officials. Agent A2 can take bribes from some client Z' and A2 being captured for bribery. According to Bac (1996a,b), these phenomena will be called external and internal corruption, respectively. The corresponding hierarchy $H3$ is presented by Figure 1.1.4; here A3 supervises A2.

Suppose that A3 (A2) detects the external corruption of A2 (A1, respectively) with some probability. In contrast to $H1$, internal corruption is not detected and therefore can be eliminated only via appropriate incentive mechanisms. A2 receives an incentive R for reporting on the corruption of A1. If the agent is caught out with bribe-taking from the client, the former is dismissed with cancelation of its wage and all incentive payments. This has interesting consequences on corruption control. Imagine that A2 decides to exact a bribe from the client, but prefers reporting on the corruption of A1. Incentive payments are such that internal corruption takes no place. In this case, the internal corruption costs of A2 are higher, since the penalty includes the loss of wage and incentive payments. Therefore, it seems easier to eliminate the external corruption of A2 than that of A1. Lower-level corruption is safer as against upper-level corruption. On the other hand, this possibly urges A2 to internal corruption. The payoff from internal corruption is greater if A2 also plans participation in external corruption. And, in this case, elimination of internal corruption causes more difficulties. Bac (1996a) considered implementation of different target levels of external corruption in the presence of internal corruption and showed that the threat of internal corruption appreciably affects the implementable range of targets.

Clearly, the studied hierarchies guarantee corruption suppression by either stimulating agents' honesty or enhancing efficient penalties (the total bribe amount) for clients. This approach fits many compulsion situations when an individual is blocked to perform an act. At the same time, what should be done in cases requiring stimulation of the agent's actions? Their analysis differs, naturally leading to alternative recommendations. For instance, in the case of extortion, negotiations on bribery, awareness structure and detection obey other rules. Assume that only A1 bears responsibility for permit issuance, whereas A2 supervises the actions of A1. The client can pass information or complain to A2 about the bribery of A1. Thus, successful detection of the corruption behavior of A1 depends on the client's actions. As far as A2 is also corrupt, the client possibly receives no compensation, but A1 has to bribe A2 for holding its job. Consequently, extortion can be less beneficial. In some cases, submitting a complaint incurs costs, and clients prefer keeping silence until extortion grows appreciably. In this case, the bribe amount of A1 is small.

Moreover, in contrast to the previous case (collusion between agent and client) when bribes from clients also reflect any expected penalty or payments of A1, here bribes can depend on a totally different set of factors. In this case, bribe depends on the partial benefit of client (rather x than F) which is unknown to A1. Therefore, A1 possibly takes a fixed bribe (similarly to monopolistic price) as an extortion payment. If bribe is fixed, then any changes in the organizational structure do not affect client until they stimulate the honesty of A1. In the previous case, even if the corruption of A1 remains invariable, the organizational structure exerts an impact on client. But some "discontinuity" exists: insofar as organizational changes do not touch bribes, client is influenced only by the fact that A1 ceases exacting bribes.

Similarly to the hierarchy $H2$, several agents may interact with a client here. Suppose that permit covers some aspects, resembling a basket of goods. There exist two options: (1) agents compete with each other for provision of the basket (recall that competition possibly reduces the client's bribe) and (2) agents answer for provision of each good separately, and client bribes each agent for permit issuance. The second option may cause hold-up-type problems. Rose-Ackerman (1978) compared these options, but the subsequent analysis of such bureaucratic structures was scanty. According to the above discussion, different organizational structures influence the corruption of officials in different ways.

The problem of corruption detection has not been posed yet. It was assumed that upper-level officials reveal the corruption of their subordinates with certain given probabilities. However, quite plausibly, these probabilities depend on the intensity of monitoring or the supervision strength of an agent performing monitoring. Now, suppose that the probability of corruption detection is defined by the supervision strength of this agent. Most likely, the success of anti-corruption measures depends on the honesty and monitoring efforts of agents.

Let the probability p of capturing individual Z by agent A1 depend on the latter's choice of its effort e_1 as follows:

$$p = e_1 / E, \quad p \in [0,1], \quad e_1 \in [0, E], \tag{1.1.6}$$

where E denotes the maximum possible effort of the agent. We believe that p is an implicit variable of the agent's choice, since effort choice unambiguously determines p. Assume that the utility functions enjoy linearity and additive separability. Then the agent's payoff makes up

$$\Pi = y - e, \tag{1.1.7}$$

where y is the expected pure income comprising incentives and bribes.

The agent submits an honest report and receives an incentive R or takes a bribe b from Z. Bribe amount depends on penalties and incentives. The agent's choice will be designated by $h, h \in \{0,1\}$, where $h = 0$ means honest report and $h = 1$ indicates of corruption. If both options are equivalent to the agent, it can choose a strategy randomly. Similarly, the decision of Z to commit a crime will be denoted by c, $c \in \{0,1\}$, where $c = 0$ corresponds to legal activity. For simplicity, consider the behavior of one individual Z with benefit x. In the sequel, we treat c and h as randomization probabilities and interpret them as the levels of crime and corruption, respectively.

Within the basic hierarchy $H0$, agent A1 chooses p and h to maximize its expected payoff. Individual Z chooses c to maximize its payoff. A Nash equilibrium is simply a vector (c^*, p^*, h^*); hence, such a choice of the individual maximizes the agent's payoff and vice versa. Let Π_Z and Π_1 signify the payoff of individual Z from crime commitment and the payoff of agent A1 under p and h, respectively. These quantities have the form

$$\Pi_Z = x - p[h(F+R)/2 + (1-h)F], \Pi_1 = c[h(F+R)/2 + (1-h)R]p - pE \qquad (1.1.8)$$

It is easy to check that, under $R < F$, agent A1 always takes a bribe and $h^* = 1$ in the equilibrium. To eliminate situations when the agent applies no efforts in the equilibrium, also suppose that E is not very large. The equilibrium (1.1.1) exists for small penalties comparable with x. However, the internal equilibrium $(2E/(F+R), 2x/(F+R), 1)$ takes place for high penalties. The equilibrium level of corruption decreases in F.

Note that c^* is positive except the limit case when F tends to infinity. This is not surprising: in the absence of crime, the agent has no incentives and bribes, thereby applying no efforts. This result preserves validity while the agent's payoffs depend on the equilibrium level of crime in such a way. The quantities P and e can be bounded below, but the following general conclusion holds true: complete elimination of corruption by this method is impossible.

In the elementary case, public welfare depends only on the level of crime and the costs of supervising efforts. Within this framework, corruption *per se* does not affect public welfare. Denote by K the pure public losses due to illegal activity and by N the costs of law enforcement. Then public welfare is defined by

$$W = -cK - N. \qquad (1.1.9)$$

The formula of N depends on a specific hierarchy: $N = pE$ (the hierarchy $H0$) and $N = pE + qE$ (the hierarchy $H1$), where q is the intensity of monitoring focused on A1 and performed by A2. Moreover, one may claim that corruption represents the major determinant of public welfare and bribery is not considered just as transfer. And this function may incorporate corresponding costs associated with h.

Comparison of H1 and H0. Let q be the probability of capturing A1 with an act of bribing. Under a given penalty G, agent A1 has to pay the bribe $G/2$ in the case of being captured. Recall that the bribe received by A1 from Z constitutes $(F+R)/2+qG/4$. Assuming that q is defined by analogy to p in (1.1.6), the payments within the hierarchy $H1$ acquire the form

$$\Pi_Z x - p[h(F+R+qG/2)/2+(1-h)F], \Pi_1 = cp[h((F+R+qG/2)/2)+(1-h)R] - pE, \quad (1.1.10)$$
$$\Pi_2 = cphqG2 - qE$$

Again, an equilibrium is (c^*, h^*, p^*, q^*). In the absence of incentives or supervision, A2 is always corrupt. In this case, the only difference consists in the effort choice by A2: the agent strives to maximize its expected income. The decision of A1 obviously depends on the supervising effort selected by A2. On the other hand, the bribe individual Z has to pay being captured by A1 depends on the choice of A2. And so, the decision of Z also depends on the choice of A2. We believe that E is insufficiently great for stimulating zero effort choice by the agents. Instead of characterizing all equilibria, let us get focused on an internal equilibrium. Under $F < R$, it is possible to establish the existence of an internal equilibrium of the form

$$c = E/R,\ p = x/F,\ q = 2(F-R)/G,\ h = 2RF/(Gx). \quad (1.1.11)$$

Note that corruption can be reduced (i.e., h decreased) via enlarging G and/or making R or F smaller. Higher values of G enhance the honesty of A1 and weaken the monitoring effort of A2. Therefore, a universal optimal strategy lies in choosing the maximum value of G. This represents an optimal way for corruption reduction within the hierarchy $H1$, which can be shown rigorously. When G admits no increase due to institutional constraints, an optimal strategy can be decreasing F and increasing R. Reduction of R is not an explicit solution, as it causes the growth of c and q. Consequently, smaller values of R definitely mean public welfare decrease, see formula (1.1.9). In this situation, the penalty F does not achieve its maximum for sure.

However, corruption uprooting is not necessarily optimal under lower bounds imposed on R. Recall that corruption uprooting means $h = 0$. This is possible only if $R > F$; then we have $h^* = q^* = 0,\ c^* = E/R,\ p^* = x/F$. So long as $R < R_0$, where R_0 is some upper bound, the public welfare (1.1.9) does not exceed $-[(E/R_0)K + xE/R_0]$. Another equilibrium can be constructed, where $R = R_0$ but $F > R$ (a certain level of corruption does exist). The parameter c remains invariable. The monitoring effort makes up $E[x/F + 2(F-R)/G]$. The values F and G can be increased so that this expression becomes smaller than Ex/R. Therefore, by applying large penalties, it is possible to obtain another equilibrium yielding a higher level of public welfare (even despite existing corruption). According to this statement, one should not insist on total elimination of corruption in any situations at any cost.

The comparative analysis of the hierarchies $H0$ and $H1$ brings to the following conclusion. An additional supervising level really increases public welfare if K takes large values and G is not bounded by small quantities. Let $R+F<2x$. In other words, the hierarchy $H0$ does not guarantee even a small corruption reduction ($c^*=1$). However, the hierarchy $H1$ ensures a limited decrease of crime in such situations. Severe penalization of A1 being possible (i.e., under great values of G), the level of crime can be reduced appreciably (small q) and the appearance of a hierarchy seems more probable. Otherwise (under small values of G), the need in supervising efforts grows (great q) and the costs of monitoring are higher. Hence, it is unreasonable to organize hierarchical monitoring and perform anti-corruption measures while losses due to illegal activity are relatively small. These results can be combined as follows.

Assertion 1 (Mishra, 2006b). Even if public welfare does not directly depend on corruption level, an optimal strategy within the hierarchy $H1$ is corruption minimization until strict constraints apply to incentive mechanism design (R, G) for the lower-level agent (A1). Welfare within $H1$ is higher than within $H0$, especially when the latter hierarchy does not counteract the illegal behavior of individuals at all.

Comparison of H1 and H2. Within the hierarchy $H2$, individual Z is monitored both by A1 and A2; and so, here a key role belongs to the sequence of their moves (decision-making). In many organizations, this sequence is defined from without. To simplify further analysis, suppose that both agents capture Z first with an identical probability. Our attention mostly focuses on the symmetrical case when both agents apply equal efforts, and hence such an assumption leads to almost no loss of generality. Recall that if agent 1 is not corrupt, then the willingness of agent 2 to release client holds things in place.

Denote by p the probability of capturing individual Z by any agent. Then the probabilities of capturing Z by one of agents and both agents constitute $p+(1-p)p$ and p^2, respectively.

Under $R>F$, the results can be derived directly. In this case, both agents are honest. However, only one of them receives an incentive. The payments make up

$$\Pi_1 = \Pi_2 = cR(p - p^2/2) - pE, \quad \Pi_Z = x - [p + p(1-p)]F. \tag{1.1.12}$$

Imagine that $F[p+(1-p)]>x$, then there exists a unique equilibrium, where $c^* = 2E/(R(2-p))$ and p satisfies the equation $2p-p^2 = x/F$. This situation can be compared with the vertical hierarchy $H1$. Note that, if $R>F$, then the second level of monitoring becomes pointless or the effort of official 2 always vanishes. Therefore, in the equilibrium we have $c^* = E/R,\ p = x/F$. It is possible to demonstrate that the hierarchy $H2$ guarantees a higher level of crime and higher costs of monitoring. The main reason here lies in duplication of officials' efforts in the horizontal case.

A somewhat more interesting situation occurs when $R<F$. Agent 2 always takes a bribe if agent 1 does not report of crime commitment. This affects bribery negotiations between client and agent 1. The bribe received by agent 1 is defined by

$$\underset{b}{\operatorname{argmax}}[F-b-p(F+R)/2][b-R]$$
$$b^* = (F+R)/2 - p(F+R)/4 \quad (1.1.13)$$

Even under $R < F$, for some values $R > R^*$ agent 1 prefers reporting of crime commitment and obtaining an incentive rather than taking a bribe. Hence, the agent's optimal strategy represents honesty (if it is first) and bribery (if it is second). When both agents adhere to identical strategies, corruption takes no place in an equilibrium. The equilibrium outcome is same as in the previous case of $R > F$. Consequently, even if $R < F$, the hierarchy $H2$ can lead to total honesty (in contrast to the hierarchy $H1$ always demonstrating a certain level of corruption). The hierarchy $H2$ is interpreted as competition between agents, and so tougher competition reduces corruption. Within the hierarchy $H2$, corruption disappears in an equilibrium for a wider range of system parameters than within the hierarchy $H1$. Despite that corruption *per se* does not affect public welfare, in this case smaller corruption causes smaller monitoring costs and, probably, increases public welfare. The following pair of statements (see Mishra, 2002) provide a partial characterization of the hierarchies $H1$ and $H2$.

Assertion 2 (Mishra, 2006b). In contrast to $H1$, the hierarchy $H2$ admits an equilibrium with honest reporting of client's crimes even if incentives are smaller than penalties. Public welfare within $H2$ is higher than within $H1$ if losses incurred by criminality and the penalty G are reasonable.

Interestingly, the monitoring costs in $H1$ go down as we increase G, and the stated assertion fails for sufficiently large G. Similarly, if G is small enough that the second level of monitoring disappears, then the horizontal case can dominate in the sense of public welfare (however, due to antipodal reasons). Now, in the horizontal case corruption is smaller, but the costs of anti-corruption measures are higher. Suppose that incentives are sufficiently great for ensuring honest reporting within the hierarchy $H2$. But, as far as G appears very small, the hierarchy $H1$ admits no internal equilibrium and $c^* = h^* = p^* = 1, q^* = 0$. Therefore, criminality is not scotched. In this case, stopping anti-corruption struggle seems a better alternative within $H1$. Nevertheless, the horizontal hierarchy $H2$ still allows reducing the level of crime under same parameter values. If the payoff gained by criminality reduction outweighs the costs of anti-corruption measures, then the horizontal hierarchy is advantageous. This immediately brings to

Assertion 3 (Mishra, 2006b). Suppose that agents' incentives and penalties are bounded so that anti-corruption struggle is impossible within the hierarchy $H1$. In this case, anti-corruption struggle can be performed within the hierarchy $H2$, which becomes a more beneficial organizational structure.

The previous subsections have demonstrated that, whenever the probability of bribery detection depends on the agent's effort, a principal suffers from being restricted in corruption suppression and crime control mechanism design. As before, a certain role belongs to higher-level monitoring. But this effect gets "blurred" if different-level agents can enter into ex ante collusion.

Consider the hierarchy $H1$. In this case, A2 applies efforts to supervising and detection the corruption of A1. They enter into collusion only after bribery detection, and A2 does not report the corruption of A1 in exchange for a bribe. Such a situation can be called ex post collusion. We have studied only this possibility so far. However, A1 and A2 can arrange things prior to effort application by A2 (i.e., A2 receives a bribe for monitoring cancellation). And the corruption of A1 is not detected at all. According to the Coase theorem-like argumentation, such a collusion becomes more beneficial for the agents: monitoring costs are saved. But this aggravates the problem for a Principal, since penalization (G) demonstrates smaller efficiency.

As a matter of fact, the described form of collusion takes place in many organizations. It is most probable in organizations with repeated interaction among different-level agents. This form is gradually institutionalized and upper-level officials simply receive their shares for ignoring corruption at lower levels. Although the both forms of collusion (ex ante and ex post) are not independent, taking into account ex ante collusion further complicates the success of anti-corruption measures.

In the context of different hierarchies, an important determining factor for the probability of corruption detection is the scope of management performed upper-level supervisors. Williamson (1967), Calvo and Wellisz (1978), Qian (1994) considered optimal organizational structures in terms of firm employees and size monitoring. The ratio of supervisors and supervisees in management often influences the probability of employee effort/evasion detection. Bac (1996a,b) and Bag (1997) adopted similar reasoning to study different hierarchies in the aspect of corruption. It is possible to construct a "steep" hierarchy (like $H1$), where a higher-level agent controls a lower-level agent A1 and, by-turn, is controlled by agent A3. On the other hand, another approach consists in authorizing agents A1 and A2 to service clients under the supervision of A3. Such a structure can be called a "flat" hierarchy. The cited authors compared these two hierarchies under different assumptions regarding the nature of control procedure.

The preceding analysis was focused par excellence on the ascending models of corruption (Rose-Ackerman, 1999). Only a lower-level official (A1) is engaged in bribery, although the real amount of bribes depends on the character of interaction between A1 and the rest part of a hierarchy. If several such agents deal with clients, it is possible to explore decentralized corruption. The paper (Shleifer and Vishny, 1993) and the book (Bardhan, 1997) noted that decentralized corruption can be worse than its centralized counterpart. Let us consider this hypothesis following (Waller et al., 2002).

Denote by x the benefit of an individual (client) from some not precisely defined action. Suppose that the benefit can be gained (the action performed) only via bribing two corrupt agents (officials) A1 and A2. In addition, these agents are controlled by third corrupt upper-level agent A3. Recall that there may exist descending or ascending corruption. In the former case, A3 establishes the bribe exacted from a client, but needs lower-level agents for client servicing (thus, A3 shares the bribe with A1 and A2). In the latter case, only lower-level agents A1 and A2 interact with a client and establish the bribe to-be-paid by it. At the same time, the upper-level agent monitors them and A1 and A2 have to share the bribe with A3 for keeping silence or protecting against punishment.

For the sake of convenience, assume that x is uniformly distributed on the segment $[0, X]$. Agents do not know x, but are aware of its distribution. Agents exact an identical bribe from each client. Let B indicate the total bribe amount a client has to pay. Clients meeting the condition $x \geq B$ perform the desired action. The participation rate of the client population is $(X-B)/X$.

First, study ascending corruption. Imagine that the lower-level agents (A1 and A2) have to give a share q of the collected bribes to the upper-level agent. Suppose that A1 and A2 do not cooperate. Designate by w the agent's wage and by b_j the bribe exacted by agent $j, j=1,2$. The payoff of agent j constitutes

$$\Pi_j = w + b_j(1-q)(X-b_1-b_2)/X. \tag{1.1.14}$$

It is possible to find an equilibrium pair of bribes (b_1^*, b_2^*) such that the agents maximize their individual payoffs under known bribes exacted by them and known share of the upper-level agent in the bribe. We easily obtain that

$$b_1 = b_2 = X/3, B = 2X/3. \tag{1.1.15}$$

The share of participation equals 1/3, whereas the total bribe amount is $2X/9$.

In the above decentralized setting, the presence of an upper-level agent does not affect the bribe of each agent or the total bribe amount. And adding another hierarchical level has no impact on corruption. A possible explanation lies in a specific model of an upper-level agent. But an alternative interpretation is that A3 controls A1 and A2 and detects corruption with probability q. In the case of detection, A3 completely grabs the bribes collected by A1 and A2, but does not initiate any punishment (e.g., deprivation of wage or application of other penalties). The outcomes remain same.

Compare these results with the case of descending corruption. Here A3 establishes bribes to-be-collected by A1 and A2. The total bribe goes to A3, and the latter returns some share t to A1 and A2. Actually, such a situation resembles centralized corruption. Agent A3 chooses B to maximize the expression $\Pi_3 = B(X-B)/X - t$. Obviously, $B^* = X/2$, i.e., each agent has to collect $b^* = B^*/2 = X/4$ from a client. As against ascending decentralized corruption, each client pays a smaller total bribe and the share of participation is higher.

Since A1 and A2 are involved in real bribery, they possibly collect more than authorized by A3. Let b be the permitted bribe and b_j specify a surplus exacted by agent j. So long as surpluses do not meet the interests of A3, it monitors A1 and A2. Suppose that A3 detects the surplus with probability q and, if this is the case, confiscates all collected bribes and dismiss the agents. Then a lower-level agent satisfies the permitted quota and $b_j = 0$ under the following condition:

$$w+t \geq (1-q)(w+t)+(1-q)b_j[(X-2b-(b_1+b_2))/X]. \tag{1.1.16}$$

Similarly to the previous case, agent j chooses b_j to maximize

$$\Pi_j = (1-q)(w+t) + (1-q)b_j[(X-2b-(b_i+b_j))/X], \text{ i,j} = 1,2. \qquad (1.1.17)$$

It is possible to show that $b_1^* = b_2^* = (X-2b)/3$. Without lower-level agent's consent, the upper-level one choose b to maximize the function

$$\Pi_3 = [2b + (2/3)q(X-2b)][(X-2b-(2/3)(X-2b))/X]. \qquad (1.1.18)$$

(Recall that $B = 2b$). Readers can easily find that

$$B^* = 2b^* = X\frac{6-8q}{4(3-2q)}. \qquad (1.1.19)$$

By substituting (1.1.19) into (1.1.18), we calculate the surpluses preferred by A1 and A2. In this case, the total bribe amount paid by a client becomes appreciably higher. Set $q = 1/2$; then the total bribe amount received from each client in the centralized case without lower-level agent's consent makes up $3X/4$. This quantity exceeds its analog in the decentralized case $2X/3$.

Assertion 4 (Mishra, 2006b). To the degree the descending system guarantees efficient centralization of bribe assignment, it leads to smaller bribes of clients in comparison with the decentralized ascending system. However, in the absence of consent between lower- and upper-level agents, the descending system yields greater bribes of clients.

Therefore, the key role belongs to the motivational constraint ensuring consent between A1 and A2. According to an important remark in Waller et al. (2002), if the upper level of the hierarchy fails to control bribes collection efficiently, then its addition simply induces another level of corruptors. Satisfaction of the condition (1.1.16) depends on several parameters X, q, w. In this trivial example, transfer t can be chosen so that (1.1.16) always holds true and the inefficiency caused by centralized bribe assignment disappears. But this may not be possible in more general statements.

Over a long period of time, internal professional advancement is considered as a motivation mechanism for struggling with employee evasion from active labor activity. In the context of corruption hierarchies, the question is how far the capabilities of internal advancement affect the motives of lower-level officials with regard to corruption. At the first glance, one can hypothesize that internal promotion increases losses due to potential dismissal, thereby reducing corruption motivation. However, internal advancement effects are not so obvious within the hierarchy, where higher levels are also corrupt. Carillo (2000) and Rauch (2001) studied the impact of internal promotion on corruption in different aspects. Consider the hierarchy $H1$. Here A2 controls A1 and the bribery of A1 is detected with probability p. If A1 takes no bribes, it advances to the position of A2 (becomes a higher-level official). Most statements claim that the income of A2 is higher, which increases the motivation of A1 for being honest. But the expected income depends on a series of factors. An advancement mechanism defines a certain degree to which the career chances of A1 depend on its attitude towards corruption. Imagine that A2 is also corrupt; being captured, then A1 can bribe A2 and receive promotion. In the limit case when extortion is possible, corrupt A2 can cancel the advancement of honest A1 and promote corrupt A1. Even if extortion takes no place but advancement obeys a quota (only n of m , $n < m$) officials A1 are promoted), then corrupt A2 can replace honest A1 by corrupt A1 in the list of advancing agents. Choosing between two candidates, corrupt A2 prefers a corrupt colleague to an honest one. In such cases, a better solution is random choice if a strong prejudice exists against corrupt A1. Alternatively, an advancement mechanism can be checked by other officials so that corrupt A1 never receives promotion.

The expected payoff of A1 also depends on its intentions at the position of A2 (honest or corrupt behavior). A1 can have strategic plans of being honest in order to deserve promotion and then exact bribes. Carillo (2000) considered a modification of the hierarchy $H1$, where A2 is controlled by a next hierarchical level (A3) composed of incorruptible officials only. According to a possible interpretation, A3 represents an external organization not entering into collusion with (internal) agents. A2 audits A1 with probability p, whereas A3 audits A2 with probability q . If A1 is captured while receiving a bribe b from a client, it can be dismissed (which causes deprivation of its wage w_1 and bribe confiscation). However, corrupt A2 can conceal this information in exchange for the bribe received from client by A1. By-turn, the bribery of A2 can be detected by A3; in this case, A2 is dismissed (again, with deprivation of its wage w_2 and bribe confiscation). Note that A1 incurs costs due to bribery only if A2 prefers honesty. Denote by x and y the partial payoffs of agents A1 and A2, respectively, gained by their job retainment or moral losses due to their dismissal. As previously, suppose that x and y obey uniform distributions on the segments [0,X] and [0,Y], respectively. Under given wages and the probabilities of monitoring/auditing, it is possible to calculate the share of agents choosing corruption strategy in an equilibrium (the quantities λ_1 and λ_2). Obviously, the decision of A1 to take bribes depends on the share of corrupt officials A2. Within this setting, higher wages and probabilities of auditing obviously suppress corruption. Even if w_1 and p are fixed, by increasing w_2 and q we reduce λ_1. In some sense, the suppression effect possesses the following trickle-down feature: higher honesty of A2 scotches the corruption of A1. Moreover, wage policy and monitoring efforts exert similar impact on corruption. Yet, internal advancements (if any) also affect these factors.

Assume that the advancement system is such that honest A2 promotes only honest A1 (after audit), whereas corrupt A2 promotes honest and corrupt A1. Actually, promotion of a corrupt subordinate by a corrupt superior is not surprising under the temptation of bribery. In addition, a corrupt superior always benefits from reducing the share of honest A2: this increases the share of corrupt subordinates, *ergo* enhances the expected corrupt income. And the share of promoted A1 makes up $\lambda_1\lambda_2 + (1 - \lambda_1)$. It is possible to find the share of agents preferring bribery. Suppose that x and y have total correlation: one can predict whether A1 described by some x becomes corrupt A2 after advancement. Let x_1, x_2 be marginal agents considering corruption and honesty of equal value at the positions of A1 and A2, respectively.

This means that all officials with $x < x_1$ choose corruption at the position of A1 (similarly, for officials $x < x_2$). If $x_1 < x_2$, all corrupt A1 and even some honest A1 become corrupt, being appointed to A2.

It is possible to discuss how advancements influence anti-corruption strategies in the model. The growth of w_2 immediately reduces the share of corrupt A2. This fact makes bribery more risky for A1, as well as weakens converse advancement effects (corrupt officials promotion) and indirectly stimulates the honesty of A1. Higher wage implies higher expected income of A1 owing to future advancement. The total effect from corruption reduction (A1) is greater than in the absence of internal advancements. In contrast, an increase of q can have mixed consequences: it cuts down the share of corrupt A2, but also curtails the expected income of officials preferring bribery after their advancement. Hence, the motive for honesty becomes weaker, generally facilitating corruption growth at the level of A1. These considerations were summarized as follows (Carrillo 2000).

Assertion 5 (Mishra, 2006b). Let $x_1 < x_2$. Increasing the wage w_2 of upper-level officials reduces the share of corrupt lower-level officials. However, higher probability q of monitoring performed by upper-level officials may cause corruption growth at the lower level.

Advancement plays a more considerable role in selection if the nature and capabilities of corruption at the two control levels differ and internal corruption takes no place. Rauch (2001) modeled a situation when A2 supplies a set of public goods under a limited budget. The corruption of A2 means embezzlement of allocated funds and desiccation of the goods. A2 uses the services of A1 for the real supply of the goods, but A1 can influence their final supply engaged in petty corruption. But A1 is monitored by A2, and the set of public goods desired by A2 can be provided. A captured official is dismissed, internal corruption does not exist.

Individuals in an organization differ in the sense of utility they can derive via efficient utilization of the authority (D) belonging to the upper level only (A2). An agent with high D consumes more time, effort and energy on subordinates monitoring to receive evidence that a desired set of public goods is realized. This means that less time and effort can be allocated to design the mechanisms and schemes of rent sources; and the grand corruption of A2 decreases. Since lower-level officials (A1) risk being dismissed due to petty corruption, then higher monitoring efforts of A2 reduce petty corruption. Therefore, corruption at the upper and lower levels demonstrates downward drift.

In this case, only honest officials have positive probability of advancement. As in the previous model, the prospect of advancement increases the alternative costs of corruption. However, these costs vary for officials with different D. A lower-level official with high D appreciates advancement as ensuring more efficient application of its authority and hence has more motives for being honesty. Corrupt officials are not promoted, and the probability of advancement becomes greater for an official with high D. If an upper-level official is selected by internal promotion (not from a whole set of officials), then the probability of having high D is also greater for it. Recall that such an upper-level official needs more effort for supervising, which leads to better selection: corrupt officials are detected more frequently. Thus, internal advancement reduces corruption at the both levels.

Internal advancement may have converse effects under corrupt high-level officials. Corrupt superiors oppress their subordinates, making the latter also corrupt. Mishra (2006a) studied a model of such a harassment and showed the existence of multiple equilibria (petty and grand corruption). Consider a group of subordinates controlled by corrupt superiors. If honest agents undergo bribery harassment, while corrupt agents avoid penalty via bribery of their superiors, the number of honest agents is likely to decrease. Agents act in an environment of distrust (everybody is viewed as a corruptor) and this incites many agents to bribery. If the lower level contains many corrupt agents, the probability of advancement and further bribery of a corrupt agent is also higher. By-turn, a corrupt superior induces the corruption behavior of the rest agents. Consequently, widespread corruption is self-reproducing.

Many countries applied anti-corruption measures, but failed in making good progress. The presence of hierarchical corruption can have appreciable contribution to these failures. When upper- and lower-level employees are corrupt, implementation of any motivational schemes faces obstacles. "Set a thief to catch a thief": this proverb seems justified only in very special cases and does not lead to a great success.

The presented results acquire negative tinge as the models take into account additional properties of the real world. When the probability of corruption detection is fixed, an appropriate hierarchy can guarantee certain harmony with law by stimulating honest behavior or increasing the costs of corruption. But this statement loses correctness under the assumption that the probability of detection depends on the choice of monitoring efforts and the possibility of ex ante collusion. In the latter case, there is no detection and hierarchical monitoring gets discredited.

Despite the performed comparison of different organizational structures, this should be comprehended as the choice of suboptimal outcomes. Furthermore, the outcomes have sensitivity to institutional specifics and constraints imposed on different tools. In principle, it is possible to design sophisticated anti-corruption mechanisms, but most real situations apply strict constraints to tools choice. The general picture arising in the course of analysis points to a close connection between the optimal motivational scheme and organizational structure.

The role of honest individuals in organizations requires a thorough study. Organizations often comprise honest employees being inefficient among very many corrupt colleagues. Being unable to introduce real changes, such employees prefer bribery or passive observance. It is possible to explore schemes, where honest employees become efficient. According to the analysis, one should be careful in staff recruitment policy and promotion schemes design. These measures may contribute to anti-corruption struggle, but sometimes it seems almost impracticable to change anything. Then alternative ways to organize the principal's activity are required (Mishra, 2006b).

The paper (Auriol, 2006) was dedicated to the problem of corruption in procurement and public purchase. The author adopted the "Principal–delegate–firms" model which was pioneered in the context of corruption by Tirole (Tirole, 1986). Analysis discriminates between the cases of capture (firms bribe for tender win) and extortion (firms pay for participation in a tender). According to Auriol's view, capture is more prejudicial: in contrast to extortion, it causes direct public losses due to inefficient resource allocation. The ratio of these losses and the bribe amount varies from 1.2 to 2.88. The main recommendation of the French researcher is to organize open tenders for large procurements and not to monitor small procurements at all (Auriol, 2006).

The paper (Lambert-Mogiliansky et al., 2007) explored petty corruption in the case when a request is approved via a bureaucratic chain. None of requests receives approval in the one-step setting. Within the framework of the repeated interaction model, the author characterized trigger strategy equilibria minimizing public losses due to corruption. It was demonstrated that the "single window" procedure of permit issuance does not necessarily reduce corruption; an ambiguous impact also belongs to bureaucratic rotation (Lambert-Mogiliansky et al., 2007).

A series of Russian investigators considered anti-corruption struggle in the activity of tax inspectorate. Alexey Savvateev's paper (2003) treated the corruption suppression problem in tax inspectorate via a two-level control structure. The upper level of this structure chooses an audit strategy taking into account an observed profile of violations (participation in collusion) of all agents. The author identified an interesting "domino effect": even agents with appreciable corruption capabilities (sufficiently high bribe amounts) sequentially scorn bribery as the number of corruptors goes down. This allows reducing the costs of anti-corruption measures significantly.

Alexander Vasin and the co-athors (Vasin and Panova, 1999; Vasin et al, 2010, 2011) analyzed the problem of an efficient control structure which guarantees law-abiding behavior and suppresses corruption under existing cost constraints. An inspection strategy is defined by the probabilities of auditing depending on incoming information on the results obtained at preceding levels. Necessary and sufficient optimality conditions were derived, which serve for calculating the corresponding probabilities of auditing. Possible applications of the theory were discussed. This direction of research also includes the paper of Vladimir Bure and Suriya Kumacheva (2010) and the dissertation of Kumacheva (2011).

The book (Vybornov, 2006) considered models of corruption using the theory of control in organizations (Novikov, 2007). The author studied game-theoretic multilevel hierarchical interaction with the following subjects (in the descending order of their authority): a common corrupt Meta-Principal, a set of corrupt Principals, and a set of corrupt Agents. Agents strive for maximization of their utilities. Next, Principals either maximize their utilities or solve complex problems, e.g., optimization of Agents' actions or anti-corruption struggle. And the Meta-Principal is interested in its utility maximization or optimization of Principals' actions or anti-corruption struggle. Vybornov systematized the hierarchical relations among the subjects and identified five major types of their interaction. The models were classified based on the number of participants, hierarchical structures, the awareness of participants and their relations.

A detailed analysis covered a wide class of problems associated with the above types of interaction, namely:

1. The tender problem ("Principal-Agent" interaction).

It was shown that corruption can be prevented in the tender problem via information control. The author proved that a bribe required for tender winning goes down due to penalty increase. Another result concerns the disadvantageousness of Agents' penalties increase for the whole set of players and the advantageousness of simultaneous penalties increase for Agents (not Principals!).

2. The resource allocation problem ("Principal-Agent" and "Principal-Principal" interactions).

The Meta-Principal payoff maximization problems were solved under two types of functions defining the probability of corruption detection for Principals. The equilibrium bribe minimization problem was treated and solved as the problems with restricted audit efforts for the two types of the probabilities of corruption detection for Principals. In addition, the author presented solutions to the resource allocation problems with internal equilibria in the games of Principals and in the games of Principals and the Meta-Principal including the existence conditions of non-corruption Nash equilibrium.

Analysis was focused on the hierarchical incentive problem in "Principal–Agent" organizational systems for preventing plan fulfillment costs overstatement by Agent. The conditions when Agent benefits from truth-telling (i.e., reporting its actual type to the Principal) were formulated. And Vybornov calculated the optimal probability of Agent's auditing by Principal under given payoff and penalty functions.

The book considered the hierarchical incentive problem of collective activity ("Principal" + "Agent" – "Meta-Principal"), as well as some its modifications. The conditions when Principal benefits from choosing strategies without costs overstatement were suggested. And finally, the author established the conditions preventing the Principal's corruption behavior under given payoff functions, costs and the additional assumption of Agents' symmetry (Vybornov, 2006).

The paper (Mikhailov, 1999) examined hierarchical models of corruption in authorities, which are derivatives of the "authority-society" model further analyzed in (Mikhailov and Lankin, 2006). We outline the essential distinctions of this framework in comparison with numerous models of corruption introduced by other researchers: the number of levels in a hierarchy can be infinitely large; system description employs mathematical physics equations.

The author suggested the following classification of corruption:

1. common corruption (acts performed by a law-abiding authority according to its official instructions, but in exchange for a bribe);
2. inactivity corruption (acts not performed by an authority owing to a bribe);
3. hyperactivity corruption (acts performed by a corrupt authority "in excess of the plan."

The hierarchy in models is described by the authority tree topology, the number of incoming instances and the level of their power, as well as by some behavioral characteristics of bureaucrats. The basic parameters of interaction among instances, e.g., the levels of power, are described by an integral-differential equation under the assumption of sufficiently many hierarchical levels. An authority hierarchy represents a line segment with instances placed in the descending order of their power. The model also incorporates functional parameters describing the "occupancy" of each level and possible directions of orders. Orders are power "flows" from superior bureaucrats to their subordinates (not necessarily direct ones). The degree of corruption at each level and moment is defined as the sum of corruption acts of the above types normalized by the number of correct actions.

It was demonstrated that the intensity of power flows varies in comparison with the non-corruption case: certain flows lose their intensity due to passivity corruption, whereas new flows appear due to hyperactivity corruption. Hence, for power retainment a bureaucrat has to guarantee the difference in powers coinciding with the corresponding value in the non-corruption case. Based on this statement, the authors constructed the equation of the "power retainment law" in the presence of corruption and orders passed according to the existing hierarchy. Furthermore, public losses and total public losses were evaluated for each type of corruption. And finally, corruption suppression costs were estimated depending on the corruptor's position in a power hierarchy and efficient allocation of financial resources assigned to corruption suppression was considered.

The paper (Mikhailov and Lankin, 2006) presented the results of numerical calculations for the chain- and tree-shaped hierarchies of the model considered in (Mikhailov, 1999). For the chain-shaped hierarchy, the authors evaluated the efficiency of corruption suppression depending on the degree of power centralization (the distribution of powers among different levels) and obtained the following results (in the descending order of the degree of power centralization):

- the efficiency of suppressing lower-, middle- and upper-level officials decreases for all types of corruption;
- in all cases, the efficiency achieves its maximum (minimum) under suppressing lower-level officials (extreme-level officials, respectively);
- starting from weakly decentralized hierarchies, the efficiency achieves its maximum (minimum) under suppressing extreme-level officials (upper- or middle-level officials, respectively);
- as the degree of power decentralization grows, the ratio of the maximum and minimum efficiencies tends to unity (for all types of corruption!).

For the tree-shaped hierarchy, Mikhailov and Lankin arrived at a series of conclusions based on numerical experiments:

- the efficiency of corruption suppression of lower- and extreme-level officials demonstrates non-monotonic behavior as the number of officials at an appropriate level grows;
- in comparison with less branched hierarchies, police actions of corruption suppression in strongly branched ones have smaller efficiency;
- in all cases, the efficiency achieves its maximum (minimum) under suppressing lower-level officials (extreme- or upper-level officials, respectively), see (Mikhailov, 1999; Mikhailov and Lankin, 2006).

Model identification. Most mathematical models of corruption mentioned in the survey to some extent employ empirical data. Sometimes, authors describe the identification procedures of their models (with a certain level of detail). Such an approach seems reasonable, as basing on real data is almost necessary in an applied research. One way or another, the measurement problem has to-be-solved also in theoretical models: science does not exist without measurement. However, the problem of empirical data search and usage in corruption model identification appears extremely cumbersome, labor-intensive and thankless.

In the first place, a natural procedure to solve this problem is involving standard econometric methods (Dougherty, 1992) and identification methods (Ljung, 1987). Nevertheless, correct application of these methods often requires rather long homogeneous time series (obviously!) unavailable for such a subtle and delicate phenomenon as corruption.

According to Georgy Satarov, there exist two basic approaches to corruption measurement, *viz.*, the sociological approach (surveys with results processing) and the empirical approach (international indices assessing corruption in different countries), see (Levin et al., 2011, p. 251). The empirical approach also includes statistical models, e.g., lobbying (Levin and Levina, 2001). But this approach is not suitable for identifying the main group of optimization and game-theoretic models which describe the mechanisms and regularities of corruption behavior.

A detailed treatment and illustrative application of the sociological approach to corruption study were given in the fundamental monograph by Satarov (Russian Corruption, 2013). The authors correctly noted that measurement is not just a certain procedure of assigning numerical values to something, but the most widespread and fundamental form of modeling. Using a series of sociological studies conducted by INDEM foundation within the period from 2001 to 2010, the cited researchers developed a methodology of sociological modeling of corruption including different aspects such as analysis of corruption and other informal practices, spatial and social geography of corruption, dispositions and causes of corruption behavior. The main tools were depth interviews and analysis of quantitative data. Satarov and the colleagues suggested several generalized variables and indexes characterizing the level of corruption and its dynamics, as well as described their design methodology. However, all these innovations served for the specific goals of investigations instead of data accumulation for constructing mechanism-type models of corruption.

Thus and so, we declare that the identification problem is still open for the mathematical models of corruption.

Conclusions. The performed analysis brings to the following conclusions.

1. mathematical models of corruption describe the strategic behavior of active agents, thereby mostly involving the framework of optimization and game theory. Researchers also employ empirical-statistical models and few models of other types.
2. Generally, the models belong to the static class or reflect the dynamics of decision-making (multistep games). Optimal control models and differential games with explicit description of controlled system dynamics are not so common. At the same time, scientists often adopt probabilistic models, as such an approach is conventional in modern contract theory and microeconomic models.
3. The mathematical models of corruption are identified using standard methods of applied statistics; however, their application faces the problem of empirical data on corruption. Organizing special mathematical and sociological studies seems a most adequate approach here, but this is associated with obvious organizational and financial difficulties and happens rarely.
4. The methodological basis of corruption modeling is the approach pioneered by Gary Becker and further developed by Susan Rose-Ackermann, which balances the benefit from prevented corruption losses and the costs of anti-corruption struggle.
5. From the substantial viewpoint, corruption modeling embraces very many aspects: different scales (petty and grand corruption), types (extortion and capture), domains

(economics, politics, management), kinds (business and social corruption), forms (governmental and corporate corruption), activities (levying of taxes, permit issuance), branches of industry and regions, and so on.

6. An important place among corruption models belongs to the description of corruption relations in hierarchical structures. Here most attention is paid to the issue regarding corruption control efficiency in the case when supervisors are also corrupt. And many real factors lead to the negative answer to it.
7. We emphasize some striking conclusions drawn as the result of modeling:
   - game-theoretic models admit the existence of multiple "good" and "bad" equilibria corresponding to small and high levels of corruption, respectively, in a society; in "bad" equilibria, anti-corruption measures (penalty increase, frequent inspections) even cause counter-intuitive consequences intensifying corruption;
   - competition among officials exerts ambiguous impact on corruption and depends on a series of factors, particularly, on the professional development costs of license applicants; this thesis holds true for other popular anti-corruption measures such as the single window procedure and rotation of officials;
   - high natural rent intensifies corruption only in the case of weak democratic institutions;
   - in the presence of corruption, struggle against shadow economy seems pointless.

The next section introduces an original concept of mathematical modeling of corruption in hierarchical systems based on sustainable management.

1.2. The Concept of Corruption Modeling Based on Sustainable Management

The original concept of corruption modeling in hierarchical systems proceeds from theory of sustainable management (Ougolnitsky, 2002, 2005, 2010, 2011). As a matter of fact, this theory includes three basic interconnected elements. In what follows, we provide their brief description.

1. *Control methods*. The Leader-Follower system has three methods of hierarchical control, namely: 1) compulsion when Leader forces Follower to facilitate the achievement of the former's goals, ignoring the latter's goals and interests (impact on the Follower's set of admissible strategies); 2) impulsion when Leader creates certain conditions so that Follower benefits from facilitating the achievement of the former's goals and does not benefit from the converse behavior (impact on the Follower's payoff function with feedback); 3) collaboration when the relations between these subjects become mutually beneficial. Table 1.2.1 provides a compact characterization of these control methods; for detailed treatment, an interested reader is referred to the monograph (Ougolnitsky, 2011).

2. *Sustainable development*. The notion of sustainable development (SD) applies to the impact of a society on environment and, moreover, to any dynamic system involving active agents. In fact, the SD requirements include three conditions: homeostasis, trade-off and dynamic consistency. For a certain system, homeostasis is the domain of its essential

characteristics, which corresponds to the normal functioning and evolvement of the system. The functioning of any dynamic system is described by a set of time-varying indicators. The homeostasis condition dictates that all system indicators belong to given ranges on a (sufficiently large finite or even infinite) horizon and, in the limit case, take given point values.

Table 1.2.1. A characterization of hierarchical control methods

	Compulsion	Impulsion	Collaboration
General description of the method	Leader assigns its desirable strategy to Follower by force	The strategy desirable for Leader is more beneficial to Follower than undesirable ones	Follower chooses the strategy desirable for Leader voluntarily and consciously
Nature of impact	Administrative or legislative	Economic	Social-psychological
Type of relationships	Subject-to-object	Subject-to-object with partial consideration of the Follower's interests	Subject-to-subject
Mathematical formalization	The Leader's impact on the Follower's set of admissible strategies	The Leader's impact on the Follower's payoff function	Transition of Leader and Follower to the collaboration and maximization of the coalitional payoff function

We emphasize that the SD conditions embrace not only the state of a controlled system but also impacts on it. Any complex active dynamic system is associated with a set of subjects. On the one hand, their goals and interests are more or less defined by the state and functioning of the system. On the other hand, these subjects influence the system, thereby affecting its functioning. Therefore, the SD of a system is possible only under proper consideration and coordination of interests pursued by all subjects associated with the system. In the overwhelming majority of cases, their interests and goals do not coincide, leading to conflicts. However, the interests of subjects are not opposite and a certain trade-off can be reached. In the light of the SD conditions, the trade-off has to take into account the homeostasis condition. Reaching exactly such a trade-off among associated subjects forms another prerequisite for the SD of a system. The trade-off condition in its mathematical setting means the existence of a solution for a game describing the conflict interaction of all subjects associated with a system. If a trade-off has not been reached, a system is in jeopardy of inadequate impacts potentially destroying homeostasis.

Another key problem of SD concerns the inconsistence of short- and long-term optimality criteria. The homeostasis condition possesses the long-term character: it must be satisfied over the whole period of system existence and functioning. At the same time, associated subjects are often guided by short-term criteria whose period is appreciably smaller than the system lifetime. And a reached compromise can be broken by cooperators benefiting from another strategy answering their short-time interests at a current step. In this context, the SD conditions admit implementation only for compromises preserving their optimality for all associated subjects over the whole lifetime of the system. Under the game-theoretic formalization, this principle is known as dynamic stability. Researchers discriminate between weak dynamic stability (also called time consistency) and strong dynamic stability (subgame perfectness), see (Petrosjan, 1977; Zenkevich et al., 2009; Kidland and Prescott, 1977; Differential games, 2000). A game solution enjoys dynamic stability if its truncation remains optimal in all subgames arising along the trajectory of system development (optimal one for weak and any for strong dynamic stability). This guarantees the practical implementability of a trade-off solution so that none of subjects benefits by a unilateral deviation over the whole lifetime of the system.

One can claim that the conditions of homeostasis, trade-off and dynamic stability are necessary (severally) and sufficient (jointly) conditions of SD for any dynamic system with active agents. The homeostasis condition expresses the basic requirements to all aspects of system functioning, the trade-off condition ensures adequate impacts of all associated subjects on the system (during consideration of their interests), and the dynamic stability condition means the subjects' disadvantage via any deviation from a reached compromise solution with the course of time. Table 1.2.2 gives the summary of the SD conditions.

3. *Hierarchically controlled dynamic systems.* The classical notion of a controlled dynamic system (CDS) comprises an active control subject (a control subsystem) and a passive control object (a controlled subsystem). A subject applies a control action to an object for achieving a control objective under existing constraints. A subject observes the object's state at any moment and corrects the control action if necessary (the feedback principle). However, in a series of cases, the subject's control actions predetermined by its private goals and interests may bring an object to an admissible state according to the viewpoint of a higher-level subject. This suggests an idea of introducing an additional (higher) control level to maintain "supersystem" requirements imposed on the state of a controlled object. Note that a new control subject may possess its own private interests. Pursuing its goals, a new control subject affects an initial control subject. The above considerations lead to the concept of a hierarchically controlled dynamic system (HCDS). The trivial configuration of an HCDS contains three elements:

Table 1.2.2. The SD conditions of a dynamic system with active agents

SD conditions	Conceptual description	Mathematical formalization
Homeostasis	All essential indicators of system functioning belong to given ranges	$\forall t \in [0,T]: x(t) \in X^*$, where x(t) is the system state vector (the phase vector), X* is the homeostasis domain, and T is the period of functioning (system lifetime)
Trade-off	Interests' consideration and coordination for all subjects associated with the system	The existence of a solution to the game-theoretic model of conflict interaction among the subjects
Dynamic stability	Coordination of short- and long-term optimality criteria so that any subject benefits nothing via unilateral deviation from the trade-off during the whole period of system functioning (lifetime)	Time consistency or subgame perfectness of the game-theoretic solution

- an upper-level control subject (Leader);
- a lower-level control subject (Follower);
- a controlled dynamic system (CDS).

By assumption, the relations among these elements of an HCDS are organized as follows: Leader exerts an impact on Follower, and Follower exerts an impact on CDS (the Leader's direct impact on CDS takes no place). Leader and Follower together can be considered as a joint impact subject affecting CDS and having a hierarchical structure (which explains the term of an HCDS). Of course, the general case admits more complex configurations, where a hierarchical impact subject affecting CDS represents fan-like, diamond-shaped structures, etc., as well as their combinations.

Consequently, the whole essence of the notion of HCDS consists in the following. By influencing CDS, Follower pursues well-defined goals (generally, not coinciding with CDS maintenance in a given state, see the homeostasis condition). By-turn, CDS is a passive object and cannot achieve these goals. This explains the necessity of Leader capable of affecting Follower for the above goals. Let us formulate the general hierarchical control problem of a dynamic system (Ougolnitsky, 1999):

$$x(t) \in \Omega, t = 1,2,...,T; \tag{1.2.1}$$

$$J_v = \sum_{t=1}^{T} g_v(t, v(t)) \to \max; \tag{1.2.2}$$

$$v(t) \in V(t), t = 1,2,...,T; \tag{1.2.3}$$

$$J_u = \sum_{t=1}^{T} g_u(t, x(t-1), u(t), v(t)) \to \max; \tag{1.2.4}$$

$$u(t) \in U(t, x(t-1), v(t)), t = 1,2,...,T; \tag{1.2.5}$$

$$\xi(t) \in \Xi(t), t = 1,...,T; \tag{1.2.6}$$

$$x(t+1) = x(t) + f(t, x(t), u(t), \xi(t)); \tag{1.2.7}$$

$$x(0) = x_0, t = 0,1,..., T-1. \tag{1.2.8}$$

Here $x(t) = (x_1(t),..., x_n(t))$ denotes the state vector of CDS at moment t;

$u(t) = (u_1(t),...,u_m(t))$ means the control vector applied by Follower to CDS at moment t;

$v(t) = (v_1(t),...,v_p(t))$ is the control vector applied by Leader to Follower at moment t;

$\xi(t) = (\xi_1(t),..,\xi_r(t))$ indicates the uncontrolled external disturbance vector of CDS at moment t;

$V(t)$ specifies the Leader's admissible control domain at moment t;

$U(t, x(t-1), v(t))$ designates the Follower's admissible control domain at moment t;

$\Xi(t)$ is the admissible external disturbance domain at moment t;

$g_v(t, v(t))$ describes the Leader's objective function at moment t;

J_v - stands for the Leader's total objective function over the period [0,T];

$g_u(t, x(t-1), u(t), v(t))$ represents the Follower's objective function at moment t;

J_u - the Follower's total objective function over the period [0,T];

$f(t, x(t), u(t), \xi(t))$ is the state transition operator of CDS from moment t to moment t+1 (a given nonlinear function);

$x_0 = (x_{01},..., x_{0n})$ corresponds to a known initial state of CDS;

T signifies the prediction horizon; Ω makes the desirable state domain of CDS.

The condition (1.2.1) formalizes a real control objective: it is required that at each moment CDS belongs to a given domain Ω of the state space R^n. The objective function (1.2.2) is maximized over all possible trajectories $\{v(t)\}$, meeting the condition (1.2.3). Consequently, the problem (1.2.2)-(1.2.3) is an optimization problem for Leader subject to the auxiliary obligatory constraint (1.2.1). Accordingly, the expressions (1.2.4)-(1.2.5) define an optimization problem for Follower; in the general case, the only knowledge about the external disturbances $\xi(t)$ is satisfaction of the condition (1.2.6). And finally, formulas (1.2.7)-(1.2.8) describe the controlled system dynamics under the Follower's impact, external factors and given initial conditions.

From the mathematical view, the expressions (1.2.1)-(1.2.8) determine a multistep hierarchical two-player (Leader-Follower) game under external disturbances $\xi(t)$. The formal requirements to the functions and sets embedded in this model, as well as the rules of the game are described in each specific case.

Let us define compulsion and impulsion equilibria taking into account the SD conditions and their design algorithms for two- and three-level control systems (Ougolnitsky and Usov, 2014). The original game-theoretic hierarchical model of sustainable management (SM) has the form

$$J_L(y(t)) = \int_0^T e^{-\alpha t} g_L(y(t))dt \to \max \qquad (1.2.9)$$

$$q(t) \in Q; p(t) \in P; \qquad (1.2.10)$$

$$J_F(y(t)) = \int_0^T e^{-\alpha t} g_F(y(t))dt \to \max \quad (1.2.11)$$

$$u(t) \in U; \quad (1.2.12)$$

$$\dot{x} = f(u(t), x(t)), x(0) = x_0; \quad (1.2.13)$$

$x(t) \in X^*, t \geq 0.$ (1.2.14)

Subscripts L and F indicate Leader and Follower, respectively; J_L and J_F, g_L and g_F are their integral and instantaneous payoff functions; T gives a finite or infinite horizon (the second case is more adequate to the sustainable management problem); α denotes the discount factor; $y(t) = (q(t), p(t), u(t), x(t))$; $q(t)$ forms the compulsion control vector applied by Leader; $p(t)$ is the impulsion control vector applied by Leader; $u(t)$ represents the Follower's control vector (of same dimension as $q(t)$); $x(t)$ signifies the state vector of CDS; the expression (1.2.13) describe the CDS dynamics under given initial conditions and the Follower's control actions; formulas (1.2.14) reflect the SD conditions for CDS. By assumption, Q, P, U are compact subsets of appropriate metric spaces; J_L and J_F are continuous in their arguments; the vector-function f in (1.2.13) meets the Caratheodory conditions.

Formally, the SM problem represents the differential game (1.2.9)-(1.2.13) with the phase constraints (1.2.14). Its essence is to find an acceptable trade-off among the control subjects considering the requirements to the state of CDS.

Analyze an information extension of the game (1.2.9)-(1.2.14), which corresponds to compulsion. In this case, impulsion control is not used. Leader exerts an impact on the Follower's set of admissible strategies (but not its payoff function) by choosing an open-loop strategy $q(t)$ and reporting it to Follower. A natural example of such an impact consists in the inequalities

$$u(t) \leq q(t) \quad \text{or } q(t) \leq u(t), \quad (1.2.15)$$

restricting the Follower's admissible controls above or below (depending on problem specifics). These constraints cannot be violated by Follower at the "physical" level. Being aware of $q(t)$, Follower chooses its optimal response from the set

$$R_F^{comp}(q(t)) = \{u(t) \in U : J_F^{comp}(q(t), u(t), x(t)) = \max_{v(t) \in U(t)} J_F^{comp}(q(t), v(t), x(t))\}.$$

The Leader's guaranteed result makes up

$$\gamma_L^{comp} = \sup_{q(t)\in Q} \inf_{u(t)\in R_F^{comp}(q(t))} J_L^{comp}(q(t),u(t),x(t)),$$

where the trajectory $x(t)$ is induced by the corresponding control action $u(t)$; superscript *comp* means compulsion. A compulsion equilibrium considering the SD conditions is a strategy profile

$$(q^*(t),\tilde{u}^*(t)) \in \widetilde{BR}_F : J_L^{comp}(\pi(q^*(t),\tilde{u}^*(t),x^*(t))) = \gamma_L^{comp},$$
$$\widetilde{BR}_F = \{(q(t),\tilde{u}(t)) \in Q\times\tilde{U} : u(q(t)) \in R_F^{comp}(q(t))\}$$

under the condition (1.2.14), where the trajectory $x^*(t)$ is induced by the strategy $\tilde{u}^*(t)$.

The constructed information extension is similar to the game Γ_{1t} (Kononenko, 1977) with a couple of features: (a) Leader exerts an impact on the Follower's set of admissible strategies and (b) the condition (1.2.14) has to-be-satisfied. Note that, by analogy to the static game Γ_1, here the Follower's optimal response to the Leader's choice represents an operator $\tilde{u}(t) = u(q(t))$ with the domain $R_F^{comp}(q(t))$.

The design algorithm of compulsion equilibria with the SD conditions includes the following steps.

1. Solve the parametric optimal control problem (1.2.11)-(1.2.13) associated with Follower: its solution is an operator $u^*(t) = u^*(q(t))$ inducing a unique trajectory $x^*(t)$ of CDS for each $q(t)$.
2. Solve the optimal control problem (1.2.9)-(1.2.10), (1.2.13) associated with Leader subject to the additional constraint (1.2.14), where the operator $u^*(t) = u^*(q(t))$ (see Step 1) is substituted into (1.2.9) and (1.2.13). If this problem admits a solution $q^*(t)$, then the strategy profile $(q^*(t),u^*(q(t))$ makes a compulsion equilibrium considering the SD conditions. Application of the described design algorithm may involve methods suggested in (Ougolnitsky and Usov, 2013a).

Now, consider an information extension of the game (1.2.9)-(1.2.14), which corresponds to impulsion. In this case, compulsion control is not used. Leader exerts an impact on the Follower's payoff function via choosing a feedback control mechanism $\tilde{p}(t) = p(u(t))$ and reporting it to Follower. A natural example of such an operator is the incentive–penalty mechanism

$$\tilde{p}(t) = \begin{cases} \text{giving an incentive to Follower if } u(t) \text{ satisfies Leader,} \\ \text{imposing a penalty on Follower, otherwise} \end{cases}$$

Being aware of the strategy $\tilde{p}(t)$, Follower chooses the optimal response from the set

$$R_F^{imp}(\widetilde{p}(t)) = \{u(t) \in U : J_F^{imp}(p(u(t)),u(t),x(t)) = \max_{v(t)\in U} J_F^{imp}(p(v(t)),v(t),x(t))\}.$$

Again, suppose that $u(t) = \widetilde{\widetilde{u}}(\widetilde{p}(t))$. The Leader's guaranteed payoff constitutes

$$\gamma_L^{imp} = \sup_{\widetilde{p}(t)\in\widetilde{P}} \inf_{u\in R_F^{imp}(\widetilde{p})} J_L^{imp}(\pi(\widetilde{p}(t),u(t),x(t))), \widetilde{P} = \{\widetilde{p} : U \to P\}, \widetilde{\widetilde{U}} = \{\widetilde{\widetilde{u}} : \widetilde{P} \to U\},$$

$\pi : \widetilde{P} \times \widetilde{\widetilde{U}} \times X \to P \times U \times X$ is a projection, the trajectory $x(t)$ is induced by the strategy $\widetilde{\widetilde{u}}(t)$, the superscript indicates impulsion. An impulsion equilibrium considering the SD conditions is a strategy profile

$$(\widetilde{p}^*(t), \widetilde{\widetilde{u}}^*(t)) \in B\widetilde{\widetilde{R}}_F : J_L^{imp}(\pi(\widetilde{p}^*(t), \widetilde{\widetilde{u}}^*(t), x^*(t))) = \gamma_L^{imp},$$
$$B\widetilde{\widetilde{R}}_F = \{(\widetilde{p}(t), \widetilde{\widetilde{u}}(t)) \in \widetilde{P} \times \widetilde{\widetilde{U}} : u(p(u(t))) \in R_F^{imp}(\widetilde{p}(t))\}$$

under the condition (1.2.14), where the trajectory $x^*(t)$ is induced by the strategy $\widetilde{\widetilde{u}}^*(t)$. The constructed informational extension is similar to the game Γ_{2t} (Kononenko, 1977) with the additional constraint (1.2.14). The design algorithm of impulsion equilibria considering the SD conditions includes the following steps.

1. Introduce the penalty applied by Leader to Follower, i.e., the operator $\widetilde{p}^P(t) = p^P(u(t)) : J_F^{imp}(\pi(\widetilde{p}^P(t),u(t),x(t))) = \inf_{\widetilde{p}(t)\in\widetilde{P}} J_F^{imp}(\pi(\widetilde{p}(t),u(t),x(t)))$, where the trajectory $x(t)$ is induced by the corresponding control action $u(t)$.
2. Find the Follower's guaranteed payoff under no cooperation with Leader: $L_F^{imp} = \sup_{u(t)\in U} J_F^{imp}(\pi(\widetilde{p}^P(t),u(t),x(t)))$.
3. Consider the set $D_F^* = \{(\widetilde{p}(t),u(t)) : J_F^{imp}(\pi(\widetilde{p}(t),u(t),x(t))) \geq L_F^{imp}, x(t) \in X^*, t \geq 0\}$ and the quantity $K^* = \sup_{(\widetilde{r},u)\in D_F^*} J_L^{imp}(\pi(\widetilde{p}(t),u(t),x(t)))$. For arbitrary $\varepsilon > 0$, it is possible to construct (Kononenko, 1977) open-loop strategies $p^\varepsilon(t), u^\varepsilon(t)$ and a corresponding trajectory $x^\varepsilon(t)$ such that $J_L^{imp}(p^\varepsilon(t),u^\varepsilon(t),x^\varepsilon(t)) \geq K^* - \varepsilon$, where the ε -optimal guaranteeing strategy of Follower has the form
$$\widetilde{p}^\varepsilon(t) = \begin{cases} p^\varepsilon(t), \text{ if } u(t) = u^\varepsilon(t), \\ \widetilde{p}^P(t), \text{otherwise,} \end{cases}$$

and the impulsion equilibrium considering the SD requirements is defined by $(\tilde{p}^{\varepsilon}(t), u^{\varepsilon}(t))$.

Now, consider a three-level HCDS comprising upper-, middle- and lower-level control subjects. For simplicity, further analysis gets confined to the case of one control subject at each level (denoted by UPP, MED and LOW, respectively). Only LOW exerts an impact on CDS, pursuing its individual interests. Subjects UPP and MED are concerned with the SD conditions, as well as may have individual interests. While affecting their subordinates (MED and LOW), subjects UPP and MED apply the methods of compulsion or impulsion. Consequently, there arise four information procedures in the hierarchical three-player game: 1) UPP and MED both use compulsion (CC); 2) UPP uses compulsion, whereas MED uses impulsion (CI); 3) UPP uses impulsion, whereas MED uses compulsion (IC); 4) UPP and MED both use impulsion (II).

The original game-theoretic model possesses the form

$$J_{UPP}(z(t)) = \int_0^T e^{-\alpha t} g_{UPP}(z(t))dt \to \max, \tag{1.2.16}$$

$$q(t) \in Q; p(t) \in P; \tag{1.2.17}$$

$$J_{MED}(z(t)) = \int_0^T e^{-\alpha t} g_{MED}(z(t))dt \to \max, \tag{1.2.18}$$

$$s(t) \in S; \; r(t) \in R; \tag{1.2.19}$$

$$J_{LOW}(z(t)) = \int_0^T e^{-\alpha t} g_{LOW}(z(t))dt \to \max, \tag{1.2.20}$$

$$u(t) \in U \tag{1.2.21}$$

by virtue of (1.2.13) and (1.2.14). Here $z(t) = (q(t), p(t), s(t), r(t), u(t), x(t))$; $q(t), p(t)$ denote the compulsion and impulsion control vectors, respectively, for subject UPP; $s(t), r(t)$ are the compulsion and impulsion control vectors, respectively, for subject MED; $u(t)$ means the control vector of subject LOW; $x(t)$ represents the state vector of CDS; the vectors q, s, u have identical dimension.

By assumption, the sets Q, P, S, R, U are compact subsets of appropriate metric spaces; the functions $J_{UPP}, J_{MED}, J_{LOW}$ enjoy continuity in all arguments; the function f in (1.2.13) satisfies the Caratheodory conditions.

First, consider the case when subjects UPP and MED both choose compulsion. Impulsion controls are not applied. Subject MED performs "primary" monitoring of the SD conditions, restricting the admissible control domain of subject LOW (which incurs certain costs).

Subject UPP conducts "final" monitoring of the SD conditions, restricting the admissible strategy domain of subject MED (which incurs certain costs associated with its actions and the actions of subject MED). Thus, the game-theoretic model can be rewritten as

$$J_{UPP}^{CC}(q(t),s(t),u(t),x(t))=\int_0^T e^{-\alpha t}g_{UPP}^{CC}(q(t),s(t),u(t),x(t))dt\rightarrow\max, \qquad (1.2.22)$$

$$q(t)\in Q; \qquad (1.2.23)$$

$$J_{MED}^{CC}(s(t),u(t),x(t))=\int_0^T e^{-\alpha t}g_{MED}^{CC}(s(t),u(t),x(t))dt\rightarrow\max, \qquad (1.2.24)$$

$$s(t)\in S(q(t)); \qquad (1.2.25)$$

$$J_{LOW}^{CC}(u(t),x(t))=\int_0^T e^{-\alpha t}g_{LOW}^{CC}(u(t),x(t))dt\rightarrow\max, \qquad (1.2.26)$$

$$u(t)\in U(s(q(t))) \qquad (1.2.27)$$

by virtue of (1.2.13) and (1.2.14). In the sequel, time dependence will be omitted for compactness. We have $q\in Q;\tilde{s}\in\tilde{S}=\{\tilde{s}=s(q):Q\rightarrow S\};\tilde{\tilde{u}}\in\tilde{\tilde{U}}=\{\tilde{\tilde{u}}=u(s(q)):Q\times\tilde{S}\rightarrow U\};$, subject UPP chooses a control action (constant strategy) $q\in Q$ and reports it to subject MED; next, subject MED chooses a strategy $\tilde{s}\in\tilde{S}$ such that $s=\tilde{s}(q)$ belongs to its optimal response set $R_{MED}^{CC}(q,u)=Arg\max_{s\in S}J_{MED}^{CC}(s,u,x)$ and reports this strategy to subject LOW; and finally, subject LOW chooses a strategy $\tilde{\tilde{u}}\in\tilde{\tilde{U}}$ such that $u=u(s(q))$ belongs to its optimal response set $R_{LOW}^{CC}(\tilde{s})=Arg\max_{u\in U}J_{LOW}^{CC}(u,x)$. The guaranteed result of subject UPP is $\gamma_{UPP}^{CC}=\sup_{q\in Q}\inf_{s\in R_{MED}^{CC}(q,u)}\inf_{u\in R_{LOW}^{CC}(\tilde{s})}J_{UPP}^{CC}(\pi(q,\tilde{s},\tilde{\tilde{u}},x))$ under the condition (1.2.14); the compulsion-compulsion equilibrium considering the SD conditions makes up

$$\begin{gathered}(q^*,\tilde{s}^*,\tilde{\tilde{u}}^*)\in BR^{CC}:J_B^{CC}(\pi(q^*,\tilde{s}^*,\tilde{\tilde{u}}^*,x^*))=\gamma_B^{CC},\\ BR^{CC}=\{(q,\tilde{s},\tilde{\tilde{u}})\in Q\times\tilde{S}\times\tilde{\tilde{U}}:s(q)\in R_C^{CC}(q,u),u(s(q))\in R_H^{CC}(\tilde{s})\}\end{gathered} \qquad (1.2.28)$$

under the condition (1.2.14), the trajectory x^* is induced by the control action $u^*(s^*(q^*))$.

The design algorithm of the equilibrium (1.2.28) includes the following steps.

1. Solve the parametric optimal control problem (1.2.26)-(1.2.27) of subject LOW by virtue of (1.2.13): the solution is the operator $u^*(t)=u^*(s(q(t)))$ inducing a unique CDS trajectory $x^*(t)$ for each pair (s,q).

2. Solve the parametric optimal control problem (1.2.24)-(1.2.25) of subject MED by virtue of (1.2.13) under $u^*(t) = u^*(s(q(t)))$. The solution is the operator $s^*(q(t))$.
3. Solve the optimal control problem (1.2.22)-(1.2.23) of subject UPP by virtue of (1.2.13) under the additional conditions (1.2.14). If the solution $q^*(t)$ exists, the strategy profile $(q^*, s^*(q), u^* s(q))$ is the compulsion-compulsion equilibrium considering the SD conditions (1.2.28).

Assume that subjects UPP and MED both adhere to impulsion. Compulsion control actions are not used. Subject MED stimulates subject LOW to choose strategies guaranteeing the SD conditions and taking into account its individual interests. In addition, subject UPP stimulates subject MED to choose strategies so that subject LOW maintains the SD conditions taking into account its individual interests. Therefore, the informational procedure takes the form

$$\tilde{p} \in \tilde{P} = \{\tilde{p} : R \to P\}; \tilde{\tilde{r}} \in \tilde{\tilde{R}} = \{\tilde{\tilde{r}} : \tilde{P} \times U \to R\}; u \in U;$$

subject UPP chooses the strategy $\tilde{p} \in \tilde{P}$ and reports it to subject MED; next, subject MED chooses strategy $\tilde{\tilde{r}} \in \tilde{\tilde{R}}$ such that $r = \tilde{\tilde{r}}(p(u), u)$ belongs to its optimal response set $R_{MED}^{II}(\tilde{p}, u) = Arg\max_{r \in R} J_{MED}^{II}(p(u), r, u, x)$ and reports this strategy to LOW; and finally, subject LOW chooses the optimal response $u \in R_{LOW}^{II}(\tilde{\tilde{r}}) = Arg\max_{u \in U} J_{LOW}^{II}(p(u), r, u, x)$. The guaranteed result of subject UPP constitutes $\gamma_{UPP}^{II} = \sup_{\tilde{p} \in \tilde{P}} \inf_{r \in R_{MED}^{II}(\tilde{p}, u)} \inf_{u \in R_{LOW}^{II}(\tilde{\tilde{r}})} J_{UPP}^{II}(\pi(\tilde{p}, \tilde{\tilde{r}}, u, x))$ by virtue of (1.2.14).

The impulsion-impulsion equilibrium considering the SD conditions is

$$\begin{aligned} &(\tilde{p}^*, \tilde{\tilde{r}}^*, u^*) \in BR^{II} : J_{UPP}^{II}(\pi(\tilde{p}^*, \tilde{\tilde{r}}^*, u^*, x^*)) = \gamma_{UPP}^{II}, \\ &BR^{II} = \{(\tilde{p}, \tilde{\tilde{r}}, u) \in \tilde{P} \times \tilde{\tilde{R}} \times U : r(p(u), u) \in R_{MED}^{II}(\tilde{p}, u), u \in R_{LOW}^{II}(\tilde{\tilde{r}})\} \end{aligned} \tag{1.2.29}$$

by virtue of (1.2.14), the trajectory x^* is induced by the control action u^*.

For obtaining the equilibrium (1.2.29), it seems reasonable to apply the procedure suggested in (Gorelik and Kononenko, 1982, p. 39).

1. Evaluate the maximum guaranteed payoff of subject LOW under the penalty strategies used by subjects UPP and MED: $L_{LOW}^{II} = \sup_{u \in U} \inf_{\tilde{p} \in \tilde{P}} \inf_{\tilde{\tilde{r}} \in \tilde{\tilde{R}}} J_{LOW}^{II}(\pi(\tilde{p}, \tilde{\tilde{r}}, u, x))$, where the trajectory $x(t)$ is induced by the control action $u(t)$.
2. Define the set $D_{LOW}^{II} = \{(\tilde{\tilde{r}}, u) : J_{LOW}^{II}(\pi(\tilde{p}^P, \tilde{\tilde{r}}, u, x)) \geq L_{LOW}^{II}\}$, where $\tilde{p}^P$ is the penalty strategy applied by subject UPP to subject MED.

3. Evaluate the maximum guaranteed payoff of subject MED under the penalty strategy used by subject UPP taking into account the interests of subject LOW:
$$L_{MED}^{II} = \sup_{(\tilde{r},u)\in D_{LOW}^{II}} \inf_{\tilde{p}\in\tilde{P}} J_{MED}^{II}(\pi(\tilde{p},\tilde{\tilde{r}},u,x)).$$
4. Introduce the set
$$D_{MED}^{*}=\{(\tilde{p},\tilde{\tilde{r}},u): J_{MED}^{II}(\pi(\tilde{p},\tilde{\tilde{r}},u,x))\geq L_{MED}^{II}, J_{LOW}^{II}(\pi(\tilde{p},\tilde{\tilde{r}},u,x))\geq L_{LOW}^{II}, \forall t\ x(t)\in X^{*}\}$$
which reflects the interests of subjects MED and LOW under the SD conditions.
5. Then the guaranteed payoff of subject UPP is $\gamma_{UPP}^{II} = \sup_{(\tilde{p},\tilde{\tilde{r}},u)\in D_{MED}^{*}} J_{UPP}^{II}(\pi(\tilde{p},\tilde{\tilde{r}},u,x)),$

which leads to (1.2.29). Of course, the described algorithm can be implemented only if $D_{LOW}^{II}\neq\varnothing, D_{MED}^{*}\neq\varnothing$.

And finally, consider an information extension of the game (1.2.13)-(1.2.14), (1.2.16)-(1.2.21), where subject UPP chooses compulsion and subject MED prefers impulsion. In this case, subject UPP restricts the set of admissible impulsion strategies of subject MED; using these strategies, the latter designs a feedback control mechanism and reports it to subject LOW. And so, we have

$$q\in Q; \tilde{\tilde{r}}\in\tilde{\tilde{R}}=\{\tilde{\tilde{r}}:Q\times U\to R\}; \tilde{\tilde{\tilde{u}}}\in\tilde{\tilde{\tilde{U}}}=\{\tilde{\tilde{\tilde{u}}}:\tilde{\tilde{R}}\to U\}.$$

Subject UPP selects a control action (constant strategy) $q\in Q$ and reports it to subject MED; next, subject MED chooses a strategy (control mechanism) $\tilde{\tilde{r}}\in\tilde{\tilde{R}}$ such that $r=\tilde{\tilde{r}}(q,u)$ belongs to the optimal response set $R_{MED}^{CI}(q,u) = Arg\max_{r\in R} J_{MED}^{CI}(q,r,u,x)$ and reports it to subject LOW; and the latter chooses a strategy $\tilde{\tilde{\tilde{u}}}\in\tilde{\tilde{\tilde{U}}}$ such that the optimal response $u=\tilde{\tilde{\tilde{u}}}(r(q,u))$ belongs to the set $R_{LOW}^{CI}(\tilde{\tilde{r}})=Arg\max_{u\in U} J_{LOW}^{CI}(r(u),u,x)$ (the payoff function of subject LOW is independent from q). The guaranteed payoff of player UPP constitutes

$$\gamma_{UPP}^{CI} = \sup_{q\in Q}\ \inf_{r\in R_{MED}^{CI}(q,u)}\ \inf_{u\in R(\tilde{\tilde{r}})} J(\pi(q,\tilde{\tilde{r}},u,x))$$ by virtue of (1.2.14).

The compulsion-impulsion equilibrium considering the SD conditions is

$$\begin{aligned}&(q^{*},\tilde{\tilde{r}}^{*},\tilde{\tilde{\tilde{u}}}^{*})\in BR^{CI}: J_{UPP}^{CI}(\pi(q^{*},\tilde{\tilde{r}}^{*},\tilde{\tilde{\tilde{u}}}^{*},x^{*}))=\gamma_{UPP}^{CI},\\ &BR^{CI}=\{(q,\tilde{\tilde{r}},\tilde{\tilde{\tilde{u}}}): r(q,u)\in R_{MED}^{CI}(q,u), u(r(q,u))\in R_{LOW}^{CI}(\tilde{\tilde{r}})\}\end{aligned} \tag{1.2.30}$$

by virtue of (1.2.14), the trajectory x^{*} is induced by the control action u^{*}.

The design algorithm of the equilibrium (1.2.30) includes the following steps.

1. Evaluate the maximum guaranteed payoff of subject LOW under the penalty strategies applied by subjects UPP and MED:

   $$L_{LOW}^{CI} = \sup_{\tilde{\tilde{u}} \in \tilde{\tilde{U}}} \inf_{q \in Q} \inf_{\tilde{r} \in \tilde{R}} J_{LOW}^{CI}(\pi(q,\tilde{r},\tilde{\tilde{u}},x)),$$

   where the trajectory $x(t)$ is induced by the control action $u(t)$.
2. Find the set $D_{LOW}^{CI} = \{(\tilde{r},\tilde{\tilde{u}}) : J_{LOW}^{CI}(\pi(q,\tilde{r},\tilde{\tilde{u}},x)) \geq L_{LOW}^{CI}\}$ for each $q \in Q$.
3. Evaluate the guaranteed payoff of subject MED:

   $\gamma_{MED}^{CI}(q) = \sup_{(\tilde{r},\tilde{\tilde{u}}) \in D_{LOW}^{CI}} J_{MED}^{CI}(\pi(q,\tilde{r},\tilde{\tilde{u}},x))$; denote by $\tilde{r}^*,\tilde{\tilde{u}}^*$ the strategies of subjects MED and LOW, implementing $\gamma_{MED}^{CI}(q)$ for each q (possibly, with accuracy ε).
4. Solve the optimal control problem (1.2.22)-(1.2.23), (1.2.13)-(1.2.14) of subject UPP with the phase constraints under $\tilde{r} = \tilde{r}^*, \tilde{\tilde{u}} = \tilde{\tilde{u}}^*$. If the solution $q^*(t)$ exists, the strategy profile $(q^*,\tilde{r}^*(q),\tilde{\tilde{u}}^*(r(q)))$ forms the compulsion-impulsion equilibrium considering the SD conditions (1.2.30). Implementation of this algorithm requires the non-emptiness of the set D_{LOW}^{CI} for all $q \in Q$.

The information rules of impulsion-compulsion is treated by analogy (Ougolnitsky and Usov, 2014).

Theory of sustainable management was applied to corruption modeling in the pioneering paper (Rybasov and Ougolnitsky, 2004). The authors suggested the following basic model of hierarchical control for an ecological-economic system with corruption:

$$J_v = \sum_{t=1}^{T} [g_v^t(p^t,q^t,u^t,\beta^t) - M\rho(u^t,U_v^t)] \to \max; \; p^t \in P^t, q^t \in Q^t; \qquad (1.2.31)$$

$$J_u = \sum_{t=1}^{T} [g_u(p^t,u^t,\beta^t) - M\rho(u^t,U_u^t)] \to \max; \; u^t \in U^t(q^t), \beta^t \in \mathrm{B}^t. \qquad (1.2.32)$$

Here $\beta = (\beta_1,...\beta_n) \in R_+^n$ is the set of additional control actions of Follower (in a practical interpretation, a bribe offered by Follower to Leader for enjoying certain privileges); $\mathrm{B}^t \subset R_+^n, t = 1,..., T$ stand for the sets of the Follower's admissible control actions in order to bribe Leader. The rest notation is presented in Table 1.2.3.

Table 1.2.3. The basic hierarchical control model of sustainable development

Symbol	Mathematical definition	Ecological-economic interpretation
x^t	$(x_1^t,\dots,x_k^t)\in R_+^k$	The set of ecological-economic state indicators of a hierarchically controlled system in year *t*
u^t	$(u_1^t,\dots,u_n^t)\in R_+^n$	The set of the Follower's control actions (a natural resource user) in year *t*: extraction of natural resources, production of goods, pollutants release (waste discharge)
p^t	$(p_1^t,\dots,p_m^t)\in R_+^m$	The set of the Leader's control actions (a supervising authority) affecting the Follower's objective function in year *t*: taxes, penalties
q^t	$(q_1^t,\dots,q_n^t)\in R_+^n$	The set of the Leader's control actions affecting the set of the Follower's admissible control actions: quotas, limits, norms
f	$f: R_+^k \times R_+^n \to R_+^k$	The state variation rule of the ecological-economic system under the Follower's impact
x_0	$(x_{01},\dots,x_{0k})\in R_+^k$	A given initial state of the ecological-economic system
T	$0 < T \le \infty$	Horizon (the period of hierarchical control in the system)
P^t, Q^t	$P^t \in R_+^m; Q^t \in R_+^n$; compact sets for t = 1,…,T	The sets of the Leader's admissible control actions (generally, time-varying)
$U^t(q^t)$	$U^t(q^t)\subset R_+^n$ a compact set for t = 1,…,T	The set of the Follower's admissible actions, which depends on the Leader's impact at current step
g_v^t	$g_v^t : R_+^{2n}\times R_+^k \times R_+^m \to R$ a continuous numerical function	The Leader's impact at step *t*
g_u^t	$g_u^t : R_+^n\times R_+^k \times R_+^m \to R$ a continuous numerical function	The Follower's impact at step *t*
ρ	$\rho(x^t,X)\begin{cases} = 0, x^t \in X \\ > 0, x^t \notin X \end{cases}$	A conditional function being equal to zero if at step *t* the state of the ecological-economic system belongs to the set *X*, and positive otherwise
M_v	$M_v > \max\limits_{p^t,q^t,u^t} g_v$	The Leader's penalty constant
M_u	$M_u > \max\limits_{p^t,u^t} g_u$	The Follower's penalty constant
J_v, J_u	$J_v \in R; J_u \in R$	The incomes of Leader and Follower, respectively, for period *T*
X_v^t, X_u^t	$X_v^t \subseteq R_+^k, X_u^t \subseteq R_+^k, t=1$	The target sets in the phase space for the state of the hierarchically controlled ecological-economic system at step *t* according to Leader and Follower, respectively

Let us classify corruption depending on the type of privileges offered for bribery. Separate out three classes of corruption:

1. *p-corruption.* In this case, Leader grants economic privileges (e.g., taxation) to Follower for bribery, i.e.,

$$p^t = p(\beta_p^t). \tag{1.2.33}$$

In the elementary setting, the tax rate depends on the bribe linearly: $p^t = p_0 - \gamma \beta_p^t, \gamma > 0$.

2. *q-corruption.* For this class of corruption, the determinative role belongs to the relationship between the quota assigned by Leader and the bribe:

$$q^t = q(\beta_q^t). \tag{1.2.34}$$

Similarly to *p*-corruption, the trivial model operates the linear function $q^t = q_0 - \delta \beta_q^t, \delta > 0$.

3. *a-corruption.* Here Leader extends the set of strategies answering the homeostasis condition for bribery, i.e.,

$$U_v^t = U(\beta_a^t). \tag{1.2.35}$$

In fact, under a-corruption Leader ignores the homeostasis condition via artificial extension of the set U_v, thereby liberalizing the actions of Follower. Among the above classes, a-corruption is most dangerous: neglecting the homeostasis condition causes critical consequences for an ecological-economic system.

Now, consider in detail the mentioned classes of corruption subject to the hierarchical control model of sustainable development (1.2.31)-(1.2.32) of ecological-economic systems:

Bribery affects the tax rate (*p-corruption*):

$$J_v = \sum_{t=1}^{T} [c^t p_\beta^t (1 - \beta_p^t) u_t + c^t \beta_p^t u^t - g_2(p_\beta^t, q^t) - M\rho(u^t, U_v^t)] \to \max; \tag{1.2.36}$$

$$J_u = \sum_{t=1}^{T} [c^t (1 - p_\beta^t)(1 - \beta_p^t) u^t] \to \max; \tag{1.2.37}$$

$$p_\beta^t = p_0 - \gamma \beta_p^t + d^t, \gamma > 0; \tag{1.2.38}$$

$$0 \le p_\beta^t \le 1; 0 \le q \le 1; \tag{1.2.39}$$

$$0 \le \beta_p^t \le 1; \tag{1.2.40}$$

$$0 \le u^t \le 1 - q^t; \tag{1.2.41}$$

$$U_v^t = [0, a^t], 0 \le a^t \le 1, t = 1, \ldots, T. \tag{1.2.42}$$

Here c^t is the price coefficient and g_2 represents a monotone Leader's control cost function increasing in both arguments. The bribe share β_p^t allows Follower to obtain tax privileges. The parameter d^t describes the so-called hardness of corruption. For definiteness, suppose that $d^t = 0$ corresponds to "soft" corruption (capture), whereas $d^t = \gamma$ reflects "hard" corruption (extortion). Under capture, a bribetaker provides the normative amounts of resources to a briber free of charge (and more beneficial amounts in exchange for a bribe). Under extortion, a bribetaker exacts money for the normative amounts of resources; in the case of refusal, it drives the dependent subject into less beneficial conditions than stipulated by existing legislature. Capture and extortion have similar organization for other classes of corruption.

Bribery affects the quota assigned by Leader (*q-corruption*):

$$J_v = \sum_{t=1}^{T} [c^t p^t (1-\beta_q^t) u^t + c^t \beta_q^t u^t + c^t \beta_q^t u^t - g_2(p^t, q^t) - M\rho(u^t, U_v^t)] \to \max; \tag{1.2.43}$$

$$J_u = \sum_{t=1}^{T} [c^t (1-p^t)(1-\beta_q^t) u^t] \to \max; \tag{1.2.44}$$

$$0 \le p^t \le 1; 0 \le q_\beta^t \le 1; \tag{1.2.45}$$

$$q_\beta^t = q_0 - \delta\beta_q^t + d^t, \delta > 0; \tag{1.2.46}$$

$$0 \le \beta_q^t \le 1; \tag{1.2.47}$$

$$0 \le u^t \le 1 - q_\beta^t; \tag{1.2.48}$$

$$U_v^t = [0, a^t], 0 \le a^t \le 1, t = 1, \ldots, T. \tag{1.2.49}$$

In exchange for the bribe, Follower obtains a greater amount of resource owing to a higher quota. By analogy to *p*-corruption, $d^t = 0$ corresponds to "soft" corruption and $d^t = \delta$ reflects "hard" corruption.

Bribery weakens the homeostasis condition (*a-corruption*):

$$J_v = \sum_{t=1}^{T} [c^t p^t (1-\beta_\alpha^t) u^t + c^t \beta_\alpha^t u^t - g_2(p^t, q^t) - M\rho(u^t, U_v^t(\alpha^t))] \to \max; \tag{1.2.50}$$

$$J_u = \sum_{t=1}^{T} [c(1-p^t)(1-\beta_\alpha^t) u^t] \to \max; \tag{1.2.51}$$

$$0 \le p^t \le 1;\ 0 \le q^t \le 1; \tag{1.2.52}$$

$$\alpha^t = \lambda\beta_\alpha^t + d^t, \lambda > 0; \tag{1.2.53}$$

$$0 \le \beta_\alpha^t \le 1; \tag{1.2.54}$$

$$0 \le u^t \le 1 - q^t; \tag{1.2.55}$$

$$U = [0, a^t + \alpha^t],\ 0 \le a^t + \alpha^t \le 1,\ t = 1,..., T. \tag{1.2.56}$$

In this case, Follower is permitted to increase the amount of resource owing to a wider set of strategies meeting the homeostasis condition. Similarly to *p*- and *q*-corruption, "soft" and "hard" corruption are described by $d^t = 0$ and $d^t = a^t$, respectively.

Let us analyze the described model for different classes of corruption using compulsion, impulsion and collaboration, as well as compare the results with the ones derived for the model without corruption, see (Ougolnitsky, 2010). Further exposition gets confined to the model with compulsion equilibria. The tables below also present the corresponding results for other classes of corruption (yet, without technicalities). In the sequel, we omit summation indexes *t*, as optimal solution is constructed on the whole horizon.

Compulsion equilibrium, q-corruption. By definition, we believe that $q_\beta = q - \delta\beta_q$ ("soft" corruption) and $q_\beta = q + \delta(1 - \beta_q)$ ("hard" corruption).

"Soft" corruption. The Follower's problem takes the form

$$J_u = c(1-p)(1-\beta_q)u \to \max_{u,\beta_q},\ u \in [0, 1 - q_\beta],\ q_\beta = q - \delta\beta_q.$$

Obviously, Follower uses the amount of resource coinciding with the quota assigned by Leader. Hence, $u^* = 1 - q_\beta = 1 - q + \delta\beta_q$ and the Follower's problem can be rewritten as $J_u = c(1-p)(1-\beta_q)(1-q+\delta\beta_q) \to \max_{q,\beta_q}$.

The first-order necessary optimality condition $\left(J_u'\right)_{\beta_q} = 0$ yields $\beta_q^* = \dfrac{q+\delta-1}{2\delta}$, i.e., the local minimum point of the function $J_u(\beta_q)$. Since $\beta_q \ge 0$, this dictates that $\delta \ge 1 - q$ (otherwise, $\beta_q^* = 0$). On the other hand, the constraint $u \le 1$ brings to the inequality $\delta \le 1 + q$. If not, Follower chooses the strategy ensuring no quota from Leader, i.e., under $\delta > 1 + q$ the Follower's optimal control is $\beta_q^* = \dfrac{q}{\delta}$. And so,

$$\beta_q^* = \begin{cases} 0 & ,\delta \in [0;1-q] \\ \dfrac{q+\delta-1}{2\delta} & ,\delta \in [1-q;1+q], \\ \dfrac{q}{\delta} & \delta \in [1+q;+\infty) \end{cases} \tag{1.2.57}$$

$$J_u^* = \begin{cases} c(1-p)(1-q) & ,\delta \in [0;1-q] \\ c(1-p)\dfrac{(1+\delta-q)^2}{4\delta} & ,\delta \in [1-q;1+q]. \\ c(1-p)\left(1-\dfrac{q}{\delta}\right) & ,\delta \in [1+q;+\infty) \end{cases} \tag{1.2.58}$$

Now, take the Leader's payoff function. Actually, it depends on the parameter δ :

$$J_v = \begin{cases} cp(1-q) & ,\delta \in [0;1-q] \\ c\left[p\dfrac{(1+\delta-q)^2}{4\delta} + \dfrac{(\delta+q-1)(\delta+1-q)}{4\delta}\right] & ,\delta \in [1-q;1+q]. \\ c\left[p\left(1-\dfrac{q}{\delta}\right)+\dfrac{q}{\delta}\right] & ,\delta \in [1+q;+\infty) \end{cases} \tag{1.2.59}$$

Consider each of the three cases in separate.

1) $\delta \in [0;1-q]$. It is clear from (1.2.59) that $q^* = 1-a$. Then $J_v = cpa$, i.e., the resulting equilibrium is identical to the one in the "pure" case (without corruption).
2) $\delta \in [1-q;1+q]$. The homeostasis condition requires that $u \in [0;a]$. Taking into account the Follower's optimal response, we have $\delta \le 2a-1+q$. By virtue of the obvious inequality $2a-1+q \le 1+q$, it is reasonable to find the optimal solution in δ on the segment $[1-q;2a-1+q]$. However, correct problem statement implies that $1-q \le 2a-1+q$, or $1-q \le a$.
3) $\delta \in [1+q,+\infty]$. In this case, it follows from (1.2.59) that q* = 1. Therefore, we seek for the Leader's optimal control in q under the conditions $\delta \in [1-q;2a-1+q]$ and $q \in [1-a;1]$. Then the Leader's problem possesses the solution $q_\beta^* = 1-2a\beta_q$. And $J_v^* = c(1+p)\frac{a}{2}$; $J_u^* = c(1-p)\frac{a}{2}$.

The analysis results can be rewritten as

$$(p^*, q^*, u^*, \beta^*) = (p, 1-a, 1, 1/2); J_v^* = c(1+p)a/2; J_u^* = c(1-p)a/2.$$

Consequently, "soft" q-corruption represents a tool of appreciable income increase for Leader. At the same time, the Follower's income is cut twice in comparison with the "pure" case.

"Hard" corruption. By analogy to "soft" q-corruption, the Follower's optimal control makes up $u^* = 1 - q_\beta$. The Follower's problem can be defined by

$$J_u = c(1-p)(1-\beta_q)(1-q-\delta(1-\beta_q)) \to \max_{q,\beta_q}.$$

By considering the first-order partial derivative of the function J_u with respect to β_q, we construct the local maximum point $\beta_q^* = \dfrac{2\delta + q - 1}{2\delta}$. According to the condition (1.2.47), this is valid only if $\delta \geq \dfrac{1-q}{2}$. Otherwise, the local maximum of the function J_u is achieved at the point $\beta_q^* = 0$. Thus,

$$\beta_q^* = \begin{cases} 0 & ,\delta \in \left[0; \dfrac{1-q}{2}\right] \\ \dfrac{2\delta + q - 1}{2\delta} & ,\delta \in \left[\dfrac{1-q}{2}; +\infty\right) \end{cases}, \tag{1.2.60}$$

$$J_u^* = \begin{cases} c(1-p)(1-q-\delta) & ,\delta \in \left[0; \dfrac{1-q}{2}\right] \\ c(1-p)\dfrac{(1-q)^2}{4\delta} & ,\delta \in \left[\dfrac{1-q}{2}; +\infty\right) \end{cases}.$$

Just like "soft" corruption, readers can easily observe that "hard" corruption is non-beneficial to Follower under any conditions. To evaluate the Leader's optimal strategy, consider the following cases:

Case 1: $\delta \in \left[0; \dfrac{1-q}{2}\right]$. Then the Leader's payoff function acquires the form $J_v = cp(1-q-\delta)$. Clearly, the Leader's optimal strategies are the ones satisfying $\delta + q = 1 - a$. And the optimal value of the payoff function equals $J_v^* = cpa$.

Case 2: $\delta \in \left[\dfrac{1-q}{2};+\infty\right)$. Here the Leader's payoff function admits the representation $J_v = c\left[p\dfrac{(1-q)^2}{4\delta} + \dfrac{(2\delta+q-1)(1-q)}{4\delta}\right]$. It appears from $u \le a$ that $q \in [1-2a;1]$. The payoff function is maximized under infinitely large values of the parameter δ and $q = 1-2a$: $\lim_{\delta\to+\infty} J_v = ca$. Therefore, $(p^*,q^*,u^*,\beta^*) = (p,1-a,a,1-a/N)$,

$q_\beta^* = 1-2a+N(1-\beta_q)$, where N is an infinitely large quantity; $J_v^* \approx ca, J_u^* \approx 0$.

Summarizing the outcomes, "hard" q-corruption gives full resource control to Leader and the Follower's income approach zero.

Compulsion equilibrium, a-corruption. The strategy set of sustainable development has the form $U_v = [0, a+\alpha(\beta_\alpha)]$, $\alpha(\beta_\alpha) = \lambda\beta_\alpha - d$.

"Soft" corruption.

In this case, $\alpha(\beta_\alpha) = \lambda\beta_\alpha$. The Follower's problem can be rewritten as $J_u(p,q) = c(1-p)(1-\beta_\alpha)u \to \max_{u,\beta_\alpha}$.

Obviously, $u^* = 1-q$. Taking into account the Leader's optimal strategy (which constitutes $q^* = 1-(a+\alpha(\beta_\alpha))$), we immediately obtain

$$J_u(p,q) = c(1-p)(1-\beta_\alpha)(a+\lambda\beta_\alpha) \to \max_{\beta_\alpha}.$$

By resolving the equation $\left(J_u'\right)_{\beta_\alpha} = 0$, find the local minimum point $\beta_\alpha^* = \dfrac{\lambda - a}{2\lambda}$ of the function $J_u(\beta_\alpha)$. This is valid only if $\lambda \ge a$, see the condition (1.2.54). Otherwise, Follower prefers the pure strategy, i.e., $\beta_\alpha^* = 0$. Due to the constraint $a + \alpha \le 1$, under $\lambda \ge 2-a$ Follower chooses the strategy allowing complete resource utilization, i.e., $\beta_\alpha^* = \dfrac{1-a}{\lambda}$. Consequently,

$$\beta_\alpha^* = \begin{cases} 0 & ,\lambda \in [0;a] \\ \dfrac{\lambda - a}{2\lambda} & ,\lambda \in [a;2-a] \\ \dfrac{1-a}{\lambda} & ,\lambda \in [2-a;+\infty) \end{cases},$$

$$J_u^* = \begin{cases} c(1-p)a & ,\lambda \in [0;a] \\ c(1-p)\dfrac{(\lambda+a)^2}{4\lambda} & ,\lambda \in [a;2-a] \\ c(1-p)\left(1-\dfrac{1-a}{\lambda}\right) & ,\lambda \in [2-a;+\infty) \end{cases}$$

Thus, the Follower's choice of a certain strategy depends on the size of the set of strategies answering the homeostasis condition. If this set is sufficiently wide, Follower does not bribe Leader and loses nothing in comparison with the "pure" case. Otherwise, Follower increases its income in comparison with the "pure" case through bribery. The Follower's income is an increasing function of λ .

And we have $(p^*,q^*,u^*,\beta^*) = (p,0,1,\dfrac{1-a}{2-a})$; $J_v^* = c\dfrac{p+1-a}{2-a}$; $J_u^* = \dfrac{c(1-p)}{2-a}$.

Under the Follower's optimal strategy, the Leader's payoff function becomes

$$J_v = \begin{cases} cpa & ,\lambda \in [0;a] \\ c\left[p\dfrac{(\lambda+a)^2}{4\lambda} + \dfrac{(\lambda-a)(\lambda+a)}{4\lambda}\right] & ,\lambda \in [a;2-a] \\ c\left[p\left(1-\dfrac{1-a}{\lambda}\right)+\dfrac{1-a}{\lambda}\right] & ,\lambda \in [2-a;+\infty) \end{cases}.$$

The Leader's payoff function is maximized in λ at the point $\lambda^* = 2-a$. The optimal payoff equals $J_v^* = c\dfrac{1}{2-a}(p+1-a)$.

"Hard" corruption. Similarly to the previous cases, we obtain the following results for Follower:

$$\beta_\alpha^* = \begin{cases} 1/2, \lambda \in [0,2], \\ 1/\lambda, \lambda \in (2,\infty); \end{cases} \quad J_u^* = \begin{cases} c(1-p)\lambda/4, \lambda \in [0,2], \\ c(1-p)(1-1/\lambda), \lambda \in (2,\infty) \end{cases}.$$

Here a distinction from "soft" corruption is that Follower always benefits from bribery. The Leader's payoff function is maximized at $\lambda^* = 2$, which leads to

$$(p^*,q^*,u^*,\beta^*) = (p,0,1,1/2); \quad J_v^* = c(1+p)/2; \quad J_u^* = c(1-p)/2.$$

The established results are combined in Table 1.2.4.

Table 1.2.4. Analysis of the hierarchical control model of an ecological-economic system with corruption

	p *	q *	u *	β *	J_v^*	J_u^*
Compulsion						
The "pure" case	p	$1-a$	a	-	cpa	$c(1-p)a$
p-corruption ("soft")	-	-	-	-	-	-
p-corruption ("hard")	-	-	-	-	-	-
q-corruption ("soft")	p	$1-a$	a	½	$c(1+p)a/2$	$c(1-p)a/2$
q-corruption ("hard")	p	$1-a$	a	1	ca	0
a-corruption ("soft")	p	0	1	$(1-a)(2-a)$	$\frac{c(p+1-a)}{2-a}$	$\frac{c(1-p)}{2-a}$
a-corruption ("hard")	p	0	1	1/2	$c(1+p)/2$	$c(1-p)/2$
Impulsion						
The "pure" case	1-ε	0	a	-	$c(1-\varepsilon)a$	$c\varepsilon a$
p-corruption ("soft")	1-ε	0	a	0	$c(1-\varepsilon)a$	$c\varepsilon a$
p-corruption ("hard")	(1-ε)/2	0	a	1	ca	0
q-corruption ("soft")	-	-	-	-	-	-
q-corruption ("hard")	-	-	-	-	-	-
a-corruption ("soft")	1-ε	0	1	$\frac{1-a}{2-a}$	$\frac{c(2-\varepsilon-a)}{2-a}$	$\frac{c\varepsilon}{2-a}$
a-corruption ("hard")	1-ε	0	1	1/2	$c(1-\varepsilon/2)$	$c\varepsilon/2$
Compulsion-impulsion						
The "pure" case	1-ε	$1-a$	a	-	$c(1-\varepsilon)a$	$c\varepsilon a$
p-corruption ("soft")	1-ε	$1-a$	a	0	$c(1-\varepsilon)a$	$c\varepsilon a$
p-corruption ("hard")	(1+p)/2	$1-a$	a	1	ca	0
q-corruption ("soft")	1-ε	$1-a$	a	1/2	$c(2-\varepsilon)a/2$	$c\varepsilon a/2$
q-corruption ("hard")	P	$1-a$	a	1	ca	0
a-corruption ("soft")	1-ε	0	1	$\frac{1-a}{2-a}$	$\frac{c(2-\varepsilon+a)}{2-a}$	$c\varepsilon/(2-a)$
a-corruption ("hard")	1-ε	0	1	1/2	$c(1-\varepsilon/2)$	$c\varepsilon/2$

Table 1.2.4. (Continued)

	p^*	q^*	u^*	β^*	J_v^*	J_u^*
Impulsion-compulsion						
The "pure" case	1- ε	0	a	-	$c(1-\varepsilon)a$	ca
p-corruption ("soft")	1- ε	0	a	0	$c(1-\varepsilon)a$	$c\varepsilon a$
p-corruption ("hard")	1- ε	0	a	1	ca	0
q-corruption ("soft")	-	-	-	-	-	-
q-corruption ("hard")	-	-	-	-	-	-
a-corruption ("soft")	1- ε	0	1	$\frac{1-a}{2-a}$	$\frac{c(2-\varepsilon a)}{2-a}$	$\frac{c\varepsilon}{2-a}$
a-corruption ("hard")	1- ε	0	1	½	$c(1-\varepsilon/2)$	$c\varepsilon/2$

Let us conduct comparative analysis using the data presented by Table 1.2.4. Obviously, in all cases Leader benefits from corruption. In addition, "hard" corruption is always preferable to its "soft" counterpart for Leader (and the opposite picture exists for Follower). Under compulsion, Leader gains more via "hard" a-corruption than "hard" q-corruption if $p > 2a-1$. This condition is identically true provided that $a < 1/2$. Therefore, a-corruption is more beneficial to Leader under the strong homeostasis condition, as it allows evading the latter. The potential threat of a-corruption is also its profitability for Follower in many situations. For instance, under compulsion "soft" a-corruption is more beneficial to Follower than the "pure" case. Certain conditions (i.e., $a < 1/2$) even make "hard" a-corruption more advantageous to Follower than the "pure" case. Under impulsion, "hard" a-corruption becomes more profitable to Leader than "hard" p-corruption whenever $a < 1 - \frac{\varepsilon}{2}$ (which holds almost always). According to the problem statement, Leader has two income sources: tax levying and Follower's bribery. Table 1.2.5 demonstrates the correlation of these sources for the equilibrium values of the Leader's objective function.

As illustrated by Table 1.2.5, whenever bribery occurs in an equilibrium, the Leader's corruption income exceeds the tax income. In some cases, the Leader's income falls on bribery possibly having grave consequences for an ecological-economic system.

The next model (Denin and Ougolnitsky, 2010) further developed the basic hierarchical control model of an ecological-economic system with corruption. The new features incorporated in the model include the briber's ability to give simultaneously several bribes of different nature, as well as the generalized notion of Leader's benevolence during corruption deals.

Table 1.2.5. The comparative analysis of Leader's income sources

	Tax	Bribe
Compulsion		
The "pure" case	cpa	-
p-corruption ("soft")	-	-
p-corruption ("hard")	-	-
q-corruption ("soft")	$cpa / 2$	$ca / 2$
q-corruption ("hard")	0	ca
a-corruption ("soft")	$cp /(2 - a)$	$c(1 - a)(2 - a)$
a-corruption ("hard")	$cp / 2$	$c / 2$
Impulsion		
The "pure" case	$c(1 - \varepsilon)a$	-
p-corruption ("soft")	$c(1 - \varepsilon)a$	0
p-corruption ("hard")	0	ca
q-corruption ("soft")	-	-
q-corruption ("hard")	-	-
a-corruption ("soft")	$c(1 - \varepsilon) /(2 - a)$	$c(1 - a) /(2 - a)$
a-corruption ("hard")	$c(1 - \varepsilon) / 2$	$c / 2$
Compulsion-impulsion		
The "pure" case	$c(1 - \varepsilon)a$	-
p-corruption ("soft")	$c(1 - \varepsilon)a$	0
p-corruption ("hard")	0	ca
q-corruption ("soft")	$c(1 - \varepsilon)a / 2$	$ca / 2$
q-corruption ("hard")	0	ca
a-corruption ("soft")	$c(1 - \varepsilon)(2 - a)$	$c(1 - a) /(2 - a)$
a-corruption ("hard")	$c(1 - \varepsilon) / 2$	$c / 2$
Impulsion-compulsion		
The "pure" case	$c(1 - \varepsilon)a$	-
p-corruption ("soft")	$c(1 - \varepsilon)a$	0
p-corruption ("hard")	0	ca
q-corruption ("soft")	-	-
q-corruption ("hard")	-	-
a-corruption ("soft")	$c(1 - \varepsilon) /(2 - a)$	$c(1 - a)(2 - a)$
a-corruption ("hard")	$c(1 - \varepsilon) / 2$	$c / 2$

The cited authors considered a static two-level game-theoretic model of multiple corruption using hierarchical control methods with two types of bribery under the homeostasis condition. Note that the model possesses a series of application domains. For instance, we mention ecological-economic systems (e.g., quota assignment in bioresources extraction and processing), systems of socioeconomic relations among employees and their groups (e.g., workload calculation), and so on. Further exposition adopts the terminology of ecological-economic systems, since it provides an intuitively clear description of the model.

The subjects of game interaction are (1) an official establishing quotas for some renewable resource and levying taxes for its extraction (Leader, an upper-level subject) and (2) an individual or an enterprise extracting and processing the resource (Follower, a lower-level subject).

As the basic game-theoretic model of hierarchical interaction, we employed Germeier game Γ_2 (Germeier, 1975) with an additional assumption that both players know the values of all exogenous parameters. The quantitative consideration of Leader's benevolence proceeds from newly introduced parameters (the so-called hardness of corruption). An example of non-benevolent attitude (extortion) is an overstated tax rate or an understated quota established for Follower. The value of such an over- or understatement is defined by the corresponding hardness parameter. According to the hierarchical control concept of sustainable development, the guarantor of the homeostasis condition is Leader as a subject bearing direct responsibility for rational quota assignment. Violation of this condition causes Follower's penalization by Leader if resource extraction exceeds an established quota taking into account potential bribery. Such an approach prevents from excessive resource extraction by Follower. Penalization is realized via an infinitely large constant M (1.2.72) in the last summand of the objective function (1.2.61). Tax rate represents an exogenous parameter (a statutory quantity), but Leader modifies it in exchange for bribery or owing to benevolence.

The players interact in the following way. Knowing the values of all exogenous parameters, Leader calculates the profitability of its own admissible strategies considering the optimal response of non-benevolent Follower. Then Leader realizes an impulsion mechanism and defines incentive-penalty functions $p \in P^{U(q)}$, where $P^{U(q)}$ is the set of mappings $p: U(q) \to [0,1]$. Thus, Leader makes most profitable strategies (the Follower's responses) also beneficial to the latter, yet not restricting its admissible strategy sets. At next step, Leader realizes a compulsion mechanism and defines the most profitable quota range

$$Q_v = \{q : \forall s \in [1-a, 1], \forall p \in P^{U(q)}\ J_L(p,s) \le J_L(p,q)\},$$

thereby restricting the Follower's admissible strategy set so that it comprises only the strategies beneficial to Leader. Using this information, Leader finds its optimal strategies and moves. Follower responds by choosing the bribes and the extraction shares $R(p,q) = \{(\beta_p, \beta_q, u) \in [0,+\infty) \times [0,+\infty) \times [0,a] : \forall \mu \in [0,+\infty), \forall \eta \in [0,+\infty), \forall s \in [0,a]$ $J_F(\beta_p, \beta_q, u, p, q) \ge J_F(\mu, \eta, s, p, q)\}$. The model includes two types of corruption, *viz.*, p-corruption (resource extraction tax rate decrease in exchange for bribery) and q-corruption (resource extraction quota increase in exchange for bribery).

The Leader's problem is described by the objective function

$$J_L = c_1(p_\beta u^{k_1} - M\rho(U,u)) \to \max_{q \in Q_v} \max_{p \in P^{U(q)}} \min_{u \in R(p,q)}; \tag{1.3.31}$$

subject to the constraints

$$p_\beta = p - \gamma\beta_p + d_p; \tag{1.2.62}$$

$$u \in [0, 1-q_\beta]; \quad (1.2.63)$$

$$q_\beta = q - \sigma\beta_q + d_q; \quad (1.2.64)$$

$$p, q, p_\beta, q_\beta \in [0,1]; \quad (1.2.65)$$

$$U = [0, a]; \quad (1.2.66)$$

$$a \in [0,1]; \quad (1.2.67)$$

$$d_p \in [0, \gamma]; \quad (1.2.68)$$

$$d_q \in [0, \sigma]; \quad (1.2.69)$$

$$k_1, k_2, \gamma, \sigma > 0; \quad (1.2.70)$$

$$\beta_p, \beta_q \geq 0; \quad (1.2.71)$$

$$M \to +\infty; \quad (1.2.72)$$

$$\rho(u, U) = \begin{cases} 1, u \in U \\ 0, u \notin U \end{cases}. \quad (1.2.73)$$

The model parameters have the following interpretation: U is the homeostasis domain, i.e., the set of extraction shares such that resource extraction causes no irreversible resource depletion; a means the homeostasis domain size (the maximum permissible amount of resource extraction); u indicates the extraction share of resource (a Follower's control action); p represents the tax rate applied to resource extraction (a Leader's control action); p_β gives the tax rate considering the bribe; q specifies the share of resource to-be-retained in the system for proper resource reproduction (reserve). In this case, the quota is defined as $1-q$ (a Leader's control action); q_β designates the resource share considering the bribe; M is an infinitely large penalty constant playing the role of the Follower's penalty in the case of homeostasis breach; $\rho(\cdot)$ signifies the set indicator function which detects homeostasis breach (the homeostasis condition is violated if $u \notin U$); γ denotes the efficiency of p-corruption (the tax rate decrease applied by Leader if Follower gives its income completely); σ means the efficiency of q-corruption (the extension applied by Leader to the statutory homeostasis domain if Follower gives its income completely); d_p is the hardness of p-corruption (Leader's benevolence towards Follower in terms of tax rate reduction); d_q indicates the hardness of q-corruption (Leader's benevolence towards Follower in terms of homeostasis domain extension); β_p represents the share of the Follower's income allocated to illegal tax rate variation (a Follower's control action); β_q gives the share of the Follower's income allocated to quotas increase (a Follower's control action); c_1 is the Leader's deal profitability per unit resource amount extracted by Follower; and finally, k_1 corresponds to the technological coefficient of resource utilization by Leader.

Follower has to extract resource within the quotas established by Leader and pays resource extraction taxes. However, Follower may also maximize its income via bribing Leader (i.e., offering the latter a certain share of its income).

The Follower's problem is defined by

$$J_F = c_2(1-p_\beta)u^{k_2}(1-\beta_p-\beta_q) \to \max_{u,\beta_p,\beta_q} . \qquad (1.2.74)$$

The expressions (1.2.62)-(1.2.71) are common for the Leader's problem and the Follower's problem. The parameters u, p, p_β, q, q_β, γ, σ, d_p, d_q, β_p, β_q and the constraints (1.2.62)-(1.2.71) in the Follower's problem have exactly the same interpretation as in the Leader's problem. The Follower's problem also incorporates the following auxiliary parameters: c_2 is is the Follower's deal profitability per unit resource amount extracted by it considering resource extraction and processing costs; k_2 indicates the technological coefficient of resource utilization by Follower.

At Step 1 of model exploration, the authors derived the analytical solution of the nonlinear optimization problem (1.2.62)-(1.2.71), (1.2.74) in order to identify the Follower's response domains and to find the optimal values of the Follower's control actions for each class of the identified domains. The Leader's control actions in the problem (1.2.62)-(1.2.71), (1.2.74) were treated as free parameters: according to the model structure, Follower does not affect them directly.

By solving the problem and analyzing the responses and optimal behavior strategies, the authors found and grouped similar elements in the derived formulas. As a result, a certain parameter was identified which describes corruption hardness in the model with several types of bribes. The above parameter was called the aggregate relative hardness indicator (ARHI). In the case of two types of bribes in the model, the parameter takes the form

$$I_{pq} = 1 - \frac{d_p}{\gamma} - \frac{d_q}{\sigma} \in [-1,1]. \qquad (1.2.75)$$

Further search and revelation of similar elements in the model (1.2.61)-(1.2.74) using ARHI led to the following gradation of corruption hardness (obviously, generalizing the notions of capture and extortion):

"Soft" <=> $I_{pq} = 1$;

"Semisoft" <=> $I_{pq} \in (0,1)$;

"Moderate" <=> $I_{pq} = 0$;

"Semihard" <=> $I_{pq} \in (-1,0)$;

"Hard" <=> $I_{pq} = -1$.

For each class of corruption, this gradation correlates the numerical values of hardness and efficiency with the work complication measure of Follower due to barriers set up by Leader. The subsequent study of the model yielded an objective function allowing to separate out and characterize the Follower's response domains, i.e., the so-called response characteristic function (RCF). It is defined by

$$RCF(p,q) = I_{pq} + \frac{1-p}{\gamma} + \frac{1-q}{\sigma}.$$

The RCF values together with the sign of the auxiliary expression $I_{RCF} = \gamma a - \sigma k_2$ (the specifying indicator of RCF) uniquely determine the Follower's response.

Solution of the optimization problem (1.2.62)-(1.2.71),(1.2.74) produced five domains with essential distinctions in the sense of the Follower's response. The domains guaranteeing the choice of different types of the Leader's behavior represent the intersection of the rectangle $(p,q) \in [0,1] \times [1-a,1]$ in axes p, $(1-q)$ and a set of half-planes constructed by parallel lines obeying the following systems of inequalities:

$$\mathbf{I} = RCF(p,q) < 0; \tag{1.2.76}$$

$$\mathbf{II} = \begin{cases} 0 \le RCF(p,q) \le \dfrac{k_2+2}{\gamma}; \\ RCF(p,q) > \dfrac{(k_2+2)a}{\sigma k_2} \end{cases} \tag{1.2.77}$$

$$\mathbf{III} = \begin{cases} 0 \le RCF(p,q) \le \dfrac{(k_2+2)a}{\sigma k_2}; \\ RCF(p,q) > \dfrac{k_2+2}{\gamma} \end{cases} \tag{1.2.78}$$

$$\mathbf{IV} = \begin{cases} RCF(p,q) \ge 0 \\ RCF(p,q) \le \dfrac{(k_2+2)a}{\sigma k_2}; \\ RCF(p,q) \le \dfrac{k_2+2}{\gamma} \end{cases} \tag{1.2.79}$$

$$\mathbf{V}=\begin{cases} RCF(p,q)>\dfrac{k_2+2}{\gamma} \\ RCF(p,q)>\dfrac{(k_2+2)a}{\sigma k_2} \end{cases}. \quad (1.2.80)$$

For any given set of the exogenous parameters, the above domains do not intersect and their union covers the rectangle $(p,q) \in [0,1] \times [1-a,1]$. It was established that the additional non-emptiness condition for domains **II** and **III** is the sign of the expression (1.2.63), but the domains do not exist simultaneously. It was also demonstrated that, for any given set of the exogenous parameters, there may simultaneously exist the domains of at least one and at most four types.

For each of the domains (1.2.76)–(1.2.80), the authors defined the optimal strategies of the interacting subjects. The Follower's bribe strategies on the corresponding domains have the following form:

$$\begin{pmatrix} \beta_{pI}^* \\ \beta_{qI}^* \end{pmatrix}=\begin{pmatrix} \dfrac{d_p+p-1}{\gamma} \\ \dfrac{d_q+q-1}{\sigma} \end{pmatrix} \text{ if } (p,q)\in \mathbf{I}; \quad \begin{pmatrix} \beta_{pII}^* \\ \beta_{qII}^* \end{pmatrix}=\begin{pmatrix} \dfrac{\left(1+\dfrac{C}{\sigma}-\dfrac{(k_2+1)A}{\gamma}\right)}{k_2+2} \\ \dfrac{q-(1-a)+d_q}{\sigma} \end{pmatrix} \text{ if } (p,q)\in \mathbf{II}$$

$$\begin{pmatrix} \beta_{pIII}^* \\ \beta_{qIII}^* \end{pmatrix}=\begin{pmatrix} \dfrac{p+d_p}{\gamma} \\ \dfrac{\left(k_2-2*\dfrac{C}{\sigma}+k_2\dfrac{A}{\gamma}\right)}{k_2+2} \end{pmatrix} \text{ if } (p,q)\in \mathbf{III}; \quad \begin{pmatrix} \beta_{pIV}^* \\ \beta_{qIV}^* \end{pmatrix}=\begin{pmatrix} \dfrac{\left(1+\dfrac{C}{\sigma}-\dfrac{(k_2+1)A}{\gamma}\right)}{k_2+2} \\ \dfrac{\left(k_2-\dfrac{2C}{\sigma}+\dfrac{k_2A}{\gamma}\right)}{k_2+2} \end{pmatrix} \text{ if}$$

$$(p,q)\in \mathbf{IV}; \quad \begin{pmatrix} \beta_{pV}^* \\ \beta_{qV}^* \end{pmatrix}=\begin{pmatrix} \dfrac{p+d_p}{\gamma} \\ \dfrac{q-(1-a)+d_q}{\sigma} \end{pmatrix} \text{ if } (p,q)\in \mathbf{V};$$

where $A=1-p-d_p$; $C=1-q-d_q$.

The optimal values of the objective functions provided that Leader chooses strategies from domains **I-V** are presented below.

1. $J_L^*=0$; $J_F^*=0$ if $(p,q)\in \mathbf{I}$.

If Leader chooses a control action from domain **I**, the both subjects gain nothing (resource extraction becomes non-beneficial to Follower). In this case, a major factor is high benevolence of Leader. Follower bribes Leader only to increase its benevolence to a minimum acceptable level and acquire the right of resource extraction (by assumption, Leader deprives Follower of the right by offering a negative quota or a tax rate higher than 100%). This control scheme is extremely disadvantageous to the both players.

2. $J_L^* = c_1\left[1 - \frac{\gamma}{k_2+2} RCF(p,q)\right] a^{k_1}$;

$$J_F^* = c_2\left[\frac{\gamma}{k_2+2} RCF(p,q)\right]\left(\frac{k_1+1}{k_1+2} RCF(p,q) - \frac{a}{\sigma}\right) a^{k_2} \text{ if } (p,q) \in \mathbf{II}.$$

The Leader's choice of a strategy from domain **II** leads to the following situation. Follower benefits from its income maximization owing to quota increase rather than tax rate reduction. Such an effect takes place, since Leader's benevolence in quota assignment is much higher than in tax levying. This control scheme seems somewhat advantageous for Leader as guaranteeing a positive income. On the other hand, Follower also receives a positive income.

3. $J_L^* - 0$; $J_F^* - c_2\left[1 - q - d_q\right]^{k_2}\left(1 - \frac{p+d_p}{\gamma}\right)$ if $(p,q) \in \mathbf{III}$.

Whenever Leader prefers a strategy from domain **III**, Follower benefits more from bribery for complete tax immunity than from extra payments for quota increase: Leader demonstrates appreciably higher benevolence to tax rate definition than quota assignment. This control scheme is disadvantageous to Leader, as Follower's tax immunity yields zero income to the former.

4. $J_L^* = c_1\left(\frac{\sigma k_1 k_2}{(k_1+1)\gamma}\right)^{k_1}\left(\frac{1}{k_1+1}\right)$; $J_F^* = c_2(\sigma k_2)^{k_2}\gamma\left(\frac{k_1}{(k_1+1)\gamma}\right)^{k_2+2}$ if $(p,q) \in \mathbf{IV}$.

It was shown that strategy choice from this domain globally maximizes the Leader's objective function under the constraints (1.2.63)-(1.2.74). At the same time, another influencing factor is the existence conditions of the domain, see the system of inequalities (1.2.67). Readers can easily find the values of the exogenous parameters making domain **IV** empty.

5. $J_L^* = 0$; $J_F^* = c_2 I_{pq} a^{k_2}$ if $(p,q) \in \mathbf{V}$.

If Leader chooses a control action from domain **V**, Follower acquires complete tax immunity and the maximum admissible quota a. Here we observe the extremely high benevolence of Leader to the both types of control actions under high efficiencies of the both types of corruption. This control scheme appears most preferable to Follower, but Leader adheres to such a strategy only if domains **II** and **IV** are empty: really, Leader gains nothing in domain **V**.

The choice of the Leader's control actions and the associated Follower's responses obeys the following priority (in the descending order):

1. domain **IV** (if nonempty);
2. domain **II** (if nonempty, but domain **IV** is empty);
3. any of domains **I**, **III**, **V,** if domains **II** and **IV** are empty.

Note that control choice can be performed only from nonempty domains: there must exist at least one Leader's strategy (p_0,q_0) such that the value RCF(p_0,q_0) satisfies the corresponding set of inequalities (1.2.64)-(1.2.68). Actually, this requirement essentially depends on the value set of the exogenous parameters. For any set of the exogenous parameters, at least one and at most four domains are nonempty. Hence, the total set of Leader's strategies is always a nonempty set. But the most beneficial strategy can be unachievable for Leader, e.g., in the case of empty domain **IV**. Moreover, Follower receives a nonzero income on domains **III** and **V**, and the additional assumption of Leader's benevolence to Follower in neutral situations allows the former to minimize or maximize the latter's income.

Using the constructed model (1.2.61)-(1.2.74), the researchers (Ougolnitsky and Denin, 2011) conducted computing experiments under different parameter values. As an example, consider the following set of the parameters: $\gamma = 1.63$; $\sigma = 0.171$; $d_p = 0.488$; $d_q = 0.145$; $a = 0.3$; $c_1 = 1$; $c_2 = 1$; $k_1 = 1$; $k_2 = 1$. In this case, ARHI equals $I_{pq} = 1 - \frac{0.488}{1.63} - \frac{0.145}{0.171} = -0.15$, indicating of "semihard" corruption in the model. This corruption hardness is described by the total medium non-benevolence of Leader.

Analyze the existence of different response domains: $RCF(p,q) = -0.15 + \frac{1-p}{1.63} + \frac{1-q}{0.171}$;

$\frac{k_2+2}{\gamma} \approx 1.84$; $\frac{(k_2+2)*a}{\sigma k_2} \approx 2.63$; $I_{RCF} = 0.318$.

According to (1.2.63), domain **II** becomes empty under the above parameter values. Furthermore, as far as the maximum possible value of RCF on the Leader's control domain is $RCF(0, 0.7) \approx 2.217 < 2.63$, domain **V** is also empty. The minimum value of RCF on the Leader's control domain constitutes $RCF(1,1) = -0.15$. Hence, there exist nonempty response domains **I**,**III**, and **IV**. The optimal control action should be searched for within domain **IV**. Indeed, the maximizing strategy is point $(1,\ 0.757)$ yielding the Leader's payoff $J_L^* = 0.304$. The partial hardness of resource extraction taxes and quotas make up $\frac{d_p}{\gamma} = 0.3$ and $\frac{d_q}{\sigma} = 0.85$, respectively. They stimulate Follower to purchase tax rate reduction much more than additional quota. This situation is exploited by Leader establishing tax rate 100% and exacting bribes for its reduction. As a result, Follower gives 72.4% of its income to decrease the tax rate to 31%. Simultaneously, Leader's non-benevolence to quota assignment increases the share of resource retained in the system from 0.757 to 0.902; this brings to the Follower's maximum admissible quota of resource extraction equal to $1-0.902=0.098$. Follower does not benefit from purchasing an additional quota due to low efficiency and high partial hardness of q-corruption. This stimulates Follower to extract the maximum possible resource amount without bribery. And Follower responds by the strategy $(\beta_p^*, \beta_q^*, u^*) = (0.724, 0, 0.098)$, receiving the payoff $J_F^* = 0.0186$.

Therefore, the authors (Denin and Ougolnitsky, 2010; Ougolnitsky and Denin, 2011) derived the aggregate relative hardness indicator (1.2.75) providing an adequate characterization of the joint hardness of multiple corruption. The response characteristic function was also constructed, whose values unambigously indicate of control action belonging to an appropriate response domain. The existence conditions of different response domains were established using RCF. And finally, the cited works estimated players' incomes for each response domain and stated the priority of the Leader's control choice according to the classification of its income by response domains.

Having in mind the described statements of sustainable management and the conducted analysis of the mathematical models of corruption, we formulate the major theses of an original concept of corruption modeling in hierarchical control systems (in italics) and comment them.

1. A basic scheme of modeling is the "Principal–supervisor–agent–object" hierarchical system in different modifications and its game-theoretic study. Dynamic models describe the state of an object explicitly, whereas static ones consider the agent's impact on the object only. Corruption affects middle-level control (supervisor), upper-level control (Principal) is non-corrupt and struggles against corruption.

According to the numerous models of corruption in hierarchical structures (see the survey (Mishra, 2006b) discussed above), if officials responsible for corruption control are corrupt themselves, anti-corruption struggle becomes inefficient. Thus, we postulate that Principal is non-corrupt, thereby introducing an upper bound for corruption spread in hierarchies. Such an assumption seems adequate when (at least) the upper level of government avoids corruption. We hope that this is true.

2. The sustainable development requirements of a controlled system (object) are well-defined and known. Dynamic (static) models specify them in terms of the object's state (the agent's impact on the object, respectively). If the sustainable development requirements are met, the Principal's problem is solved, even in the presence of corruption.

This thesis fixes the fundamental distinction of our concept from the approach developed by Becker and Rose-Ackerman. Instead of comparing corruption suppression costs with eliminated public losses, we formulate the anti-corruption struggle problem as the problem of satisfying the sustainable development requirements. Exactly the degree of such satisfaction characterizes public welfare. By assumption, experts choose the normative indices of homeostasis in a specific situation. For instance, natural indices of homeostasis can be statutory requirements (e.g., tax rates or resource extraction quotas): in this case, the anti-corruption struggle problem is reduced to the standard law enforcement problem.

3. "Principal–supervisor" and "supervisor–agent" pairs have Leader-Follower relations. In each pair, Leader (Principal or supervisor) pursues its individual goals using compulsion (par excellence, administrative and legislative impact) and impulsion (par excellence, economic impact); in the mathematical formalization, compulsion means the

Leader's impact on the admissible strategy set of Follower (generally, without feedback), whereas impulsion implies the Leader's impact on the payoff function of Follower (generally, with feedback).

A brief characterization of hierarchical control methods has been provided in the beginning of this section; for details, we refer to (Ougolnitsky, 2010, 2011). Game-theoretic compulsion and impulsion equilibria considering the sustainable development requirements (including the case of corruption) and corresponding construction algorithms were suggested in (Ougolnitsky and Usov, 2013a,b; 2014a,b). They are described in the monograph.

4. Corruption threatens the object's sustainable development, as a briber weakens the sustainable development requirements in exchange for a bribe. On the other hand, corruption is a specific form of feedback in hierarchical control systems, making control actions certain functions of bribe amount.

To the best of our knowledge, an explicit treatment of corruption as feedback in a control system forms is original and naturally complements the notion of a hierarchically controlled dynamic system suggested above. According to such treatment, the cybernetic meaning of corruption is that a control subject makes decisions depending on bribe amount.

5. There exists a discrimination between administrative corruption (administrative requirements weakened via bribery) and economic corruption (the economic requirements of upper-level control weakened via bribery). Modeling of administrative corruption lies in agent's compulsion by supervisor with bribe amount feedback. Modeling of economic corruption consists in agent's impulsion by supervisor with (unique or additional) bribe amount feedback.

This thesis further develops the previous one and correlates all types of corruption with the nature of control methods, see Table 1.2.1. Compulsion is a complex of administrative and legislative impact methods whose weakening via bribery represents administrative corruption. Formally speaking, an initial admissible strategy set of Follower can be extended: the function specifying such extension is the administrative corruption function with bribe amount feedback. For instance, a traffic policeman lets an offender go in exchange for a bribe.

Impulsion is a complex of economic impact methods whose distortion via bribery represents economic corruption. The character of the Leader's initial impact on the Follower's payoff function induces two possible modifications of impulsion. If this impact represents a constant parameter, then corruption makes it a certain function of bribe amount, realizing unique feedback. Imagine a tax officer dissembling nonpayment of fixed-rate taxes; as a result, tax rate becomes a certain function of bribe amount.

A more complicated modification of impulsion occurs when an initial economic impact is a function of the Follower's control variable (e.g., a differentiated tax rate). In this case, the economic corruption function has two variables and reflects the initial Follower control feedback and the additional bribe amount feedback. Imagine that innovative enterprises enjoy a lower tax rate than common ones (i.e., an economic mechanism stimulates innovative activity). Using bribery, the owner of a common enterprise can choose accounting at a preferential rate.

6. Corruption exists in the form of capture and extortion. Under capture, a statutory set of services is guaranteed and additional relaxations are granted via bribery. Under extortion, bribery is demanded for a basic set of services (otherwise, existing requirements are toughened).

We mostly adhere to the conventional approach presented by Table 1.1.1 and related comments. The corresponding definition is rigorously stated and clarified using several models in the forthcoming section.

7. The briber's behavior is characterized by compliancy (its willingness to weaken administrative or economic requirements in exchange for a bribe) and greediness (the price of such relaxations). Quantitative indexes of compliancy and greediness are proposed.

This thesis contributes to the corruption measurement problem. Empirical corruption indexes find wide application (International Handbook, 2006). Satarov and the colleagues (Satarov, 2007; Russian Corruption, 2013) introduced a series of corruption indexes based on sociological studies. Compliancy and greediness indexes are derived directly from corruption models, which facilitates their calculation (yet, does not remove the model identification problem). It seems interesting to give a more comprehensive sociological characterization of the suggested indexes and to elaborate recommendations on anti-corruption measures in appropriate terms.

8. A bribe can be a part of the agent's payoff owing to administrative or economic relaxations (kickback) or some absolute amount (buy-off). In the both cases, a convenient technique lies in considering bribe amount as a share of the agent's corruption payoff or total income, respectively.

This thesis is mostly a technicality refining the model hypotheses.

9. Descriptive and normative approaches are applicable to characterize corruption in hierarchical control systems with the sustainable development requirements. Within the descriptive approach, the administrative or economic corruption functions (i.e., the relationships between control variables and bribe amount) are assumed known; and the primary problem is to identify their parameters using statistical data. Within the normative approach, the corruption function follows from solution of an optimization or game-theoretic problem.

The descriptive approach plays a crucial role in our concept. We believe that the general regularities of corruption in hierarchical control systems can be described on the basis of plausible assumptions partly considering the previous experience of modeling. Then the model expressions (the classes of appropriate functions) are selected under these assumptions stating the required properties of the functions, with only numerical parameters being refined (see Thesis 11).

However, the normative approach is possible, too. For instance, corruption modeling via Germeier game Γ_2 defines the Leader's optimal strategy by a corresponding theorem. This also applies to dynamic problems (optimal control models, differential games).

10. Corruption analysis in the "Principal–supervisor–agent" system proceeds from three alternative positions. If the corruption function is known, from the agent's position corruption can be described by an optimization model. The supervisor's position brings to a hierarchical parametric game. And finally, from the Principal's position the anti-corruption struggle problem lies in evaluating control parameters so that the sustainable development requirements are satisfied under the supervisor's optimal strategy found.

The complexity of a corruption model is determined by the place a studied subject occupies in the "Principal–supervisor–agent" hierarchical structure. This allows constructing a hierarchical system of corruption models (see Thesis 12).

11. The identification problem (choosing the class of appropriate functions and defining the numerical values of their parameters) appears far from trivial and requires special studies and expertise procedures. The methodological sense of identification is that each set of parameter values determines a specific socioeconomic and political system with corruption.

According to the previous section of the monograph, applying common identification methods of mathematical models (econometrics, identification theory) to corruption modeling faces peculiar difficulties connected with the studied phenomenon. Within the framework of our approach, solution of arising identification problems bases on constructing sequences of gradually complicated mathematical models (Antonenko and Ougolnitsky, 2014; see Thesis 12). The solution procedure of the identification problem includes four steps as follows:

a) *descriptive* identification–choosing the class of mathematical models used to describe an issue and solve the associated problem;

b) *structural* identification–choosing the type of functions which form a model of this class;

c) *parametric* identification–establishing the physical meaning and measurement method of model parameters;

d) *numerical* identification–choosing the values of parameters incorporated in each function.

At each step, it is reasonable to design a sequence of gradually complicated mathematical models with a more and more accurate description of the reality (in the limit case–arbitrarily accurate description). For instance, for descriptive identification these are sequences of the types "an optimization problem–a two-player game–a three-player game" or "an optimal control problem–a dynamic two-player game–a dynamic three-player game." For structural identification, we have sequences of the type "a linear function–a power function–more complex functions." For parametric identification, there arise sequences of the type "a qualitative assessment–a special expert appraisal–a well-defined measurement method." A possible approach to the parametric identification of any function comprises the following stages: (1) choosing a reasonable grid (for interpretable and representatively distinguishable values of a variable), (2) conducting an expert appraisal of function values on this grid and (3) obtaining an analytic form of the function by the least-squares technique. And finally, for numerical identification one can perform exhaustive search on some grid with subsequent step decrease.

12. It is reasonable to construct sequences of gradually complicated models with a more and more accurate description of real corruption phenomena in hierarchical control systems. The main logical scheme of such complication has the form of "optimization models–hierarchical two-player games–hierarchical three-player games" (statics) and "optimal control problems–dynamic hierarchical two-player games– dynamic hierarchical three-player games."

This thesis is last but not least. Furthermore, it describes the main aim of the concept–designing a hierarchical system of interconnected gradually complicated models of corruption, which reflect the attitudes of all participants of corruption relations. The whole idea of the approach (common in mathematical modeling) consists in the following. First, construct an elementary (most simple) model reflecting merely the essential features of a studied object. Generally, such a model involves a few parameters and admits an explicit analytic treatment. Imagine that this treatment is successfully completed and certain results are established. Then a researcher finds out the scarcity of the model and the properties of the real object it neglects. Subsequently, the model undergoes complication in an appropriate direction and the procedure repeats. In the limit case, the induced sequence of gradually complicated models of a same object allows its description with arbitrarily high accuracy ("true in the limit"). The stated approach seems a key one to answer an important question: Are mathematical models able to provide an adequate description of complex systems? Actually, it is applicable to identification problems, as well.

The residual of the book is dedicated to the theoretical and applied models of corruption proceeding from the above theses.

Chapter 2

THEORETICAL MODELS OF CORRUPTION IN HIERARCHICAL CONTROL SYSTEMS

Chapter 2 of the monograph considers the theoretical models of corruption in hierarchical control systems. The logic of exposition is defined by the matrix "statics – dynamics" and "administrative corruption – economic corruption." Under administrative (economic) corruption, a briber relaxes administrative (economic, respectively) requirements of an upper-level control subject. In the sense of modeling, administrative corruption means agent's compulsion by a supervisor with bribe amount feedback, whereas economic corruption represents agent's impulsion by a supervisor with unique or additional bribe amount feedback. In all cases, we construct a sequence of gradually complicated models providing a more and more accurate description of real corruption phenomena in hierarchical control systems. The main logical scheme of such complication is "optimization models – hierarchical two-player games – hierarchical three-player games" (in statics) and "optimal control problems – hierarchical dynamic two-player games – hierarchical dynamic three-player games" (in dynamics).

In addition, Chapter 2 describes a simulation complex for static models of corruption. We characterize the regularities of corruption behavior depending on the model parameters, as well as formulate appropriate recommendations on anti-corruption measures. The definitions of compulsion equilibria and impulsion equilibria are given for dynamic models considering sustainable development requirements in the conditions of corruption, including some algorithms of their evaluation.

2.1. STATIC MODELS

The notion of administrative corruption is widespread in scientific literature on the subject. According to the monograph (Russian Corruption, 2013), "the prevailing manifestations of corruption consisting in bribery for "rendering of services" or "elimination of barriers" are often called administrative corruption" (p. 54). The term of economic corruption also appears, indicating of the same phenomenon in the economic sphere (in contrast to politics).

Based on these approaches, this book introduces somewhat different definitions of administrative and economic corruption, proceeding from compulsion and impulsion of sustainable management theory. The main theses of the original concept of corruption modeling in hierarchical control systems using this theory have been stated in the previous chapter. In the static setting, corruption is studied in the "Principal–supervisor–agent" system. An upper-level control subject (Principal) is not corrupt. It establishes sustainable development requirements whose satisfaction forms the aim of anti-corruption struggle. However, real monitoring of these requirements is performed by supervisor; in exchange for a bribe from an interested agent, supervisor can weaken them. "Principal–supervisor" and "supervisor–agent" pairs have Leader-Follower relations. In each pair, Leader (Principal or supervisor) pursues its individual goals using compulsion (par excellence, administrative and legislative impact) and impulsion (par excellence, economic impact); in the mathematical formalization, compulsion means the Leader's impact on the admissible strategy set of Follower (generally, without feedback), whereas impulsion implies the Leader's impact on the payoff function of Follower (generally, with feedback)

In the case of administrative corruption, administrative requirements are weakened via bribery. Economic corruption corresponds to a situation when the economic requirements of upper-level control are weakened via bribery. Modeling of administrative corruption lies in agent's compulsion by supervisor with bribe amount feedback. Modeling of economic corruption consists in agent's impulsion by supervisor with (unique or additional) bribe amount feedback.

To describe corruption, it is reasonable to construct sequences of gradually complicated models with a more and more accurate description of real corruption phenomena in hierarchical control systems. The main logical scheme of such complication in the static mode has the form of "optimization models–hierarchical two-player games–hierarchical three-player games." Therefore, the system of static models of corruption in hierarchical control systems possesses the logical structure illustrated by Table 2.1.1. Now, we consider them in detail.

Table 2.1.1. Static models of corruption in hierarchical control systems

	Administrative corruption	Economic corruption
The agent's level	Optimization problem	Optimization problem (in two settings)
The supervisor's level	Two-player hierarchical game with the rule Γ_2	Two-player hierarchical game with the rule Γ_2 (in two settings)
The Principal's level	Three-player hierarchical game	Three-player hierarchical game (in different settings)

Administrative corruption: the agent's level. In the absence of corruption, the agent's problem can be formulated in the following way:

$$g_0(u) \to \max, \quad 0 \le u \le s_0 \quad (0 \le s_0 \le 1). \tag{2.1.1}$$

The agent's activity is described by its effort u. For convenience, suppose that this variable represents a share of the maximum possible effort, i.e., $0 \le u \le 1$. The agent's payoff function $g_0(u)$ can be increasing (e.g., resource extraction) or decreasing (labor effort reduction). In the former case, the sustainable development requirements dictate imposing upper bounds on the agent's activity (in the latter case, lower bounds are necessary). The both cases are treated by analogy. For definiteness, further analysis covers the former case, see the model (2.1.1). Assume that g_0 is a strictly increasing function such that $g(0) = 0, \lim_{u\to\infty} g_0(u) = \infty$.

The parameter s_0 plays the role of "a quota" assigned by Principal to agent. Under $s_0 = 0$, the agent's activity is absolutely prohibited; if $s_0 = 1$, no restrictions actually apply. The condition $u \le s_0$ is interpreted as the sustainable development requirement in the static mode.

Administrative corruption consists in that supervisor (responsible for quota control) relaxes the existing requirements via bribery. This is expressed by the administrative corruption function

$$s(b) = s_0 + w(b). \qquad (2.1.2)$$

Here $w(b)$ is an increasing function reflecting weakened administrative restrictions in exchange for a bribe, $w(0) = 0$; $b \in [0,1]$ means the share of the agent's payoff (income) allocated to the supervisor's bribe. Therefore, $s(0) = s_0$ and the function (2.1.2) corresponds to capture: the cases $s(0) < s_0$ (extortion) and $s(0) > s_0$ (weak control) can be studied by analogy. Then the model

$$g(u,b) = (1-b)g_0(u) \to \max,\ 0 \le u \le s(b),\ 0 \le b \le 1$$

describes the agent's optimization problem in the conditions of administrative corruption. So long as the function $g_0(u)$ strictly increases, it suffices to consider the above problem as the following one-dimensional optimization problem:

$$g(b) = (1-b)g_0(s(b)) \to \max, \quad 0 \le b \le 1. \qquad (2.1.3)$$

To characterize corruption behavior, introduce the following indicators: $\hat{s} = \min\{1, s(1)\}$ –compliancy (maximum possible relaxation by a bribetaker); $\hat{b} = \min\{b; s(b) = \hat{s}\}$–greediness (the price of this relaxation). Suppose that really agent allocates to bribery at most a share $\bar{b}$ of its payoff. In this case, the conditional classification of compliancy and greediness is given by Table 2.1.2.

Table 2.1.2. The conditional classification of compliancy and greediness

The levels of compliancyand greediness	Minimum	Low	Medium	High	Maximum	Exorbitant
$\hat{s}$	s_0	$(s_0, \frac{1-s_0}{2})$	$\frac{1-s_0}{2}$	$(\frac{1-s_0}{2}, 1)$	1	-
$\hat{b}$	0	$(0, \bar{b}/2)$	$\bar{b}/2$	$(\bar{b}/2, \bar{b})$	$\bar{b}$	$(\bar{b}, 1]$

As an illustration, consider the linear parameterization of the model (2.1.3): set $s(b) = s_0 + Ab,\ A \geq 0,\ g_0(u) = u$. Then the model (2.1.3) acquires the form

$$g(b) = (1-b)(s_0 + Ab) \to \max, \quad 0 \leq b \leq 1. \tag{2.1.4}$$

Clearly, the parameter A determines the qualitative characteristics of the bribetaker's behavior. Under $A = 0$, corruption takes no place at all. Higher values of A increase bribetaker's appeasability and reduce its greediness. Here a threshold is $A = 1 - s_0$: in this case, we have $s(1) = 1$, i.e., the limit level of greediness guarantees maximum appeasability. If $A < 1 - s_0$, greediness becomes exorbitant and appeasability does not achieve its maximum level (in other words, for any bribe some quota smaller than 1 has to-be-satisfied). If $A > 1 - s_0$, agent can ignore the quota in exchange for a reasonable bribe (maximum appeasability and small greediness).

The paper (Descriptive Approach, 2011) performed differential identification of the model (2.1.4) for Caucasian regions using expert appraisal. A natural assumption is that typical values are $A < s_0$ (central Russia regions) and $A > 1 - s_0$ (Caucasian regions). The range $s_0 \leq A \leq 1 - s_0$ represents their intersection (such a situation occurs in the both groups of regions). Therefore, officials in Caucasian regions are more likely to bribery and wink at quota nonobservance for a comparatively small amount of money. At the same time, in central Russia regions officials are harder-to-please: even if they agree to bribery, the matter concerns appreciably higher amounts of money and smaller quota relaxations.

Let us revert to the optimization problem (2.1.4). We obtain $g(0) = s_0,\ g(1) = 0,\ \frac{dg(b)}{db} = A - s_0 - 2Ab,\ \frac{d^2 g(b)}{db^2} = -2A < 0$, so that $b^* = \frac{A - s_0}{2A}$ is the maximum point, $g(b^*) = \frac{(A + s_0)^2}{4A} > g(0)$.

Note that $b^* \begin{cases} > 0, & A > s_0, \\ < 0, & A < s_0, \end{cases}$ hence, $g_{\max} = \begin{cases} g(b^*), & A > s_0, \\ g(0), & A < s_0. \end{cases}$

Consequently, the key role also belongs to the parameter A defining two qualitatively different behavioral strategies of agent. If $A < s_0$, bribery makes no sense, agent receives its maximum income s_0 for $b = 0$. Under $A > s_0$, the optimal bribe share makes up $b^* = \frac{A - s_0}{2A}$, yielding the agent's income $\frac{(A + s_0)^2}{4A} > s_0$.

Interestingly, in a more general case with the agent's income function parameterized by $g(b) = (1-b)(s_0 + Ab)^k, k \le 1$, the maximum income has the formula $g_{\max} = \begin{cases} g(0), & A < s_0 / k, \\ g(b^*), & A > s_0 / k, \end{cases}$ where $b^* = \frac{kA - s_0}{(1+k)A}$.

Administrative corruption: the supervisor's level. Consider the static model of administrative corruption in the two-level "supervisor–agent" hierarchical control system (Antonenko et al., 2013):

$$g_1(s,u,b) \to \max_{s \in [0 \div \bar{s}]}, \quad g_2(s,u,b) \to \max_{u \in [0,1-s];\, b \in [0,\bar{b}]}, \tag{2.1.5}$$
$$\frac{\partial g_1}{\partial u} \ge 0, \ \frac{\partial g_1}{\partial b} \ge 0, \ \frac{\partial g_1}{\partial s} \le 0, \ \frac{\partial g_2}{\partial u} \ge 0, \ \frac{\partial g_2}{\partial b} \le 0, \ \frac{\partial g_2}{\partial s} \le 0.$$

Here g_1, g_2 denote the payoff functions of supervisor and agent, respectively; s is the administrative control action applied by supervisor; $\bar{s}$ means the maximum possible value of this control action in the given conditions ($0 \le \bar{s} \le 1$); u specifies the agent's action (effort) measured in the percentage of the maximum effort; b indicates the share of the agent's income passed to supervisor as a bribe; and finally, $\bar{b}$ is the maximum share of the agent's income allocated to bribery ($0 \le \bar{b} \le 1$).

By assumption, the agent's action u (its payoff function $g_2(s,u,b)$ increases in u) may break the homeostasis condition $u \le 1 - s_0$, where s_0 is the statutory value of S. The responsibility for homeostasis maintenance belongs to a Principal; in the two-level model, it is comprehended as an appropriate value of s_0 such that the homeostasis condition holds true. The quantity $1 - s$ is called the quota. However, in the two-level control system the quota is established by supervisor via the variable S, representing the object of administrative corruption. Really, supervisor strives for maximizing its income regardless of the homeostasis condition. The case of $s = 0$ corresponds to the absence of administrative control. Next, the case of $s = s_0$ describes satisfaction of the statutory requirements. And the case of $s = 1$ (actually, $s = \bar{s} < 1$) answers to the tightest control possible.

Let us consider the variable s as a nonincreasing function of corruption (bribery) on the segment $[0,1]$ or the quota relaxed via bribery with the property that $\exists b_0 > 0: \ s(b_0) < s_0$. That is, in exchange for a bribe, supervisor agrees to weaken the statutory requirements, thereby facilitating homeostasis breach. This function describes qualitative beliefs about the nature of corruption; however, its identification can be performed using statistical data (if available).

We say that there exists capture if $s(0) = s_0$ and extortion if $s(0) > s_0$. The case of $s(0) < s_0$ (no legislative regulation) will be not analyzed. Under capture, a statutory set of services is guaranteed and additional relaxations are granted via bribery. Under extortion, bribery is demanded even for a basic set of services (in this case, $s = s_0$). To parameterize the corruption relationship, for convenience we employ the linear function $s(b) = A - Bb$, where the parameter $A \ge s_0$ describes the initial level of corruption ($A = s_0$ under capture and $A > s_0$ under extortion) and the parameter $B \ge 0$ reflects bribe sensitivity ($B = 0$ if no corruption exists; higher values of B increase the sensitivity). Figure 2.1.1 provides a qualitative illustration of the corruption function (linear parameterization in the case of capture), as well as the indicators of appeasability and greediness in the following situations: (a) $\hat{s} = 0, \hat{b} = b_1$; (b) $\hat{s} = 0, \hat{b} = 1$; (c) $\hat{s} = s_1, \hat{b} = 1$; (d) no corruption

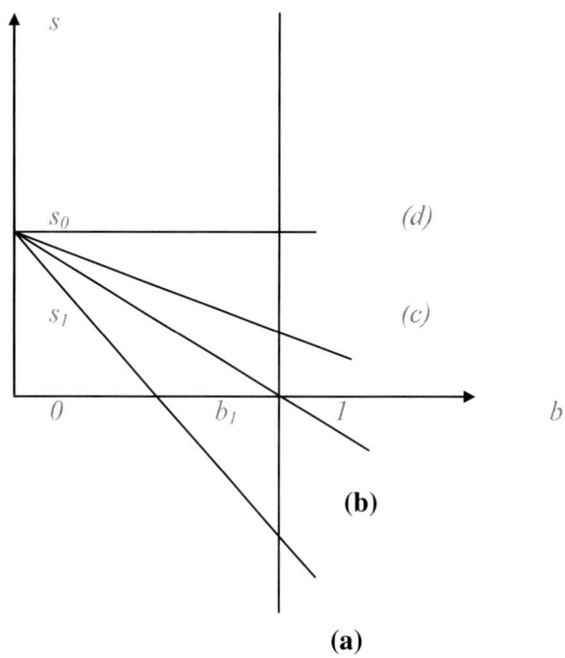

Figure 2.1.1. The indicators of appeasability and greediness under the linear function of administrative corruption.

As an example of the model (2.1.5), consider the two-player hierarchical game

$$g_1(s,u,b) = bf(u) \to \max_{s\in[0,\bar{s}]}, \quad g_2(s,u,b) = (1-b)f(u) \to \max_{u\in[0,1-s],\, b\in[0,\bar{b}]}, \tag{2.1.6}$$

where $f(u)$ designates the agent's income functions. By virtue of its properties, the function $f(u)$ does not decrease, and the optimal action of agent is $u^* = 1 - s$. The compulsion problem (2.1.6) is reduced to Germeier game Γ_2 of the form

$$g_1(s,b) = bf(1-s) \rightarrow \max_{s\in[0,\bar{s}]}, \quad g_2(s,b) = (1-b)f(1-s) \rightarrow \max_{b\in[0,\bar{b}]}.$$

Further exposition needs the Germeier theorem, see (Gorelik and Kononenko, 1982).

The Germeier theorem. Suppose that the payoff functions of players 1 and 2, $M_1(x_1, x_2)$ and $M_2(x_1, x_2)$, enjoy continuity on the compact sets X_1 and X_2 (the admissible strategy sets of the players). Introduce the following functions: $x_1^P(x_2)$ as the penalty strategy of player 2 according to the rule $M_2(x_1^P, x_2) = \min_{x_1\in X_1} M_2(x_1, x_2)$, and $x_1^D(x_2)$ as the dominant strategy of player 1, which meets the condition $M_1(x_1^D, x_2) = \max_{x_1\in X_1} M(x_1, x_2)$. In addition, introduce the following quantities and sets:

$$L_2 = \max_{x_2\in X_2} M_2(x_1^P(x_2), x_2);\ E_2 = \{x_2 \in X_2 : M_2(x_1^P(x_2), x_2) = L_2\};$$
$$D_2 = \{(x_1, x_2) \in X_1 \times X_2 : M_2(x_1, x_2) > L_2\};$$
$$K_1 = \sup_{(x_1,x_2)\in D_2} M_1(x_1, x_2) \leq M_1(x_1^\varepsilon, x_2^\varepsilon) + \varepsilon \quad (D_2 = \varnothing \Rightarrow K_1 = -\infty);$$
$$K_2 = \min_{x_2\in E_2} \max_{x_1\in X_1} M_1(x_1, x_2).$$

Then the guaranteed payoff of player 1 (Leader) in the game Γ_2 (the game, where player 1 has information on the choice of player 2) is $w_1 = \max(K_1, K_2)$ and the corresponding ε-optimal guaranteeing strategy takes the form

$$\tilde{x}_1^\varepsilon(x_2) = \begin{cases} x_1^\varepsilon, & x_2 = x_2^\varepsilon, K_1 > K_2, \\ x_1^D(x_2), & x_2 \in D_2, K_1 \leq K_2, \\ x_1^P(x_2), & \text{otherwise}, \end{cases}$$

with x_1^ε and x_2^ε described above.

By applying the Germeier theorem to the model function $f(u) = \sqrt{u}$, we obtain:

$$s^D(b) \equiv 0;\ s^P(b) \equiv \bar{s};\ \hat{s} = \sqrt{1-\bar{s}};\ L_2 = \hat{s}\max_{b\in[0,\bar{b}]}(1-b) = \hat{s};\ E_2 = \{0\};$$
$$D_2 = \{(s,b) : (1-b)\sqrt{1-s} > \hat{s}\};\ K_2 = \max_{s\in[0,\bar{s}]} g_1(s,0) = 0;\ K_1 = \sup_{D_2} b\sqrt{1-s}.$$

The global maximum g_1 is achieved for $s = 0, b = \bar{b}$. The interests of the players with respect to the variable s do coincide; hence, $s^* = 0$. Next, if $1-\bar{b} > \hat{s}$, then $b^* = \bar{b}$ (otherwise, the condition $1-\bar{b} > \hat{s}$ implies $b^* = 1-\hat{s}-\varepsilon$). And so,

$$b^{\varepsilon} = \begin{cases} \bar{b}, \bar{b} < 1 - \hat{s}, \\ 1 - \hat{s} - \varepsilon, \text{otherwise}, \end{cases}$$

i.e., $b^{\varepsilon} = 1 - \hat{s} - \varepsilon = K_1$ anyway. As far as $K_1 > 0 = K_2$, the maximum guaranteed payoff of supervisor equals K_1, and its ε -optimal guaranteeing strategy has the form

$$\tilde{s}^*(b) = \begin{cases} 0, \; b = 1 - \varepsilon - \hat{s}, \\ \bar{s}, \; \text{otherwise}. \end{cases}$$

Thus, $\hat{s} = 0$ (maximum possible appeasability) and $\hat{b} = b^{\varepsilon}$. For instance, the parameter values $\bar{b} = \bar{s} = 1/2$ bring to $K_1 = 1 - \sqrt{2}/2 - \varepsilon$,

$$\tilde{s}^*(b) = \begin{cases} 0, \quad b = 1 - \varepsilon - \sqrt{2}/2, \\ 1/2, \quad \text{otherwise}. \end{cases}$$

Therefore, in the given conditions, for a comparatively fare payment $b \cong 0.15 - \varepsilon$ the corrupt supervisor completely removes the statutory homeostasis requirements.

Economic corruption: the agent's level. In the absence of corruption, similarly to (2.1.1) the agent's problem can be formulated as

$$(1 - r_0) g_0(u) \to \max, \quad 0 \le u \le 1 \;\; (1 \le r_0 \le 1). \tag{2.1.7}$$

The parameter r_0 plays the role of tax rate established by Principal. If $r_0 = 0$, no taxes are levied; under $r_0 = 1$, the agent's income is completely confiscated as taxes. In the static setting, tax collection at a rate r_0 plays the role of the sustainable development requirement.

Economic corruption lies in the following. Being responsible for tax collection control, supervisor relaxes the existing requirements via bribery. This situation is characterized by the economic corruption function

$$r(b) = r_0 - w(b). \tag{2.1.8}$$

Here $w(b)$ represents an increasing function such that $w(0) = 0$, which reflects tax rate reduction in exchange for a bribe; $b \in [0,1]$ is the share of the agent's payoff (income) allocated to the supervisor's bribe. In a practical interpretation, corrupt supervisor (a tax inspector) dissembles full or partial nonpayment of taxes by agent. Then the model

$$g(b) = (1 - b - r(b)) g_0(u) \to \max, \; 0 \le u \le 1, \quad 0 \le b \le 1$$

describes the agent's optimization problem in the conditions of economic corruption. Since the variable u does not affect corruption, it suffices to consider the one-dimensional optimization problem

$$b + r(b) \to \min, \quad 0 \le b \le 1. \tag{2.1.9}$$

The indicators of appeasability and greediness are introduced by analogy to the case of administrative corruption. Under the linear parameterization $r(b) = r_0 - Ab$, the agent's cost minimization model (2.1.9) acquires the form

$$g(b) = r_0 + (1 - A)b \to \min_{0 \le b \le 1}, \tag{2.1.10}$$

where A is the model parameter. Note that $A > 0$, so long as the economic corruption function $r(b) = r_0 - Ab$ strictly decreases. On the other hand, the total costs $g(b)$ are nonnegative, and so $A \le 1 + r_0$. This leads to the range $0 < A \le 1 + r_0$.

Just like for administrative corruption, the parameter A defines the qualitative behavioral characteristics of the bribetaker. If $A = 0$, corruption takes no place at all. Higher values of A increase the bribetaker's appeasability and reduce its greediness. The threshold is $A = r_0$: in this case, $r(1) = 0$ (limit greediness guarantees maximum possible appeasability). Under $A < r_0$, greediness is exorbitant and appeasability does not achieve its maximum level (i.e., for any bribe agent still pays some positive tax). If $A > r_0$, agent even pays no taxes for a comparatively fare bribe (maximum appeasability and small greediness).

The paper (Descriptive Approach, 2011) performed differential identification of the model (2.1.10) for Caucasian regions using expert appraisal. It seems reasonable to assume that $0 \le A \le 2 - r_0$ (central Russian regions) and $r_0 \le A \le 1 + r_0$ (Caucasian regions). The range $r_0 \le A \le 2 - r_0$ represents their intersection (such a situation occurs in the both groups of regions). Therefore, officials in Caucasian regions are more likely to bribery and wink at nonpayment of taxes for a comparatively small amount of money. Yet, in central Russia regions officials are harder-to-please: even if they agree to bribery, the matter concerns appreciably higher amounts of money and smaller tax privileges.

Now, switch to the optimization problem (2.1.10). Since $\frac{dg(b)}{db} = 1 - A$, for $0 < A < 1$ the function g strictly increases and its minimum value is achieved at the left bound of the admissible range: $g_{\min} = g(0) = r_0$. Accordingly, for $1 < A < 1 + r_0$ the function g strictly decreases and its minimum values is achieved at the right bound of the admissible domain: $g_{\min} = g(1) = 1 + r_0 - A < r_0$. The degenerate case when $A = 1$ yields $g(b) \equiv r_0$ (bribery is pointless, no corruption takes place).

Therefore, the key role is also played by the parameter A defining two qualitatively different behavioral strategies of agent. If $0 < A < 1$, the agent's total costs $g(b)$ grow, and the rational action is to reject bribery and honestly pay taxes at the rate r_0. Under $1 < A < 1 + r_0$, the agent's costs $g(b)$ go down, and it is economically sound to bribe and pay the amount $1 + r_0 - A < r_0$ at the actual rate.

Consider the following (more general) economic corruption function:

$$g(b) = b + r(b) = b + r_0 - Ab^k \ (k > 0). \tag{2.1.11}$$

We have

$$\frac{dg}{db} = 1 - kAb^{k-1} = 0 \Rightarrow b^* = (kA)^{\frac{1}{1-k}}; \frac{d^2 g}{db^2} = k(1-k)Ab^{k-2}; \ \frac{d^2 g(b^*)}{db^2} = (1-k)(kA)^{\frac{1}{k-1}}.$$

Consequently,

$$\frac{d^2 g(b^*)}{db^2} \begin{cases} > 0,\ 0 < k < 1 \Rightarrow b^* \text{ is the minimum point;} \\ < 0,\ k > 1 \Rightarrow b^* \text{ is the maximum point.} \end{cases}$$

If b^* b^* is the maximum point, then $\min_b g(b) = \begin{cases} g(0) = r_0,\ 0 < A < 1, \\ g(1) = r_0 + 1 - A,\ 1 < A < 1 + r_0. \end{cases}$

And we finally obtain that $b_{\min} = \begin{cases} (kA)^{\frac{1}{1-k}},\ 0 < k < 1; \\ 0,\ k > 1 \wedge 0 < A < 1; \\ 1,\ k > 1 \wedge 1 < A < 1 + r_0 \end{cases}$

(the case of $k = 1$ is considered in detail separately).

An alternative (more complicated) setting of the economic corruption model is possible. Assume that, in the absence of corruption, the agent's optimization problem has the form

$$(1 - r_0(u))g_0(u) \to \max, \quad 0 \le u \le 1,$$

where the tax rate $r_0(u)$ represents an agent's activity function, e.g.,

$$r_0(u) = \begin{cases} r_1, & u \in [0, a), \\ r_2, & u \in [a, 1], \end{cases} \quad r_2 < r_1.$$

In this case, the economic corruption function $r(u, b)$ becomes a two-variable function with additional feedback by bribe amount, e.g.,

$$r(u,b)=\begin{cases} r_0(u), & b<b_0, \\ r_2, & b\geq b_0 \end{cases}.$$

Accordingly, the economic corruption model is reduced to a two-dimensional optimization problem with the objective function

$$g(u,b)=(1-b-r(u,b))g_0(u)\to \max,\quad 0\leq u\leq 1,\quad 0\leq b\leq 1. \tag{2.1.12}$$

Actually, economic control mechanisms with feedback are typical for impulsion. Tax rates may vary for large- and small-scale business or traditional and innovative enterprises. Therefore, the model (2.1.12) shows higher adequacy than the model (2.1.9), but entails larger difficulties in the sense of identification and analysis.

Economic corruption: the supervisor's level. As the basic model, let us consider the two-player hierarchical game with the rule Γ_2:

$$\begin{aligned} g_S(r,b)&=b+pr(b)\to \max,\quad 0\leq r\leq r_0, \\ g_A(r,b)&=b+r(b)\to \min,\quad 0\leq b\leq 1. \end{aligned} \tag{2.1.13}$$

Here g_S and g_A denote the payoff (income) functions of supervisor and agent, respectively; $p\geq 0$ means the share of tax revenues assigned by Principal to supervisor (wage, bonuses); r_0 is a statutory tax rate. At the supervisor's level the quantity p is assumed constant. Agent has the same objective function as in the model (2.1.9) (costs minimization), while the supervisor's payoff comprises the official and corruption incomes. No doubt, the both sums in the right-hand sides of (2.1.13) represent the shares of the agent's income $g_0(u)$ independent from b . Hence, optimization with respect to b neglects them.

By the Germeier theorem, the ε -optimal strategy of supervisor in the simple model (2.1.13) has the expression

$$r^*(b)=\begin{cases} 0, & b=r_0-\varepsilon, \\ r_0, & otherwise \end{cases} \tag{2.1.14}$$

Formula (2.1.14) explains high public danger of corruption: almost all taxes go to a briber (not government), but this situation is beneficial to a taxpayer.

Of course, in this case an alternative setting of the model is possible when tax rate represents a control mechanism with feedback $r_0(u)$. Then the corruption model becomes a game Γ_2 of the form

$$\begin{aligned} g_S(r,b,u)&=(b+pr(b,u))g_0(u)\to \max,\quad 0\leq r\leq r_0, \\ g_A(r,b,u)&=(1-b-r(b,u))g_0(u)\to \max,\quad 0\leq u\leq 1,\quad 0\leq b\leq 1. \end{aligned} \tag{2.1.15}$$

Here the second variable could not be neglected, which complicates analytic definition of the ε -optimal strategy of supervisor.

Administrative corruption: the Principal's level. Consider the basic model

$$g_P(q,s) = M\,|\,s - s_0\,| + h(q) \to \min, \quad s_0 \le q \le 1;$$
$$g_S(q,s,b) = bg_0(s) \to \max, \quad s_0 \le s \le q; \qquad (2.1.16)$$
$$g_A(s,b) = (1-b)g_0(b) \to \max, \quad 0 \le b \le 1.$$

Here the notation is same as in the model (2.1.5) and we comment the Principal's payoff function g_P only. Principal seeks to maintain the homeostasis condition $s = s_0$, see the first summand. The quantity $M >> 1$ is the penalty coefficient applied to Principal if the homeostasis condition fails. To guarantee homeostasis via compulsion, Principal restricts the supervisor's admissible strategy domain from above by its control variable q . To avoid the trivial solution $q = s_0$, the model takes into account the control costs using a decreasing function $h(q)$ such that $h(1) = 0$. The correlation between the first and second summands in the Principal's payoff function determines the comparative significance of the homeostasis condition and the control costs for it.

Economic corruption: the Principal's level. In this case, the objective functions of the players can be defined by

$$g_P = (1-p)r - M\,|\,r - r_0\,| \to \max, \quad 0 \le p \le 1;$$
$$g_S = pr + b \to \max, \quad 0 \le r \le r_0; \qquad (2.1.17)$$
$$g_A = r + b \to \min, \quad 0 \le b \le 1,$$

where b signifies the share of the agent's income allocated to bribery (the agent's strategy); r is tax rate (the supervisor's strategy); p gives the share of the supervisor's incentive in the amount of collected taxes (the Principal's strategy); M denotes the penalty coefficient applied to Principal if the homeostasis condition $r = r_0$ fails; the subscripts *P*, *S*, *A* indicate the objective functions of Principal, supervisor and agent, respectively.

Let r_0 be a statutory tax rate and $r(b)$ represent the amount of collected taxes considering relaxations due to bribery, $\Delta r = r_0 - r(b) > 0$. Clearly, the bribery profitability condition takes the form $b < \Delta r$ (for briber–agent) and $b > p\Delta r$ (for bribetaker–supervisor). The general bribery profitability condition is described by

$$p\Delta r < b < \Delta r\,. \qquad (2.1.18)$$

This two-sided inequality always holds true, since $p < 1$ (really, even $p << 1$). Hence, the model (2.1.17) makes bribery beneficial anyway, and bribe amount within the range (2.1.18) can be the bargained by agent and supervisor.

The general control model in the three-level system with corruption. The game-theoretic control model of corruption in the three-level hierarchical system admits the following general representation:

$$J_P(y) \to \max_y; \quad J_S(y) \to \max_y; \quad J_A(y) \to \max_y. \tag{2.1.19}$$

Here J_P, J_S, J_A designate the payoff functions of Principal, supervisor and agent, respectively; $y = (p, q_r, q_s, r, s, u, b_r, b_s)$; p is the economic control action applied by Principal ($0 \le p \le 1$); q_r, q_s indicate its administrative control actions intended for the economic and administrative activities of supervisor, respectively ($0 \le q_r \le 1$; $0 \le q_s \le 1$); r means the economic control action applied by supervisor (tax) $(q_r \le r \le \bar{r})$; s specifies the administrative control action applied by supervisor (quota) ($q_s \le s \le \bar{s}$); u is the agent's action ($0 \le u \le 1 - s$); and finally, b_r, b_s denote the shares of tax and quota bribes, respectively ($b_r \ge 0; b_s \ge 0;\ b_r + b_s \le 1$).

By assumption, there exist minimum admissible values of tax r_0 and quota s_0 satisfying the homeostasis requirements for the controlled system (the latter has no explicit representation in the static model). The functions $r = r(b_r), s = s(b_s)$ describe economic and administrative corruption, respectively. Within the framework of the model (2.1.19), the Principal's anti-corruption struggle problem is solved by the following two-step optimization algorithm:

1) fix the values of the Principal's control variables and find the solution of the parametric "supervisor-agent" game of type Γ_2;
2) select the values of the Principal's control variables guaranteeing the supervisor's choice of the homeostatic control actions r_0, s_0 in the obtained solution of the above parametric game.

Suppose that a single control method (administrative or economic control) is applied at the Principal's level and the supervisor's level. In this case, there arise four settings of the anti-corruption struggle problem as follows: compulsion-compulsion, compulsion-impulsion, impulsion-compulsion and impulsion-impulsion. As an example, consider the compulsion-compulsion model (since economic methods take no place, i.e., $p = const$, denote $q_s = q, b_s = b$):

$$J_P(q,s,u,b) = -M\,|\,s - s_0\,| \to \max_{q \in [0,1]}; \quad J_S(q,s,u,b) = bf(u) \to \max_{s \in [q,\bar{s}]};$$
$$J_A(q,s,u,b) = (1-b)f(u) \to \max_{u \in [0,1-s],\ b \in [0,\bar{b}]}. \tag{2.1.20}$$

The Principal's payoff function reflects the unalterable requirement that supervisor chooses the value $s = s_0$, ensuring the homeostasis condition $u \le 1 - s_0$. If $s < s_0$, then Principal suffers from arbitrarily large penalty $(M >> 1)$. Without loss of generality, set $f(u) = \sqrt{u}$ and fix q to construct game Γ_2 of the form

$$J_S(s,b) = b\sqrt{1-s} \to \max_{q \le s \le \bar{s}}; \quad J_A(s,b) = (1-b)\sqrt{1-s} \to \max_{0 \le b \le \bar{b}}. \tag{2.1.21}$$

Similarly to the two-level model, apply the Germeier theorem to obtain the supervisor's maximum guaranteed payoff $K_1 = b^\varepsilon \sqrt{1-q} = (1 - \sqrt{(1-\bar{s})/(1-q)} - \varepsilon)\sqrt{1-q}$ and its ε-optimal guaranteeing strategy $\tilde{s}^*(b) = \begin{cases} q, b = b^\varepsilon, \\ \bar{s}, \text{otherwise.} \end{cases}$

Therefore, by choosing $q = s_0$, Principal ensures the homeostasis condition $s = s_0$. In the impulsion-compulsion analog of the model (2.1.20) (which is also reducible to a game Γ_2 similar to (2.1.21)), the supervisor's ε-optimal guaranteeing strategy has the form $\tilde{s}^*(b) = \begin{cases} 0, b = b^\varepsilon, \\ \bar{s}, \text{otherwise.} \end{cases}$

Here Principal appears unable to meet the condition $s = s_0$ by an appropriate choice of p: the economic struggle problem against administrative corruption admits no solution in this setting. The rest two settings of the anti-corruption struggle problem yield the same result, see (Antonenko et al., 2013).

Now, address the corruption model in the hierarchical control system with the sustainable development requirements in a modified form (Rozin et al., 2011):

$$\begin{gathered}
g_P(\cdot) = (1-p)rf(u) - \frac{q_r}{K_r - q_r} - \frac{q_s}{K_s - q_s} - M_r\rho(r,r_0) - M_s\rho(s,s_0) \to \max \\
0 \le p \le p_0; \quad 0 \le q_r \le r_0; \quad 0 \le q_s \le s_0; \\
g_S(\cdot) = (pr + b_r + b_s)f(u) \to \max \\
q_r \le r \le r_0; \quad q_s \le s \le s_0; \\
g_A(\cdot) = (1 - r - b_r - b_s)f(u) \to \max \\
0 \le u \le 1 - s; \quad b_r + b_s \le \bar{b}; \quad b_r \ge 0; \quad b_s \ge 0; \\
\rho(r,r_0) = \begin{cases} 0, \ r = r_0; \\ 1, \ r \ne r_0; \end{cases} \quad \rho(s,s_0) = \begin{cases} 0, \ s = s_0; \\ 1, \ s \ne s_0. \end{cases}
\end{gathered} \tag{2.1.22}$$

Here g_P, g_S, g_A are the payoff functions of Principal, supervisor and agent, respectively; the symbol $(\cdot)$ indicates the strategy profile of the game; p means the Principal's economic control parameter; p_0 gives its maximum admissible value; q_r, q_s

denote the Principal's control parameters with respect to the supervisor's economic and administrative activities, respectively; K_r, K_s answer for the Principal's control capability parameters; M_r, M_s are the significance coefficients of economic and administrative homeostasis conditions for Principal; r, s designate the supervisor's economic and administrative control variables, respectively; r_0, s_0 specify their homeostatic (statutory) values; u is the agent's action (a share of the maximum action); $f(u)$ represents the agent's income function; b_r, b_s signify the bribe shares in the agent's income under economic and administrative corruption, respectively; and $\bar{b}$ stands for the agent's bribery capability parameter.

The agent's action u yields an income $f(u)$ redistributed among all control levels. The variable r characterizes supervisor's economic control (taxes, penalties, subsidies, privileges) and the variable s describes its administrative control (quotas, limits, licenses). By assumption, the values r_0, s_0 of these variables ensure the homeostasis requirements. Client may benefit from relaxing the requirements for income shares (bribes) b_r, b_s; in this case, the homeostasis conditions are violated. Noncorrupt Principal chooses the economic parameter p (e.g., the share of officials' wage in collected taxes) and the parameters q_r, q_s of agent's activity control (audits, inspections, revisions, sanctions). Such control incurs certain costs, see the second and third terms in the Principal's payoff function. The fourth and fifth terms in this function represent penalties for homeostasis requirements breach.

The general corruption model (2.1.22) has the parameters

$$p_0 \in [0,1]; r_0 \in [0,1]; s_0 \in [0,1]; K_r \in [r_0,1]; K_s \in [s_0,1]; M_r \geq 0; M_s \geq 0; \bar{b} \in [0,1-r_0],$$

as well as the parameters of the functions $r(b)$, $s(b)$, $f(u)$ (their number depends on the class of functions selected for approximation). Here the identification problem (choice of an appropriate class of functions and evaluation of their parameters) is far from trivial and requires special studies and expert appraisals. The methodological meaning of identification consists in that each set of parameter values defines a concrete socioeconomic and sociopolitical system with corruption. Therefore, the matter concerns differential identification discriminating objects of research based on their structural and numerical parameters.

The admissible range of each scalar parameter represents a segment with boundaries defining qualitatively opposite types of its meaning content. The results of such analysis can be found in Table 2.1.3. Clearly, the boundary values specified in this table are almost nonimplementable in practice, but provide a qualitative picture via real value closeness.

Using expert appraisals, we have formed two sets of differentiated parameter values answering two test regions (Central Russia and Caucasus), see Table 2.1.4.

Within the framework of the model (2.1.22), it seems methodologically reasonable to study administrative and economic corruption separately. The administrative corruption model has the form

$$g_P(\cdot) = (1-p)rf(u) - \frac{q_s}{K_s - q_s} - M_s\rho(s,s_0) \to \max$$
$$0 \le p \le p_0; \quad 0 \le q_s \le s_0;$$
$$g_S(\cdot) = (pr + b_s)f(u) \to \max$$
$$q_s \le s \le s_0; \tag{2.1.23}$$
$$g_A(\cdot) = (1 - r - b_s)f(u) \to \max$$
$$0 \le u \le 1 - s; \quad 0 \le b_s \le \bar{b};$$
$$\rho(s,s_0) = \begin{cases} 0, \; s = s_0; \\ 1, \; s \ne s_0. \end{cases}$$

Table 2.1.3. Parameter identification of the corruption model (2.1.22)

Parameter	Interpretation	Boundary values and their meaning
p_0	The maximum share of officials' wage in tax income	$p_0 = 0$ – tax income is not intended for officials' wage at all; $p_0 = 1$ – tax income is completely allocated to officials' wage.
r_0	A statutory tax rate or another economic impact parameter	$r_0 = 0$ – complete immunity from taxes; $r_0 = 1$ – all income is collected as taxes.
s_0	A statutory quota or another administrative impact parameter	$s_0 = 0$ – no administrative restrictions; $s_0 = 1$ – business activity is prohibited.
K_r	The Principal's control capabilities with respect to agent's satisfaction of economic requirements	$K_r = r_0$ – complete control of economic requirements satisfaction is possible under infinite costs only; $K_r = 1$ – complete control is possible under reasonable costs
K_s	The Principal's control capabilities with respect to agent's satisfaction of administrative requirements	$K_s = s_0$ – complete control of administrative requirements satisfaction is possible under infinite costs only; $K_s = 1$ – complete control is possible under reasonable costs
M_r	The Principal's penalty coefficient for economic requirements nonsatisfaction	$M_r < 1$ – the economic homeostasis requirements are not so important for Principal; $M_r >> 1$ – the economic homeostasis requirements are unalterable for Principal
M_s	The Principal's penalty coefficient for administrative requirements nonsatisfaction	$M_s < 1$ – the administrative homeostasis requirements are not so important for Principal; $M_s >> 1$ – the administrative homeostasis requirements are unalterable for Principal
$\bar{b}$	The maximum bribe share in the client's income	$\bar{b} = 0$ – complete refusal from bribery; $\bar{b} = 1$ – readiness to allocate all income to bribery (willfully or under pressure)

Table 2.1.4. The test parameter values of the corruption model (2.1.22)

Parameter	Central Russia region	Caucasian region
p_0	0.025	0.1
r_0	0.2	0.4
s_0	0.4	0.6
K_r	0.7	0.6
K_s	0.8	0.6
M_r	5	10
M_s	5	10
$\bar{b}$	0.1	0.3

Set $f(u) = \sqrt{u}$; obviously, client always chooses the optimal value $u^* = 1 - s$. Consider the "supervisor-agent" Germeier game of type Γ_2 with the Principal's parameters $p \in [0, p_0], q_s \in [0, s_0]$:

$$g_S(s, b_s) = (pr + b_s)\sqrt{1-s} \to \max, \quad q_s \le s \le 1 - s_0; \tag{2.1.24}$$

$$g_A(s, b_s) = (1 - r - b_s)\sqrt{1-s} \to \max, \quad 0 \le b_s \le \bar{b} \le 1. \tag{2.1.25}$$

By applying Germeier's theory to this model (Gorelik and Kononenko, 1982), we find the client's optimal strategy (bribe) $b_s{}^*$ and the supervisor's optimal guaranteeing strategy $\tilde{s}^*(b_s)$ in the following form:

$$b_s{}^* = \begin{cases} \bar{b}, & \bar{b} < \dfrac{(1-r)(\sqrt{1-q_s} - \sqrt{s_0})}{\sqrt{1-q_s}}, \\ \dfrac{(1-r)(\sqrt{1-q_s} - \sqrt{s_0})}{\sqrt{1-q_s}}, & \text{otherwise;} \end{cases} \qquad \tilde{s}^*(b_s) = \begin{cases} q_s, & b = b_s{}^*, \\ 1 - s_0, & \text{otherwise} \end{cases}$$

By choosing $q_s = s_0$, Principal solves the sustainable management problem (ensures the condition $\tilde{s}^* = s_0$). In this case, $b_s{}^* = 0$: the equilibrium is corruption-free. The payoffs of all players under appropriate assumptions on the parameter values are demonstrated by Table 2.1.5. Clearly, Caucasian region players are at an advantage over their Central Russia opponents.

Table 2.1.5. The payoffs of the players in the model (2.1.23)

Parameter	Central Russia region	Caucasian region
r	0.2	0.2
p	0.01	0.04
g_P	-2.875	-1.851
g_S	0.0013	0.0062
g_A	0.506	0.62

The economic corruption model is constructed and analyzed by analogy to the models (2.1.23), (2.1.24)-(2.1.25). Here the agent's optimal strategy and the supervisor's optimal guaranteeing strategy acquire the form

$$b_r{}^* = \bar{b}, \quad \tilde{r}^*(b_r) = \begin{cases} r_0 - \bar{b} - \varepsilon, & b_r = \bar{b}, \\ r_0, & \text{otherwise.} \end{cases}$$

Hence, under economic corruption, Principal is unable to ensure the homeostasis condition $r = r_0$; giving the maximum bribe $b_r = \bar{b}$, client reduces the tax rate by the quantity $\bar{b} + \varepsilon$. Table 2.1.6 shows the payoffs of all players.

Table 2.1.6. The payoffs of the players in the economic corruption model

Parameter	Central Russia region	Caucasian region
r	0.2	0.2
p	0.01	0.04
g_P	-4.875	-9.875
g_S	0.1885	0.3856
g_A	0.4428	0.3873

In this case, the payoff of Caucasian Principal is smaller against its Central Russia colleague: the homeostasis condition fails and sensitivity to its breach is higher. Client gains less, too; at the same time, briber still has a higher payoff (Rozin et al., 2011). The next section presents a simulation complex for static models of corruption.

2.2. Software Complex for Static Models of Corruption

The software complex for static models of corruption (Antonenko, 2012) has been developed in Microsoft Visual Studio 2010. It includes the following modules:

1. input module;
2. calculation module;

3. graphics module;
4. output module.

The structure of the complex is shown by Figure 2.2.1.

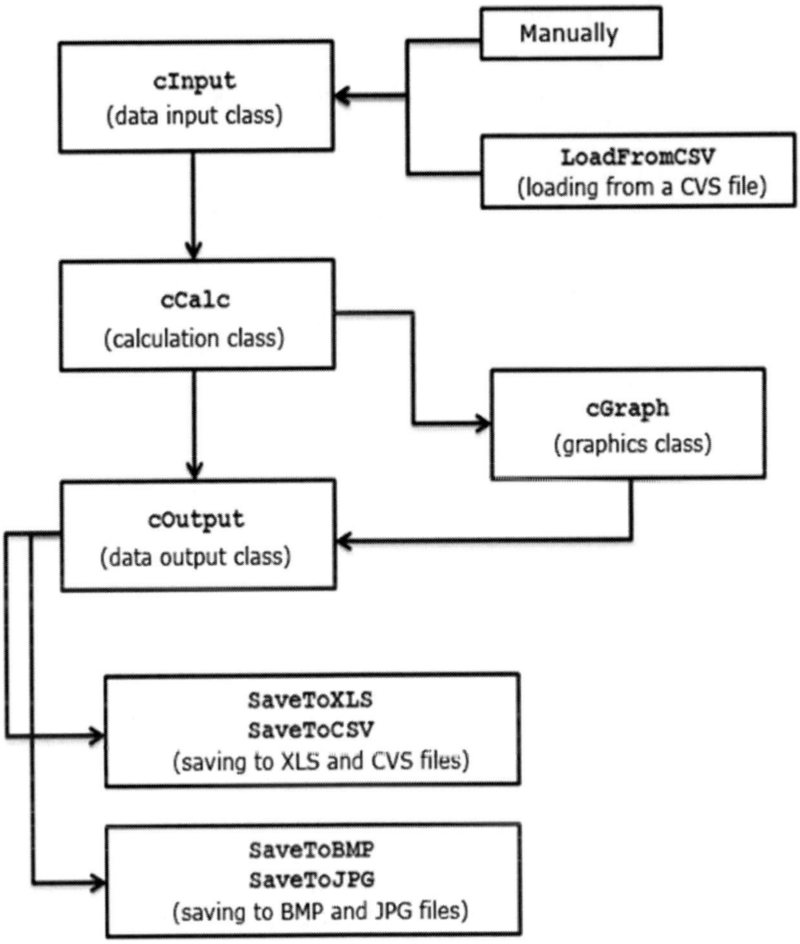

Figure 2.2.1. The structure of the main classes in the software complex.

Input module loads the initial data of static models in the CSV format, converts these data into a given format and assesses the correctness of resulting data according to model constraints.

Input data have several categories depending on the type of models and corruption. They can be divided into groups as follows.

Optimization models: general models of administrative corruption, models of administrative corruption in real estate development projects (ICPs), general models of economic corruption, models of economic corruption in ICPs.

Two-level models: general models of economic corruption, models of economic corruption, models of administrative corruption.

Three-level models: an example of the general three-level model, an example of the three-level model of corruption in ICPs.

Each of these groups is associated with (static or dynamic) model parameters. Static parameters represent model indicators which are defined initially and remain invariable during calculations. For instance, such parameters include statutory tax rates (r_0) or quotas (s_0), the probability of bribery detection (p), the raising coefficient γ of commercial real estate price and the estimated share in the model of administrative corruption in ICPs management. As its static parameters, the above model also incorporates the parameters ξ, u, r characterizing social real estate market.

Dynamic parameters are quantities varying in the course of calculations. The quantity A is a common dynamic parameter of all models in the software complex. This parameter characterizes the influence of bribe on bribetaker (supervisor). Other dynamic parameters are the quantities (the exponents of the corruption functions in appropriate models). Following software complex start, all static parameters receive their default values, in the manual or automatic mode (loading from an external CSV file). Dynamic parameters allow assessing the result under different conditions, i.e., provide a more comprehensive picture of the result. The parameters of bribe (b) and the payoff functions of Principal, supervisor and agent belong to analyzed parameters: they vary during calculations and *ergo* represent dynamic parameters.

By pressing the button "Calculate" in the main window of the software complex, a user transmits data to calculation module, where different solution methods are applied depending on the model type. Optimization models undergo simulation, solution of two-level models bases on Germeier theorem usage with simulation methods and gradient search. Solution of three-level models includes two stages: (1) the Germeier theorem yields a solution to the two-level "supervisor-agent" problem and (2) the resulting data are used to solve the Principal's optimization problem.

Graphics module displays the strategy domains of Principal, supervisor and agent in the 3D space. This visually explains the meaning of model parameters to a user, as well as shows the response of payoff functions to model parameters variations. 3D visualization employs linear algebra algorithms (particularly, affine transformations for two- and three-dimensional points in the space). Standard primitives are used such as lines, points and painted polygons. For better comprehension, all graphs are plotted in the isometric projection; yet, a user can change the angle of view with the mouse. The option of scaling fits a large graph into the window rectangle.

Output module shows the results of several experiments, as well as saves text output data in the CSV format or uploads them into Microsoft Excel. Graphic data are saved in the BMP or JPEG formats. Calculation module compiles a table of the parameter values and results of a given model. This table is displayed by output module and graphics module uses it to plot a 3D graph.

The realization efficiency of the algorithms based on model analysis is confirmed by high-speed calculations. For instance, the software complex performs up to 200 iterations per second for optimization models. This indicator makes up about 130 game iterations per second for two-level models and 110 game iterations per second for three-level models. Such a slight difference between two- and three-level models can be explained as follows. For the both models, calculations have a same scenario and computing costs, but the Principal's optimal strategy is also found in three-level models. We have performed calculations on a computer with Intel Core 2 Quad 2.4 GHz CPU and 6 Gb RAM. Note that the speed of calculations increases approximately by 200 iterations in the case of graphics module disconnection as CPU releases from graph plotting tasks.

As an example of software complex operation, consider the general model of administrative corruption under $s_0 = 0.35$. The parameter A varies from 0 to 6 with increment 1.2, the exponent of the function takes values 0.1, 1.1, and 2.6. The parameter varies from 0.1 to 3.3 with increment 0.8.

Table 2.2.1. The dependence of the agent's payoff function on model parameters (the general model of administrative corruption)

The exponent of the function f-the agent's production function (equals 0.1)								
	A (the influence of bribe on supervisor)							
the exponent k of the corruption function		0	1.2	2.4	3.6	4.8	6	
	0.1	0.9	1	1.054	1.09	1.118	1.141	*Payoff (G)*
		0	0.01	0.01	0.01	0.01	0.01	*Bribe (b)*
	0.9	0.9	0.9	0.901	0.906	0.914	0.924	*Payoff (G)*
		0	0	0.01	0.02	0.03	0.04	*Bribe (b)*
	1.7	0.9	0.9	0.9	0.9	0.9	0.9	*Payoff (G)*
		0	0	0	0	0	0	*Bribe (b)*
	2.5	0.9	0.9	0.9	0.9	0.9	0.9	*Payoff (G)*
		0	0	0	0	0	0	*Bribe (b)*
	3.3	0.9	0.9	0.9	0.9	0.9	0.9	*Payoff (G)*
		0	0	0	0	0	0	*Bribe (b)*
The exponent of the function f-the agent's production function (equals 1.1)								
	A (the influence of bribe on supervisor)							
the exponent k of the corruption function		0	1.2	2.4	3.6	4.8	6	
	0.1	0.315	1.209	2.206	3.248	4.323	5.422	*Payoff (G)*
		0	0.07	0.08	0.09	0.09	0.09	*Bribe (b)*
	0.9	0.315	0.52	0.873	1.247	1.634	2.031	*Payoff (G)*
		0	0.36	0.43	0.45	0.46	0.47	*Bribe (b)*
	1.7	0.315	0.348	0.561	0.792	1.032	1.278	*Payoff (G)*
		0	0.48	0.58	0.6	0.62	0.62	*Bribe (b)*
	2.5	0.315	0.315	0.415	0.582	0.756	0.935	*Payoff (G)*
		0	0	0.66	0.69	0.7	0.71	*Bribe (b)*
	3.3	0.315	0.315	0.33	0.461	0.597	0.738	*Payoff (G)*
		0	0	0.72	0.74	0.75	0.76	*Bribe (b)*
The exponent of the function f-the agent's production function (equals 2.6)								
	A (the influence of bribe on supervisor)							
the exponent k of the corruption function		0	1.2	2.4	3.6	4.8	6	
	0.1	0.065	1.83	7.745	19.5	38.498	65.976	*Payoff (G)*
		0	0.16	0.18	0.19	0.19	0.2	*Bribe (b)*
	0.9	0.065	0.523	2.065	5.073	9.893	16.825	*Payoff (G)*
		0	0.62	0.66	0.67	0.68	0.68	*Bribe (b)*
	1.7	0.065	0.31	1.205	2.945	5.731	9.733	*Payoff (G)*
		0	0.75	0.78	0.79	0.8	0.8	*Bribe (b)*
	2.5	0.065	0.22	0.851	2.077	4.035	6.851	*Payoff (G)*
		0	0.81	0.84	0.85	0.85	0.86	*Bribe (b)*
	3.3	0.065	0.171	0.658	1.604	3.114	5.287	*Payoff (G)*
		0	0.85	0.87	0.88	0.89	0.89	*Bribe (b)*

Table 2.2.1 shows the dependence of the agent's payoff function and bribe on model parameters. This table is the result of software complex operation. Several graphs (see below) are plotted using these data. Each row in the table answers to an appropriate graph. Graphs are constructed by graphics module and can be saved in BMP or JPG formats (for further usage in presentations or reports). Text data can be uploaded to CSV or XLS format, which eases subsequent manipulation of the results yielded by the software complex.

Analysis of the results generated by the software complex for the general model of administrative corruption leads to the following conclusion. Agent maximizes its gain only in the case of strongly corrupt supervisor. This seems obvious; however, according to the corruption function, maximum gain can be achieved under different bribes. Rather acceptable profits appear even without bribery when the exponent of the payoff function is approximately zero. The agent's intention to bribe supervisor grows simultaneously with the exponent as this appreciably increases its profits. Yet, higher exponent of the corruption function reduces the agent's intention to bribe supervisor, even though guarantees larger profits.

Thus, it is necessary to control and (as far as possible) decrease the supervisor's bribe sensitivity (the parameter A). Such an approach makes bribery pointless, see the leftmost column in the table. One should also keep the corruption function in a close neighborhood of zero. In this case, agent benefits nothing from bribery.

Below we show the agent's payoff as a function of bribe and the parameter A. In Figures 2.2.2-2.2.5, the exponents of the functions and have different values for a proper illustration of the calculations. Vertical axes answer for the agent's payoff and horizontal ones correspond to b and A (bribe and the briber's quantitative characteristic).

In Figure 2.2.2, agent obtains maximum gain under maximum value of the parameter A and a small bribe given to supervisor. On the other hand, if $A = 0$, agent guarantees its maximum payoff without bribery at all.

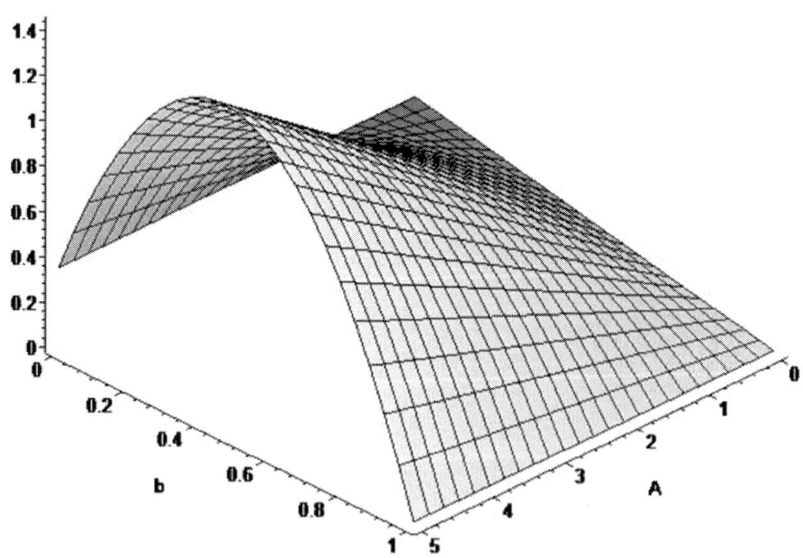

Figure 2.2.2. The agent's payoff as a function of the bribe b and the parameter A. (the exponents of the functions $f(x)$ and $s(b)$ equal 1).

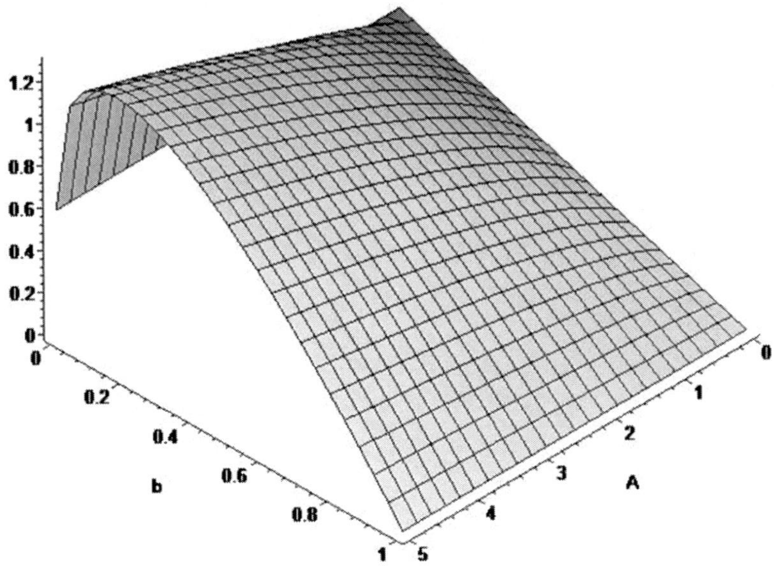

Figure 2.2.3. The agent's payoff as a function of the bribe b and the parameter A.
(the exponents of the functions $f(x)$ and $s(b)$ equal 0.5).

Similarly to Figure 2.2.2, here agent maximizes its payoff under largest parameter A, but the bribe required is smaller (the exponents of the production function and corruption function are decreased). Figure 2.2.4 is analogous to the previous ones, except that the agent's payoff reaches its maximum under $b \approx 0.7$.

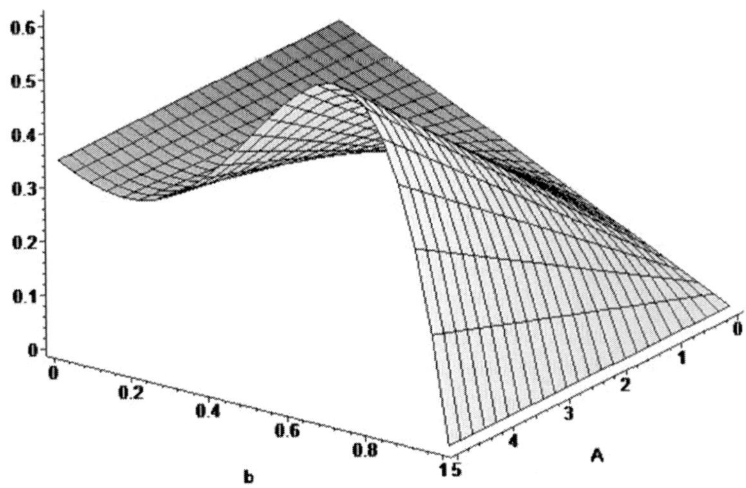

Figure 2.2.4. The agent's payoff as a function of the bribe b and the parameter A.
(the exponents of the functions $f(x)$ and $s(b)$ equal 1 and 3, respectively).

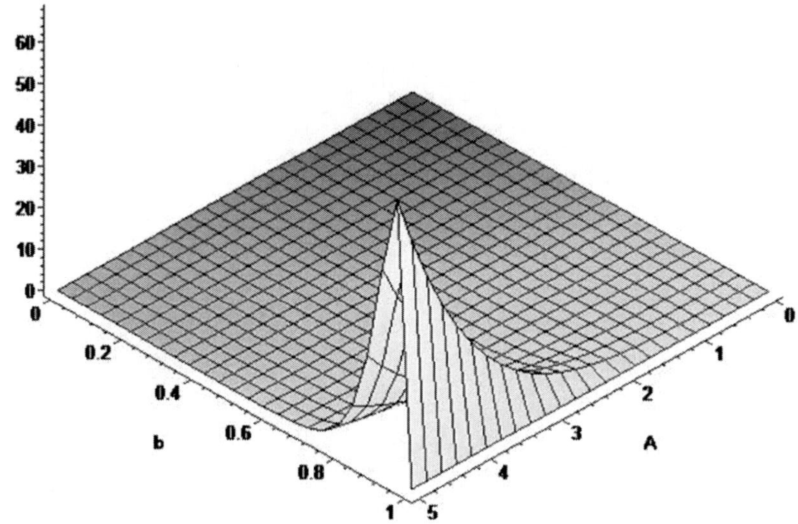

Figure 2.2.5. The agent's payoff as a function of the bribe b and the parameter A.
(the exponents of the functions $f(x)$ and $s(b)$ equal 5).

Further growth of the exponents of the production function and corruption function enlarges the agent's maximum payoff. However, it is necessary to give bribe $b \approx 0.9$ to supervisor, see Figure 2.2.5.

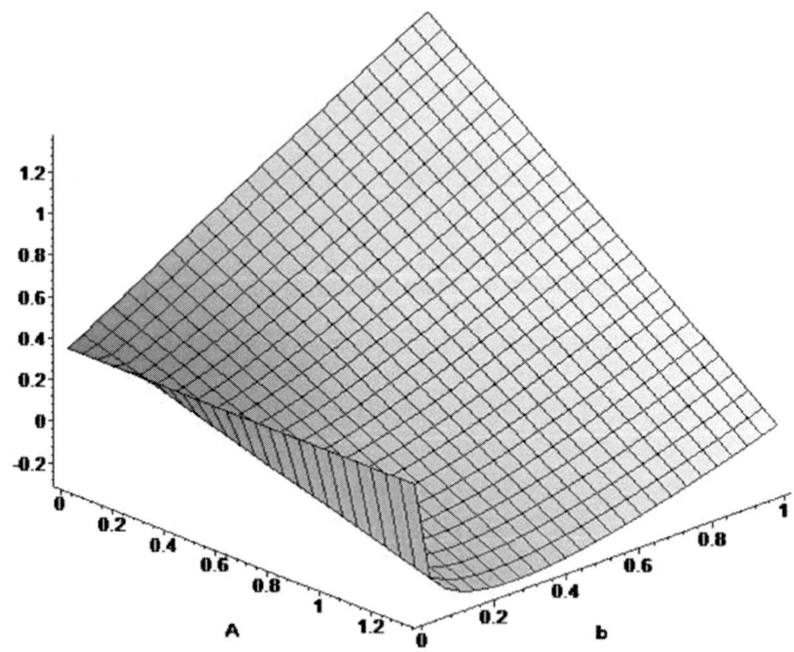

Figure 2.2.6. The agent's costs (vertical axis) as a function of the bribe b and the parameter A (the exponent $k = 0.3$).

Table 2.2.2. The dependence of the agent's payoff function on model parameters (the general model of economic corruption)

	A (the influence of bribe on supervisor)								
		0	0.225	0.45	0.675	0.9	1.125	1.34	
k (Показатель The exponent of the corruption function	0.1	0.35	0.218	0.063	0.005	0.002	0.007	0.001	Payoff (G)
		0	0.02	0.03	0.24	0.49	0.75	0.99	Bribe (b)
	0.6	0.35	0.346	0.325	0.28	0.207	0.1	0.001	Payoff (G)
		0	0.01	0.04	0.1	0.21	0.37	0.99	Bribe (b)
	1.1	0.35	0.35	0.35	0.35	0.35	0.227	0.015	Payoff (G)
		0	0	0	0	0	0.99	0.99	Bribe (b)
	1.6	0.35	0.35	0.35	0.35	0.35	0.233	0.021	Payoff (G)
		0	0	0	0	0	0.99	0.99	Bribe (b)
	2.1	0.35	0.35	0.35	0.35	0.35	0.238	0.028	Payoff (G)
		0	0	0	0	0	0.99	0.99	Bribe (b)
	2.6	0.35	0.35	0.35	0.35	0.35	0.244	0.035	Payoff (G)
		0	0	0	0	0	0.99	0.99	Bribe (b)
	3.1	0.35	0.35	0.35	0.35	0.35	0.25	0.041	Payoff (G)
		0	0	0	0	0	0.99	0.99	Bribe (b)

Let us discuss the numerical results obtained for the general model of economic corruption. The function means the total costs (payment of taxes and bribery) to-be-minimized by agent, $r_0 = 0.35$, *A* denotes the supervisor's bribe sensitivity (as before). In this model, it varies from 0 to 1.34 with increment 0.225. And finally, *k* is the exponent of the corruption function, taking values from 0.1 to 3.1 with increment 0.5. The results generated by the software complex are described by Table 2.2.2.

In the model of economic corruption, it is necessary to find parameter values in order to minimize the function $g(b)$. Clearly, the most beneficial case to agent makes *A* = 1.34, *k* = 0.1 under the bribe $b = 0.99$. The corresponding costs constitute 0.001, i.e., they almost vanish. Similar result can be achieved if *k* = 0.6. Note that the whole column *A* = 1.34 is most desired for agent, even in the case of maximum bribe. However, the table has domains free of bribery, see the red rectangle; here *k* increases from 1 and *A* < 1. Within these domains, agent prefers payment of statutory taxes. Hence, for bribery reduction in the general model of economic corruption one should keep the supervisor's bribe sensitivity inside the interval (0,1) and maximize the parameter (the exponent of the corruption function). Figures below demonstrate these relationships.

Consider Figure 2.2.6. First, by implication the corruption function is positive (agent pays taxes, not receives them). Second, for *k* = 0.3 the agent's costs achieve minimum under a rather small bribe (within the range from 0 to 0.1) depending on the parameter *A*. Hence, agent benefits from bribery and minimizes the total costs.

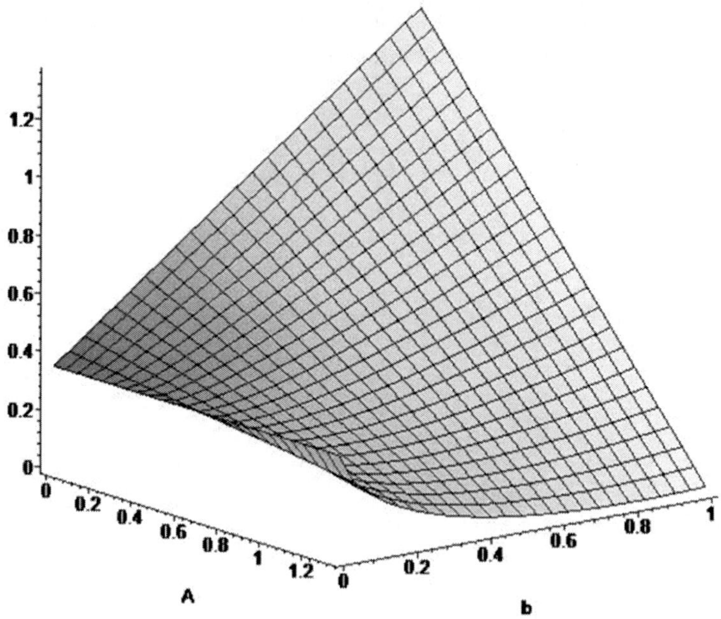

Figure 2.2.7. The agent's costs (vertical axis) as a function of the bribe b and the parameter A (the exponent $k = 0.7$).

Figure 2.2.7 qualitatively resembles Figure 2.2.6, except that the agent's costs are maximized via bribe $b \approx 1$ under $A \geq 1$.

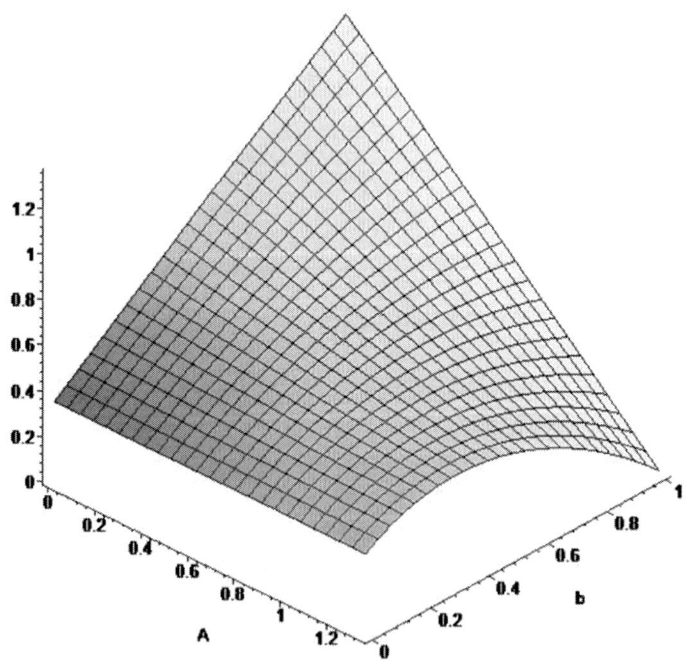

Figure 2.2.8. The agent's costs (vertical axis) as a function of the bribe b and the parameter A (the exponent $k = 1.7$).

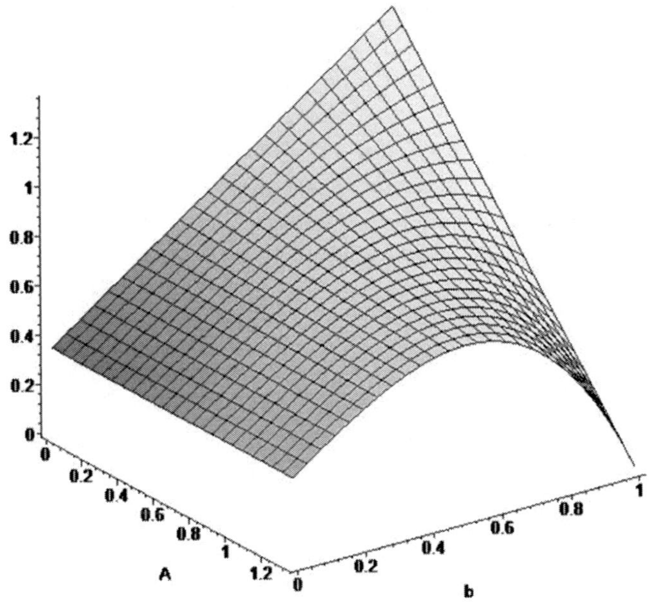

Figure 2.2.9. The agent's costs (vertical axis) as a function of the bribe b and the parameter A (the exponent $k = 3.1$).

Figure 2.2.8 illustrates the following. As the parameter A approaches or exceeds 1, agent incurs almost no costs via bribe from 0.8 to 1.

The qualitative picture remains the same in Figure 2.2.9. Here large values of A and b allow minimizing the agent's general costs.

By examining the above graphs, we make a more concrete conclusion for the model under consideration. For corruption prevention, one should decrease the parameter as close to zero as possible (i.e., reduce the supervisor's aspiration for bribery, e.g., via establishing sufficiently high penalties or sanctions for bribetaker.

Therefore, the created software complex visually illustrates the derived analytical results or performs numerical simulation of corruption models in the absence of such results. Moreover, another field of its application concerns learning. Section 3.1 describes how the software complex can be used for numerical simulation of corruption models in management of real estate development projects.

2.3. Dynamic Models

This section is a logical continuation of the sections dedicated to static models of anti-corruption drive: here we explore corresponding dynamic models. Within the original concept, description of corruption and anti-corruption measures in the dynamic setting proceeds from a series of theses.

1. A basic scheme of modeling is the "Principal–supervisor–agent–object" hierarchical system in different modifications and its game-theoretic study by optimal control and dynamic games methods. Corruption affects middle-level control (supervisor), upper-

level control (Principal) is non-corrupt and struggles against corruption. In several cases, the "bribetaker–briber" (supervisor–agent–object) simplified model is considered, where non-corrupt upper-level subject (Principal) has implicit (parametric) description.
2. Both Leader (Principal or supervisor) and Follower (supervisor or agent, respectively) pursue individual goals using compulsion (par excellence, administrative and legislative impact) and impulsion (par excellence, economic impact); in the mathematical formalization, compulsion means the Leader's impact on the admissible strategy set of Follower (without feedback), whereas impulsion implies the Leader's impact on the payoff function of Follower (with feedback).
3. There exists a discrimination between administrative corruption (administrative requirements weakened via bribery) and economic corruption (the economic requirements of upper-level control weakened via bribery). Modeling of administrative corruption lies in agent's compulsion by supervisor with bribe amount feedback. Modeling of economic corruption consists in agent's impulsion by supervisor with additional bribe amount feedback.
4. Corruption exists in the form of capture and extortion. Under capture, a statutory set of services is guaranteed and additional relaxations are granted via bribery. Under extortion, bribery is demanded for a basic set of services (otherwise, existing requirements are toughened).
5. Descriptive and normative approaches are applicable to characterize corruption in hierarchical control systems with the sustainable development requirements. Within the descriptive approach, the administrative or economic corruption functions are assumed known and the primary problem is to identify their parameters using statistical data. Within the normative approach, the corruption function follows from solution of an optimization or game-theoretic problem.
6. Corruption analysis in the "Principal–supervisor–agent" system proceeds from three alternative positions. If the corruption function is known, from the agent's position corruption can be described by an optimal control model. The supervisor's position brings to Germeier hierarchical parametric game of the type Γ_{2t} (its general solution in the form of the corruption function with bribe amount feedback is known). And finally, from the Principal's position the anti-corruption struggle problem lies in evaluating control parameters so that the sustainable development requirements of a controlled dynamic system (object) are satisfied under the supervisor's optimal strategy found.
7. It is reasonable to construct sequences of gradually complicated models with a more and more accurate description of real corruption phenomena in hierarchical control systems. The main logical scheme of such complication has the form of "optimal control problems – dynamic hierarchical two-player games – dynamic hierarchical three-player games." Each type of models admits several modifications, inducing sequences in the form of "networks."

The dynamic aspects of control systems functioning can be divided into two groups as follows. First, this is controlled system dynamics, i.e., its state variations with the course of time due to internal driving forces and control impacts. And theory of dynamic systems acts as the main mathematical framework involved. Second, this is decision-making processes dynamics expressed in an action sequence of control subjects and their information exchange. The latter aspect to a large degree determines control system hierarchy, i.e., the inequitable status of its elements depending on their place and role in the rules of interaction. Here dynamic games theory prevails in mathematical formalization. Consequently, while defining the sustainable development conditions of hierarchically controlled dynamic systems, one should state some requirements both to controlled subsystem dynamics and impacts exerted on it.

Analysis of dynamic hierarchical control models demonstrates that the basic results in the field were obtained within the framework of dynamic Stackelberg games (Basar and Olsder, 1999) and their special case known as dynamic Germeier games (Gorelik et al., 1991). In comparison with static settings, the dynamic ones possess a series of new features, namely:

1. *Decision-making dynamics and controlled system dynamics*. Decision-making can be implicitly considered as a process in any hierarchical game, since Leader and Follower move sequentially. In multistep games, decision-making dynamics is described in an explicit and detailed way, bringing to specific solutions in dynamic games of the types Γ_{1t} and Γ_{2t} and its design methods (Gorelik et al., 1991). Controlled system dynamics has no characterization in the static case; it can be described in discrete or continuous time. The former approach involves difference games, whereas the latter operates differential games.
2. *Information structure*. Information structure is appreciably richer and more diverse in the dynamic setting than in the static one. According to our viewpoint, here two "watersheds" appear of utmost importance. First, the presence of state feedback in the controlled system: a strategy is defined for a whole horizon (open-loop strategy) or it depends on the state of the controlled system (closed-loop strategy). Possible subclasses of closed-loop strategies (e.g., a strategy depends on the current state, on the whole prehistory or its part, etc.) seem not so crucial, although induce mathematical variations. Second, the presence of control feedback: Leader makes decisions regardless of the Follower's behavior or depending on it. This discrimination becomes salient in dynamic games (see Table 2.3.1).
3. *Dynamic stability*. In a practical interpretation, this major notion of dynamic game theory means that none of players benefits by deviating from an initial agreement (solution) over the whole duration of the game (Zenkevich et al., 2009; Basar and Olsder, 1999). As is well-known, a Stackelberg equilibrium in open-loop strategies does not enjoy time consistency, whereas a Stackelberg equilibrium in closed-loop strategies is subgame perfect. Below we concretize some notions introduce in Section 1.2.

Table 2.3.1. Dynamic games: A classification

Control dependence \ State dependence	No (open-loop strategies)	Yes (closed-loop strategies)
No (Stackelberg games)	Γ_{1t}	Γ_{1x}
Yes (Germeier games)	Γ_{2t}	Γ_{2x}

Partial Classes of Dynamic Hierarchical Games

For simplicity and definiteness, as the initial "generic" model consider two-player (Leader-Follower) differential games in open-loop strategies of the form

$$J_L(p,q,u,x) = \int_0^{\infty} e^{-\alpha t} g_L(p(t),q(t),u(t),x(t))dt \to \max \tag{2.3.1}$$

$$p(t) \in P, \quad q(t) \in Q \tag{2.3.2}$$

$$J_F(p,u,x) = \int_0^{\infty} e^{-\alpha t} g_F(p(t),u(t),x(t))dt \to \max \tag{2.3.3}$$

$$u(t) \in U(q), \tag{2.3.4}$$

$$\dot{x} = f(x(t),u(t)), \quad x(0) = x_0, \tag{2.3.5}$$

where are the payoff functions of Leader and Follower, respectively, $p(t)$ or $q(t)$ and $u(t)$ represent their open-loop strategies, denote the corresponding sets of admissible strategies, is the discount factor; means the state vector of the controlled dynamic system described by equation (2.3.5), $x(t) = x(u(t),t)$; $x(t) \in X$; X stands for the set of admissible system states.

By assumption, P, Q, U, X, and X^* form compact sets in appropriate spaces; the payoff function J_L is continuous on $P \times Q \times U \times X$; the payoff function J_F is continuous and strictly convex on $P \times U \times X$; the strategies p, q, and u are piecewise continuous in t ; and finally, the function f is continuously differentiable with respect to x and u, as well as meets the Lipschitz condition in x. The above infinite-horizon setting is most adequate to the sustainable management problem.

We believe that the model (2.3.1)–(2.3.5) possesses a couple of features. First, the dynamics of (2.3.5) depends explicitly only on the Follower's impact; Leader controls the state of the system (2.3.5) indirectly by influencing Follower. And second, the both players have interests of either same direction in u (i.e., $\sup_{u \in U(q)} J_L(p,q,u,x) = \sup_{u \in U(q)} J_F(p,u,x); \forall p(t) \in P; q(t) \in Q$) or opposite direction in u ($\sup_{u \in U(q)} J_L(p,q,u,x) = \inf_{u \in U(q)} J_F(p,u,x); \forall p(t) \in P; q(t) \in Q$).

In the former case, a basic (though, not unique) practical interpretation is that the Follower's activity yields an income shared by the players. In the latter case, Follower, e.g., saves its labor efforts, whereas Leader tries to increase them. Further exposition accepts the hypothesis on the same-direction interests of the players (the other case is treated by analogy).

Under the above assumptions, study some particular classes of dynamic hierarchical games attracting certain interest for modeling of hierarchically controlled dynamic systems, both in the sense of theory and applications (Ougolnitsky and Usov, 2013b).

Dynamic hierarchical games with control feedback. In this case, the Leader's strategy depends on the Follower's strategy: $p(t)=p(u(t))$ or $q(t)=q(u(t))$. This class of games corresponds to dynamic Germeier games of the type Γ_{2t}. Concerning practical interpretations, the models describe internal adaptation in a system and corruption is a striking example. Note that games in closed-loop strategies serve as external adaptation models.

Dynamic hierarchical compulsion and impulsion games. We comprehend compulsion as the Leader's impact on the set of the Follower's admissible strategies only (generally, without control feedback) and impulsion as the Leader's impact on the Follower's payoff function only (generally, with control feedback). Therefore, compulsion games involve $U=U(q)$, where q is the Leader's strategy (the function $p=p(t)$ is defined and fixed), while impulsion games operate $J_F=J_F(p,u,x)$ (the function $q=q(t)$ is defined and fixed). In its practical interpretation, this class of models characterizes compulsion and impulsion as the basic methods of hierarchical control (administrative-legislative and economic ones) (Ougolnitsky, 2010).

Table 2.3.2. Game-theoretic models of hierarchical control and their interpretation

No.	Model	Interpretation
1	Stackelberg compulsion game (Germeier game of the type Γ_{2t}) with control feedback	Administrative corruption
2	Stackelberg impulsion game (Germeier game of the type Γ_{2t}) with additional control feedback	Economic corruption
3	Stackelberg compulsion game (Germeier game of the type Γ_{2t}) with requirements to controlled dynamic system	Sustainable management via compulsion
4	Stackelberg impulsion game (Germeier game of the type Γ_{2t}) with requirements to controlled dynamic system	Sustainable management via impulsion
5	Stackelberg compulsion game (Germeier game of the type Γ_{2t}) with control feedback and requirements to controlled dynamic system	Sustainable management via compulsion under administrative corruption
6	Stackelberg impulsion game (Germeier game of the type Γ_{2t}) with additional control feedback and requirements to controlled dynamic system	Sustainable management via impulsion under economic corruption

Dynamic games with requirements to controlled dynamic system. Here Leader has to guarantee certain requirements to the state of the controlled dynamic system (CDS), which can be expressed as $\forall t \in [0,T]: x(t) \in X^*$ (the Lagrange stability), where X^* designates the set of admissible states of the controlled system. These requirements are rewritten using a penalty term in the Leader's payoff function, i.e., $g_L(p(t),q(t),u(t),x(t)) = \overline{g}_L(p(t),q(t),u(t),x(t)) - M\rho(x(t),X^*)$, where $\rho(x(t),X^*) = \begin{cases} 0, & x(t) \in X^*, \\ 1, & otherwise \end{cases}$ signifies the indicator function and $M >> 1$ is a penalty constant. This class of models is used to describe the sustainable management problem (Ougolnitsky, 2010; Ougolnitsky and Usov, 2014a). By combining the mentioned conditions, one can construct particular classes of practical models, see their names and interpretations in Table 2.3.2.

Game-Theoretic Models, Interpretation, Optimality Principles

Let us describe in detail the mentioned particular classes of dynamic game-theoretic models of hierarchical control.

Model 1: Stackelberg compulsion game (Germeier game of the type Γ_{2t}) with control feedback. In this case, the model (2.3.1)–(2.3.4) acquires the form

$$J_L(q,u,b,x) = \int_0^\infty e^{-\alpha t} g_L(q(t),u(t),b(t),x(t))dt \to \max \tag{2.3.6}$$

$$q(t) \in Q^{B(t)}; \tag{2.3.7}$$

$$J_F(u,b,x) = \int_0^\infty e^{-\alpha t} g_F(u(t),b(t),x(t))dt \to \max \tag{2.3.8}$$

$$u(t) \in U(q(t)); \quad b(t) \in B(t); \tag{2.3.9}$$

The dynamic equation (2.3.5) remains unchanged. The model (2.3.5)–(2.3.9) is interpreted as the model of administrative corruption, where $q(t)$ denotes Leader's compulsion control ("quota"); $u(t)$ means the Follower's action assigned a quota; $b(t)$ is a bribe for quota increase; $Q(t),U(q(t)),B(t)$ indicate the admissible control sets of the subjects; $Q^{B(t)}$ represents the set of all mappings from $B(t)$ into $Q(t)$; and finally, $x(t)$ designates the controlled system state determined by the Follower's actions only.

Definition 2.3.1. A triplet (q^*,u^*,b^*) is called a Stackelberg compulsion equilibrium in open-loop strategies with control feedback if

$$J_L(q^*,u^*,b^*,x^*) = \sup_{q\in Q^B} \sup_{u\in U(q)} \inf_{b\in R_u(q)} J_L(q,u,b,x),$$

where $x^*, x \in X$ specify the corresponding trajectories of the CDS belonging to the admissible state set of the system; $R_u(q) = \{b \in B(t) : \forall c \in B(t)\, J_F(u,b,x) \geq J_F(u,c,x)\}$ gives the set of the Follower's optimal responses in the variable b to the Leader's compulsion strategy q under a fixed function $u(t) = u(q(t),t) \in U(q)$.

The equilibrium design algorithm in the model (2.3.5)–(2.3.9) includes the following steps:

1) Introduce the penalty strategy

$$q^P(t) : J_F(u(q^P(t),t), b(t), x(t)) = \inf_{q(t)\in Q} J_F(u(q(t),t), b(t), x(t))$$

applied by Leader to Follower.

Evaluate the Follower's guaranteed payoff under no cooperation with Leader:

$$L_F = \sup_{b(t)\in B(t),\, u(t)\in U(q^P(t))} J_F(u(t), b(t), x(t)).$$

2) Solve the optimal control problem (2.3.5)–(2.3.7), (2.3.9) subject to the additional constraint $L_F < J_F(u(t), b(t), x(t))$.

Under the assumption regarding the same-direction interests of the both players, maximize the expression (2.3.6) in the three functions $q(t), u(t), b(t)$. Denote by $q^R(t), u^R(t)$, $b^R(t)$ the solution of the stated optimal control problem, where $q^R(t)$ is the incentive strategy applied by Leader to Follower under compulsion.

3) Leader submits to Follower the feedback strategy (corruption control mechanism)

$$\hat{q}(b(t),t) = \begin{cases} q^R(t), & \text{if } \; b(t) = b^R(t) \; \text{for } \forall t \in [0,\infty) \\ q^P(t), & \text{otherwise.} \end{cases}$$

4) Follower being economically wise, the equilibrium in the model (2.3.5)–(2.3.9) has the form $\left(q^R(t), u^R(t), b^R(t)\right)$.

Consider an operator $A_q : U(q) \to X$ defined by (2.3.5). Denote

$$A_q^{-1}(X) = \left\{u \in U(q) : A_q u \in X\right\}.$$

Assertion 2.3.1. The model (2.3.5) – (2.3.9) admits an equilibrium according to Definition 2.3.1 if $S_1 = \{q(t) \in Q(t); b(t) \in B(t); \quad u(t) \in A_q^{-1}(X) : L_F < J_F(u(t), b(t), x(u(t)))\} \neq \varnothing$ under a given function $p(t) \in P$.

Proof. Due to the properties enjoyed by the sets $B(t), Q(t), U(q(t))$, $A_q^{-1}(X), X$ and the payoff function J_F, whenever $S_1 \neq \varnothing$ we have that

$$\sup_{(u(t),b(t),q(t))\in S_1} J_F(u(q(t),t),b(t),x(t)) = \max_{(u(t),b(t),q(t))\in S_1} J_F(u(q(t),t),b(t),x(t))$$
$$= J_F(u_1(q_1(t),t),b_1(t),x_1(t)); \quad (u_1(t),b_1(t),q_1(t)) \in S_1.$$

The triplet $(u_1(t),b_1(t),q_1(t))$ forms an equilibrium in the model (2.3.5)–(2.3.9) according to Definition 2.3.1. The proof is complete.

Model 2: Stackelberg impulsion game with additional control feedback
In this case, the model (2.3.1)–(2.3.4) takes the form

$$J_L(p,u,b,x) = \int_0^\infty e^{-\alpha t} g_L(p(t),u(t),b(t),x(t))dt \to \max \tag{2.3.10}$$

$$p(t) \in P^{U(t)*B(t)}; \tag{2.3.11}$$

$$J_F(p,u,b,x) = \int_0^\infty e^{-\alpha t} g_F(p(t),u(t),b(t),x(t))dt \to \max \tag{2.3.12}$$

$$u(t) \in U(t); \quad b(t) \in B(t); \tag{2.3.13}$$

The model (2.3.10)–(2.3.13), (2.3.5) is interpreted as the model of economic corruption, where $p(t)$ means Leader's impulsion control ("tax"); $u(t)$ indicates the Follower's action liable to the tax; $b(t)$ denotes a bribe for tax reduction; and finally, $P^{U(t)\times B(t)}$ represents the set of all mappings from the Cartesian product $U(t)\times B(t)$ into $P(t)$.

Definition 2.3.2. A triplet (p^*,u^*,b^*) is called a Stackelberg impulsion equilibrium in open-loop strategies with additional control feedback if

$$J_L(p^*,u^*,b^*,x^*) = \sup_{p\in P^{U\times B}} \sup_{u\in U(t)} \inf_{b\in R_u(p)} J_L(p,u,b,x),$$

where $R_u(p) = \{b \in B(t) : \forall c \in B(t)\ J_F(p,u,b,x) \geq J_F(p,u,c,x)\}$ forms the set of the Follower's optimal responses to the Leader's impulsion strategy p under a fixed function $u(t) = u(t) \in U(t)$.

The equilibrium design algorithm in the model (2.3.10)–(2.3.13), (2.3.5) includes the following steps.

1) Introduce the penalty strategy

$$p^P(t) : J_F(p^P(t),u(t),b(t),x(t)) = \inf_{p(t)\in P} J_F(p(t),u(t),b(t),x(t)); u(t) \in U(t)$$

applied by Leader to Follower.

Evaluate the Follower's guaranteed payoff under no cooperation with Leader:

$$L_F = \sup_{b(t)\in B(t);u(t)\in U(t)} J_F(u(t),b(t),x(t)).$$

2) Solve the optimal control problem (2.3.10), (2.3.11), (2.3.13), (2.3.5) subject to the additional constraint $L_F < J_F(p(t),u(t),b(t),x(t))$. Maximize (2.3.10) in the three functions $p(t),u(t),b(t)$. Denote by $p^R(t),u^R(t),b^R(t)$ the solution of the stated optimal control problem, where $p^R(t)$ is the incentive strategy applied by Leader to Follower under compulsion.

3) Leader submits to Follower the feedback strategy (corruption control mechanism)

$$\hat{p}(u(t),b(t),t)=\begin{cases} p^R(t), & \text{if } b(t)=b^R(t);u(t)=u^R(t)\forall t\in[0,\infty) \\ p^P(t), & \text{otherwise.}\end{cases}$$

4) Follower being economically wise, the equilibrium in the model (2.3.10)–(2.3.13), (2.3.5) has the form $\left(p^R(t),u^R(t),b^R(t)\right)$.

Assertion 2.3.2. The model (2.3.10)–(2.3.13), (2.3.5) admits an equilibrium according to Definition 2.3.2 if $S_2=\{p(t)\in P(t);b(t)\in B(t);\quad u(t)\in A_q^{-1}(X):$ $L_F < J_F(p(t),u(t),b(t),x(u(t)))\} \neq \varnothing$ under a given function $q(t)\in Q$.

This result is proved by analogy to Assertion 2.3.1.

Model 3: Stackelberg compulsion game with requirements to controlled dynamic system. The model (2.3.1)–(2.3.4) acquires the form

$$J_L(q,u,x)=\int_0^\infty e^{-\alpha t} g_L(q(t),u(t),x(t))dt \to \max \quad (2.3.14)$$

$$q(t)\in Q(t); \tag{2.3.15}$$

$$J_F(u,x)=\int_0^\infty e^{-\alpha t} g_F(u(t),x(t))dt \to \max \tag{2.3.16}$$

$$u(t)\in U(q(t)); \tag{2.3.17}$$

$$x(t)=x(u(t))\in X^*. \tag{2.3.18}$$

The model (2.3.14)–(2.3.18), (2.3.5) is interpreted as the model of sustainable management via compulsion. The condition (2.3.18) describes the sustainable development requirements to the controlled dynamic system.

Definition 2.3.3. A pair (q^*, u^*) is called a Stackelberg compulsion equilibrium in open-loop strategies with requirements to the CDS if

$$J_L(q^*,u^*,x^*) = \sup_{q\in Q_X} \inf_{u\in R_1(q)} J_L(q,u,x),$$

where $R_1(q) = \{u \in U(q(t)) : \forall w \in U(q(t))\ J_F(u,x) \geq J_F(w,x)\}$ forms the set of the Follower's optimal responses to the Leader's compulsion strategy q; $Q_X = \{q(t) \in Q(t) : \forall u(t) \in R_1(q(t)), x(u(t)) \in X^*,\ t \geq 0\}$ is the set of admissible compulsion controls applied by Leader taking into account the requirements to the CDS. If $Q_X = \varnothing$, no equilibria exist.

The equilibrium design algorithm in the model (2.3.14)–(2.3.18), (2.3.5) includes the following steps.

1) Perform optimization of the functional (2.3.16) subject to the constraints (2.3.17) and construct the Follower's optimal strategies depending on the Leader's controls, i.e., a function $u^*(t) = u^*(q(t),t)$.

2) Substitute the function $u^*(t) = u^*(q(t),t)$ obtained at Step 1 into (2.3.14), (2.3.5). Solve the optimal control problem (2.3.14), (2.3.5) subject to the additional constraints (2.3.15) and the phase constraints (2.3.18). The Leader's optimal function is $q^*(t)$ maximizing the expression (2.3.14) under the conditions (2.3.15), (2.3.18) taking into account (2.3.5).

3) The equilibrium in Model 3 has the form $(q^*(t), u^*(q^*(t),t))$.

If there exist several maximum points of the Follower's payoff function, Leader displays caution according to Germeier's principle of guaranteed result.

Assertion 2.3.3. The model (2.3.14), (2.3.15), (2.3.18), (2.3.5) admits an equilibrium according to Definition 2.3.3 if

$$S_3 = \{q(t) \in Q(t) : u^*(p(t), q(t), t) \in A_q^{-1}(X^*)\} \neq \varnothing$$

under a given function $p(t) \in P$.

Proof. By virtue of the properties of the sets $Q(t), U(q(t)), A_q^{-1}(X^*), X^*$ and the functional J_F, whenever $S_3 \neq \varnothing$ we have that

$$\sup_{q(t)\in S_3} J_F(u(q(t),t),x(t)) = \max_{q(t)\in S_3} J_F(u(q(t),t),x(t))$$

$$= J_F(u_1(q_1(t),t),x_1(t));q_1(t)\in S_3.$$

The pair of functions $(u_1(q_1(t),t),q_1(t))$ is an equilibrium of the model (2.3.14), (2.3.15), (2.3.18), (2.3.5) according to Definition 2.3.3. This concludes the proof.

Model 4: Stackelberg impulsion game with requirements to controlled dynamic system. The model (2.3.1)–(2.3.4) acquires the form

$$J_L(p,u,x) = \int_0^\infty e^{-\alpha t} g_L(p(t),u(t),x(t))dt \to \max \tag{2.3.19}$$

$$p(t) \in P^{U(t)}; \tag{2.3.20}$$

$$J_F(p,u,x) = \int_0^\infty e^{-\alpha t} g_F(p(t),u(t),x(t))dt \to \max \tag{2.3.21}$$

$$u(t) \in U(t). \tag{2.3.22}$$

The dynamic equation (2.3.5) and the condition (2.3.18) remain unchanged. The model (2.3.19)–(2.3.22), (2.3.5), (2.3.18) is interpreted as the model of sustainable management via impulsion. Here $P^{U(t)}$ represents the set of all mappings from $U(t)$ into $P(t)$.

Definition 2.3.4. A pair (p^*,u^*) is called a Stackelberg impulsion equilibrium in open-loop strategies with requirements to the CDS if

$$J_L(p^*,u^*,x^*) = \sup_{p\in P_X} \inf_{u\in R_1(p)} J_L(p,u,x),$$

where $R_1(p) = \{u \in U(t): \forall w \in U(t)\ J_F(p,u,x) \geq J_F(p,w,x)\}$ forms the set of the Follower's optimal responses to the Leader's impulsion strategy p; $P_X = \{p(t) \in P^{U(t)}: \forall u(t) \in R_1(p(t))\quad x(u(t)) \in X^*; t \geq 0\}$ is the set of admissible impulsion controls applied by Leader taking into account the requirements to the CDS. If $P_X = \varnothing$, no equilibria exist.

The equilibrium design algorithm in the model (2.3.18)–(2.3.22), (2.3.5) includes the following steps.

1) Perform optimization of the functional (2.3.21) subject to the constraints (2.3.22) and construct the Follower's optimal strategies depending on Leader's controls, i.e., a function $u^*(t) = u^*(p(t),t)$.

2) Substitute the function $u^*(t)=u^*(p(t),t)$ obtained at Step 1 into (2.3.19), (2.3.5). Solve the optimal control problem (2.3.19), (2.3.5) subject to the additional constraints (2.3.20) and the phase constraints (2.3.18). The Leader's optimal function is $p^*(t)$ maximizing the expression (2.3.19) under the conditions (2.3.18), (2.3.20) taking into account (2.3.5).

3) The equilibrium in Model 4 has the form $(p^*(t),u^*(p^*(t),t))$.

If there exist several maximum points of the Follower's payoff function, Leader displays caution according to Germeier's principle of guaranteed result, similarly to Model 3.

Assertion 2.3.4. The model (2.3.18)–(2.3.20), (2.3.5) admits an equilibrium according to Definition 2.3.4 if

$$S_4 = \{p(t) \in P(t) : u^*(p(t),q(t),t) \in A_q^{-1}(X^*)\} \neq \varnothing$$

under a given function $q(t) \in Q$.

This result is established by analogy to Assertion 2.3.3.

Model 5: Stackelberg compulsion game with control feedback and requirements to controlled dynamic system.

Model 5 is described by a system of functionals and control constraints, see (2.3.5)–(2.3.9), subject to the additional condition (2.3.18) reflecting the sustainable development requirement of the system. This model is interpreted as the model of sustainable management via compulsion under administrative corruption.

Definition 2.3.5. A triplet (q^*, u^*, b^*) is called a Stackelberg compulsion equilibrium in open-loop strategies with control feedback and requirements to the CDS if

$$J_L(q^*,u^*,b^*,x^*) = \sup_{(q,u)\in Q_X} \inf_{b\in R_u(q)} J_L(q,u,b,x),$$

where $Q_X = \{q(t) \in Q^{B(t)}; u(t) \in U(q(t))\, x(u(t)) \in X^*, t \geq 0\}$. If $Q_X = \varnothing$, no equilibria exist.

The equilibrium design algorithm in the model (2.3.5)–(2.3.9), (2.3.18) includes the following steps.

1) Introduce the penalty strategy

$$q^P(t) : J_F(u(t),b(t),x(t)) = \inf_{q(t)\in Q} J_F(u(t),b(t),x(t))$$

applied by Leader to Follower.

Evaluate the Follower's guaranteed payoff under no cooperation with Leader:

$$L_F = \sup_{b(t)\in B(t):u(t)\in U(q^P(t))} J_F(u(t),b(t),x(t)).$$

2) Solve the optimal control problem (2.3.5)–(2.3.7), (2.3.9) subject to the additional constraint $L_F < J_F(u(t),b(t),x(t))$ and the phase constraint (2.3.18).

Under the assumption regarding the same-direction interests of the both players, maximize (2.3.6) in the three functions $q(t)$, $u(t)$, $b(t)$. Denote by $(q^R(t),u^R(t),b^R(t))$ the solution of the stated optimal control problem, where $q^R(t)$ is the incentive strategy applied by Leader to Follower under compulsion.

3) Leader submits to Follower the feedback strategy (corruption control mechanism)

$$\hat{q}(b(t),t) = \begin{cases} q^R(t), & \textit{if } b(t) = b^R(t) \textit{ for } t \in [0,\infty) \\ q^P(t), & \textit{otherwise.} \end{cases}$$

4) Follower being economically rational, the equilibrium in the model (2.3.5)–(2.3.7), (2.3.9), (2.3.18) has the form $\left(q^R(t),u^R(t),b^R(t)\right)$, where $u(t)\in R(q^R)$.

Assertion 2.3.5. The model (2.3.10), (2.3.11), (2.3.13), (2.3.5), (2.3.18) admits an equilibrium according to Definition 2.3.5 if

$$S_5 = \{q(t)\in Q(t); b(t)\in B(t); u(t)\in A_q^{-1}(X^*):$$
$$L_F < J_F(u(t),b(t),x(u(t)))\} \neq \varnothing$$

under a given function $p(t) \in P$. The proof is similar to that of Assertion 2.3.1.

Model 6: Stackelberg impulsion game with additional control feedback and requirements to controlled dynamic system

Model 6 is described by a system of functionals and control constraints, see (2.3.10)–(2.3.13), (2.3.5), subject to the additional condition (2.3.18) reflecting the sustainable development requirement of the system. This model is interpreted as the model of sustainable management via impulsion under economic corruption.

Definition 2.3.6. A triplet (p^*,u^*,b^*) is called a Stackelberg impulsion equilibrium in open-loop strategies with control feedback and requirements to the CDS if

$$J_L(p^*,u^*,b^*,x^*) = \sup_{(p,u)\in P_X} \inf_{b\in R_u(p)} J_L(p,u,b,x),$$

where $P_X = \{p(t)\in P^{U(t)\times B(t)}; u(t)\in U(t) x(u(t))\in X^*, t\geq 0\}$. If $P_X = \varnothing$, no equilibria exist.

The equilibrium design algorithm in the model (2.3.10)– (2.3.13), (2.3.5), (2.3.18) includes the following steps.

1) Introduce the penalty strategy

$$p^P(t): J_F(p^P(t),u(t),b(t),x(t)) = \inf_{p(t)\in P(t)} J_F(p(t),u(t),b(t),x(t)); \quad u(t)\in U(t)$$

applied by Leader to Follower.

Evaluate the Follower's guaranteed payoff under no cooperation with Leader:

$$L_F = \sup_{b(t)\in B(t);u(t)\in U(t)} J_F(u(t),b(t),x(t)).$$

2) Solve the optimal control problem (2.3.10), (2.3.11), (2.3.13), (2.3.5) subject to the additional constraint $L_F < J_F(p(t),u(t),b(t),x(t))$ and the phase constraint (2.3.18).

Maximize (2.3.10) in the three functions $p(t),u(t),b(t)$. Denote by $p^R(t),u^R(t),b^R(t)$ the solution of the stated optimal control problem, where $p^R(t)$ is the incentive strategy applied by Leader to Follower under impulsion.

3) Leader submits to Follower the feedback strategy (corruption control mechanism)

$$\hat{p}(u(t),b(t),t) = \begin{cases} p^R(t), & \text{if } b(t)=b^R(t); u(t)=u^R(t) \text{ for } t\in[0,\infty) \\ p^P(t), & \text{otherwise.} \end{cases}$$

4) Follower being economically wise, the equilibrium in the model (2.3.10), (2.3.11), (2.3.13), (2.3.5), (2.3.18) has the form $\left(p^R(t),u^R(t),b^R(t)\right)$.

Assertion 2.3.6. The model (2.3.10), (2.3.11), (2.3.13), (2.3.5), (2.3.18) admits an eq uilibrium according to Definition 2.3.6 if

$$S_6 = \{p(t)\in P(t); b(t)\in B(t); u(t)\in A_q^{-1}(X^*): L_F < J_F(p(t),u(t),b(t),x(u(t)))\} \neq \varnothing$$

under a given function $q(t)\in Q$.

This result is shown by analogy to Assertion 2.3.1.

An Analysis Method for the Differential Game Models of Control Systems: A Three-Level Control System

For convenient interpretation and without loss of generality, consider the optimal bioresource management problem. Its modeling proceeds from the three-level control system, see (Ougolnitsky and Usov, 2014b). For the sake of simplicity, study the case of a single control subject at each level (denote them by subjects P, S and A, respectively). Only subject A (agent) exerts an impact on the CDS, pursuing its individual interests. Subject P (Principal) is concerned with the sustainable development (SD) conditions. Moreover, just like subject S (supervisor), Principal may have individual interests, too. The controlled dynamic system evolves according to the differential equation with given initial conditions

$$\frac{dx}{dt} = h(x(t)) - u(t)x(t), \quad x(0) = x_0. \qquad (2.3.23)$$

Here means the biomass of an exploited population (e.g., fish); is the share of fish catch (at moment t); represents some function of heterogenous population size dynamics (e.g., the one adopted in the Malthus model, the Verhulst-Pearl model, the Ricker model, etc.); and finally, specifies the initial biomass (at the initial moment). As an example, take the linear Malthus function $h(x(t)) = \varepsilon x(t); \varepsilon = const$.

The total income from fishery makes up aux, where a designates the unit price of biomass (for simplicity, we will omit time dependence). Suppose that a certain share of this income is confiscated by subject P (government), whereas the share is left to subject A (fish artel). Note that can be treated as a tax rate. The economic impact variable may have other interpretations (e.g., penalty). By-turn, subject P gives a share of its residual income to subject S (fishery agency official) as a wage or bonus and leaves the share to itself. Therefore, the objective function of subject P is defined by

$$J_A(r(\cdot),u(\cdot)) = \int_0^T \left(a(1-r(t))u(t) - cu^2(t)\right)x(t)dt \to \max \quad (2.3.24)$$

Here indicates the agent's costs of catching the share $u(t)$; stands for the planning horizon. By incorporating the control constraints

$$0 \le u(t) \le 1, \quad (2.3.25)$$

we arrive at the optimal control problem (2.3.23)-(2.3.25).

The objective function of subject S takes the form

$$J_C(p(\cdot),r(\cdot),u(\cdot)) = \int_0^T p(t)r(t)au(t)x(t)dt \to \max \ . \quad (2.3.26)$$

By assumption, subject S applies impulsion via the control variable meeting the constraint

$$0 \le r(t) \le r_0 \, . \quad (2.3.27)$$

And finally, the objective function of subject P can be expressed in the form

$$J_P(p(\cdot),r(\cdot),u(\cdot)) = \int_0^T [au(t)x(t)(1-p(t))r(t) - M(x(t)-\bar{x})^2]dt \to \max. \quad (2.3.28)$$

Here indicates the optimal biomass in the sense of sustainable development of the population; is a penalty imposed on subject P for a deviation of the current biomass from its optimal counterpart. The first term in the above integrand answers for the income of subject P, while the second one corresponds to its penalty.

We believe that subject P, just like subject S, uses impulsion through the control variable satisfying the inequality

$$0 \le p(t) \le 1 \cdot \tag{2.3.29}$$

Generally, the expressions (2.3.23)-(2.3.29) determine a differential hierarchical three-player game of the form or depending on accepted information rules.

Introduce the operator according to (2.3.23). Denote

$$A^{-1}(X) = \{u \in U : Au = x;\ x(t) \in X\}.$$

While exploring the model (2.3.23)-(2.3.29), suppose that the functions are piecewise continuous in and $A^{-1}(X) \cap U \ne \{\varnothing\} \cdot$

Generally, the expressions (2.3.23)-(2.3.29) determine a differential hierarchical three-player game. Below we present some equilibrium design algorithms for the model.

Equilibrium Design Algorithms

There exist four possible information rules in the hierarchical three-player game: 1) subjects P and S both apply compulsion; 2) subjects P and S apply compulsion and impulsion, respectively; 3) subjects P and S apply impulsion and compulsion, respectively; 4) subjects P and S both apply impulsion. Further exposition scrutinizes the last case (the rest cases are treated by analogy).

And so, subjects P and S both apply impulsion. Compulsion takes no place. Subject S stimulates subject A to choose strategies ensuring satisfaction of the former's interests. In addition, subject P stimulates subject S to choose strategies ensuring the SD conditions, with consideration of the former's interests.

The framework of the model (2.3.24)-(2.3.29) brings to the following possible combinations of equilibria in dynamic Germeier games of the form Γ_{1t} and Γ_{2t} between different-level control subjects:

1. construct an equilibrium in Germeier game Γ_{1t} (for subjects P and S) and Γ_{2t} (for subjects S and A);
2. construct an equilibrium in Germeier game Γ_{2t} (for subjects P and S) and Γ_{1t} (for subjects S and A);
3. construct an equilibrium in Germeier game Γ_{2t} for the both pairs of control subjects;
4. construct an equilibrium in Germeier game Γ_{1t} for the both pairs of control subjects.

Let us consider the last two cases.

In Germeier game Γ_{2t} (case 3), the information rules of the game have the following form: subject P chooses a strategy and reports it to subject S; next, subject S chooses a strategy such that belongs to the optimal response set $R_C^{II}(\tilde{p},u) = Arg\max_{r \in R} J_C(p(u),r,u,x)$ and reports it to subject A; and subject A chooses the optimal response $u \in R_A^{II}(\tilde{\tilde{r}}) = Arg\max_{u \in U} J_A(p(u), r, u, x)$. The guaranteed result of subject P is $\gamma_{\Pi}^{II} = \sup_{\tilde{p} \in \tilde{P}} \inf_{r \in R_C^{II}(\tilde{p}, u)} \inf_{u \in R_A^{II}(\tilde{\tilde{r}})} J_{\Pi}(\pi(\tilde{p}, \tilde{\tilde{r}}, u, x))$.

The impulsion-impulsion equilibrium in Germeier game Γ_{2t} makes up

$$(\tilde{p}^*, \tilde{\tilde{r}}^*, u^*) \in BR^{II} : J_P(\pi(\tilde{p}^*, \tilde{\tilde{r}}^*, u^*, x^*)) = \gamma_P^{II},$$

$$BR^{II} = \{(\tilde{p}, \tilde{\tilde{r}}, u) \in \tilde{P} \times \tilde{\tilde{R}} \times U : r(p(u), u) \in R_S^{II}(\tilde{p}, u), u \in R_A^{II}(\tilde{\tilde{r}})\},$$

where the trajectory is induced by the control action u^*. Equilibrium design employs the procedure proposed in the papers (Ougolnitsky and Usov, 2010-2014).

1. Evaluate the maximum guaranteed payoff of subject A under the penalty strategies applied by subjects P and S:

$$L_A^{II} = \sup_{u \in U} \inf_{\tilde{p} \in \tilde{P}} \inf_{\tilde{\tilde{r}} \in \tilde{\tilde{R}}} J_A(\pi(\tilde{p}, \tilde{\tilde{r}}, u, x)),$$

where the trajectory is induced by the control action $u(t)$.

2. Define the set $D_A^{II} = \{(\tilde{\tilde{r}}, u) : J_A(\pi(\tilde{p}^P, \tilde{\tilde{r}}, u, x)) \geq L_A^{II}\}$, where is the penalty strategy of subject S.

3. Evaluate the maximum guaranteed payoff of subject S considering the interests of subject A under the penalty strategy applied by subject P:

$$L_S^{II} = \sup_{(\tilde{\tilde{r}}, u) \in D_A^{II}} \inf_{\tilde{p} \in \tilde{P}} J_S(\pi(\tilde{p}, \tilde{\tilde{r}}, u, x)).$$

4. Introduce the set

$$D_S^* = \{(\tilde{p}, \tilde{\tilde{r}}, u) : J_S(\pi(\tilde{p}, \tilde{\tilde{r}}, u, x)) \geq L_S^{II}, J_A(\pi(\tilde{p}, \tilde{\tilde{r}}, u, x)) \geq L_A^{II}, \forall t\ x(t) \in X^*\}$$

describing the interests of subjects S and A under the SD conditions.

5. Then the guaranteed payoff of subject P is $\gamma_{\Pi}^{II} = \sup_{(\tilde{p}, \tilde{\tilde{r}}, u) \in D_C^*} J_{\Pi}(\pi(\tilde{p}, \tilde{\tilde{r}}, u, x))$. Of course, implementation of this algorithm requires that $D_A^{II} \neq \varnothing, D_C^* \neq \varnothing$.

In Stackelberg game Γ_{1t} (case 4), the equilibrium design algorithm for the games of both subjects P and S, subjects S and A, includes the following steps:

1) Maximize the functional (2.3.24) subject to the constraints (2.3.25) in the function to find the optimal strategies of subject A depending on the control actions of subject S $(u^*(r(t), t))$.
2) Substitute the optimal strategy of subject A found at Step 1 into formula (2.3.26). Solve the parametric optimal control problem (2.3.26), (2.3.27). Denote by the resulting optimal strategy of subject S.

3) Substitute the strategies and found at Steps 1-2 into formulas (2.3.28), (2.3.29). Solve the optimal control problem (2.3.28), (2.3.29). Denote by the resulting optimal strategy of subject P.
4) Both for subjects P and S, subjects S and A, the equilibrium in Germeier game Γ_{1t} has the form $\left(p^*(t), r^*(p^*(t),t), u^*(r^*(p^*(t),t),t)\right)$.

Both for subjects P and S, subjects S and A, the equilibrium in Germeier game Γ_{1t} exists if the optimal control problem at Step 3 is feasible, i.e.,

$$\exists\, p(t) \in \Omega : u^*(r^*(p(t),t),t) \in A^{-1}(X) \cap U \,.$$

In the presence of several maximum points of the Follower's payoff function, Leader displays caution according to Germeier's principle of guaranteed result, similarly to Model 3.

A Multistep-Differential Counterpart of the Differential Model

In what follows, we suggest an analysis method of differential control models based on transition from an original differential model to its multistep-differential counterpart (Ougolnitsky and Usov, 2013).

In a real control system, subjects cannot change their strategies at any moment desired; their strategies remain constant over a certain time interval. Without loss of generality, assume that strategies of all control subjects are constant on same time intervals, i.e.,

$$s(t) = \begin{cases} s_1, & \text{если } 0 \le t < t_1, \\ s_2, & \text{если } t_1 \le t < t_2, \\ \dots & \\ s_N, & \text{если } t_{N-1} \le t < T, \end{cases} \tag{2.3.30}$$

where $s_i = const$; $t_i = i\,\Delta t$; $\Delta t = T/N$; N is the number of control constancy intervals; denotes the control action applied by subject A, subject S or subject P. Further exposition focuses on the case of impulsion in Germeier game Γ_{1t}, either for subjects P and S, or subjects S and A.

By virtue of (2.3.30), the problem (2.3.23)–(2.3.29) acquires the form

— the functional (2.3.24)

$$J_A(\{r_i\}_{i=1}^N, \{u_i\}_{i=1}^N) = \sum_{i=1}^{N} \left(a(1-r_i)u_i - cu_i^2\right) \int_{t_{i-1}}^{t_i} x(t)dt \to \max(\{u_i\}_{i=1}^N); \tag{2.3.31}$$

— the conditions (2.3.25)

$$0 \le u_i \le 1; \; i = 1,2,\dots,N;, \tag{2.3.32}$$

— the functional (2.3.26)

$$J_C(\{p_i\}_{i=1}^N, \{r_i\}_{i=1}^N, \{u_i\}_{i=1}^N) = \sum_{i=1}^N ap_i r_i u_i \int_{t_{i-1}}^{t_i} x(t)dt \to \max(\{r_i\}_{i=1}^N); \qquad (2.3.33)$$

— the conditions (2.3.27)

$$0 \le r_i \le r_0;\ i = 1,2,...,N; \qquad (2.3.34)$$

— the functional (2.3.28)

$$J_\Pi(\{p_i\}_{i=1}^N, \{r_i\}_{i=1}^N, \{u_i\}_{i=1}^N) = \sum_{i=1}^N \left(a(1-p_i)r_i u_i \int_{t_{i-1}}^{t_i} x(t)dt - M \int_{t_{i-1}}^{t_i} (x(t)-\overline{x})^2 dt \right)$$

$$\to \max(\{p_i\}_{i=1}^N \qquad (2.3.35)$$

— the conditions (2.3.29)

$$0 \le p_i \le 1;\ i = 1,2,...,N, \qquad (2.3.36)$$

Under $h(x(t)) = \varepsilon x(t); \varepsilon = \text{const}$, the solution of (2.3.23) at the points is described by $x(t_i) = x(t_{i-1})e^{(\varepsilon - u_i)\Delta t}; i = 1,2,...,N.$

Therefore, solution of the optimization problem (2.3.23)–(2.3.29) has been reduced to analysis of the model (2.3.23), (2.3.31)–(2.3.35). Note that (2.3.31), (2.3.33), (2.3.35) represent objective functions of 2*N* and 3*N* variables (not functionals!) and their optimization runs with respect to *N* variables.

Here is the algorithm for solving the problem (2.3.23), (2.3.31)–(2.3.35).

1. By performing parametric optimization of the $2N$-variable function (2.3.31) (*N* parameters $\{r_i\}_{i=1}^N$) subject to the constraints (2.3.32) with respect to *N* variables $\{u_i\}_{i=1}^N$, define the optimal strategies of subject A depending on control actions applied by subject S, i.e., the quantities $\{u_i^*\}_{i=1}^N = \{u_i^*(r_i)\}_{i=1}^N$.

2. Substitute the quantities found at Step 1 into the expression (2.3.33). Solve the parametric optimization problem of the $2N$ variable function (*N* parameters $\{p_i\}_{i=1}^N$) with respect to *N* variables $\{r_i\}_{i=1}^N$. Evaluate the optimal strategies of subject S depending on control actions applied by subject P, i.e., the quantities $\{r_i^*\}_{i=1}^N = \{r_i^*(p_i)\}_{i=1}^N$.

3. Substitute the quantities and found at Steps 1-2 into the expressions (2.3.35), (2.3.23). Solve equation (2.3.23), either analytically or numerically. The optimal strategies of subject P are the quantities maximizing (2.3.35).

4. The set is said to be the equilibrium in dynamic game Γ_{1t}.

The multistep-differential model (2.3.23), (2.3.30)–(2.3.36) is equivalent to the model (2.3.23)–(2.3.29) in the following sense. If the triplet of functions is an equilibrium of the differential model, then strategy constancy of control subjects on the time intervals implies that

$$u^*(t)=\begin{cases} u_1^*, & \text{if} \quad 0 \le t < t_1, \\ u_2^*, & \text{if} \quad t_1 \le t < t_2, \\ & \dots \\ u_N^*, & \text{if} \quad t_{N-1} \le t < T, \end{cases} \qquad r^*(t)=\begin{cases} r_1^*, & \text{if} \quad 0 \le t < t_1, \\ r_2^*, & \text{if} \quad t_1 \le t < t_2, \\ & \dots \\ r_N^*, & \text{if} \quad t_{N-1} \le t < T, \end{cases}$$

$$p^*(t)=\begin{cases} p_1^*, & \text{if} \quad 0 \le t < t_1, \\ p_2^*, & \text{if} \quad t_1 \le t < t_2, \\ & \dots \\ p_N^*, & \text{if} \quad t_{N-1} \le t < T, \end{cases}$$

And the set $\{u_i^*\}_{i=1}^N$, $\{r_i^*\}_{i=1}^N$, gives the solution to the problem (2.3.23), (2.3.31)–(2.3.36).

In contrast to (2.3.23)–(2.3.29), the problem (2.3.23), (2.3.30)–(2.3.36) is an optimization problem of multivariable function (not of functionals!) under the existing hierarchy of the control subjects. If equation (2.3.23) admits analytical solution, then this problem is easily studied using Lagrange's method of multipliers; otherwise, simulation modeling is required.

The simulation modeling algorithm for the three-level model (2.3.23), (2.3.31)–(2.3.36) bases on direct ordered constant-step enumeration and includes the following steps.

1. Specify the form and values of all input functions and parameters of the model in question.
2. Specify the current strategy of subject P, i.e., a grid function .
3. Specify the current strategy of subject S, i.e., a grid function .
4. By direct ordered constant-step enumeration of admissible responses of subject A to the current strategy of subject S, find the best response of subject A, i.e., a grid function for which the objective function (2.3.31) takes its largest value among all considered.
5. Compare the current strategy of subject S with the best strategy (2.3.33) found to this moment. Whenever necessary, make the current strategy the optimal one.
6. If the number of iterations for subject S is not exhausted, choose its new strategy by considering a different scenario or by perturbing the current strategy of this subject. Then get back to Step 4 of the algorithm.
7. Solve the differential equation (2.3.23) numerically, e.g., by the finite difference method or the Runge-Kutta method. Compare the current strategy of subject P with the best strategy (2.3.35) found to this moment. Whenever necessary, make the current iteration the optimal one.

8. If the number of iterations for subject P is not exhausted, choose its new strategy by considering a different scenario or by perturbing the current strategy of this subject. Then get back to Step 3 of the algorithm.

The above algorithm yields an approximation to the system equilibrium, i.e., the set of quantities $\left(\{p_i^*\}_{i=1}^N, \{r_i^*(p_i^*)\}_{i=1}^N, \{u_i^*(r_i^*)\}_{i=1}^N\right)$.

New current strategy choice for subjects P, S or A employs, e.g., direct ordered constant- or variable-step enumeration. An approximate equilibrium of the system can be further refined using bitwise search for all control subjects. The uncertainty interval for the strategy of subject P, S or A makes up $2\frac{b-a}{M+1}$, where is the number of partition points for the admissible control domain of an appropriate subject, a and b indicate the left and right boundaries of the admissible control domain. The error of optimal strategy evaluation equals $\varepsilon = \frac{b-a}{M+1}$. For instance, in the case of subjects P and A we have (for subject S, the boundaries are $a = 0;\ b = r_0$).

Consequently, at a finite number of iterations the suggested simulation modeling algorithm constructs an approximate solution for the model (2.3.23), (2.3.31)–(2.3.36) or demonstrates that no Stackelberg equilibria actually exist. The reliability and efficiency of the algorithm follow from the properties of direct ordered constant-step enumeration in simulation experiments. All calculations have been implemented in C#.

Testing on Numerical Examples

Example 2.3.1. (equilibrium design in Stackelberg game Γ_{1t} for the both pairs of control subjects, S and A, P and S). Under $\varepsilon = 0.5\, days^{-1}$; $a = 2\,\frac{\$}{kg}$; $r_0 = 0.7$; $x_0 = 100\ kg$; T = 720 days ; $\bar{x} = 100\,kg$; $M = 10\frac{\$}{kg^2}$; $c = 3\frac{\$}{kg}$, the incomes of the control subjects constitute $J_P = \$62$; $J_S = \$31$ y.e. $J_A = \$6.66$. As the unit price of biomass increases ($a = 10\,\frac{\$}{kg}$), the incomes grow and reach the values $J_P = \$933;\ J_S = \$466;\ J_A = \$700$. When the optimal biomass of the population (in the sense of its sustainable development) deviates from the initial biomass ($\bar{x} = 80\ kg$), the incomes of the control subjects go down abruptly, even despite smaller penalty ($M = 0.1\$/kg^2$): $J_P = -\$57;\ J_S = \$31;\ J_A = \$6.66$. In the case of high catching costs ($c = 5\$/kg$), we have $J_P = J_S = 0,\ J_A = \$33$.

Example 2.3.2. (equilibrium design in Germeier game Γ_{2t} for the both pairs of control subjects, S and A, P and S). Here $L_S^{II} = 0$. The same input data as in Example 2.3.1 bring to $L = 0; J_P = \$93; J_S = 14; J_A = \$6.66$. Higher unit price of biomass ($a = 10 \frac{\$}{kg}$) yields $L_A^{II} = \$200; J_P = \$1866; J_S = \$18; J_A = \$233$. In the case of $\bar{x} = 80\,kg$ and $M = 0.1\$/kg$, the result is $L_A^{II} = \$0; J_P = -\$26; J_S = \$21; J_A = \$6.66$. For $c = 5\$/kg$ we obtain $L_A^{II} = \$0; J_P = \$31; J_S = \$12; J_A = \$22$.

Example 2.3.3. (equilibrium design in Germeier game Γ_{2t} for subjects S and A and in Germeier game Γ_{1t} for subjects P and S). The same input data as in Example 2.3.1 bring to $L_A^{II} = \$0; J_P = \$62; J_S = \$31; J_A = \$6.66$. If $a = 10\$/kg$, the result is $L_A^{II} = \$200; J_P = \$1244; J_S = \$622; J_A = \$233$. In the case of $\bar{x} = 80\,kg$ and $M = 0.1\$/kg$, we have $L_A^{II} = \$0; J_P = -\$57; J_S = \$31; J_A = \$6.66$. For $c = 5\$/kg$, calculations yield $L_A^{II} = \$0; J_P = \$20; J_S = \$10; J_A = \$2.2$.

Example 2.3.4. (equilibrium design in Germeier game Γ_{1t} for subjects S and A and in Germeier game Γ_{2t} for subjects P and S). Here $L_S^{II} = 0$. The same input data as in Example 2.3.1 bring to $J_P = \$82; J_S = \$10; J_A = \$6.66$. For $a = 10\$/kg$, the result is $J_P = \$1244; J_S = \$155; J_A = \$700$. In the case of $\bar{x} = 80\,kg$ and $M = 0.1\$/kg$, we obtain $J_A = 6.66; J_P = -\$37; J_S = \$10$. Under higher catching costs, it is impossible to make stimulation more beneficial for subject S than penalty. The given control method becomes inefficient.

Subjects P and S prefer playing Germeier game Γ_{2t} in their relations with subjects S and A, respectively. Subjects A and S prefer playing Stackelberg game Γ_{1t} in their relations with subjects S and P. Note that dynamic games Γ_{2t} (for subjects P and S) and Γ_{1t} (for subjects S and A) may have no equilibria. Subject S may possess insufficient power for implementing control actions for subject A.

A System of Dynamic Models of Administrative Corruption

Consider a series of administrative corruption models. For convenient interpretation and without loss of generality, we will study optimal bioresource management problems.

The total income from fishery equals aux, where a specifies the unit price of biomass (time dependence is omitted for the sake of simplicity), the share of fish catch is bounded above by a statutory quota s_0. In exchange for a bribe, supervisor increases the quota of fish catch from to $s_0 + s(b(t))$. The function $s(b(t))$ characterizes the supervisor's quota increase for bribery. Agent allocates a share of its additional income to bribe supervisor. This additional income appears owing to the quota of fish catch established by supervisor ($s_0 + s(b(t))$), which actually exceeds the statutory quota due to corruption. Therefore, the agent's objective functional can be expressed as

$$J_A(s(\cdot),u(\cdot),b(\cdot)) = \int_0^T \left(au(t) - cu^2(t) - \max(0, b(t)(u(t) - s_0))\right)x(t)dt \to \max. \quad (2.3.37)$$

Here denotes the agent's catching costs of the share $u(t)$; is the planning horizon; means a bribe as the additional payment for unit catch "above quota"; corresponds to the payment for catch "above quota" (kickback). The functional (2.3.37) is considered under the following constraints on the control actions:

$$0 \le b(t) \le 1;\ 0 \le u(t) \le s_0 + s(b(t)), \quad (2.3.38)$$

i.e., the problem includes bound constraints.

Under administrative corruption, the quota of fish catch represents a certain function of the bribe share. If analysis proceeds from the agent's position, this function is given. For instance, take the nonlinear capture function of the form

$$s(b(t)) = (1 - s_0)b^k(t);\ k = const \quad (2.3.39)$$

where $s(0) = 0,\ s(1) = 1 - s_0$. By substituting (2.3.39) into (2.3.38), we obtain

$$0 \le u(t) \le s_0 + (1 - s_0)b^k(t)\ . \quad (2.3.40)$$

Consequently, there arises the optimal control problem with bound constraints (2.3.23), (2.3.37) - (2.3.40). Of course, alongside with (2.3.39), one may choose other functions of administrative corruption. It seems very interesting to perform parameter identification of the function based on actual corruption data. Theoretical study of different classes of the function makes sense, too.

From the supervisor's position, the function is constructed as a solution of Germeier game between supervisor and agent (Gorelik et al., 1991). The supervisor's objective functional can be defined by

$$J_S(q(\cdot),s(\cdot),u(\cdot),b(\cdot)) = \int_0^T \left(\max(0, b(t)(u(t) - s_0)x(t) - K\mu s(t)\right)dt \quad \to \max\ . \quad (2.3.41)$$

Here optimization runs subject to the control action constraints

$$0 \le s(t) \le q(t). \tag{2.3.42}$$

The second term in the integrand of formula (2.3.41) represents a penalty imposed on supervisor in the case of "above quota" catch detection; is a penalty coefficient; gives the probability of corruption detection; indicates an upper bound applied to by Principal. The values of and characterize the Principal's anti-corruption capabilities (maintenance of the condition $s(t) = s_0$) via compulsion (an administrative impact on the admissible control domain of supervisor). The expressions (2.3.23), (2.3.37), (2.3.38), (2.3.40)-(2.3.42) describe a differential hierarchical two-player game of the type Γ_{2t}.

And finally, the Principal's objective functional can be written as

$$J_P(q(\cdot),s(\cdot),u(\cdot),b(\cdot)) = \int_0^T [C(q(t)) + M(x(t) - \bar{x})^2]dt \to \min \tag{2.3.43}$$

Here specifies the optimal biomass according to the sustainable development of the fish population; designates a penalty coefficient applied to Principal in the case of a deviation between the current biomass and its optimal counterpart; is a convex decreasing control cost function such that $C(0) = \infty; C(1 - s_0) = 0$. For instance, choose $C(q(t)) = C_1 \frac{1 - s_0 - q}{q}$.

By assumption, Principal uses compulsion via the control variable

$$0 \le q(t) \le 1 - s_0. \tag{2.3.44}$$

The first term in the integrand of (2.3.43) corresponds to the Principal's control costs, while the second term answers for the penalty imposed on Principal in the case of violating the sustainable development requirements.

The expressions (2.3.23), (2.3.37), (2.3.38), (2.3.40)-(2.3.42) determine a differential hierarchical three-player game. Its rules depend on control methods chosen by Principal. If the latter prefers compulsion, then the game between Principal and supervisor is (the function is time-varying only) or (this function also depends on the supervisor's action). The game between supervisor and agent always has the type Γ_{2t}, since the presence of bribe amount feedback is crucial in corruption modeling. Direct interaction between Principal and agent is not considered.

Therefore, using the bioresource management problem, we have defined a sequence of dynamic models of administrative corruption in the form "optimal control problem – dynamic hierarchical two-player game – dynamic hierarchical three-player game." Further exposition describes some analysis algorithms for them. By assumption, only compulsion takes place in the system.

A One-Level Model of Optimal Bioresource Management Considering Administrative Corruption

Let us study the administrative corruption model described by formulas (2.3.23), (2.3.24)-(2.3.40). The functional (2.3.23) reflects the profits of a fishing artel as a potential briber. The realized profits partially go to taxes and, possibly, to a bribe for a fishery agency official. The quota of fish catch is defined by bribe amount: the higher is the latter, the greater is the actual quota. If corruption takes no place (zero bribe), a statutory quota is applied. Obviously, quota relaxations in exchange for a bribe have to compensate corruption costs (otherwise, corruption makes no sense for the fishing artel). This poses an optimal control problem with bound constraints; we will consider two settings of the problem, depending on existing control constraints. The first setting is when

$$b(t)=0;\ 0\le u(t)\le s_0, \quad (2.3.45)$$

and the second setting corresponds to the case of

$$0\le b(t)\le 1;\ s_0\le u(t)\le s_0+s(b(t)). \quad (2.3.46)$$

The both settings of the problem are solved using Pontryagin's maximum principle. The Hamilton function for the first setting has the form

$$H(u(t), y(t), x(t)) = au(t)x(t) - cu^2(t)x(t)+y(t)x(t)(\varepsilon-u(t)),$$

where means the state variable, is the control variable and denotes the conjugate variable (all representing time-varying functions). Hence,

$$\frac{\partial H}{\partial u} = ax(t)-2cx(t)u(t)-y(t)x(t)=0\ .$$

Therefore, within the domain (2.3.45) a "potential" maximum point is defined by

$$u^0(t)=\frac{a-y(t)}{2c}, \quad (2.3.47)$$

where

$$-\frac{\partial H}{\partial x}=\frac{dy}{dt}=cu^2(t)-au(t)+(u(t)-\varepsilon)y(t);\ y(T)=0. \quad (2.3.48)$$

Substitute (2.3.47) into (2.3.48) and solve the resulting differential equation with separable variables to obtain

$$T-t=\int_0^T \frac{dy}{B+Ey+0.25y^2/c}=\begin{cases}\frac{2}{D}arctg\frac{y/(2c)+E}{D}\Big|_0^y, & \text{if} \quad E^2<B/c\\ \frac{1}{D}\ln\frac{y/(2c)+E-D}{y/(2c)+E+D}\Big|_0^y, & \text{if} \quad E^2>B/c,\\ -\frac{1}{d}\frac{1}{y+2Ec}\Big|_0^y, & \text{if} \quad E^2=B/c,\end{cases}$$

where $B=\frac{a^2}{2c}\left(a-\frac{1}{2}\right)$; $E=\varepsilon-\frac{a^2}{2c}$.; $D=\sqrt{|B/c\text{-}E^2|}$. And it follows that

(2.3.49) In this case, the second derivative of the Hamilton function is negative. And for each t the optimal share of fish catch makes up

$$u^*(t)=\begin{cases}u^0(t), & \text{if} \quad 0\le u^0(t)\le s_0\\ s_0 & \text{if} \quad u^0(t)>s_0\\ 0, & \text{if} \quad u^0(t)<0\end{cases} \tag{2.3.50}$$

For the second setting (2.3.46), the Hamilton function acquires the form

$$H(u(t),b(t),y(t),x(t))=\left(au(t)x(t)-\ cu^2(t)x(t)-b(t)(u(t)-s_0)+y(t)x(t)(\varepsilon-u(t))\right),$$

Hence, and maximum can be achieved only on the boundary of the admissible control domain. The boundaries and have been analyzed before for the first setting of the problem. In the case of $b(t)\equiv 1$, the Hamilton function becomes

$$H\,(u(t),\,y(t),\,x(t))\;=\;au\,(t)\,x(t)\;-\;cu^2(t)x(t)+(s_0-u(t))x(t)+y(t)x(t)(\varepsilon-u(t)),$$

Then it appears that

$$\frac{\partial H}{\partial u}=(a-2cu(t)-1-y(t))x(t)=0\ ,$$

i.e., within the domain (2.3.46) a “potential” maximum point is defined by

$$u^{(1)}(t)=[a-1-y(t)]/(2c) \tag{2.3.51}$$

$$-\frac{\partial H}{\partial x}=\frac{dy}{dt}=cu^2(t)-au(t)+u(t)-s_0+(u(t)-\varepsilon)y(t);\ y(T)=0. \tag{2.3.52}$$

Substitution of (2.3.51) into (2.3.52) yields a differential equation with separable variables. Its solution is defined by formula (2.3.49), in the case of $E=\varepsilon+\frac{1}{2c}-\frac{a}{2c}$. The Hessian matrix is negative definite on the found solution. Hence, for each t the optimal strategies of the control subjects have the following form (see (2.3.51), (2.3.52)):

$$(u^*(t),b^*(t))=\begin{cases}(u^{(1)}(t),1), & \text{if} \quad s_0\le u^{(1)}(t)\le 1-s_0\\ (s_0,1), & \text{if} \quad u^{(1)}(t)<s_0\\ (1-s_0,1), & \text{if} \quad u^{(1)}(t)>1-s_0\end{cases}. \qquad (2.3.53)$$

On the boundary the Hamilton function becomes

$$b^{k+1}(t)(1-s_0)x(t)+b(t)s_0x(t)+y(t)x(t)(\varepsilon-u(t)).$$

Hence, it follows that

$$\frac{\partial H}{\partial b}=(kb^{k-1}(t)a(1-s_0)-2kb^{2k-1}(t)c(1-s_0)^2-(k+1)b^k(t)(1-s_0)$$
$$+s_0-y(t)kb^{k-1}(t)(1-s_0))=0.$$

As a result, in this case the stationary points obey the equation

$$kb^{k-1}(t)(a-y(t))(1-s_0)-2kb^{2k-1}(t)c(1-s_0)^2-(k+1)b^k(t)(1-s_0)+s_0=0, \qquad (2.3.54)$$

which can be solved numerically (e.g., by the Newton method).

Therefore, one of the following pairs of points is optimal: (2.3.50), (2.3.53) or the solution (2.3.54). By substituting the found solution into (2.3.37), we evaluate the agent's optimal payoff.

A Two-Level Model of Optimal Bioresource Management Considering Administrative Corruption

Consider the administrative corruption model described by (2.3.23), (2.3.37), (2.3.38), (2.3.41), (2.3.42). In contrast to the case of economic corruption, modeling of administrative corruption from the agent's position leads to an optimization problem with bound constraints. Define the admissible control sets of supervisor and agent under a given function $q(t)$:

$$U(s(t))=\{0\le u(t)\le s_0+s(t);0\le t\le T\};$$
$$B=\{0\le b(t)\le 1;0\le t\le T\},$$

the sets associated with the information structure of the problem

$$\tilde{S} = \{\tilde{s} = s(u,b) : U \times B \to S\}; \ \tilde{\tilde{U}} = \{\tilde{\tilde{u}} = u(\tilde{s}) : \tilde{S} \to U\},$$

and a projection $\pi : \tilde{S} \times \tilde{\tilde{U}} \times B \times X \to S \times U \times B \times X$.

We suggest the following algorithm of equilibrium design.

1. Evaluate the maximum guaranteed payoff of agent under the penalty strategy applied by supervisor:

$$L_A = \sup_{(\tilde{\tilde{u}},b) \in \tilde{\tilde{U}} \times B} \inf_{\tilde{s} \in \tilde{S}} J_A(\pi(\tilde{s}, \tilde{\tilde{u}}, b, x)) .$$

To calculate L_A, solve an optimal control problem with bound constraints, which reflects the specifics of administrative corruption. Denote by $s^P(t), u^P(t), b^P(t)$ the functions implementing the quantity L_A.

2. Define the set $D_A = \{(\tilde{s}, \tilde{\tilde{u}}, b) : J_A(\pi(\tilde{s}, \tilde{\tilde{u}}, b, x)) \geq L_A\}$.

3. Evaluate the maximum guaranteed payoff of supervisor considering the interests of agent: $L_S = \sup_{(\tilde{s}, \tilde{\tilde{u}}, b) \in D_A} J_S(\pi(\tilde{s}, \tilde{\tilde{u}}, b, x))$, and its optimal strategies $(s^*, u^*, b^*) \in \arg \sup_{(\tilde{s}, \tilde{\tilde{u}}, b) \in D_A} J_S(\pi(\tilde{s}, \tilde{\tilde{u}}, b, x))$. This algorithm can be realized only if $D_A \neq \varnothing$.

The penalty strategy applied by supervisor to agent (see Step 1) lies in choosing (no quota increase). In this case, agent does offer a bribe $(b^P(t) \equiv 0)$, and the optimal share of fish catch (the function $u^P \equiv u^P(t)$) results from solving the optimal control problem studied for the one-level model under (2.3.45). The solution has the form (2.3.50), and

$$L_A = \int_0^T \left(au^P(t) - c(u^P)^2(t)\right) x^P(t) dt, \text{ where } x^P(0) = x_0.$$

The function is defined by formula (2.3.50).

The problem arising at Step 3 of the above algorithm has numerical solution.

A Three-Level Model of Optimal Bioresource Management Considering Administrative Corruption

Consider the administrative corruption model described by (2.3.23), (2.3.37), (2.3.38), (2.3.41)-(2.3.44). The essence of administrative corruption is compulsion strategy variation for the agent's benefit via bribery. Principal must guarantee the sustainable development requirements through compulsion of supervisor. Define the sets associated with the informational structure of the problem:

$$\tilde{Q}=\{\tilde{q}=q(s):S\to Q\};\ \tilde{\tilde{S}}=\{\tilde{\tilde{s}}=s(\tilde{q},u,b):\tilde{Q}\times U\times B\to S\};$$
$$\tilde{\tilde{\tilde{U}}}=\{\tilde{\tilde{\tilde{u}}}=u(\tilde{\tilde{s}}):\tilde{\tilde{S}}\to U\},$$

and a projection $\pi_1:Q\times\tilde{\tilde{S}}\times\tilde{\tilde{\tilde{U}}}\times B\times X\to Q\times S\times U\times B\times X$.

We suggest an equilibrium design algorithm based on the following procedure.

1. Evaluate the maximum guaranteed payoff of agent under the penalty strategies applied by Principal and supervisor: $L_A=\sup\limits_{(\tilde{\tilde{\tilde{u}}},b)\in\tilde{\tilde{\tilde{U}}}\times B}\ \inf\limits_{\tilde{q}\in\tilde{Q}}\ \inf\limits_{\tilde{\tilde{s}}\in\tilde{\tilde{S}}} J_A(\pi_1(\tilde{q},\tilde{\tilde{s}},\tilde{\tilde{\tilde{u}}},b,x))$.

Similarly to the two-level model, calculate by solving an optimal control problem with bound constraints, which reflects the specifics of administrative corruption. Denote by the functions realizing the quantity L_A.

2. Define the set $D_A=\{(\tilde{\tilde{s}},\tilde{\tilde{\tilde{u}}},b):J_A(\pi_1(q^P,\tilde{\tilde{s}},\tilde{\tilde{\tilde{u}}},b,x))\ge L_A\}$, where is the penalty strategy applied by Principal to supervisor, i.e., $J_S(\pi_1(q^P,\tilde{\tilde{s}},\tilde{\tilde{\tilde{u}}},b,x))=\min\limits_{\tilde{q}\in\tilde{Q}} J_S(\pi_1(\tilde{q},\tilde{\tilde{s}},\tilde{\tilde{\tilde{u}}},b,x))$.

3. Evaluate the maximum guaranteed payoff of supervisor considering the agent's interests under the penalty strategy applied by Principal: $L_S=\sup\limits_{(\tilde{\tilde{s}},\tilde{\tilde{\tilde{u}}},b)\in D_A} J_S(\pi_1(\tilde{q}^P,\tilde{\tilde{s}},\tilde{\tilde{\tilde{u}}},b,x))$.

4. Introduce the set

$$D_S^*=\{(\tilde{q},\tilde{\tilde{s}},\tilde{\tilde{\tilde{u}}},b):J_S(\pi(\tilde{q},\tilde{\tilde{s}},\tilde{\tilde{\tilde{u}}},b,x))\ge L_S,J_A(\pi_1(\tilde{q},\tilde{\tilde{s}},\tilde{\tilde{\tilde{u}}},b,x))\ge L_A\},$$

which reflects the interests of supervisor and Principal under the sustainable development requirements with economic corruption.

5. Then the Principal's guaranteed payoff makes up $\gamma_P=\sup\limits_{(\tilde{q},\tilde{\tilde{s}},\tilde{\tilde{\tilde{u}}},b)\in D_S^*} J_P(\pi(\tilde{q},\tilde{\tilde{s}},\tilde{\tilde{\tilde{u}}},b,x))$, leading to the equilibrium strategies $(q^*,s^*,u^*,b^*)=\arg\sup\limits_{(\tilde{q},\tilde{\tilde{s}},\tilde{\tilde{\tilde{u}}},b)\in D_S^*} J_P(\pi(\tilde{q},\tilde{\tilde{s}},\tilde{\tilde{\tilde{u}}},b,x))$. This algorithm can be realized only if $D_A\ne\varnothing,D_S^*\ne\varnothing$. The agent's objective functional does not depend on the Principal's control actions. Hence, the quantity (Step 1 of the algorithm) is defined by the formulas obtained for the two-level model. The problems at Steps 3–5 have numerical solution. In what follows, we test the models using a series of numerical examples.

Testing on Numerical Examples

The optimal control problem in the one-level case is solved via enumerating the points (2.3.50), (2.3.53) and resolving equations (2.3.54). Equation (2.3.54) is solved by the Newton method with the initial estimate $b(t) \equiv 0$. In the two- and three-level models, equilibria are constructed numerically after their discretization using direct ordered enumeration of appropriate admissible control domains.

Example 2.3.5. (The one-level model of optimal bioresource management considering administrative corruption). Under

$$\varepsilon = \frac{0.5}{360} day^{-1};\ a = 1\frac{c.u.}{kg};\ k = 0.5;\ s_0 = 0.6;\ c = 2\frac{c.u.}{kg}$$

$$x_0 = 1000\,kg;\ \mathrm{T} = 360\ \mathrm{days}$$

(c.u.–conventional units), the agent's income constitutes $J_A = 12355 c.u.$ As the statutory quota of fish catch or the population growth rate increases, agent's payoff goes up. For instance, for we have $_A = 21087\,c.u.$; if $\varepsilon = \frac{0.9}{360} day^{-1}$, the result is $J_A = 19502\,c.u.$. In the case of higher exponent of the corruption function or higher catch costs of unit biomass, the agent's payoff decreases: for $k = 2$, we have $J_A = 5402 c.u.$; if $c = 3\frac{c.u.}{kg}$, the result is $J_A = 7360 c.u.$

Example 2.3.6. (The two-level model of optimal bioresource management considering administrative corruption). Under $s_0 = 0.3;\ c = 2\frac{c.u.}{kg}$ $x_0 = 1000 kg; \mathrm{T} = 360$ days, $K = 100\ c.u.;\ \mu = 0.1$, within the framework of this model agent benefits nothing from continuation of its activity: its control actions equal zero. The payoffs of all subjects vanish. Suppose that we reduce the catch costs ($c = 0.2\frac{c.u.}{kg}$). Then fish catching becomes profitable in the conditions of corruption: the payoffs of the subjects make up $L_A = 326\,c.u.;\ J_A = 365\,c.u.;\ J_S = 693\,c.u.$ Higher statutory quota of fish catch ($s_0 = 0.9$) increases the agent's payoff and decreases the supervisor's payoff, while the system has no corruption ($L_A = 1134\,c.u.;\ J_A = 1151\,c.u.;\ J_S = 340\,c.u.$). As we enlarge the population growth rate ($\varepsilon = \frac{0.9}{360} day^{-1}$) or reduce the probability of corruption detection, the payoffs of the both subjects grow in the conditions of corruption:

$L_A = 485\,c.u.;\ J_A = 526\,c.u.;\ J_S = 798\,c.u.$ and

$L_A = 536\,c.u.;\ J_A = 2765\,c.u.;\ J_S = 875\,c.u.$, respectively.

Example 2.3.7. (the three-level model of optimal bioresource management considering administrative corruption). Under

$$\varepsilon = \frac{0.5}{360} day^{-1};\ a = 1\frac{c.u.}{kg}; k = 0.5;\quad x_0 = 1000 kg, \mathrm{T} = 360 \text{ day}$$

$K = 100\ c.u.; \mu = 0.1$; $M = 0.004\frac{c.u.}{kg}$; $C_1 = 2\frac{c.u.}{kg}$, agent and Principal obtain positive payoffs in the conditions of corruption, while supervisor sustains losses: $J_A = 345\,c.u.;\ J_S = -102\,c.u.; J_P = 290\,c.u.$. In the case of supervisor's smaller penalty for a deviation from the statutory tax rate ($K = 50\ c.u$), the payoffs of agent and supervisor grow under corruption, whereas the Principal's payoff goes down ($L_A = 236\,c.u.;\ L_S = 37\,c.u.;\ J_A = 281\,c.u.;\ J_S = 41\,c.u.; J_P = 221\,c.u.$). Smaller catch costs ($c = 0.1\frac{c.u.}{kg}$) or higher statutory quota of fish catch ($s_0 = 0.8$) increase the agent's payoff, but decreases the payoffs of supervisor and Principal: $L_A = 1180\,c.u.;\ L_S = -38\,c.u.;$ $J_A = 1198\,c.u.;\ J_S = -20\,c.u.; J_P = -711\,c.u.$). And finally, as we enlarge the optimal biomass required for population sustainable development ($\overline{x} = 1050\ kg$), the opposite picture shows up: the agent's payoff is reduced, while the payoffs of supervisor and Principal rise ($L_A = 236\,c.u.;\ L_S = 37\,c.u.;\ \ J_A = 241\,c.u.;\ J_S = 43\,c.u.;\ \ J_P = 329\,c.u.$).

Therefore, the conducted studies using the suggested models have demonstrated the following. Successful struggle against administrative corruption is possible through increasing the statutory quota of fish catch or strengthening supervisor's control.

A System of Dynamic Models of Economic Corruption

Consider a series of economic corruption models. Recall some notions introduced above. For convenient interpretation and without loss of generality, again choose the optimal bioresource management problem. The controlled dynamic system evolves according to the differential equation with given initial conditions

$$\frac{dx}{dt} = h(x(t)) - u(t)x(t), \quad x(0) = x_0. \tag{2.3.55}$$

Here means the biomass of an exploited population (e.g., fish); is the share of fish catch (at moment t); represents some function of heterogenous population size dynamics (e.g., the one adopted in the Malthus model, the Verhulst-Pearl model, the Ricker model, etc.); and finally, specifies the initial biomass (at the initial moment). As an example, take the linear Malthus function $h(x(t)) = \varepsilon x(t); \varepsilon = const$.

The total income from fishery makes up aux , where designates the unit price of biomass (for simplicity, we will omit time dependence). Suppose that a certain share of this income is confiscated by Principal (government), whereas the share is left to agent (fish artel). Note that can be treated as a tax rate. The economic impact variable may have other interpretations (e.g., penalty). By-turn, Principal gives a share of its residual income to supervisor (fishery agency official) as a wage or bonus and leaves the share to itself. And finally, agent allocates a share of its additional income to bribe supervisor so that the latter decreases the statutory tax rate r_0. Therefore, the agent's objective functional can be expressed as

$$J_A(r(\cdot),u(\cdot),b(\cdot)) = \int_0^T \left(a(1-r(t))u(t) - ab(t)(r_0 - r(t))u(t) - cu^2(t)\right)x(t)dt \to \max . \quad (2.3.56)$$

Here denotes the agent's catching costs of the share $u(t)$; is the planning horizon; indicates tax arrears (the agent's savings due to tax underpayment dissembled by supervisor for bribery); specifies the agent's kickback to supervisor from this sum.

Under economic corruption, the tax rate represents a certain function of the bribe share which defines the kickback amount. If analysis proceeds from the agent's position, this function is given. For instance, take the nonlinear capture function

$$r(b(t)) = r_0(1 - b^k(t)); k = const \quad (2.3.57)$$

Here the left-hand side has the actual tax rate, the first term in the right-hand side is its statutory value and the second term describes its relaxation due to bribery. Particularly, $r(0) = r_0$, $r(1) = 0$. Substitute (2.3.57) into (2.3.56) to obtain

$$J_A(r(\cdot),u(\cdot),b(\cdot)) = \int_0^T \left(a(1 - r_0 + r_0 b^k(t) - r_0 b^{k+1}(t))u(t) - cu^2(t)\right)x(t)dt \cdot \quad (2.3.58)$$

And finally, add the control constraints

$$0 \le b(t) \le 1;\ 0 \le u(t) \le 1 \quad (2.3.59)$$

to arrive at the optimal control problem (2.3.55), (2.3.58), (2.3.59). Of course, alongside with (2.3.57), one may choose other functions of economic corruption. It seems very interesting to perform parameter identification of the function based on actual corruption data. This problem can be the subject of independent investigations.

From the supervisor's position, the function is constructed as a solution of the Germeier game between supervisor and agent. The supervisor's objective functional can be defined by

$$J_S(p(\cdot),r(\cdot),u(\cdot),b(\cdot)) = \int_0^T \left([p(t)r(t)+b(t)(r_0-r(t))]au(t)x(t) - K\mu(r_0-r(t))\right)dt\,. \tag{2.3.60}$$

Here optimization runs subject to the control action constraints

$$0 \le r(t) \le r_0\,. \tag{2.3.61}$$

The second term in the integrand of formula (2.3.60) represents a penalty imposed on supervisor in the case of tax arrears detection; is a penalty coefficient; gives the probability of corruption detection. The values of and characterize the Principal's anti-corruption capabilities (maintenance of the condition $r(t) = r_0$) via compulsion (an economic impact on the supervisor's payoff function). The expressions (2.3.55), (2.3.56), (2.3.59)-(2.3.61) describe a differential hierarchical two-player game of the type Γ_{2t}.

And finally, the Principal's objective functional can be written as

$$J_P(p(\cdot),r(\cdot),u(\cdot),b(\cdot)) = \int_0^T [au(t)x(t)(1-p(t))r(t) - M(x(t)-\bar{x})^2]dt\,. \tag{2.3.62}$$

Here specifies the optimal biomass according to the sustainable development of the fish population; designates a penalty coefficient applied to Principal in the case of a deviation between the current biomass and its optimal counterpart. By assumption, Principal uses compulsion via the control variable

$$0 \le p(t) \le 1\,. \tag{2.3.63}$$

The first term in the integrand of (2.3.63) corresponds to the Principal's income, while the second term answers for the penalty imposed on Principal in the case of violating the sustainable development requirements. The expressions (2.3.55), (2.3.56), (2.3.59)-(2.3.63) determine a differential hierarchical three-player game. Its rules depend on control methods chosen by Principal. If the latter prefers impulsion, then the game between Principal and supervisor is (the function is time-varying only) or (this function also depends on the supervisor's action). The game between supervisor and agent always has the type Γ_{2t}, since the presence of bribe amount feedback is crucial in corruption modeling.

Therefore, using the bioresource management problem, we have defined a sequence of dynamic models of economic corruption in the form "optimal control problem – dynamic hierarchical two-player game – dynamic hierarchical three-player game." Further exposition describes some analysis algorithms for them. By assumption, only impulsion takes place in the system.

A One-Level Model of Optimal Bioresource Management Considering Economic Corruption

Let us study the economic corruption model described by formulas (2.3.55), (2.3.58), (2.3.59). The functional (2.3.55) reflects the profits of a fishing artel as a potential briber. The realized profits partially go to taxes and, possibly, to a bribe for a fishery agency official. Accrued taxes are defined by bribe amount: the higher is the latter, the smaller are the actual taxes paid. If corruption takes no place (zero bribe), a statutory tax rate is applied. Obviously, tax relaxations in exchange for a bribe have to compensate corruption costs (otherwise, corruption makes no sense for the fishing artel). This leads to an optimal control problem which can be solved using Pontryagin's maximum principle. The Hamilton function for the problem (2.3.55), (2.3.58), (2.3.59) has the form

$$H(u(t),b(t),y(t),x(t)) = a(1-r_0+r_0b^k(t)-r_0b^{k+1}(t))u(t)x(t)-$$
$$cu^2(t)x(t)+y(t)x(t)(\varepsilon-u(t)),$$

where means the state variable, is the control variable and denotes the conjugate variable (representing a time-varying function). Hence,

$$\frac{\partial H}{\partial b} = r_0au(t)x(t)b^{k-1}(t)(k-(k+1)b(t)) = 0;$$

i.e., within the domain (2.3.59) a "potential" maximum point is defined by

$$b^0(t) = \frac{k}{k+1};\ u^0(t) = \frac{A-y(t)}{2c}, \tag{2.3.64}$$

where $A = a\left(1-r_0+\frac{r_0}{k+1}\left(\frac{k}{k+1}\right)^k\right);$

$$-\frac{\partial H}{\partial x} = \frac{dy}{dt} = cu^2(t)-(1-r_0+\frac{r_0}{k+1}\left(\frac{k}{k+1}\right)^k)au(t)+(u(t)-\varepsilon)y(t);\ y(T)=0. \tag{2.3.65}$$

Substitute (2.3.64) into (2.3.65) and solve the resulting differential equation with separable variables to obtain

$$T-t=\int_0^T\frac{dy}{B+Ey+0.25y^2/c}=\begin{cases}\left.\frac{2}{D}arctg\frac{y/(2c)+E}{D}\right|_0^y, & \text{if}\quad E^2<B/c\\ \left.\frac{1}{D}\ln\frac{y/(2c)+E-D}{y/(2c)+E+D}\right|_0^y, & \text{if}\quad E^2>B/c,\\ \left.-\frac{1}{d}\frac{1}{y+2Ec}\right|_0^y, & \text{if}\quad E^2=B/c\end{cases}$$

where $B=\frac{A^2}{2c}\left(a-\frac{1}{2}\right)$; $E=\varepsilon-\frac{Aa}{2c}$.; $D=\sqrt{\left|B/c-E^2\right|}$. And it follows that

$$y(t)==\begin{cases} 0.5c\left(Dtg\left(0.5D(T-t)+arctg\left(E/D\right)\right)-E\right), & \text{if} \quad E^2<B/c \\ 0.5c\left(2D\frac{E+D}{E-D}e^{-D(T-t)}-E-D\right), & \text{if} \quad E^2>B/c \\ 4cE^2\frac{T-t}{2-TE+Et}, & \text{if} \quad E^2=B/c \end{cases},$$

(2.3.66)

Calculate the Hessian matrix in (2.3.64):

$$\left.\frac{\partial^2 H}{\partial b^2}\right|_{(u^0(t),b^0(t))}=-kr_0au^0(t)x(t)(b^0(t))^{k-2};\ \left.\frac{\partial^2 H}{\partial u\partial t}\right|_{(u^0(t),b^0(t))}=0\cdot$$

Due to the negative definiteness of the Hessian matrix in (2.3.64) and the constraints (2.3.59), the optimal strategies of the control subjects are defined by the following formula (see also (2.3.64), (2.3.66)):

$$(u^*(t),b^*(t))=\begin{cases}(u^0(t),\frac{k}{k+1}), & \text{if} \quad 0\le u^0(t)\le 1\\ (1,\frac{k}{k+1}), & \text{if} \quad u^0(t)>1\\ (0,0), & \text{if} \quad u^0(t)<0\end{cases}$$

(2.3.67)

And finally, substitute (2.3.66) and (2.3.67) into the expression (2.3.58) to find the equilibrium payoff of agent.

A Two-Level Model of Optimal Bioresource Management Considering Economic Corruption

Consider the economic corruption model described by (2.3.55), (2.3.56), (2.3.59)-(2.3.61). Define the admissible control sets of supervisor and agent:

$$R=\{r(t)\in L_2:0\le r(t)\le r_0;\forall t:0\le t\le T\};$$
$$B=\{b(t)\in L_2:0\le b(t)\le 1;\forall t:0\le t\le T\},$$

the sets associated with the information structure of the problem

$$\tilde{R} = \{\tilde{r} = r(u,b) : U \times B \to R\}; \; \tilde{\tilde{U}} = \{\tilde{\tilde{u}} = u(r(u,b)) : \tilde{R} \to U\},$$

and a projection $\pi : \tilde{R} \times \tilde{\tilde{U}} \times B \times X \to R \times U \times B \times X$.

We suggest the following algorithm of equilibrium design.

1. Evaluate the maximum guaranteed payoff of agent under the penalty strategy applied by supervisor: $L_A = \sup\limits_{(\tilde{\tilde{u}},b) \in \tilde{\tilde{U}} \times B} \inf\limits_{\tilde{r} \in \tilde{R}} J_A(\pi(\tilde{r},\tilde{\tilde{u}},b,x))$.

2. Define the set $D_A = \{(\tilde{r},\tilde{\tilde{u}},b) : J_A(\pi(\tilde{r},\tilde{\tilde{u}},b,x)) \geq L_A\}$.

3. Evaluate the maximum guaranteed payoff of supervisor considering the interests of agent: $L_S = \sup\limits_{(\tilde{r},\tilde{\tilde{u}},b) \in D_A} J_S(\pi(\tilde{r},\tilde{\tilde{u}},b,x))$, and its optimal strategies

$$(r^*, u^*, b^*) = \arg \sup_{(\tilde{r},\tilde{\tilde{u}},b) \in D_A} J_S(\pi(\tilde{r},\tilde{\tilde{u}},b,x)).$$

This algorithm can be realized only if $D_A \neq \varnothing$.

The penalty strategy applied by supervisor to agent (see Step 1) lies in choosing the maximum admissible tax rate from (2.3.61). In this case, agent does offer a bribe ($b^p = 0$), and the optimal share of fish catch (the function $u = u(t)$) results from solving a corresponding optimal control problem by Pontryagin's maximum principle. The Hamilton function for this problem acquires the form

$$H(u(t), y(t), x(t)) = \big(a(1 - r_0)u(t)x(t) - cu^2(t)x(t) + y(t)x(t)(\varepsilon - u(t))\big),$$

with same notation as before. Hence,

$$\frac{\partial H}{\partial u} = (1 - r_0)ax(t) - 2cx(t)u(t) - y(t)x(t) = 0 .$$

A similar line of reasoning as in the previous case leads to the following. Within the A similar line of reasoning as in the previous case leads to the following. Within the domain (2.3.59) a "potential" maximum point is defined by where

$$-\frac{\partial H}{\partial x} = \frac{dy}{dt} = cu^2(t) - (1 - r_0)au(t) + (u(t) - \varepsilon)y(t); \; y(T) = 0.$$

This differential equation possesses the solution (2.3.66), with $A = a(1 - r_0)$.

The second derivative of the Hamilton function is negative. Consequently, the optimal share of fish catch under the penalty strategy apllied by supervisor for each t makes up

$$u^P(t) = \begin{cases} u^0(t), & \text{if} \quad 0 \le u^0(t) \le 1 \\ 1 & \text{if} \quad u^0(t) > 1 \\ 0, & \text{if} \quad u^0(t) < 0 \end{cases}$$, and

$$L_A = \sup_{0 \le u^P \le 1} \int_0^T \left(a(1-r_0)u^P(t) - c(u^P)^2(t)\right)x^P(t)dt,$$

where $\dfrac{dx^P}{dt} = (\varepsilon - u^P(t))x(t), \quad x^P(0) = x_0.$

The problem arising at Steps 2 and 3 of the algorithm is solved numerically.

A Three-Level Model of Optimal Bioresource Management Considering Economic Corruption

Consider the economic corruption model described by (2.3.55), (2.3.56), (2.3.59) - (2.3.63. The essence of economic corruption is impulsion strategy variation for the agent's benefit via bribery. Principal must guarantee the sustainable development requirements through impulsion of supervisor. Define the sets associated with the information structure of the problem:

$$\tilde{P} = \{\tilde{p} = p(r) : R \to P\};\ \tilde{\tilde{R}} = \{\tilde{r} = r(\tilde{p},u,b) : \tilde{P} \times U \times B \to R\};$$

$$\tilde{\tilde{\tilde{U}}} = \{\tilde{\tilde{\tilde{u}}} = u(r(\tilde{p},u,b)) : \tilde{\tilde{R}} \to U\},$$

and a projection $\pi_1 : P \times \tilde{R} \times \tilde{\tilde{\tilde{U}}} \times B \times X \to P \times R \times U \times B \times X$.

We suggest an equilibrium design algorithm based on the following procedure, see (Gorelik and Kononenko, 1982).

1. Evaluate the maximum guaranteed payoff of agent under the penalty strategies applied by Principal and supervisor: $L_A = \sup\limits_{(\tilde{\tilde{u}},b) \in \tilde{\tilde{U}} \times B} \inf\limits_{\tilde{p} \in \tilde{P}} \inf\limits_{\tilde{r} \in \tilde{\tilde{R}}} J_A(\pi_1(\tilde{p},\tilde{\tilde{r}},\tilde{\tilde{\tilde{u}}},b,x))$.

2. Define the set $D_A = \{(\tilde{\tilde{r}},\tilde{\tilde{\tilde{u}}},b) : J_A(\pi_1(\tilde{p}^P,\tilde{\tilde{r}},\tilde{\tilde{\tilde{u}}},b,x)) \ge L_A\}$, where is the penalty strategy applied by Principal to supervisor, i.e., $J_S(\pi_1(\tilde{p}^P,\tilde{\tilde{r}},\tilde{\tilde{\tilde{u}}},b,x)) = \min\limits_{\tilde{p} \in \tilde{P}} J_S(\pi_1(\tilde{p},\tilde{\tilde{r}},\tilde{\tilde{\tilde{u}}},b,x))$.

3. Evaluate the maximum guaranteed payoff of supervisor considering the agent's interests under the penalty strategy applied by Principal:

$$L_S = \sup_{(\tilde{\tilde{r}},\tilde{\tilde{\tilde{u}}},b) \in D_A} J_S(\pi_1(\tilde{p}^P,\tilde{\tilde{r}},\tilde{\tilde{\tilde{u}}},b,x)).$$

4. Introduce the set

$$D_S^* = \{(\tilde{p},\tilde{\tilde{r}},\tilde{\tilde{\tilde{u}}},b) : J_S(\pi(\tilde{p},\tilde{\tilde{r}},\tilde{\tilde{\tilde{u}}},b,x) \geq L_S, J_A(\pi(\tilde{p},\tilde{\tilde{r}},\tilde{\tilde{\tilde{u}}},b,x) \geq L_A\}.$$

which reflects the interests of supervisor and Principal under the sustainable development requirements with economic corruption.

5. Then the Principal's guaranteed payoff makes up $\gamma_P = \sup_{(\tilde{p},\tilde{\tilde{r}},\tilde{\tilde{\tilde{u}}},b)\in D_S^*} J_P(\pi(\tilde{p},\tilde{\tilde{r}},\tilde{\tilde{\tilde{u}}},b,x))$,

leading to the equilibrium strategies $(p^*,r^*,u^*,b^*) = \arg \sup_{(\tilde{p},\tilde{\tilde{r}},\tilde{\tilde{\tilde{u}}},b)\in D_S^*} J_P(\pi(\tilde{p},\tilde{\tilde{r}},\tilde{\tilde{\tilde{u}}},b,x))$. This algorithm can be realized only if $D_A \neq \varnothing, D_S^* \neq \varnothing$.

The agent's objective functional does not depend on the Principal's control actions. Hence, the quantity (Step 1 of the algorithm) is defined by the formulas obtained for the two-level model. The problems at Steps 3–5 have numerical solution. In what follows, we test the models using a series of numerical examples.

Testing on Numerical Examples

The optimal control problem in the one-level case is solved analytically (formulas (2.3.66), (2.3.67)). In the two- and three-level models, equilibria are constructed numerically after their discretization using direct ordered enumeration of appropriate admissible control domains.

Example 2.3.8. (The one-level model of optimal bioresource management considering economic corruption).

Under $\varepsilon = \frac{0.5}{360} days^{-1}; a = 1\$/kg; k = 0.5; r_0 = 0.4; c = 2\$/kg; x_0 = 1000kg; T = 360 days$, the agent's income constitutes $J_A = \$12715$. As we reduce the statutory tax rate or increase the growth rate of the population, the agent's income rises. For instance, if $r_0 = 0.1$, the result is $J_A = \$36087$; for $\varepsilon = \frac{0.1}{360} days^{-1}$, we have $J_A = \$8502$. In the case of a higher exponent of the corruption function or higher catch costs of unit biomass, the agent's payoff decreases: for $k = 2$, we obtain $J_A = \$2402$; if $c = 1\$/kg$, the result is $J_A = \$33960$.

Example 2.3.9. (The two-level model of optimal bioresource management considering economic corruption). Under

$\varepsilon = \frac{0.5}{360} days^{-1}; a = 1\$/kg; k = 0.5; r_0 = 0.4; c = 2\$/kg; x_0 = 1000kg; T = 360 days; K = \$100; \mu = 0.1$, within the framework of this model agent benefits nothing from continuation of its activity: its control actions equal zero. The payoffs of all subjects vanish. Suppose that we reduce the catch costs $(c = 0.5\$/kg)$. Then fish catching becomes profitable in the conditions of corruption: the payoffs of the subjects make up $L_A = \$236; J_A = \$265; J_S = \$563$. Lower statutory tax rate ($r_0 = 0.1$) increases the agent's payoff and decreases the supervisor's payoff, while the system has no corruption $(L_A = \$944; J_A = \$951; J_S = \$140)$. As we enlarge the population growth rate $(\varepsilon = \frac{0.9}{360} day^{-1})$ or reduce the probability of corruption detection, the payoffs of the subjects grow in the conditions of corruption: $J_P = \$285; J_S = \$326; J_A = \$798$ and $J_P = \$236; J_S = \$2765; J_A = \$875$, respectively.

Example 2.3.10. (the three-level model of optimal bioresource management considering economic corruption). Under

$$\varepsilon = \frac{0.5}{360} days^{-1}; a = 1\$/kg; k = 0.5; r_0 = 0.4; c = 2\$/kg; x_0 = 1000kg; T = 360\,days; K = \$100; \mu = 0.1;$$
$$M = 0.004\$/kg,$$

agent and Principal obtain positive payoffs in the conditions of corruption, while supervisor sustains losses: $L_A = \$236; L_S = -\$143; J_A = \$245; J_S = -\$102; J_P = \$290$. In the case of a smaller supervisor's penalty for a deviation from the statutory tax rate $(K = \$50)$, the payoffs of agent and supervisor grow under corruption, whereas the Principal's payoff goes down $L_A = \$236; L_S = \$37; J_A = \$281; J_S = \$41; J_P = \$221$.

Smaller catch costs $(c = 0.1\$/kg)$ or a higher statutory tax rate ($r_0 = 0.1$) increase the agent's payoff, but decreases the payoffs of supervisor and Principal: $L_A = \$1180; L_S = -\$38; J_A = \$1198; J_S = -\$20; J_P = -\$711$. And finally, as we enlarge the optimal biomass required for population sustainable development $(\bar{x} = 1050\,kg)$, the opposite picture shows up: the agent's payoff is reduced, while the payoffs of supervisor and Principal rise $L_A = \$236; L_S = \$37; J_A = \$241; J_S = \$43; J_P = \$329$.

Therefore, the conducted studies using the suggested models have demonstrated the following. Successful struggle against economic corruption is possible through relaxing tax rates or strengthening supervisor's control.

Summarizing the outcomes, Chapter 2 has proposed general design principles for dynamic models of anti-corruption struggle. Particularly, we have constructed the "genetic sequences" of dynamic models of administrative and economic corruption in the form "optimal control problem – dynamic hierarchical two-player game – dynamic hierarchical three-player game" with application to optimal bioresource management. Analysis has proceeded from authors' concept of hierarchically controlled dynamic systems and the notions of compulsion and impulsion equilibria considering the sustainable development requirements, including the case of corruption.

Chapter 3

APPLIED MODELS OF CORRUPTION IN HIERARCHICAL CONTROL SYSTEMS

This chapter shows the capabilities of the suggested original concept of corruption modeling in several application domains. In Section 3.1 we describe control models for real estate development projects (REDPs) with corruption. Analytical treatment results are provided for (a) optimization models of REDP control considering corruption based on the descriptive approach to modeling from the agent's position (a developer) and (b) game-theoretic models of REDP control considering corruption based on the normative approach to modeling from the supervisor's position (an official issuing permits) and from the Principal's position (a government authority–a subject of anti-corruption struggle). In addition, we discuss some numerical simulation results of the above models using the software complex, see Section 2.2. Next, Section 3.2 gives a characterization for a sequence of gradually complicated quality control models in production systems with corruption (which realizes the idea of quality management compliance with sustainable development in organizational control), as well as considers a hierarchical system of electricity stealing prevention models. In Section 3.3 we introduce analysis models for (im)proper resource utilization in hierarchical control systems. And finally, Section 4 designs and explores quality control models of water resources in hierarchical ecological-economic systems, which involve the definitions of compulsion and impulsion equilibria with due consideration of sustainable development requirements in the conditions of corruption (including some algorithms of their evaluation). The created software tools and the results of numerical experiments are demonstrated.

3.1. CONTROL MODELS OF REAL ESTATE DEVELOPMENT PROJECTS

A real estate development project (REDP) is comprehended as "a project implementing a complete cycle of investments in construction of an object (from initial investments of capital to achievement of all project goals and completion of all project works)" (Zarenkov, 2006). The paper (Ougolnitsky, 2009) proposed a classification of optimization and game-theoretic models of REDP control and studied a series of such models. The basic role in the proposed system belonged to the aggregated models of a separate developer (investment and construction) company. First, these are static optimization models intended for optimal real estate pricing taking into account the existing restrictions on effective demand and repayment of credits. By assumption, building volume is defined by the REDP concept, and a developer establishes prices for its products (real estate objects). Second, these are dynamic search models of an optimal ratio of sales to leasing in the course of REDP planning in the field of commercial real estate. There exist two natural alternatives to generalize the basic model of a developer. According to the first alternative, developers interact as equal-right economic agents. By-turn, two possible settings arise here: (a) normal-form games of several players (competitive relations of developers without coalition formation) and (b) cooperative games or games in the characteristic function representation (cooperation among developers). The second alternative implies that developers enter into economic relations with organizations of other types. These relations often have the hierarchical character, and a developer acts as Leader (e.g., in relations with suppliers) or Follower (e.g., in relations with investors, finance and credit organizations, government authorities). And hierarchical game-theoretic models appear immediately (Ougolnitsky, 2009).

The life cycle of an REDP comprises four main phases: 1) the initial phase (including preliminary feasibility studies and receipt of all necessary permits and approvals); 2) the basic phase (including engineering survey, contracts conclusion, design and building of the object); 3) the completion phase (including commissioning and sales of the object); 4) the project warranty phase. In the current section, we study the following aspects of corruption impact at different phases of an REDP (see Figure 3.1.1): *initiation* (implicit consideration of corruption costs in assessment of project implementation prospects and evaluation of its resulting profitability); *elaboration and planning* ("shadow" budgeting taking into account corruption costs); *works execution* (permit issuance with corruption, shorter certification periods); *ICP completion* (final calculation with considering corruption), see (Antonenko, 2012).

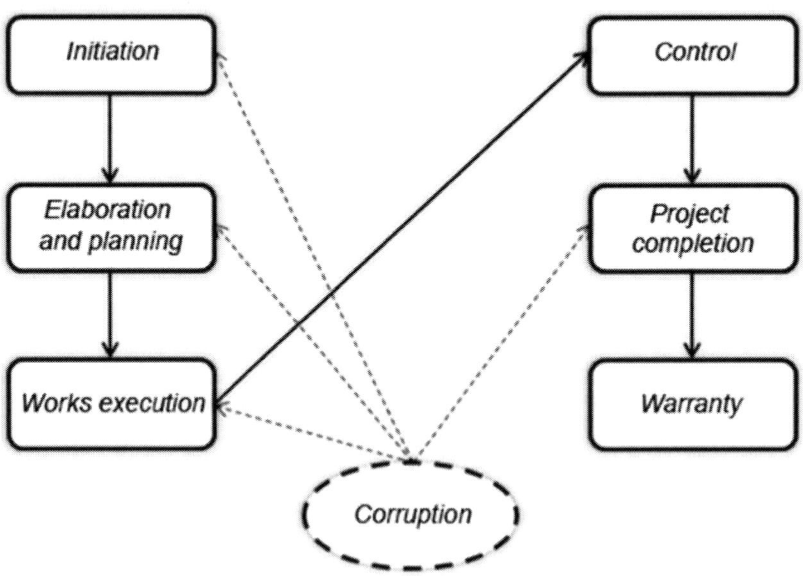

Figure 3.1.1. Corruption at different phases of REDP life cycle.

Modeling proceeds from the following conceptual scheme. A developer organizes building of social and commercial real estate. A share of social real estate is purchased by government at a guaranteed price (possibly, with corruption), the rest is sold by the company independently. Commercial real estate is sold by the company separately at a higher price.

Similarly to the general case, REDP control distinguishes between economic and administrative corruption models. *The economic corruption model at the agent's level* can be defined by

$$g(b) = (1 - b)[r(b) + \xi(1 - r(b))] \rightarrow \max, \quad 0 \le b \le 1, \tag{3.1.1}$$

where $g(b)$ means the agent's payoff function (income from project realization considering corruption costs (bribery); b denotes the economic bribe variable as a share of the agent's income; $r(b)$ is the share of social real estate purchased by government at a fixed price (this share can be increased for a bribe); ξ indicates the share of social real estate sold by agent independently at the same price.

Here $r(b)$ represents the economic corruption function (a known function within the description approach). By implication, this is monotone increasing function on [0,1]; in the case of capture, we have $r(0) = r_0$, where r_0 specifies a statutory value of (its satisfaction agrees with the sustainable development requirements in investment and construction projects). Note that the case of extortion is analyzed by analogy. Take the economic corruption function

$$r(b) = r_0 + Ab^k \quad (A > 0), \quad 0 \le r(b) \le 1. \tag{3.1.2}$$

First, consider linear parametrization (k=1). Formula (3.1.2) then leads to $r(b) = \min\{r_0 + Ab, 1\}, A > 0$. The sensitivity parameter A determines the qualitative characteristics of the briber's behavior. If $A = 0$, corruption is absent. Higher values of A increase bribetaker's appeasability and reduce its greediness. The threshold equals $A = 1 - r_0$: in this case, $r(1) = 1$ (extreme greediness guarantees maximum appeasability). Under $A < 1 - r_0$, greediness becomes exorbitant, and appeasability does not achieve its maximum (for any bribe a certain share of social real estate is still sold independently). If $A > 1 - r_0$, agent (developer) sells to government all social real estate at the fixed price in exchange for a reasonable bribe (maximum appeasability and small greediness). The optimization problem (3.1.1) acquires the form

$$g(b) = (1 - b)[r_0 + Ab + \xi(1 - (r_0 + Ab))] \rightarrow \max, \quad 0 \le b \le 1.$$

Hence,

$$g(0) = r_0 + \xi(1 - r_0),\ g(1) = 0,\ \frac{dg(b)}{db} = -2A(1 - \xi)b + A - A\xi - r_0 - \xi + \xi r_0.$$

The first-order necessary optimality conditions $\dfrac{dg(b)}{db} = 0$ yield the maximum point $b^* = \dfrac{(A - r_0)(1-\xi) - \xi}{2A(1-\xi)}$, since $\dfrac{dg^2(b^*)}{db^2} = -2A(1-\xi) < 0$. By the design procedure (see Figure 3.1.1), we have that

$$g_{\max} = \begin{cases} g(0) = r_0 + \xi(1 - r_0), & A < \dfrac{r_0(1-\xi)+\xi}{1-\xi}, \\ g(b^*) > g(0), & \text{otherwise.} \end{cases} \tag{3.1.3}$$

Thus, the agent's optimal strategy is defined by the correlation of the parameters A, r_0, ξ according to (3.1.3). In the first case, the optimal strategy forms zero bribe. In the second case, it is the bribe $b^* > 0$, bringing to the income $g(b^*) > g(0)$.

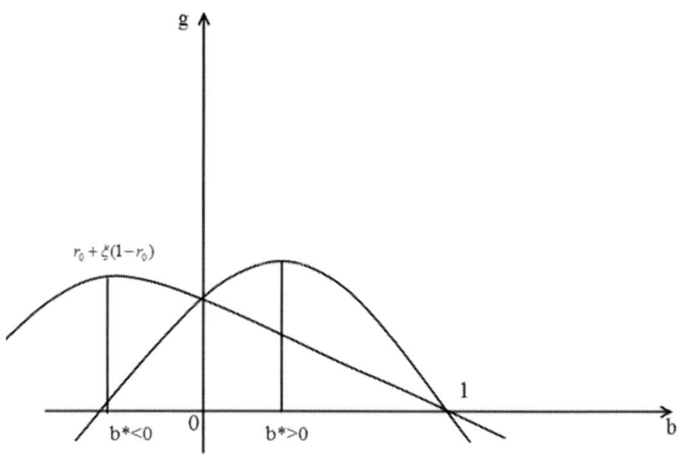

Figure 3.1.1. The agent's income as a function of the parameter A in the linear case.

Now, explore quadratic parametrization of the function (3.1.2), i.e., set k = 2 to obtain $r(b) = \min\{r_0 + Ab^2, 1\}$, $A > 0$. This function shows a same qualitative behavior as in the case of linear parametrization. The optimization problem (3.1.1) acquires the form

$$g(b) = (1-b)[r_0 + Ab^2 + \xi(1-(r_0 + Ab^2))] \to \max, \quad 0 \le b \le 1.$$

We have

$$g(0) = r_0 + \xi(1 - r_0),\ g(1) = 0,\ \frac{dg(b)}{db} = -3A(1-\xi)b^2 + 2A(1-\xi)b - (\xi + r_0(1-\xi)).$$

The first-order necessary optimality conditions $\frac{dg(b)}{db}=0$ yield $b^*=\frac{A(1-\xi)\pm\sqrt{A(1-\xi)[A-3(\xi+r_0(1-\xi))]}}{3A(1-\xi)}$. Furthermore, denote by b_+^*, b_-^*, the roots of the quadratic equation $\frac{dg(b)}{db}=0$; $b_+^*\geq 1/3 \Rightarrow b_+^*$ is the maximum point, whereas $b_-^*<1/3 \Rightarrow b_-^*$ is the minimum point. This leads to the following general picture (here D means quadratic discriminant):

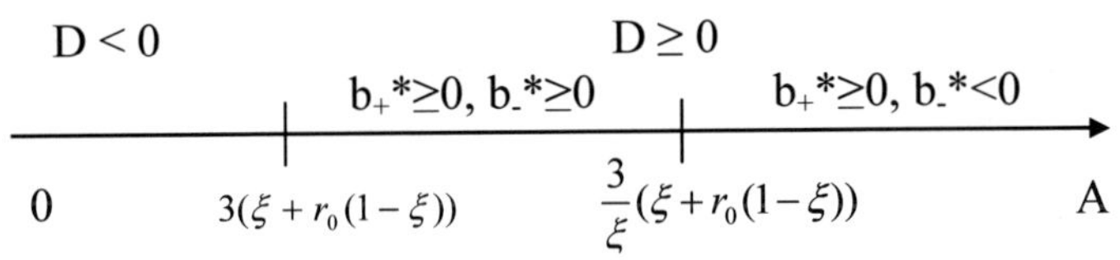

Therefore, if $A>\frac{3}{\xi}(\xi+r_0(1-\xi))$, we obtain that $b_-^*<0\leq b_+^*$ and, by construction, $g_{\max}=g(b_+^*)$ (see Figure 3.1.2); for $3(\xi+r_0(1-\xi))<A<\frac{3}{\xi}(\xi+r_0(1-\xi))$ the result is $b_+^*\geq 0, b_-^*\geq 0$, and $g_{\max}=\max\{g(b_+^*), g(0)\}$. Here numerical simulation is required.

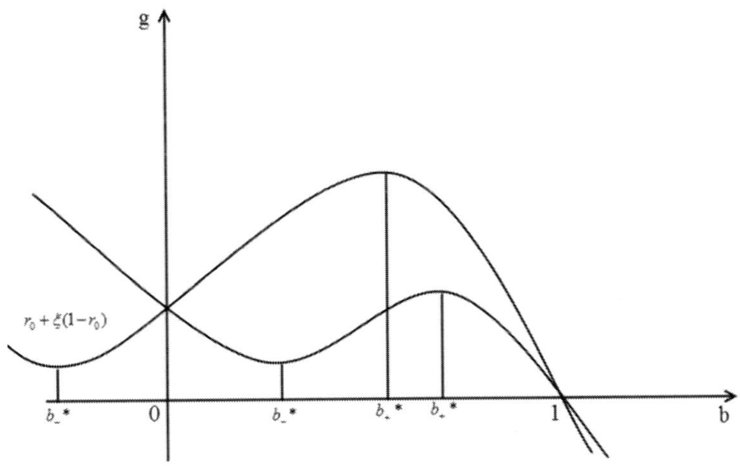

Figure 3.1.2. The agent's income as a function of the parameter A in the quadratic case/

And finally, study power parametrization of the function (3.1.2), i.e., set k = 1/2, which brings to $r(b)=\min\{r_0+A\sqrt{b},1\}$, $A>0$. The qualitative behavior of this function is same as in the previous cases. The optimization problem (3.1.1) becomes

$$g(b)=(1-b)[r_0+A\sqrt{b}+\xi(1-(r_0+A\sqrt{b}))]\rightarrow\max,\quad 0\leq b\leq 1.$$

As before, $g(0) = \xi + r_0(1-\xi)$, $g(1) = 0$. The first-order necessary optimality conditions have the form $3A(1-\xi)b + 2(\xi + r_0(1-\xi))\sqrt{b} - A(1-\xi) = 0$. As far as $\frac{d^2 g(b)}{db^2} = 3A(1-\xi) + \frac{\xi + r_0(1-\xi)}{\sqrt{b}} > 0$, the solution b^* of the above equation represents the minimum point. Let $t = \sqrt{b} \geq 0$, then the quadratic equation $3A(1-\xi)t^2 + 2(\xi + r_0(1-\xi))t - A(1-\xi) = 0$ possesses the solution

$$t = \frac{-(\xi + r_0(1-\xi)) \pm \sqrt{(\xi + r_0(1-\xi))^2 + 3A^2(1-\xi)^2}}{3A(1-\xi)}.$$

Only the positive root makes sense:

$$b^* = \frac{2(\xi + r_0(1-\xi))[\xi + r_0(1-\xi) - \sqrt{(\xi + r_0(1-\xi))^2 + 3A^2(1-\xi)^2}\,] + 3A^2(1-\xi)^2}{9A^2(1-\xi)^2}.$$

Table 3.1.1. The dependence of the agent's payoff function on model parameters in the economic corruption model of REDP

		A (the influence of bribe on supervisor)						
		0	1,2	2,4	3,6	4,8	6	
k (the exponent of the corruption function)	0.2	0.475	0.905	1.385	1.871	2.359	2.847	*Payoff (G)*
		0	0.1	0.12	0.14	0.14	0.15	*Bribe (b)*
	0.5	0.475	0.682	0.987	1.303	1.622	1.943	*Payoff (G)*
		0	0.18	0.24	0.27	0.28	0.29	*Bribe (b)*
	0.8	0.475	0.566	0.782	1.016	1.255	1.496	*Payoff (G)*
		0	0.21	0.32	0.36	0.38	0.39	*Bribe (b)*
	1.1	0.475	0.494	0.654	0.838	1.029	1.222	*Payoff (G)*
		0	0.21	0.38	0.43	0.45	0.47	*Bribe (b)*
	1.4	0.475	0.475	0.565	0.716	0.874	1.035	*Payoff (G)*
		0	0	0.42	0.48	0.51	0.52	*Bribe (b)*
	1.7	0.475	0.475	0.499	0.626	0.761	0.899	*Payoff (G)*
		0	0	0.45	0.52	0.55	0.57	*Bribe (b)*
	2	0.475	0.475	0.475	0.557	0.674	0.795	*Payoff (G)*
		0	0	0	0.55	0.59	0.6	*Bribe (b)*

We show some numerical results for the economic corruption model of REDP, which have been obtained using the software complex (see Section 2.2). The parameter values are $r_0 = 0.25$, $\xi = 0.3$. In this mode, the parameter A (a qualitative characteristic of the briber) varies from 0 to 6 with increment 1.2, k takes values within the interval (0.2, 2) with increment 0.3, as illustrated by Table 3.1.1.

The parameter values A = 6 and k = 0.2 are most beneficial to agent, i.e., the minimum value of k in combination with the maximum value of A guarantee the highest payoff to agent under small bribe b. And the anti-corruption organization prefers the diametrically opposed situation: the minimum value of A in combination with the maximum value of k make bribery nonbeneficial for agent. Analysis of other situations shows that higher exponent of the corruption function corresponds to higher bribe maximizing the agent's payoff.

The dependence of the agent's payoff on the bribe, the exponent and the parameter A is further visualized by the graphs drawn using the software complex (see Figs. 3.1.3–3.1.6).

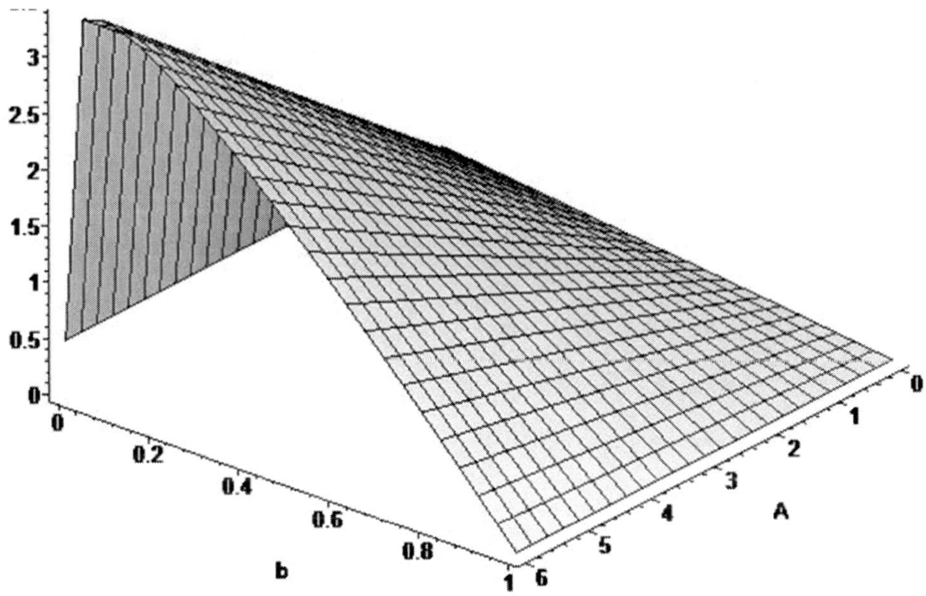

Figure 3.1.3. The agent's payoff (vertical axis) as a function of the bribe b and the parameter A (the exponent k = 0.1).

Figure 3.1.3 demonstrates the following. In the case of k = 0.1, agent is interested in bribery, since (a) bribe appears very small and (b) it is sufficient for considerable income growth. Figure 3.1.4 is in qualitative terms same as Figure 3.1.3, except that higher exponent of the corruption function increases the bribe required for income growth (agent is again interested in bribery). At the same time, Figure 3.1.5 corresponds to another situation: agent can offer a bribe within the range 0.6–0.7 (slightly improving its income) or choose honesty (gaining its legal payoff). Here a major role belongs to supervisor highly interested in additional income in the form of bribe: by imposing a due impact on agent, the former urges the latter to corruption. The last graph in the group (Figure 3.1.6) presents a situation, where agent benefits nothing from bribery (under k=7 and higher values). As a matter of fact, as A approaches 15, bribery can be attractive for agent again.

Thus, for corruption suppression one should either reduce to zero the parameter A (the bribe sensitivity) or increase the exponent k of the corruption function. In the former case, supervisor does not take a bribe even if agent tries to give it; in the latter case, agent benefit nothing from giving a bribe even if supervisor tries to receive it. A deeper practical interpretation of the mentioned parameters in terms of real anti-corruption strategies should be the subject of special sociological studies.

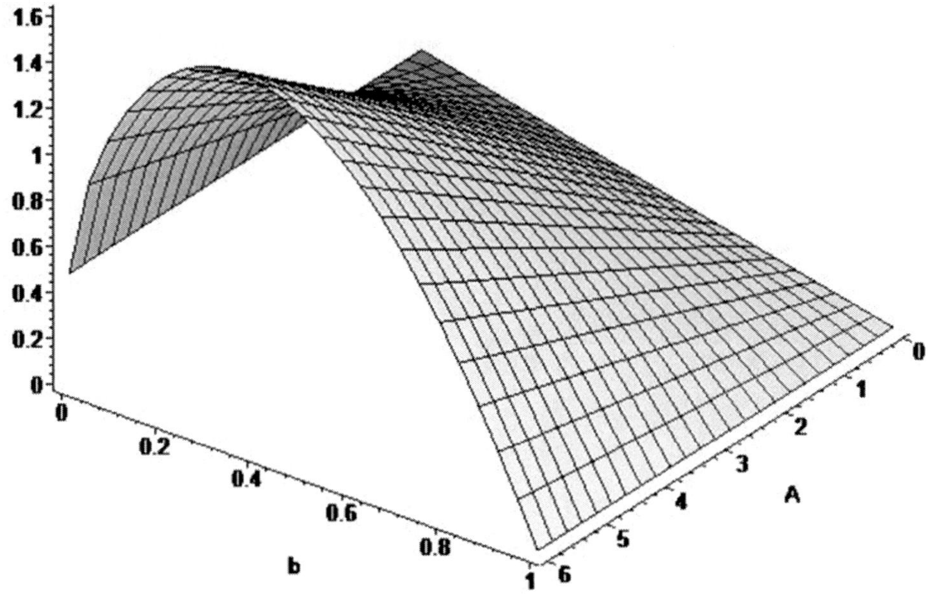

Figure 3.1.4. The agent's payoff (vertical axis) as a function of the bribe b and the parameter A (the exponent $k = 0.7$).

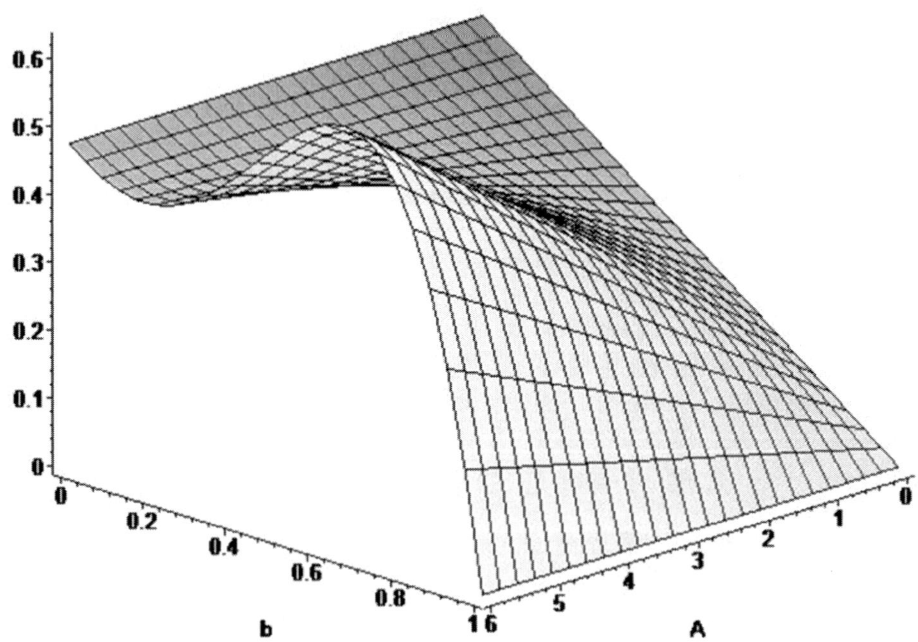

Figure 3.1.5. The agent's payoff (vertical axis) as a function of the bribe b and the parameter A (the exponent $k = 2.7$).

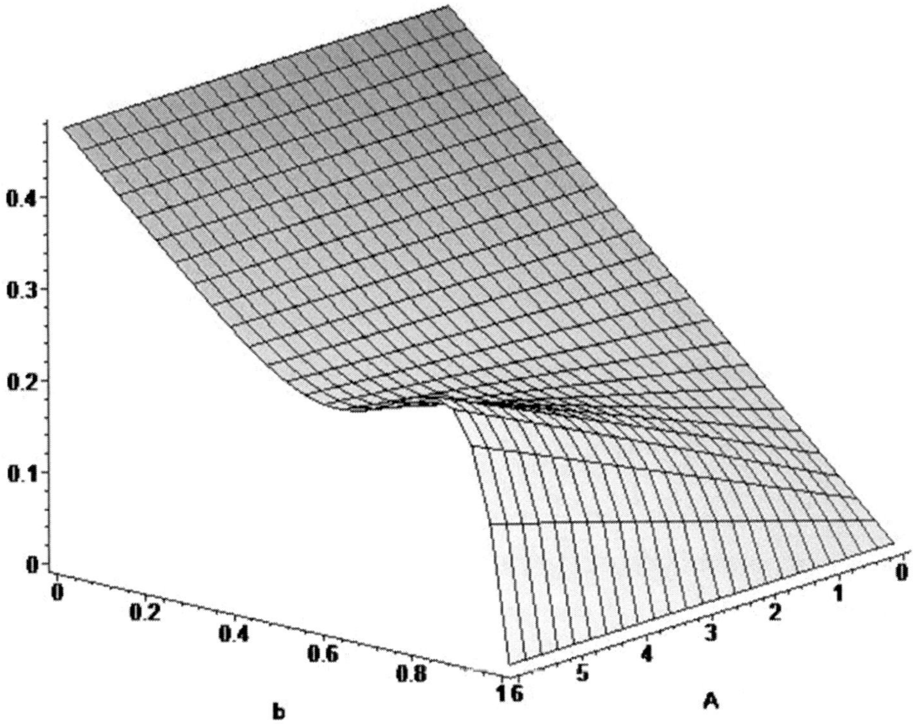

Figure 3.1.6. The agent's payoff (vertical axis) as a function of the bribe b and the parameter A (the exponent $k = 7$).

Now, consider administrative corruption models in REDP control at the agent's level. The following optimization problem arises then:

$$G(b,u) = (1-b)[ru + \xi(1-r)u + \gamma\eta(\gamma)(1-u)] \to \max, \quad s(b) \le u \le 1, \quad 0 \le b \le 1, \tag{3.1.4}$$

where $G(b,u)$ is the agent's payoff function (sales income from all types of real estate objects taking into account corruption); b means administrative bribe (a share of the income); u indicates the share of social real estate in the total building volume; r gives the share of social real estate with guaranteed government purchase at a fixed price; ξ is the estimated share of social real estate sold independently by agent at the same price; $\gamma > 1$ specifies the price coefficient for higher-class real estate; $\eta(\gamma)$ denotes the estimated share of higher-class real estate sold independently by agent; and finally, $s(b)$ stands for the minimum admissible quota of social real estate in the total building volume (which can be reduced for bribery).

Note that the optimization problem (3.1.4) has a two-variable objective function. The admissible domain of the variables under the linear corruption function is shown by Figure 3.1.7. Let us analyze the problem (3.1.4):

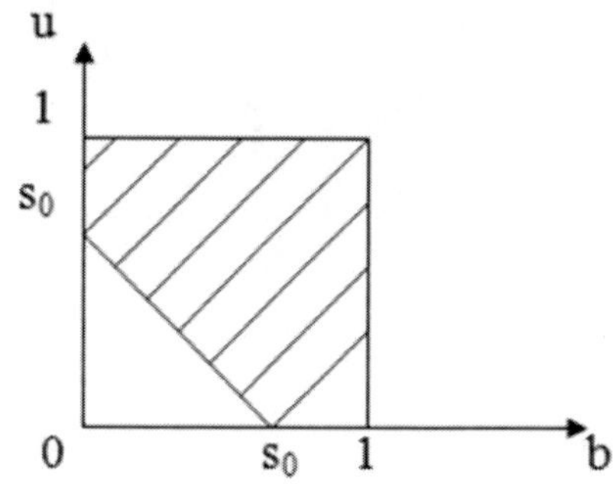

Figure 3.1.7. The admissible domain in the problem (3.1.4) under the linear corruption function

$$\frac{\partial G}{\partial b} = -[(r+\xi(1-r)-\gamma\eta)u+\gamma\eta];$$

$$\frac{\partial G}{\partial b} = 0 \Rightarrow u^* = \frac{\gamma\eta}{\gamma\eta-(r+\xi(1-r))} > 0, \quad r+\xi(1-r) < \gamma\eta;$$

$$\frac{\partial^2 G}{\partial b^2} = 0; \quad \frac{\partial^2 G}{\partial b \partial u} = \gamma\eta-(r+\xi(1-r));$$

$$\frac{\partial G}{\partial u} = (1-b)(r+\xi(1-r)-\gamma\eta); \frac{\partial G}{\partial u} = 0 \Rightarrow b^* = 1$$

$$\frac{\partial^2 G}{\partial u^2} = 0; \quad \frac{\partial^2 G}{\partial u \partial b} = \gamma\eta-(r+\xi(1-r)).$$

The Hessian matrix takes the form

$H = \begin{Vmatrix} 0 & \gamma\eta-(r+\xi(1-r)) \\ \gamma\eta-(r+\xi(1-r)) & 0 \end{Vmatrix}$, and its determinant makes up

$|H| = -[\gamma\eta-(r+\xi(1-r))]^2 < 0.$ The pair (b^*, u^*) is a saddle point and the function $G(b,u)$ reaches its maximum on the boundary of the admissible domain. We have

$$G(1,u) = 0; \quad G(0,1) = r+\xi(1-r)-\gamma\eta;$$
$$G(0,s_0) = r+\xi(1-r)+(1-s_0)\gamma\eta > G(0,1); \quad G(0,s_0) > 0;$$

Therefore, anyway the function $G(b,u)$ is maximized at $u = s(b)$. This leads to the one-dimensional (bribe amount) optimization problem $g(b) = (1-b)[(r+\xi(1-r)-\gamma\eta)s(b)+\gamma\eta] \to \max, \quad 0 \le b \le 1.$ Denote $C = \gamma\eta > 0, \quad D = \gamma\eta-(r+\xi(1-r)).$ Interestingly, if $D < 0$, it is more profitable to sell social real estate than commercial one; reducing the social real estate quota via bribery becomes pointless. Hence, rewrite the agent's payoff function as

As before, express the administrative corruption function in the form

$$s(b) = s_0 - Ab^k \quad (A > 0), \quad 0 \le s(b) \le 1,$$

where s_0 means a statutory quota. Consider the cases of linear (k = 1) and quadratic (k = 2) parametrization of this function.

The linear administrative corruption function.

$$s(b) = s_0 - Ab \; (A > 0);$$
$$g(b) = (1-b)(C - Ds_0 + ADb) = C - Ds_0 + (D(A + s_0) - C)b - ADb^2;$$
$$\frac{\partial g}{\partial b} = AD(1-2b) = 0 \Rightarrow b^* = 1/2;$$
$$\frac{\partial^2 g}{\partial b^2} = -2AD < 0 \Rightarrow b^* \quad \text{– maximum point}$$
$$g(0) = C - Ds_0; \quad g(1) = 0; \quad g(b^*) = \frac{2C + D(A - 2s_0)}{4}.$$

Consequently,

$$g^{\max} = \begin{cases} g(b^*), & D(A + 2s_0) > 2C, \\ g(0), & \text{otherwise.} \end{cases}$$

The reasonability of bribery depends on the interrelation of the model parameters. Note that in the case of $b = b^*$ the agent's payoff is positive whenever $s_0 < \frac{2C + AD}{2D}$, i.e., the statutory social real estate quota appears rather small.

The quadratic administrative corruption function.

$$s(b) = s_0 - Ab^k \quad (A > 0);$$
$$g(b) = (1-b)(C - Ds_0 + ADb^2) = C - Ds_0 - (C + Ds_0)b + ADb^2 - ADb^3;$$
$$\frac{\partial g}{\partial b} = -(C + Ds_0) + 2ADb - 3ADb^2 = 0 \Rightarrow b^* = \frac{AD \pm \sqrt{AD(AD - 3(C + Ds_0))}}{3AD}.$$

If the discriminant is nonnegative, then the positive root of the equation $\frac{\partial g}{\partial b} = 0$ represents a local maximum point of the function $g(b)$ and $g^{\max} = \max\{g(b^*), g(0)\}$. Otherwise, we necessarily have that $g^{\max} = g(0)$. Thus, the agent's optimal strategy again depends on the model parameters.

Now, consider the results of calculations performed using the software complex under the parameter values $r = 0.2, \xi = 0.4, \gamma = 3, \eta = 0.7, s_0 = 0.35$. To make the picture complete, the parameter A varies from 0 to 6 with increment 1.2 and the parameter k varies from 0.1 to 2.8 with increment 0.3. Table 3.1.2 demonstrates the agent's payoff and the corresponding bribe under the above model parameters.

Analysis of Table 3.1.2 brings to the following conclusion. The agent's payoff achieves its maximum under the highest value of the parameter A which characterizes supervisor's response to bribe (the bribe is minimum). On the other hand, the growing exponent of the corruption function reduces the agent's payoff and simultaneously increases bribe amount (the arrow indicates bribe amount growth and agent's payoff reduction). Starting from some threshold exponent of the function $s(b)$, bribery becomes pointless regardless of the parameter A.

Table 3.1.2. The dependence of the agent's payoff function on model parameters in the administrative corruption model of REDP

	A(the influence of bribe on supervisor)						
k (the exponent of the corruption function)	0	1.2	2.4	3.6	4.8	6	
0.1	1.547	2.805	4.145	5.493	6.845	8.198	*Payoff (G)*
	0	0.05	0.06	0.07	0.07	0.08	*Bribe (b)*
0.4	1.547	2.076	2.835	3.629	4.435	5.247	*Payoff (G)*
	0	0.12	0.18	0.21	0.23	0.24	*Bribe (b)*
0.7	1.547	1.742	2.238	2.797	3.375	3.961	*Payoff (G)*
	0	0.14	0.25	0.3	0.33	0.34	*Bribe (b)*
1	1.547	1.563	1.879	2.301	2.748	3.207	*Payoff (G)*
	0	0.09	0.3	0.36	0.4	0.42	*Bribe (b)*
1.3	1.547	1.547	1.638	1.966	2.328	2.703	*Payoff (G)*
	0	0	0.31	0.41	0.45	0.48	*Bribe (b)*
1.6	1.547	1.547	1.547	1.723	2.024	2.341	*Payoff (G)*
	0	0	0	0.45	0.5	0.52	*Bribe (b)*
1.9	1.547	1.547	1.547	1.547	1.794	2.067	*Payoff (G)*
	0	0	0	0	0.53	0.56	*Bribe (b)*
2.2	1.547	1.547	1.547	1.547	1.613	1.852	*Payoff (G)*
	0	0	0	0	0.56	0.59	*Bribe (b)*
2.5	1.547	1.547	1.547	1.547	1.547	1.678	*Payoff (G)*
	0	0	0	0	0	0.62	*Bribe (b)*
2.8	1.547	1.547	1.547	1.547	1.547	1.547	*Payoff (G)*
	0	0	0	0	0	0	*Bribe (b)*

In what follows, we present the graphs of the agent's payoff as a function of the bribe amount and the parameter A. In Figs. 3.1.8 - 3.1.11, the exponent of the corruption function $s(b)$ takes different values for proper illustration of the calculations. Vertical axes correspond to the agent's payoff, whereas horizontal axes answer for the parameters b and A (the bribe amount and the briber's qualitative characteristic, respectively).

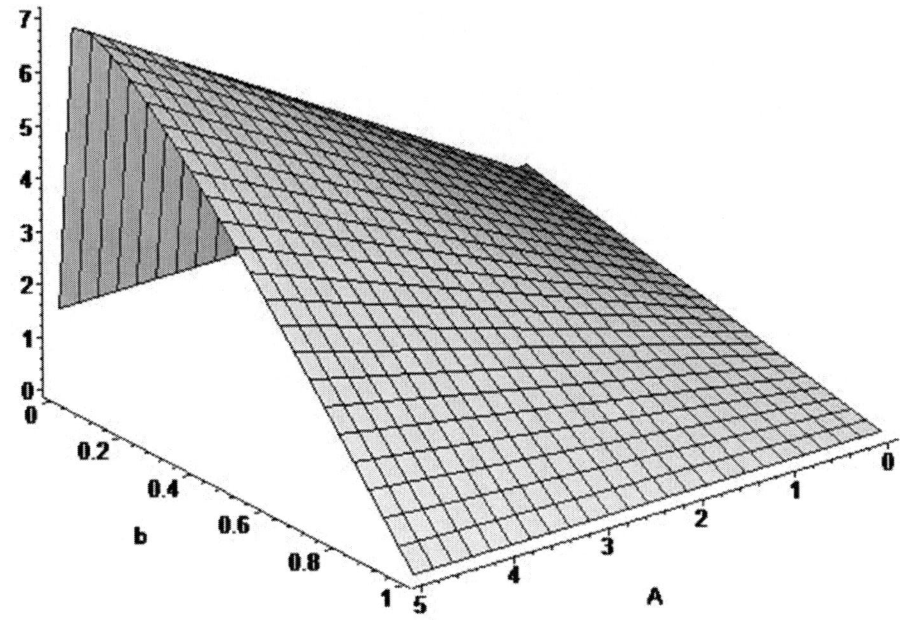

Figure 3.1.8. The agent's payoff (vertical axis) as a function of the bribe b and the parameter A (the exponent $k = 0.1$).

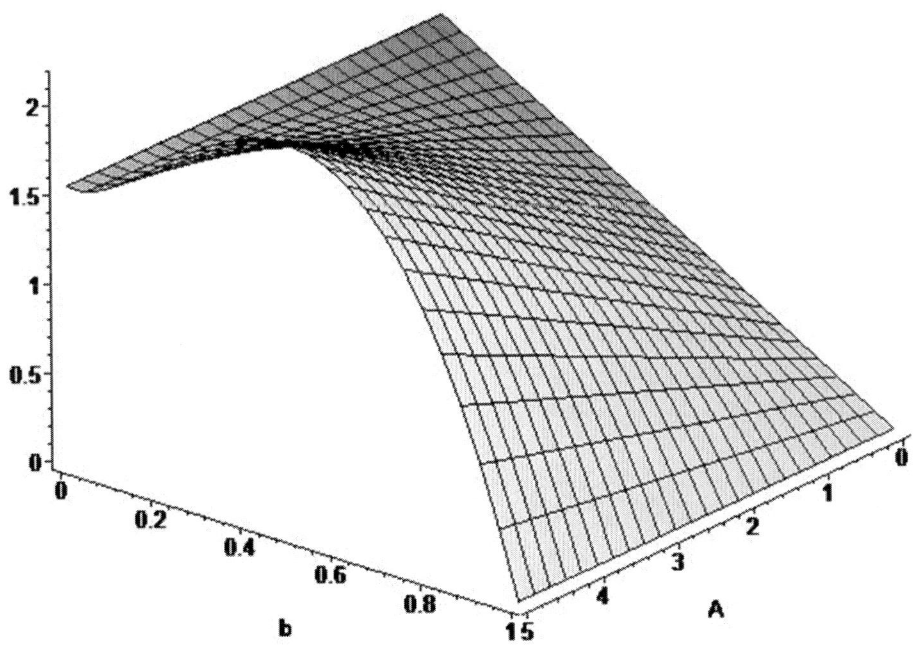

Figure 3.1.9. The agent's payoff (vertical axis) as a function of the bribe b and the parameter A (the exponent $k = 1.5$).

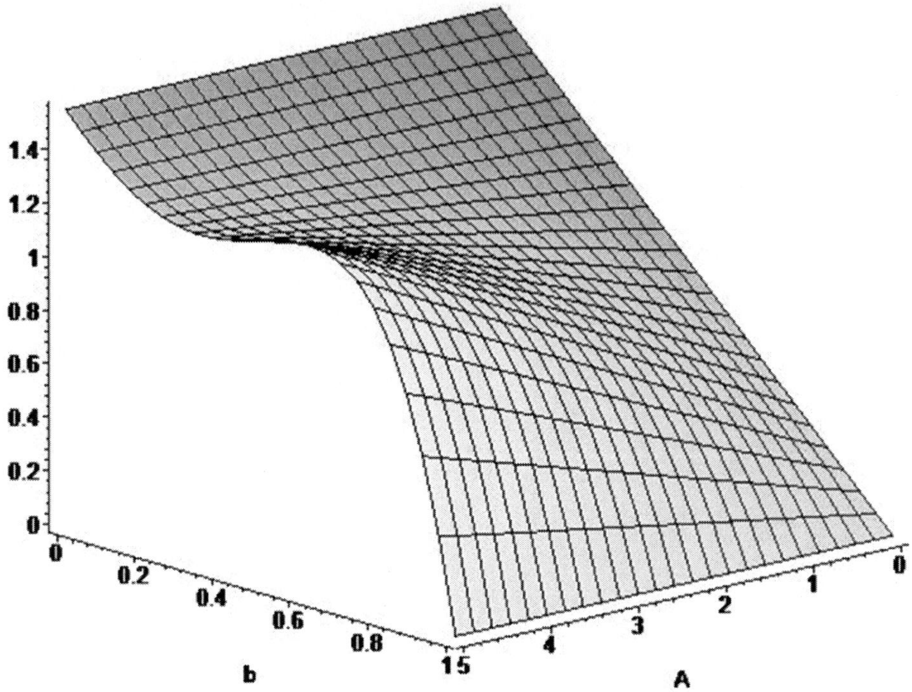

Figure 3.1.10. The agent's payoff (vertical axis) as a function of the bribe b and the parameter A (the exponent $k = 3$).

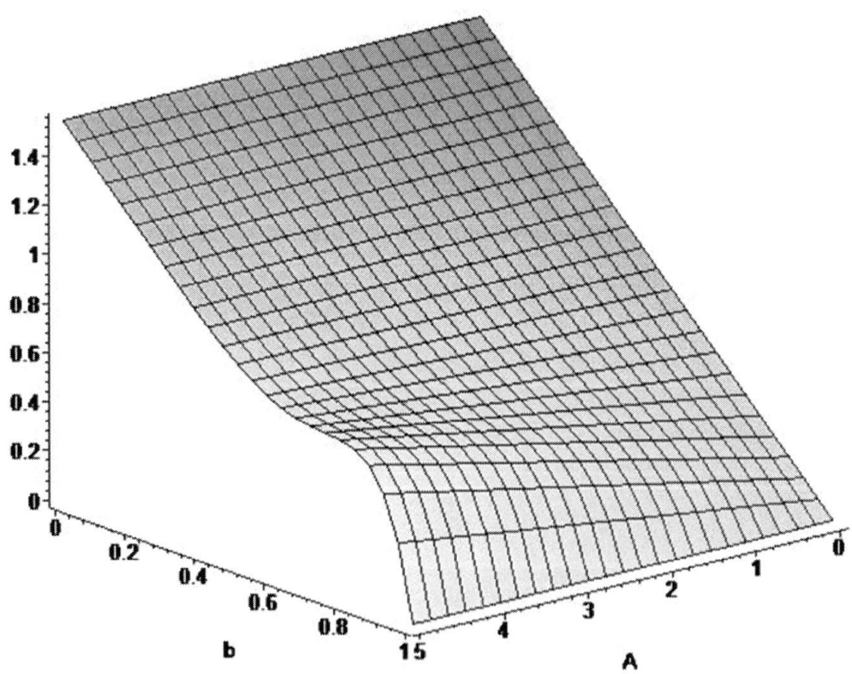

Figure 3.1.11. The agent's payoff (vertical axis) as a function of the bribe b and the parameter A (the exponent $k = 7$).

Figure 3.1.8 shows a jump in the agent's payoff under a small bribe, with gradual payoff decrease down to zero. In this situation, it is necessary to reduce the parameter *A,* and then agent's bribery becomes pointless for the briber. According to the graph in Figure 3.1.9, bribery again takes place, but within the range 0.4-0.6. Here one should weaken the supervisor's inclination for bribery. Under $A = 1.3$ and smaller values, bribery is unreasonable for agent. Figs. 3.1.10 - 3.1.11 illustrate that, since a sufficiently large value of *k,* bribery makes no sense for any *A* (see also the results in Table 3.1.2).

Therefore, it is necessary to decrease the supervisor's corruption level, reduce its bribe sensitivity (the parameter A). Furthermore, by keeping the exponent of the corruption function (the parameter k) at a sufficiently high level, agent's bribery can be made unreasonable under any value of A. Yet, excessive decreases of the parameter k would stimulate agent's bribery. In this case, even a small bribe guarantees an appreciable growth of the agent's payoff.

Two-level models of REDP control with corruption. Let us consider an administrative corruption model in the "supervisor–agent" system. With regard to REDP, the role of agent belongs to a developer and some authority acts as supervisor. Suppose that the action u specifies the share of real estate completely meeting certain quality standards. Then the requirement $u \geq s_0$ states the homeostasis condition, where $0 \leq s_0 \leq 1$ is a statutory quantity (satisfied without corruption). Supervisor guarantees the restrictions on the agent's action $s \leq u \leq 1$ by assigning a quota s. The equality $s = s_0$ holds true in the absence of corruption. If $s > s_0$, extortion occurs; further exposition ignores this case. And so, assume that $0 \leq s \leq s_0$ (if $s < s_0$, we face capture to-be-studied below). Introduce the following notation: is the bribe share in the agent's income $(0 \leq b \leq 1)$; $f_2(u)$ designates the agent's income from real estate building (a decreasing function of quality assurance costs); $f_1(s)$ specifies the supervisor's penalty in the case of any deviations from the quality standards (a decreasing function of quota hardness); p is the probability of deviation detection (i.e., briber catch). Without loss of generality, we believe that $f_i : [0,1] \rightarrow [0,1], i = 1,2$.

This leads to the administrative corruption model in the two-level control system of the form

$$
\begin{aligned}
&g_1(s,b,u) = bf_2(u) - pf_1(s) \rightarrow \max, 0 \leq s \leq s_0;\\
&g_2(s,b,u) = (1-b)f_2(u) \rightarrow \max, 0 \leq b \leq 1, s \leq u \leq 1.
\end{aligned}
$$

Due to the decreasing property of the function $f_2(u)$, its maximum value makes up $f_2^{\max}(u) = f_2(s)$. The variable u can be then eliminated and we obtain the two-player hierarchical game

$$
\begin{aligned}
&g_1(s,b) = bf_2(s) - pf_1(s) \rightarrow \max, 0 \leq s \leq s_0;\\
&g_2(s,b) = (1-b)f_2(s) \rightarrow \max, 0 \leq b \leq 1.
\end{aligned}
\tag{3.1.5}
$$

The supervisor's strategy represents a function with feedback $\tilde{s} = s(b)$, and the model (3.1.5) is treated as Germeier game Γ_2. We accordingly employ Germeier's theorem to evaluate the leader's (i.e., supervisor's) optimal guaranteeing strategy, see Section 2.1. Perform the following parameterization of the monotone decreasing functions f_1, f_2 on the segment [0,1]:

$$f_1(s) = 1 - \frac{A_1}{s_0} s^{k_1}, \quad f_2(s) = 1 - A_2 s^{k_2}, \, A_1 > 0, \, A_2 > 0, \, k_1 > 0, \, k_2 > 0.$$

In this case, the model (3.1.5) can be rewritten as

$$g_1(s,b) = b(1 - A_2 s^{k_2}) - p(1 - \frac{A_1}{s_0} s^{k_1}) \to \max, \, 0 \le s \le s_0;$$
$$g_2(s,b) = (1-b)(1 - A_2 s^{k_2}) \to \max, \, 0 \le b \le 1. \qquad (3.1.6)$$

The parameters A_1, A_2 characterize the "hardness" of the functions $f_1(s), f_2(s)$, respectively (see Figure 3.1.12a,b).

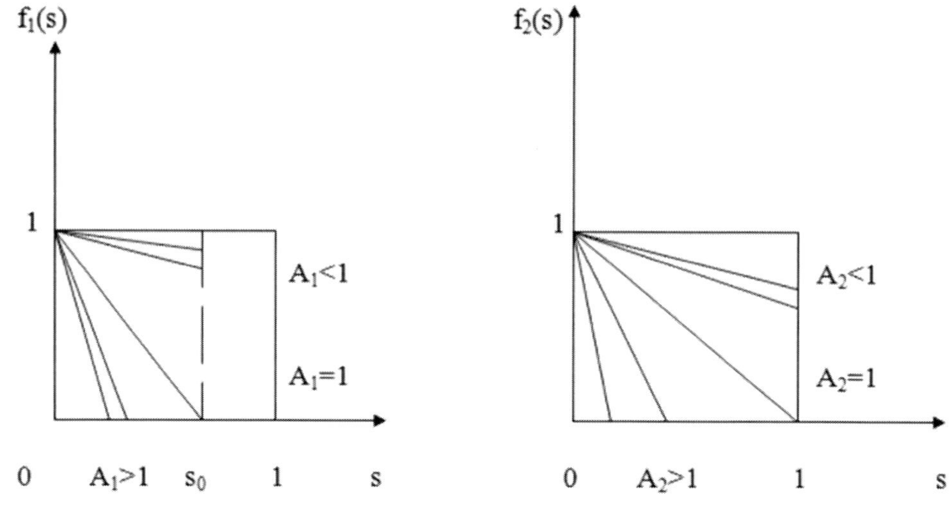

Figure 3.1.12. (a) the dependence of the function $f_1(s)$ on the parameter A_1 (the linear case); (b) the dependence of the function $f_2(s)$ on the parameter A_2 (the linear case)

Consequently, we obtain the following cases for the function $f_1(s)$:

1) $A_1 = 1 \Rightarrow f_1(s_0) = 0, \, f_1(s) > 0, \, s < s_0$,

i.e., under any detected deviations from the quality standards supervisor pays a positive penalty; the penalty vanishes only when the quality standards are fully met;

2) $A_1 < 1 \Rightarrow f_1(s_0) > 0$, i.e., supervisor pays a penalty even under the perfect quality of real estate objects it is responsible for. This case corresponds to extortion by upper-level authorities (Principal) and will not be considered;

3) $A_1 > 1 \Rightarrow f_1(s) = 0, s < s_0$, i.e., supervisor may avoid penalty even under some deviations from the quality standards. This is the most realistic hypothesis.

By analogy, the following cases apply to the function $f_2(s)$:

1) $A_2 = 1 \Rightarrow f_2(1) = 0,\ f_2(s) > 0,\quad s < s_0$, i.e., perfect quality assurance requires developer's complete refusal of profits;

2) $A_2 < 1 \Rightarrow f_2(1) > 0$, i.e., even under perfect quality a positive income is possible (the most realistic hypothesis);

3) $A_2 > 1 \Rightarrow f_2(s) < 0,\ s < 1$, i.e., losses may occur even under imperfect quality (this case will not be studied).

Therefore, fix $A_1 \geq 1, 0 \leq A_2 \leq 1$ and consider different correlation of the parameters k_1, k_2. Let $k_1 = k_2 = 1$ and $A_1 = A_2 = 1$ for simplicity. The model (3.1.6) takes the form

$$g_1(s,b) = b(1-s) - p(1-\frac{s}{s_0}) \to \max,\ 0 \leq s \leq s_0;$$

The function

$$g_2(s,b) = (1-b)(1-s) \to \max,\quad 0 \leq b \leq 1.$$

$$g_1(s,b) = b - p + (\frac{p}{s_0})s \begin{cases} \text{increases in } s, \frac{p}{s_0} > b, \\ \text{decreases in } s, \frac{p}{s_0} < b. \end{cases}$$

And it appears that $g_1^{\max} = \begin{cases} g_1(0) = b - p, \frac{p}{s_0} < b, \\ g_1(s_0) = b(1-s_0), \frac{p}{s_0} > b. \end{cases}$ Calculation of the quantities figuring in Germeier's theorem brings to the following results:

$$s^P \equiv s_0;\ s^D = \begin{cases} 0, \frac{p}{s_0} < b, \\ s_0, \frac{p}{s_0} > b. \end{cases}$$

$L_2 = 1 - s_0;\ E = \{b = 0\};\ D_2 = \{(s,b) : (1-b)(1-s) > 1 - s_0\};$

$$K_2 = \min_{b\in E_2} \max_{0\le s\le s}[b(1-s) - p(1-\frac{s}{s_0})] = p \min_{0\le s\le s_0}(1-\frac{s}{s_0}) = 0 \quad (s = s_0).$$

To evaluate K_1, we have to solve the optimization problem

$$g_1(s,b) = b - p + (\frac{p}{s_0})s \to \max_{b,s}$$
$$g_2(s,b) = (1-b)(1-s) > 1 - s_0, 0 \le s \le s_0, 0 \le b \le 1.$$

The constraint $g_2(s,b) > 1 - s_0$ gives $b < \frac{s_0 - s}{1-s}$. Set $b^* = \frac{s_0 - s}{1-s} - \varepsilon$, then

$$s^* = \begin{cases} 0, & b^* > \frac{p}{s_0}, \\ s_0, & b^* < \frac{p}{s_0}; \end{cases} \quad K_1 = \begin{cases} \frac{s_0 - s - (\varepsilon + p)(1-s)}{1-s}, & b^* > \frac{p}{s_0}, \\ \frac{s_0 - s - \varepsilon(1-s)}{1-s}(1-s_0), & b^* < \frac{p}{s_0}, \end{cases}$$

and anyway $K_1 > 0 = K_2$. Thus and so,

$$\tilde{s}^*(b) = \begin{cases} s^*, b = b^*, \\ s_0, \text{otherwise} \end{cases} = \begin{cases} 0, b = b^* > \frac{p}{s_0}; \\ s_0, \text{ otherwise.} \end{cases} \qquad (3.1.7)$$

The whole essence of the strategy (3.1.7) consists in the following. If agent agrees to pay the bribe $b = b^*$, then supervisor completely refuses to perform quality control; otherwise, it performs as strict quality control as possible. The strategy (3.1.7) is efficient (credible), i.e., $g_2(0,b^*) > g_2(s_0,0)$, if $2s_0 - p > 1 + \varepsilon$. This condition means that agent really benefits from accepting the supervisor's offer. In the general case ($k_1 \ne 1, k_2 \ne 1$), Germeier's theorem usage requires numerical simulation.

As an analytical illustration, analyze another trivial case by choosing $p = 0$ (the briber's total impunity). For simplicity, set $A_1 = A_2 = k_2 = 1$. Then the model (3.1.6) is described by

$$g_1(s,b) = b(1-s) \to \max, 0 \le s \le s_0,$$
$$g_2(s,b) = (1-b)(1-s) \to \max, 0 \le b \le 1,$$

i.e., the players have same-direction interests in s and opposite-direction interests in b. We obtain that

$$s^P \equiv s_0;\ s^D \equiv 0;\ L_2 = (1-s_0)\max_b(1-b) = 1-s_0;\ E_2 = \{b=0\};$$
$$D_2 = \{(s,b) : (1-b)(1-s) > 1-s_0\};\ K_2 = \min_{E_2}\max_{X_1} b(1-s) = 0.$$

To find K_1, solve the optimization problem

$$b(1-s) \to \max$$
$$(1-b)(1-s) > 1-s_0,\ 0 \le b \le 1,\ 0 \le s \le s_0.$$

Suppose that $s_0 = 1$, i.e., the quality standards must be met by 100%. Then the stated optimization problem possesses the solution

$$b^* = 1-\varepsilon,\ s^* = \varepsilon,\ \text{and}\ K_1 = (1-\varepsilon)^2 > 0;$$
$$\tilde{s}^*(b) = \begin{cases} \varepsilon, b = 1-\varepsilon, \\ s_0, \text{otherwise.} \end{cases} \quad (3.1.8)$$

The strategy (3.1.8) has the same sense as (3.1.7). In this case, $g_2(0,s_0) = 1-s_0 = 0,\ g_2(b^*,s^*) = \varepsilon(1-\varepsilon) > 0,$ i.e., the strategy (3.1.8) is efficient (credible). The results accumulated using the software complex under $s_0 = 0.5, p = 0.2$ are presented by Tables 3.1.3-3.1.4.

Each row in the tables is associated with some system state. By varying different parameters, we observe the dynamics of the whole system. For instance, higher k_2 increases the agent's payoff (see the column g_2). As we reduce k_1, the supervisor's payoff goes down. Moreover, starting from some parameter values, agent ceases to bribe supervisor. The corresponding values change under slight variations of other parameters. The absence of corruption can be therefore established only with a certain error for definite parameter values.

Table 3.1.3. The optimal sustainable development strategy (b^*,s^*) as a function of the parameters k_1 and k_2 (here $A_1 = A_2 = 1$)

k_1	K_2	b^*	s^*	$g_1(s^*,b^*)$	$g_2(s^*,b^*)$	$g_1(s0,0)$	$g_2(s0,0)$
5.2	0.1	0.931	0	0.731	0.069	-0.1891	0.067
4.49	1.1	0.456	0	0.256	0.544	-0.1821	0.5335
3.77	2.1	0.223	0	0.023	0.777	-0.1707	0.7667
3.06	3.1	0.109	0	-0.091	0.891	-0.1519	0.8834
2.34	4.1	0	0.5	-0.1212	0.9417	-0.1212	0.9417
1.63	5.1	0	0.5	-0.0706	0.9708	-0.0706	0.9708
0.91	6.1	0	0.5	0.0122	0.9854	0.0122	0.9854
0.2	7.1	0	0.5	0.1482	0.9927	0.1482	0.9927

Table 3.1.4. The optimal sustainable development strategy (b^*,s^*) as a function of the parameters A_1 and A_2 (here k_1 = 5.2 and k_2 = 0.1)

A_1	A_2	b^*	s^*	$g_1(s^*,b^*)$	$g_2(s^*,b^*)$	$g_1(s0,0)$	$g_2(s0,0)$
1	1	0.931	0	0.731	0.069	-0.1891	0.067
1.5	0.86	0.798	0	0.598	0.202	-0.1837	0.2003
2	0.71	0.665	0	0.465	0.335	-0.1782	0.3335
2.5	0.57	0.532	0	0.332	0.468	-0.1728	0.4668
3	0.43	0.399	0	0.199	0.601	-0.1674	0.6001
3.5	0.29	0.266	0	0.066	0.734	-0.1619	0.7334
4	0.14	0.133	0	-0.067	0.867	-0.1565	0.8667
4.5	0	0	0.5	-0.151	1	-0.151	1

In the current situation, corruption disappears when the parameters k_1 and k_2 have close values: the turning point is $k_1 = 3.06$, $k_2 = 3.1$. Under greater k_1 or smaller k_2, supervisor exacts a bribe from agent. If the parameter values vary in the opposite directions, agent refuses to pay a bribe and supervisor modifies the penalty strategy. In other words, it demands statutory quota fulfillment from agent.

Thus, reduction or total elimination of corruption requires close values of the parameters k_1 and k_2.

Table 3.1.4 shows that the presence or absence of corruption depends on the hardness of parameters A_1 and A_2. As a matter of fact, $A_2 \approx 1$ promotes corruption, but smaller values of this parameter decrease the bribe down to 0. If A_1 approximates 1, the dependence on this parameter becomes minimal. The growth of A_1 reduces the probability of corruption detection in principle. For $A_1 = 5$, there exists a single corruption state (row in Table 3.1.4), whereas for $A_1 > 6$ they totally disappear.

Summarizing the outcomes: corruption elimination is possible under close values of the parameters k_1, k_2 and increase of the parameter A_1; sufficiently large values of this parameter whittles away the impact of A_2.

Now, consider an *economic corruption model in the two-level "supervisor–agent" control system*. Let supervisor apply economic control methods (taxes, tariffs, subsidies, privileges, etc.).

Suppose that the action u specifies the share of real estate, $0 \le u \le 1$; $f(u)$ is the agent's income from real estate building (a monotone increasing function), $f : [0,1] \to [0,1]$; means a tax rate which can be relaxed via bribery, i.e., supervisor does not prosecute agent for nonpayment of tax (the economic corruption function), $0 \le r(b) \le r_0 \le 1$; r_0 denotes a statutory tax rate necessarily observed in the absence of corruption, and the equality $r = r_0$ states the homeostasis condition; b is a share of the agent's income intended for bribery, $0 \le b \le 1$; and finally, c gives a share of tax revenues in the budget, which is allocated to the supervisor's wage, $0 \le c \le 1$. We naturally arrive at the economic corruption model of the form

$$g_1(r,b,u) = (b+cr)f(u) \rightarrow \max, 0 \le r \le r_0;$$
$$g_2(r,b,u) = (1-b-r)f(u) \rightarrow \max, 0 \le u \le 1; 0 \le b \le 1.$$

The maximum value of the increasing function $f(u)$ makes up $f_{\max} = f(1)$. Hence, it suffices to study the two-player hierarchical game

$$g_1(r,b) = f(1)(b+cr) \rightarrow \max, 0 \le r \le r_0;$$
$$g_2(r,b) = f(1)(1-b-r) \rightarrow \max, 0 \le b \le 1. \quad (3.1.9)$$

The supervisor's strategy again represents a function with feedback $\tilde{r} = r(b)$, and the model (3.1.9) is treated as Germeier game Γ_2. Employ Germeier's theorem to evaluate the leader's (i.e., supervisor's) optimal guaranteeing strategy. This yields $r^P \equiv r^D \equiv r_0$, i.e., the supervisor's penalty strategy is a warning to agent;

$$L_2 = (1-r_0)f(1);\ E_2 = \{b=0\};\ D_2 = \{(r,b): 1-b-r > 1-r_0\};$$
$$K_2 = \min_{b \in E_2} \max_{0 \le r \le r_0} [f(1)(b+cr)] = cf(1) \max_{0 \le r \le r_0} r = cf(1)r_0;$$

to evaluate K_1, solve the optimization problem

$$f(1)(b+cr) \rightarrow \max_{r,b}$$
$$b + r < r_0; 0 \le r \le r_0; 0 \le b \le 1, \quad (3.1.10)$$

which is actually a linear programming problem with two variables and a strict inequality constraint; Figure 3.1.13 demonstrates its admissible domain.

And so, $b^* = r^* = r_0 - \varepsilon$, $K_1 = f(1)\max\{r_0 - \varepsilon, cr_0 - \varepsilon)\} = f(1)(r_0 - \varepsilon)$;
$K_1 > K_2$ for $(1-c)r_0 > \varepsilon$, or $c < 1 - \varepsilon$.

In this case,

$$\tilde{r}^*(b) = \begin{cases} 0, b = r_0 - \varepsilon \wedge c < 1 - \dfrac{\varepsilon}{r_0}, \\ r_0, \text{otherwise.} \end{cases}$$

If $c < 1 - \dfrac{\varepsilon}{r_0}$ (almost always!) and agent agrees to pay the bribe b^*, then supervisor reduces the real tax rate to 0 (and applies the penalty strategy, otherwise).

Consider the economic corruption model in another setting:

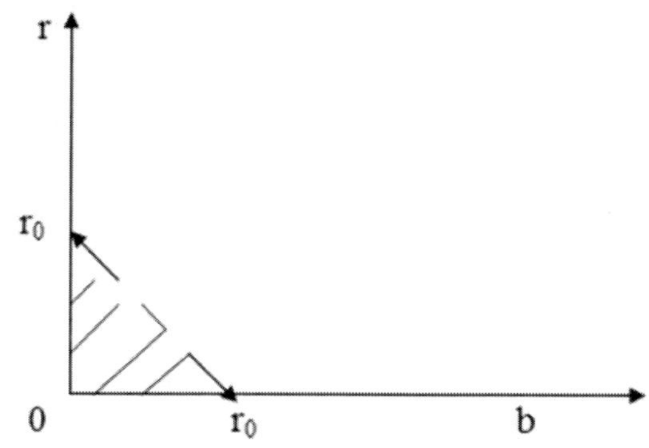

Figure 3.1.13. The admissible domain in the optimization problem (3.1.10)

$$g_1(r,b) = (k+b)f(r) - pMb \to \max, \quad 0 \le r \le 1;$$
$$g_2(r,b) = (1-b)f(r) \to \max, \quad 0 \le b \le 1. \tag{3.1.11}$$

Suppose that agent participates in a tender organized by supervisor; here r is a resource share allocated to agent in case of tender win; $f(r)$ indicates the agent's income from resource usage; k designates the degree of the supervisor's interest in efficient resource usage (in fractions of 1); b means bribe amount; p defines the probability of corruption detection; and finally, M specifies the supervisor's penalty in case of corruption detection.

Set $f(r) = a\sqrt{r}$ and assume that $\tilde{r} = r(b)$. Germeier's theory yields

$$r^P(b) \equiv 0;\ r^D(b) \equiv 1;\ L_2 = 0;\ E_2 = [0,1];\ D_2 = \{(r,b) : a(1-b) > 0\};$$
$$K_2 = \min_{0\le b\le 1}\max_{0\le r\le 1}[a(k+b)\sqrt{r} - pMb] = \min_{0\le b\le 1}[(a-pM)b + ak] = \begin{cases} ak, & a > pM; \\ a(k+1) - pM - pM, & a < pM; \end{cases}$$
$$K_1 = \begin{cases} (1-\varepsilon)(a-pM) + ak, & a > pM, \\ ak, & a < pM. \end{cases}$$

Therefore, $K_1 > K_2$ anyway and

$$\tilde{r}^*(b) = \begin{cases} 1, & b = b^* = \begin{cases} 1, & a > pM, \\ 0, & a < pM; \end{cases} \\ 0, & \text{otherwise.} \end{cases} \tag{3.1.12}$$

The strategy (3.1.12) is efficient for $a > pM$; in this case, we have $g_1(r^*, b^*) = a > 0 = g_1(0,0)$. Whenever $a < pM$, the strategy (3.1.12) is formally efficient, since the agent's optimal strategy lies in refusal of bribery and $g_1(0,0) = g_1(r^P, 0) = 0$. Consequently, corruption becomes economically unreasonable for agent if its construction capabilities are smaller than the supervisor's losses in case of corruption detection; otherwise, agent has to pay the maximum bribe.

We endeavor to generalize the model (3.1.11) to the tree-type control structure with single supervisor and several agents:

$$g_S(r,b)=\sum_{i=1}^{n}(k+b_i)a_i\sqrt{r_i}-pM\sum_{i=1}^{n}b_i\to\max,\ \sum_{i=1}^{n}r_i=1,\quad r_i\geq 0;$$

$$g_i(r_i,b_i)=a_i(1-b_i)\sqrt{r_i}\to\max,\quad 0\leq b_i\leq 1,\quad i=1,\dots,n.$$

Here $a_i\sqrt{r_i}$ is the production function of agent i and a_i means the agent's type characterizing its production capabilities (real estate building); r_i indicates the resource amount allocated to agent i in exchange for bribe a b_i. The total income of the system is defined by the quantity $G=\sum_{i=1}^{n}a_i\sqrt{r_i}$; the condition $G\geq A$ expresses the homeostasis requirement.

First, consider a resource allocation mechanism without corruption, where agents receive resources proportionally to their production capabilities:

$$\tilde{r}^0{}_i=r_i(a_1,\dots,a_n)=\frac{a_i}{\sum_{j=1}^{n}a_j},\quad b_i=0,\quad i=1,\dots,n.$$

In this case, we have $G^0=\dfrac{\sum_{i=1}^{n}a_i\sqrt{a_i}}{\sqrt{\sum_{j=1}^{n}a_j}},\quad g^0{}_S=kG^0.$

Now, study a resource allocation mechanism with corruption, where agents receive resources proportionally to their bribe amounts:

$$\tilde{r}^b{}_i=r_i(b_1,\dots,b_n)=\frac{b_i}{\sum_{j=1}^{n}b_j},\quad i=1,\dots,n.$$

The following normal-form game naturally arises at the lower level of control:

$$g_i(b_1,\dots,b_n)=\frac{a_i(1-b_i)\sqrt{b_i}}{\sqrt{\sum_{j=1}^{n}b_j}}\to\max,\quad 0\leq b_i\leq 1,\quad i=1,\dots,n. \tag{3.1.13}$$

For Nash equilibrium evaluation in this game, solve the system of equations $\frac{\partial g_i}{\partial b_i} = 0, \quad i = 1,\dots,n,$ whence it appears that

$$a_i \frac{\left(\frac{1}{2\sqrt{b_i}} - \sqrt{b_i} - \frac{b_i}{2\sqrt{b_i}}\right)\sqrt{\sum_{j=1}^{n} b_j} - \sqrt{b_i}(1-b_i)\frac{1}{2\sqrt{\sum_{j=1}^{n} b_j}}}{\sum_{j=1}^{n} b_j} = 0;$$

$$\frac{1-b_i-2b_i}{2\sqrt{b_i}}\sqrt{\sum_{j=1}^{n} b_j} = \sqrt{b_i}(1-b_i)\frac{1}{2\sqrt{\sum_{j=1}^{n} b_j}};$$

$$(1-3b_i)\sum_{j=1}^{n} b_j = b_i(1-b_i);$$

$$\frac{b_i(1-b_i)}{1-3b_i} = \sum_{j=1}^{n} b_j, \quad i = 1,\dots,n;$$

$$\frac{b(1-b)}{1-3b} = nb;$$

$$b^* = \frac{n-1}{3n-1}.$$

Therefore, the game (3.1.13) possesses the Nash equilibrium

$b_1 = \dots = b_n = b^*$, and so $r_i(b^*,\dots, b^*) = 1/n, \quad i = 1,\dots, n.$ Then we obtain that

$$G^b = \frac{1}{\sqrt{n}}\sum_{i=1}^{n} a_i; \quad g^b{}_S = \frac{1}{\sqrt{n}}\left(k + \frac{n-1}{3n-1}\right)\sum_{i=1}^{n} a_i - \frac{pMn(n-1)}{3n-1}.$$

To compare the cases with and without corruption, choose $n = 2$ and consider two characteristic settings as follows.

1. $a_1 = a_2 = a$.

$$G^0 = \frac{2a\sqrt{a}}{\sqrt{2a}} = a\sqrt{2}; \quad g^0{}_S = ka\sqrt{2};$$

$$G^b = \frac{1}{\sqrt{2}} 2a = a\sqrt{2} = G^0; \quad g^b{}_S = \frac{1}{\sqrt{2}}(k + 1/5)2a = \frac{(5k+1)a\sqrt{2} - 2pM}{5};$$

$$g^b{}_S - g^0{}_S = \frac{a\sqrt{2} - 2pM}{5}.$$

Therefore, under identical production capabilities of the agents, the total incomes of the system do coincide in the cases with and without corruption. To make the resource allocation mechanism with corruption nonbeneficial to supervisor, one should satisfy the condition $2pM > a\sqrt{2}$.

2. $a_1 = 2a, a_2 = a$.

$$G^0 = \frac{2a\sqrt{2a} + a\sqrt{a}}{\sqrt{a+2a}} = \frac{a\sqrt{3}(2\sqrt{2}+1)}{3}; \quad g^0{}_S = kG^0;$$

$$G^b = \frac{1}{\sqrt{2}} 3a = \frac{3a\sqrt{2}}{2}; \quad g^b{}_S = \frac{3a(\sqrt{2}) - 4pM}{10};$$

$$G^0 - G^b = \frac{a}{2}(2\sqrt{6} + \sqrt{3} - 3\sqrt{2}) \approx 1.2a > 0;$$

$$g^b{}_S - g^0{}_S = \frac{5ka(9\sqrt{2} - 4\sqrt{6} - 2\sqrt{3}) + 9a\sqrt{2} - 12pM}{30} \approx \frac{a(12.7 - 0.25k) - 12pM}{30}.$$

Consequently, if the production capabilities of agents differ twofold, the total income of the system goes down in the presence of corruption. To make corruption nonbeneficial to supervisor, one should satisfy the (approximate) condition $12pM > a(12.7 - 0.25k)$.

Now, consider the generalized model of corruption in the two-level control system, which covers administrative and economic corruption as special cases. The supervisor's control variable c plays the role of quota (administrative corruption) or penalty/tax (economic corruption). The supervisor's payoff function decreases in c (control costs). Similarly, the agent's payoff function decreases in c (activity constraints). Therefore, the interests of the both players have same direction in c. The game (conflict of interests) arises in terms of the variable b (bribe): supervisor benefits from higher bribe amount, whereas agent strives for its minimization. In the elementary setting, the game-theoretic model can be expressed in the form

$$g_S(c,b) = b(1-c) \to \max, \quad 0 \le c \le 1;$$
$$g_A(c,b) = (1-b)(1-c) \to \max, \quad 0 \le b \le 1. \qquad (3.1.14)$$

Analysis of the model (3.1.14) using Germeier's theory gives the following results:

$c^D(b) \equiv 0;\ c^P(b) \equiv 1;\ L_A = 0;\ E_A = [0,1];\ D_A = \{(c,b) : (1-b)(1-c) > 0\};$

$K_2 = \min_{0 \le b \le 1} \max_{0 \le c \le 1} b(1-c) = 0;$

to evaluate K_1, solve the optimization problem

$$b(1-c) \to \max$$
$$(1-b)(1-c) > 0;\ 0 \le b \le 1;\ 0 \le c \le 1.$$

Obviously, $c^* = 0, b^* = 1-\varepsilon, K_1 = 1-\varepsilon > 0 = K_2$. Then the supervisor's optimal guaranteeing strategy is defined by

$$\tilde{c}^*(b) = \begin{cases} 0, b = b^* = 1-\varepsilon, \\ 1, \text{otherwise.} \end{cases} \tag{3.1.15}$$

Let us make several remarks.

1. The strategy (3.1.15) represents bluffing, since penalty strategy usage leads to $g_S(c^P, b) = \min_c g_S(c,b)$. However, this bluffing is correct, as far as $g_A(c^*, b^*) = \varepsilon > 0 = g_A(c^P, 0)$, and agent benefits from accepting the supervisor's offer (3.1.15) even despite that $g_S(c^*, b^*) = 1-\varepsilon,\ g_A(c^*, b^*) = \varepsilon$, i.e., supervisor takes almost all payoff (not all, as in the case of penalty).
2. Within the framework of the model (3.1.14), the homeostasis condition is stated as $c \ge c_0 > 0$ and takes no place under the strategy (3.1.15). Therefore, we have to introduce the upper level of control (Principal) responsible for sustainable development maintenance. Such models are studied below.

Three-level control models for investment and construction projects with corruption. In the general form, the mathematical model of hierarchical control in a three-level system can be defined by

$$\begin{aligned} & g_1(x_1, x_2) \to \max, \quad x_1 \in X_1; \\ & g_2(x_2, x_3) \to \max, \quad x_2 \in X_2(x_1); \\ & g_3(x_2, x_3) \to \max, \quad x_3 \in X_3(x_2). \end{aligned} \tag{3.1.16}$$

Here x_1, x_2, x_3 denote the control vectors of Principal, supervisor and agent, respectively. Principal controls the admissible control domain of supervisor, while supervisor controls the admissible control domain of agent. We suggest the following two-stage solution procedure for the problem (3.1.16) (Antonenko et al, 2011).

Stage 1. Fix the Principal's control x_1 as a parameter and consider the hierarchical supervisor-agent game

$$g_2(x_2, x_3) \to \max, \quad x_2 \in X_2(x_1);$$
$$g_3(x_2, x_3) \to \max, \quad x_3 \in X_3(x_2).$$

The supervisor's optimal guaranteeing strategy $\tilde{x}_2{}^*(x_3)$ calculated by Germeier's theory represents a function $x_2(x_1)$ of the Principal's control actions.

Stage 2. Principal solves the optimization problem

$g_1(x_1, x_2(x_1)) \to \max, \quad x_1 \in X_1$ taking into account the sustainable development requirements $x_2 \in X_2{}^*$.

To proceed, illustrate this procedure for different models of administrative and economic corruption in the three-level controls systems for ICPs. Consider the administrative corruption model

$$\begin{aligned} &g_P(q,s) = p_1(s - s_0) - \frac{q}{s_0 - q} \to \max, \quad 0 \le q \le s_0; \\ &g_S(s,b) = p_2(s - s_0) + bc[(r + \xi(c)(1-r))u + \gamma\eta(\gamma)(1-u)] \to \max, \quad q \le s \le s_0; \\ &g_A(b,u) = c(1-b)[(r + \xi(c)(1-r))u + \gamma\eta(\gamma)(1-u)] \to \max, s \le u \le 1, 0 \le b \le 1. \end{aligned} \tag{3.1.17}$$

Here u is the share of social real estate in the total building volume of agent; b designates the bribe share of the income; c indicates the price of social real estate; r gives the share of social real estate with guaranteed government purchase at the price c; $\xi(c)$ is the estimated share of social real estate sold independently by agent at the price c; $\gamma > 1$ specifies the price coefficient for higher-class real estate; $\eta(\gamma)$ denotes the estimated share of higher-class real estate sold independently by agent; s is the quota of social real estate; s_0 signifies the statutory minimum share of social real estate in the total building volume; q acts as the Principal's control parameter of quota fulfillment; and finally, $p_1, p_2 > 0$ are the penalty coefficients of Principal and supervisor, respectively, for nonfulfilling social real estate quotas.

The administrative corruption model assumes that $r = const$, $\tilde{s} = s(b)$. The homeostasis condition has the form $s \ge s_0$; in case of its breach, Principal and supervisor are imposed penalties with the coefficients p_1 and p_2, respectively. According to the suggested procedure, at Stage 1 we study the hierarchical supervisor-agent game. Note that the function g_A achieves its maximum in u independently from u. Owing to the linearity of the function g_A in u, the agent's problem has the solution

$$u^* = \begin{cases} 1, & r + \xi(c)(1-r) \ge \gamma\eta(\gamma), \\ s, & \text{otherwise}. \end{cases}$$

Consider these cases in separate.

1. $r+\xi(c)(1-r)\geq\gamma\eta(\gamma)$, i.e., sales of cheap social real estate are more profitable in comparison with expensive higher-class real estate. Here the game disappears: for $u=1$ the function g_A does not depend on s. The agent's optimization problem possesses the trivial solution $b=0$, i.e., corruption takes no place.

2. $r+\xi(c)(1-r)<\gamma\eta(\gamma)$, which means that sales of expensive real estate are more attractive. This case brings to the hierarchical two-player game

$$g_S(s,b)=p_2(s-s_0)+cb[r+\xi(c)(1-r)-\gamma\eta(\gamma)]\to\max,\quad q\leq s\leq s_0;$$
$$g_A(s,b)=c(1-b)[(r+\xi(c)(1-r)-\gamma\eta(\gamma))s+\gamma\eta(\gamma)]\to\max, 0\leq b\leq 1.$$

Germeier's theory yields

$$s^P(b)\equiv s_0;\quad s^D(b)=\begin{cases}s_0, & p_2>bc(r+\xi(c)(1-r)-\gamma\eta(\gamma)),\\ q, & \text{otherwise;}\end{cases}$$

$$L_A=c[(r+\xi(c)(1-r)-\gamma\eta(\gamma))s_0+\gamma\eta(\gamma)];\ E_A=\{b=0\};$$
$$D_A=\{(s,b):g_A(s,b)>L_A\}=\varnothing,\ \text{so long as}$$
$$(1-b)[(r+\xi(c)(1-r)-\gamma\eta(\gamma))s+\gamma\eta(\gamma)]\leq(r+\xi(c)(1-r)-\gamma\eta(\gamma))s_0+\gamma\eta(\gamma)$$

under $0\leq b\leq 1, q\leq s\leq s_0$. Here we believe that $K_1=-\infty<K_2$, and therefore

$$\tilde{s}^*(b)=\begin{cases}s^D(b), & b=0,\\ s_0, & \text{otherwise,}\end{cases}=\begin{cases}q, & p_2<bc(r+\xi(c)(1-r)-\gamma\eta(\gamma))\wedge b=0,\\ s_0, & \text{otherwise.}\end{cases}$$

However, the conditions $p_2<bc(r+\xi(c)(1-r)-\gamma\eta(\gamma))$ and $b=0$ are inconsistent, and so $\tilde{s}^*(b)\equiv s_0$. The agent's optimization problem has the solution $b^*=0$ (no corruption), $u^*=s_0$, and the Principal's interference for sustainable development maintenance is not required. Accordingly, at Stage 2 Principal merely faces the control costs minimization problem $\frac{q}{s_0-q}\to\min,\quad 0\leq q\leq s_0,$ which possesses the trivial solution $q^*=0$ (as the Principal's interference is unnecessary).

Consider the administrative corruption model in a slightly modified setting:

$$g_P(q,s)=p_1(s-s_0)-\frac{q}{s_0-q}\to\max,\quad 0\leq q\leq s_0;$$
$$g_S(s,b)=p_2(s-s_0)+bc[u+m(1-u)]\to\max,\quad q\leq s\leq s_0; \tag{3.1.18}$$
$$g_A(b,u)=(1-b)c[u+m(1-u)]\to\max,\quad s\leq u\leq 1,\quad 0\leq b\leq 1.$$

As against the model (3.1.17), we have added $m > 1$ as the price coefficient for higher-class real estate. Recall that the function g_A decreases in u. Hence, $u^* = s$ and the following two-player hierarchical game occurs at Stage 1:

$$g_S(s,b) = p_2(s - s_0) + bc[m - (m-1)s] \to \max, \quad q \le s \le s_0;$$
$$g_A(s,b) = c(1-b)[m - (m-1)s] \to \max, \quad 0 \le b \le 1.$$

Application of Germeier's theory leads to

$$s^D(b) = \begin{cases} s_0, & p_2 > bc(m-1), \\ q, & \text{otherwise}; \end{cases} \quad s^P(b) \equiv s_0; \quad L_A = c(m - (m-1)s_0); \quad E_A = \{b = 0\};$$

$K = p \max\limits_{q \le s \le s_0} (s - s_0) = 0$ as far as again

$D_A = \{(s,b) : (1-b)(m-(m-1)s) > m - (m-1)s_0\} = \varnothing$, then $K_1 = -\infty < K_2$,

and

$$\tilde{s}^*(b) = \begin{cases} s^D(b), & b = 0, \\ s_0, & \text{otherwise}, \end{cases} = \begin{cases} q, & p_2 < bc(m-1) \wedge b = 0, \\ s_0, & \text{otherwise}, \end{cases} \equiv s_0.$$

Consequently, in this model corruption vanishes, the homeostasis condition holds true and Principal's control becomes unreasonable ($q^* = 0$).

Consider the economic corruption model in the three-level control system

$$g_P = H(c) + M(r_0 - r) \to \min, \quad 0 \le c \le 1;$$
$$g_S = f(1)(b + cr) \to \max, \quad 0 \le r \le r_0;$$
$$g_A = f(1)(1 - b - r) \to \max, \quad 0 \le b \le 1,$$

which generalizes the model (3.1.9). Here $H(c)$ is an increasing costs function of Principal and M denotes its penalty coefficient in case of breaking the homeostasis condition $r = r_0$. The supervisor's optimal guaranteeing strategy has the form

$$\tilde{r}^*(b) = \begin{cases} 0, \; b = r_0 - \varepsilon \wedge c < 1 - \dfrac{\varepsilon}{r_0}, \\ r_0, \; \text{otherwise.} \end{cases}$$

If $b \ne r_0 - \varepsilon$, then $r \equiv r_0$ and the Principal's optimization problem possesses the trivial solution $c = 0$. Under $b = r_0 - \varepsilon$, Principal ensures the homeostasis condition only by choosing $c = 1$. Therefore, its optimization problem has the solution

$$c^* = \begin{cases} 1, & H(1) < Mr_0, \\ 0, & \text{otherwise.} \end{cases}$$

Principal has to compare the penalty for homeostasis breach with the costs of its maintenance. And finally, consider the generalized model of corruption in the three-level control system, which covers administrative and economic corruption as special cases. The model is described by

$$g_P(a,c) = k_1(c - c_0) - \frac{k_2 a}{c_0 - a} \to \max, \quad 0 \le a \le c_0;$$
$$g_S(c,b) = b(1-c) \to \max, \quad a \le c \le 1;$$
$$g_A(c,b) = (1-b)(1-c) \to \max, \quad 0 \le b \le 1.$$

The supervisor's control variable c plays the role of quota (administrative corruption) or penalty/tax (economic corruption). The supervisor's payoff function decreases in c (control costs). Similarly, the agent's payoff function decreases in c (activity constraints). Therefore, the interests of the both players have same direction in c. The game (conflict of interests) arises in terms of the variable b (bribe): supervisor benefits from higher bribe amount, whereas agent strives for its minimization. The Principal's control variable a affects the actual value of c; the coefficient $k_1 > 0$ defines the unit penalty imposed on Principal for breaking the homeostasis condition $c \ge c_0$; the coefficient $k_2 > 0$ determines the control costs of quota fulfillment. Germeier's theory yields

$c^P(b) \equiv 1$; $c^D(b) \equiv a$; $L_A = 1 - a$; $E_A = \{b = 0\}$; $D_A = \{(c,b) : (1-b)(1-c) > 1 - a\} = \varnothing$, hence, $K_1 = -\infty < 0 = K_2$, and the supervisor's optimal strategy takes the form

$$\tilde{c}^*(b) = \begin{cases} a, & b = 0, \\ 1, & \text{otherwise.} \end{cases}$$

This strategy seems rather paradoxical: under refusal of bribery (the agent's worst strategy for supervisor), supervisor still chooses $c = a$ (most profitable option for agent); in the rest cases, supervisor applies the penalty strategy. The total satisfaction of the homeostasis condition ($a = c_0$) requires infinitely large costs from Principal. Therefore, the latter prefers its optimal strategy $a^* = c_0 - \sqrt{\frac{k_2 c_0}{k_1}}$, as a sufficiently good approximation of the solution to the sustainable management problem.

3.2. Control Models of Production Systems

Consider quality assessment models in production systems with corruption (Kornienko, 2011; Kornienko and Ougolnitsky, 2010). According to the rigorous definition in the Russian legislature, corruption is abuse of office, giving a bribe, taking of a bribe, abuse of power, secret commission or other illegal use of official capacity by an individual in contravention of legal interests of a society and government for the sake of deriving gains in the form of money, valuables, other property or associated services, other property rights, either for this individual or for third parties.

Models will comprehend a gains-deriving individual as an individual assessing the quality of a production system (inspector). It is responsible for measuring quality indices and supervising satisfaction of certain requirements established by Principal (some government authority). Principal applies sanctions to an enterprise in case of requirements nonsatisfaction. An abuse is any information misrepresentation to Principal and any expansion of admissible ranges for measured indices. By assumption, gains have the form of money bribes.

Our intention is endeavoring to apply hierarchical control models of sustainable development to problems arising in the optimization-based quality management model. Hierarchical control and optimization methods have to-be-designed at the next level when Principal varies appropriate parameters in order to affect the solution of an associated hierarchical game and solve its own optimization problem. We also employ quality management principles including the process approach as a fundamental idea (Deming, 2007). Integration of quality management and sustainable management was proposed in the monograph (Ougolnitsky, 2011).

$$p(q) - r \rightarrow \max, \quad (q, r) \in S, \tag{3.2.1}$$

where $q = (q_1, \ldots, q_m)$ is the quality indices vector, r means production costs, $p(q)$ specifies the sales income from products with the quality indices q, S forms the set of admissible production strategies.

Quality indices describe consumer- and production-related attributes of products (e.g., environmental impact). We believe that all indices are normalized and take values from the range [0, 1], and for each index comparison relations enjoy transitivity. The boundaries of the range (0 and 1) are not necessarily achieved. The production system model under consideration is static, which means that income and costs are calculated for the whole reference period. The control subject cannot change its strategy during this period. Decision-making takes place at the beginning of the reference period. The set S is Pareto optimal, i.e., better value of a quality index corresponds to higher costs:

$\forall\, (q_1, r_1) \in S, (q_2, r_2) \in S : (q_1 > q_2) \Rightarrow (r_1 > r_2)$, where by definition $q_1 > q_2$, if $\forall i \in 1, \ldots, m : q_{1i} \geq q_{2i}$, $\exists j \in 1, \ldots, m : q_{1j} > q_{2j}$.

The set S may have different structure (e.g., discrete, continuous or piecewise continuous) depending on feasible alternatives in production strategies choice.

Therefore, we consider an image S of the production control parameters set P on the plane (q, r) such that $S = PO(f(P))$, where $P = \{(p_1, \ldots, p_n)\}$, f denotes the production function, and PO is the transformation function of the initial set to the Pareto optimal one. Each parameter p_i possesses its definition domain and corresponds, e.g., to different raw material suppliers, a selected production technology, the presence of intermediate quality control at some stage, concentrations of certain substances, i.e., generally belongs to an arbitrary-structure set.

Suppose that for each element in the set S one can define its preimage in the set P, i.e., values of the control parameters $p \in P$ leading to given $(r,q) \in S$. Whenever such a correspondence appears nonunique, all alternatives within the model are assumed to have identical economic efficiency and we simply choose any of them. Consequently, it suffices (a) to solve the posed problem on the set S instead of the whole set P and (b) apply the inverse function f^{-1} to the obtained solution. In this case, we comprehend the solution of the problem (3.2.1) as a pair $(q,r) \in S$ and as a corresponding set of parameters $(p_1,..., p_n) \in P$.

The homeostasis condition implies that all essential indices of system functioning belong to given ranges. For an enterprise, the homeostasis requirement includes quality production, adequate wages of employees, environmental safety of production in terms of natural resources usage and pollution. The formal homeostasis conditions for index i can be expressed by

$$q_i \geq a_i, \quad 0 \leq a_i \leq 1, \quad i = 1,..., m, \tag{3.2.2}$$

where a_i determines the minimum admissible value of this index. If an index has no imposed constraints, then $a_i = 0$. Figure 3.2.1 demonstrates an example of the set S for the quality index. Here oblique crosses indicate admissible strategies outside S, since they are dominated by other strategies. The points q_1, q_2 do not satisfy the homeostasis condition $q_i \geq a_0$. In this example, q_3 is the optimal point for agent.

And so, we explore the *problem considering the homeostasis requirements*:

$$p(q) \to \max, \quad (q,r) \in S \cap A, \quad A = [a_1,1] \times ... \times [a_m,1] \times [0,\infty). \tag{3.2.3}$$

Since the homeostasis conditions narrow the set S, the maximum profits evaluated under these conditions decrease or remain same. This creates prerequisites for neglecting the homeostasis conditions in pursuit of higher profits.

According to ISO 9000 standards, any activity has to-be-treated as a manufacturing process (GOST R ISO, 2008). Within an organization, these processes interact in a complicated way, thereby forming a system or network of processes. Each process transforms some labor object and has an input and an output. Output means (material and nonmaterial) products yielded by a process. For instance, an output is a document, a software product, a chemical substance, a bank service, medical equipment or intermediate products of any general category. An input of a process is material or nonmaterial products or natural raw materials.

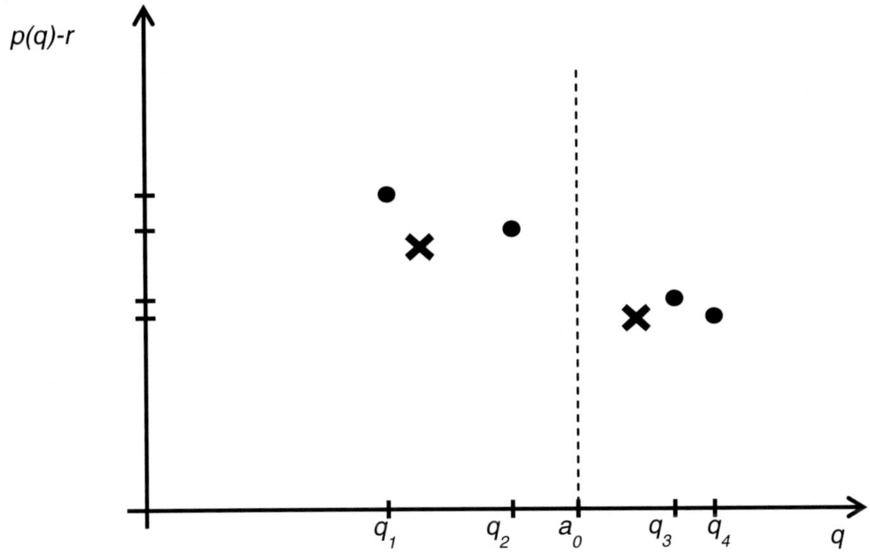

Figure 3.2.1. An example of the set S.

ISO 9000 standards proceed from an assumption that each organization performs work on product value adding. This work is performed through a network of processes. The network has a complex structure, as most processes interact with each other. Therefore, organization management is impossible without control of its processes.

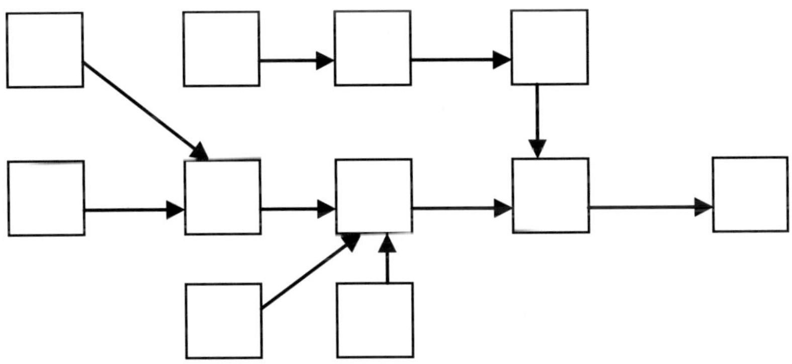

Figure 3.2.2. An example of a tree-type production structure.

Consider a production system (Figure 3.2.2) representing a tree D = (X,U), oriented to the root. Let X be the set of processes (vertices) and U denote the set of product flows between these processes (arcs).

During transition from one process to another, product flow is characterized by two quantities, *viz.*, the quality indices vector q and the production costs r. Each process of the production system has an associated process function, i.e., an input-output flow transformation. This function is multidimensional so that each its component answers to a quality index and the last one reflects the costs. All components satisfy nonstrict monotonicity with respect to each variable. And so, each process corresponds to a set of process functions. By-turn, each element of this set corresponds to a certain strategy for the process. For instance, the matter concerns different production technologies, different types of resources or different levels of intermediate quality control. Moreover, processes can have different number of strategies. Agent aims at choosing an optimal set of strategies yielding maximum profits. This set shows which strategy should be applied for each process. In the general case, a process includes several input flows. Then output flow characteristics represent some functions of all these variables. The initial process has no input flow. The output of the last process comes to a client and exactly its characteristics determine the agent's profits.

The above description of the production system allows constructing the Pareto optimal strategy set S step-by-step, from one process to another. Here we employ the dynamic programming principle: for each process, find the set of all undominated output flows and for each such flow find the optimal strategy set comprising the strategy for this process and all preceding processes.

Really, monotonicity of process functions guarantees the following. Whenever an input flow is dominated by another one, for any strategy the output flow of the former is not better than that of the latter. Hence, at each step we cast away all strategy sets a fortiori yielding nonoptimal results. This eliminates the need for considering all admissible combinations of process strategies. And the set of undominated flows of the last process corresponds to the desired set S.

To solve the problem (3.2.3) by the described method, we have developed an application using *Java* platform and *NetBeans 6.9* package.

A major difficulty in programming has been the need for independent input of appropriate functions by a user. *Java* is an object-oriented language and functions can be defined only as methods of classes. A possible solution lies in choosing a function from a given set and specifying associated parameters. Here one should create an interface for a process function and several classes realizing this interface. However, such an approach makes the resulting application inflexible and rules out rather complicated and nontrivial functions as input data.

An alternative solution implies creating a dedicated class for expression identification, which dramatically enlarges the class of input parameters. However, this solution seems comparatively slow and causes certain problems connected with realization of complex functions (e.g., the ones containing conditional operators and loops). The set of elementary functions available in expressions becomes limited, too.

We have selected a third approach employing *ScriptEngine* class from *javax.script.** package. This class executes a *JavaScript* code. As a result, *Parser* class has been defined with the static method *double eval(String s, ArrayList<Double> q, double r)*. The role of input parameters belongs to the characteristics of process input flow and a string containing the *JavaScript* code of a function. The method returns the value of a function described by s depending on specified characteristics. To construct the set S, we have adopted the following classes: *Stream*, which stores flow characteristics and the numbers of process strategies inducing this flow; *Process*, which stores process name, the strategy set, and a calculation method for the Pareto optimal set of all admissible output flows; *Agent*, which contains information on the set of processes and income functions. It includes calculation methods for the set S (considering the homeostasis conditions or not) and profits yielded by each strategy.

For the sake of easy data input, the application also generates process functions of a given form with random parameters. To construct the set S, appropriate methods are sequentially called all processes starting from the first process. For each admissible input flow, the application finds all admissible output flows (depending on process strategies). Output flows are placed in a special set; whenever their adding violates Pareto optimality, unnecessary elements are removed. The application constructs the set S, as well as evaluates the strategies yielding the maximum profits (subject to the homeostasis conditions or not).

Now, consider *the corruption model in the two-level inspector-agent control system*. As we have mentioned, the homeostasis conditions are not always beneficial for agent. Establishing these conditions, Principal has to control their satisfaction. Principal often represents a legislative body, a local authority or a certifying organization. Hence, direct control of homeostasis maintenance by Principal is hardly possible, which leads to the need for inspectors. Let us analyze the following scheme of hierarchical system operation. An organization (i.e., a production enterprise) acts as a controlled system. A control subject is agent, *viz*., organization's top management choosing a production strategy. The model is static, and we believe that agent knows the system response (the quality indices vector q and the costs r) to each control vector p. In addition, agent knows the homeostasis conditions established by Principal (which forms an external subject in the model).

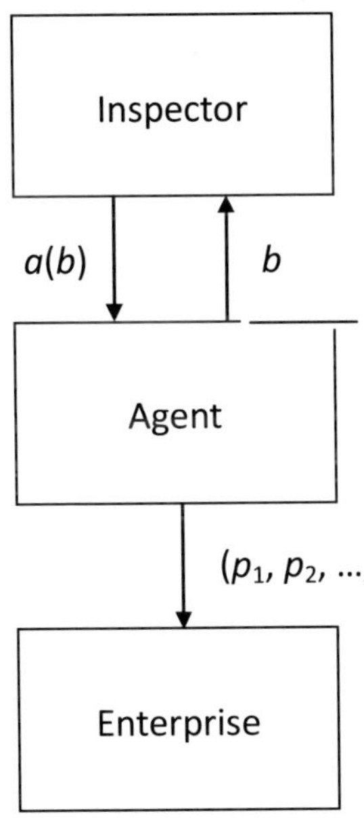

Figure 3.2.3. The two-level inspector-agent hierarchical system with impact exerted on enterprise.

The second subject is inspector as a person responsible for homeostasis conditions control in the system. For simplicity, we begin with the assumption that inspector controls a quality index and receives adequate accurate information about its value. If the homeostasis conditions hold true, additional measures are not required. Whenever they are violated, agent has to eliminate this drawback. Furthermore, an additional penalty can be imposed for homeostasis breach. Its amount depends on the existing deviation between the real value of the quality index and its statutory value. Ideally, inspector is an unbiased person without personal interests, performing its functions honestly. Inspector has a fixed payoff (wage) predefined by Principal. The agent's penalty (if any) goes completely to Principal. However, the case can be somewhat different in practice.

Modify the described model as follows. Suppose that inspector can expand the homeostasis domain for a controlled quality index. Of course, this is done for some compensation from agent. Such a situation occurs when an audit performed by inspector reveals homeostasis breach. The inspector-agent hierarchical system is shown by Figure 3.2.3.

The audit procedure of quality index i includes the following sequence of actions:

1. Principal reports the admittance limits vector determining the homeostasis conditions: component i of this vector is a_0.
2. Agent chooses a control strategy which makes control index i equal to q_T and incurs costs r_T. Note that the homeostasis condition can be violated.
3. Inspector checks the value of quality index i and finds q_T.
4. If $q_T < a_0$, inspector reports a function $a(b)$ to agent. This function shows the dependence of the tolerance limit a on bribe amount b.
5. Agent chooses bribe amount b, pays it to inspector and passes to a new production strategy which satisfies the new tolerance limit $q_T \geq a(b)$. Moreover, passing to the new strategy, agent suffers from additional costs due to production changes and (if necessary) pays penalties for initial norms nonfulfilment.

Imagine that agent has no idea about the interval of quality audit and quality index to-be-checked. In this case, corruption in the two-level system affects only actions 3-5. Here the reference period starts when agent passes to the new production strategy (more specifically, when the tolerance limit for the quality index is satisfied, whether it has be modified or not). We proceed to the mathematical description of this model as a complicated version of the model (3.2.3). The agent's objective function g_2 is its profits as the income from new quality indices minus the new production costs, the paid bribe and the penalty function for changed strategy:

$$g_2(a,b,q,r) = p(q) - r - b - d(q,q_T) \to \max,\ b \geq 0, (q,r) \in S, q_i \geq a(b), \quad (3.2.4)$$

where i designates the number of audited quality index; b specifies the bribe paid to inspector; $a(b)$ gives the new tolerance limit for quality index i; q forms the new quality indices vector; r describes the new production costs; S is the admissible strategy set; and finally, d represents the penalty function for transition from the old strategy ensuring the quality indices q_T to the new strategy. This function covers additional costs due to production changes and penalties for initial norms nonfulfilment.

The role of controlled parameters belongs to the new production strategy and the bribe amount offered to inspector. The domain of the production strategy is the admissible strategy set with the new admittance limit for checked quality index i. The domain of the bribe amount on [0, +∞) is defined by the function $a(b)$.

The inspector's objective function also answers its profits, with elimination of its fixed wage. Actually, it coincides with the bribe amount paid by agent:

$$g(a,b) = b \to \max_{a(b)}. \tag{3.2.5}$$

Inspector implements control by choosing $a(b)$. This function has to obey the following constraints:

$$a(0) = a, \quad q_T \le a(b) \le a_0. \tag{3.2.6}$$

The equality constraint means that inspector applies capture, i.e., the statutory admittance limits are guaranteed in the absence of bribery. According to the two-sided inequality constraint, inspector can extend the admittance limit up to the current value of the checked quality index. Further extension seems pointless, as agent disagrees to reduce a quality index if the current strategy is admissible. Another reasonable condition is the nonstrict monotonicity of $a(b)$: higher bribe amounts correspond to same or greater admittance limits.

The above statement of the problem is game-theoretic, as far as subjects pursue different interests. Higher bribe amounts appear beneficial to inspector and nonbeneficial to agent. The objective functions of both players depend on the opponent's strategies. This game is hierarchical in the following sense. The first move belongs to inspector, who reports the response function to bribe amount. And the next move is made by agent, who chooses the bribe amount and the values of controlled parameters. Of course, moving first, inspector (Leader) strives for maximizing its guaranteed payoff after strategy choice of agent (Follower). Here Germeier game Γ_2 seems most adequate. However, the agent's objective function possesses too complex form.

For reducing this game to the canonical form Γ_2, let us slightly modify the agent's objective function. Making its move, agent chooses the bribe amount and the production strategy. The latter choice does not affect the inspector's objective function. At the same time, this choice depends on the admittance limit.

Introduce the function

$$u(a) = \max_{(q,r)\in S, q_i \ge a} (p(q) - r - d(q, q_T)), \tag{3.2.7}$$

which describes the solution to the profits maximization problem under the given tolerance limit a. For each a, agent can evaluate this function without information about the inspector's strategy. According to formula (3.2.7), the above function is nonincreasing and defined on the whole segment [0,1]. It gets maximized at the point q_T, as agent benefits nothing from further decrease of the quality index.

Therefore, the problem (3.2.4)-(3.2.6) can be rewritten in the form

$$g_1(a,b) = b \to \max, \quad q_T \le a \le a_0, \quad a(0) = a_0;$$
$$g_2(a,b) = u(a) - b \to \max, \quad b \ge 0. \tag{3.2.8}$$

This model fits Germeier game Γ_2 with inspector as Leader and agent as Follower. The above considerations are easily applied to the case when inspector audits several quality indices simultaneously. Then the inspector's strategy becomes a multidimensional vector, and the dimensionalities of the set D_2 and the function u both grow, too. The solution procedure and the final result remain unchanged: the inspector's optimal strategy contains two points corresponding to the current system state and the homeostasis conditions.

To construct the solution of the game (3.2.8), we again employ Germeier's theorem, see Section 2.1. The inspector's objective function has no explicit dependence on the established tolerance limit. Hence, the Leader's dominating strategy $a^D(b)$ is any value of a. The choice of a_0 as the limit seems most grounded: inspector has not to break the law: $a^D(b) = a_0$, $g_1(a^D(b),b) = \max\limits_{a\in[q_T,a_0]} g_1(a,b) = b$.

The Leader's penalty strategy $a^P(b)$ lies in agent's compulsion to homeostasis condition fulfillment: $a^P(b) = a_0$. The Follower's maximum payoff under the Leader's penalty strategy makes up $L_2 = \max\limits_{b\ge 0} g_2(a_0,b) = u(a_0)$. In this case, agent varies the production strategy so that the checked quality index obeys the statutory admittance limits. Of course, here bribery is unnecessary and the Follower's optimal strategy under the Leader's penalty strategy takes the form $E_2 = \{0\}$.

Consider the set $D_2 = \{(a,b): u(a) - b > u(a_0)\}$. An example of the set D_2 is shown by Figure 3.2.4. The step boundary of this set answers the shape of the function $u(a)$. The quantity b^* is the maximum bribe amount agent can offer inspector for establishing the admittance limit $a = q_T$.

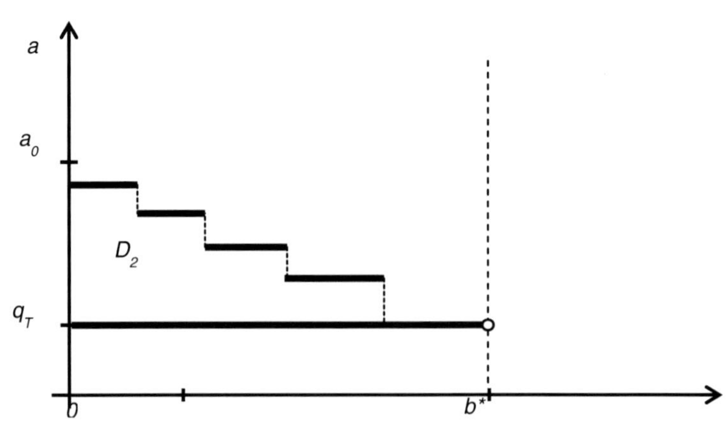

Figure 3.2.4. An example of the set D_2.

Bribery is economically sound for agent exactly under such combinations of the bribe amount and the tolerance limit. Next, we have that

$$K_1 = \sup_{(a,b)\in D_2} g_1(a,b) = b^*; \quad (x_1^\varepsilon, x_2^\varepsilon): g_1(x_1^\varepsilon, x_2^\varepsilon) \geq K_1 - \varepsilon; \quad x_1^\varepsilon = q_T, x_2^\varepsilon = b^* - \varepsilon;$$

$$K_2 = \max g_1(a,0) = 0.$$

Since $K_1 > K_2$, the Leader's optimal strategy

$$a^\varepsilon(b) = \begin{cases} q_T, b = b^* - \varepsilon, \\ a_0, \quad otherwise. \end{cases} \tag{3.2.9}$$

To evaluate b^*, construct the set D_2 on the plane $(u(a), b)$. The function $u(a)$ is monotone and the domain D_2 has the form illustrated by Figure 3.2.5. Clearly, $b^* = u(q_T) - u(a_0)$. Thus, the solution of the game (3.2.8) is the pair $(a^\varepsilon(b), u(q_T) - u(a_0))$, and the associated values of the objective functions make up $g_1^* = u(q_T) - u(a_0) - \varepsilon, \; g_2^\varepsilon = u(a_0) - \varepsilon$.

A considerable disadvantage of the Leader's optimal strategy (3.2.9) is that inspector must know the function $u(a)$. According to (3.2.7), this function has a rather complex structure, being defined by the profit function, production costs and the penalty function. During audit, inspector acquires reliable information on the current value of the checked quality index merely.

Inspector actually does not need the full knowledge of the function u. For optimal strategy evaluation it suffices to have estimates for two points. Suppose that inspector possesses sufficient information about the market to construct the distribution of the values $u(q_T), u(a_0)$ (denote them by u_T, u_0, respectively): $u_0 \in N(\mu_1, \sigma_1), u_T \in N(\mu_2, \sigma_2)$. In this case,

$$b^* \in N(\mu_2 - \mu_1, \sqrt{\sigma_1^2 + \sigma_2^2}) = N(\mu, \sigma).$$

Inspector chooses some value b_0 as the estimate of u^* and employs it to design the corruption strategy

$$a_0^\varepsilon(b) = \begin{cases} q_T, b \geq b_0, \\ a_0, otherwise. \end{cases}$$

The strategy is reported to agent and there appear two possible situations:

1. The point (q_T, b_0) belongs to the domain D_2. In this case, Follower gives the bribe b_0, and inspector dissembles the detected breach. The corresponding payoffs of the players make up $g_1^* = u(q_T) - u(a_0) - b_0$, $g_2^* = b_0$.
2. The point (q_T, b_0) belongs to the domain D_2. Agent chooses zero bribe and achieves the homeostasis conditions. Inspector receives nothing: $g_1^* = u(q_T) - u(a_0)$, $g_2^* = 0$.

Inspector knows the distribution of b^* and calculates the probability

$$P(b^* > b_0) = \frac{1}{\sigma\sqrt{2\pi}} \int_{b_0}^{\infty} e^{-\frac{(s-\mu)^2}{2\sigma^2}} ds.$$

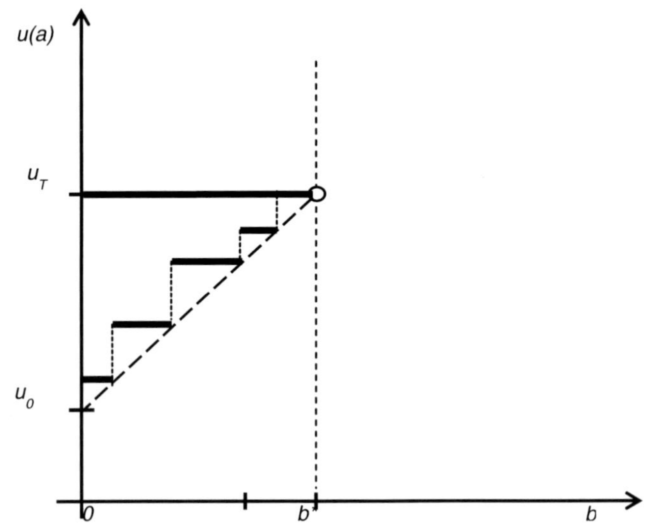

Figure 3.2.5. The set D_2 on the plane $(b, u(b))$.

Hence, the inspector's objective function can be modified as follows:

$$f(b_0) = \begin{cases} b_0, b^* > b_0, \\ 0, \textit{otherwise}. \end{cases}$$

This brings to *the maximization problem of the inspector's expected payoff*

$$E[f(b_0)] = \frac{b_0}{\sigma\sqrt{2\pi}} \int_{b_0}^{\infty} e^{-\frac{(s-\mu)^2}{2\sigma^2}} ds \to \max_{b_0}. \quad (3.2.10)$$

The central limit theorem justifies the choice of the normal distribution. We believe that production costs comprise very many random factors such as purchase prices, employee wages, equipment maintenance costs. However, such an approach is imperfect. For instance, the normal distribution yields a nonzero probability of $b^* = 0$. This complicates petty corruption modeling (small bribes), and, in this case, one should prefer other distributions without the described drawback (e.g., the lognormal distribution or the Rayleigh distribution). In this situation, agent can make the first move by reporting an amount it is willing to pay to inspector. Inspector compares this value with the expected payoff and, depending on its attitude to risks, agrees with the offered bribe or suggests another strategy.

Using *Maple*, we have solved the problem (3.2.10) under different distribution parameters of b^*. Figure 3.2.6 demonstrates the inspector's payoff function and its derivative for $b^* \in N(50,15)$.

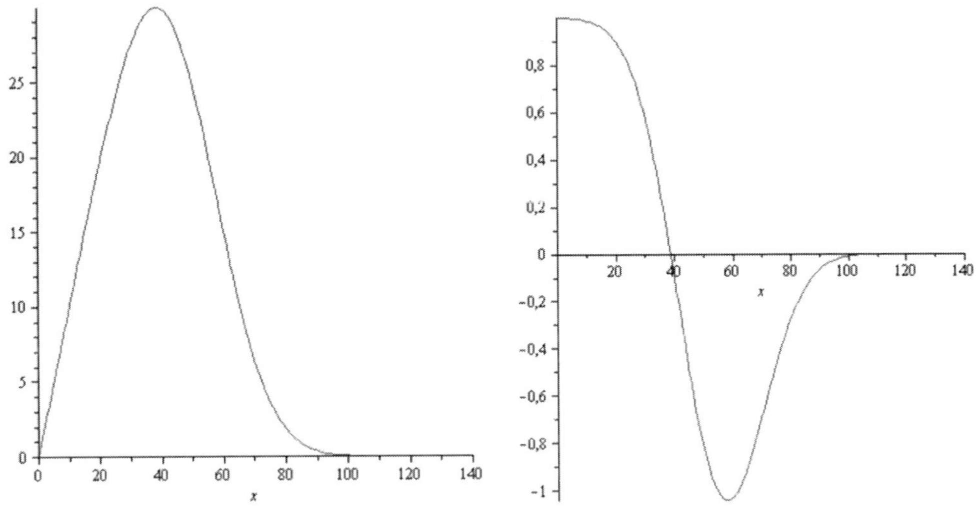

Figure 3.2.6. The inspector's payoff function and its derivative for the normal distribution.

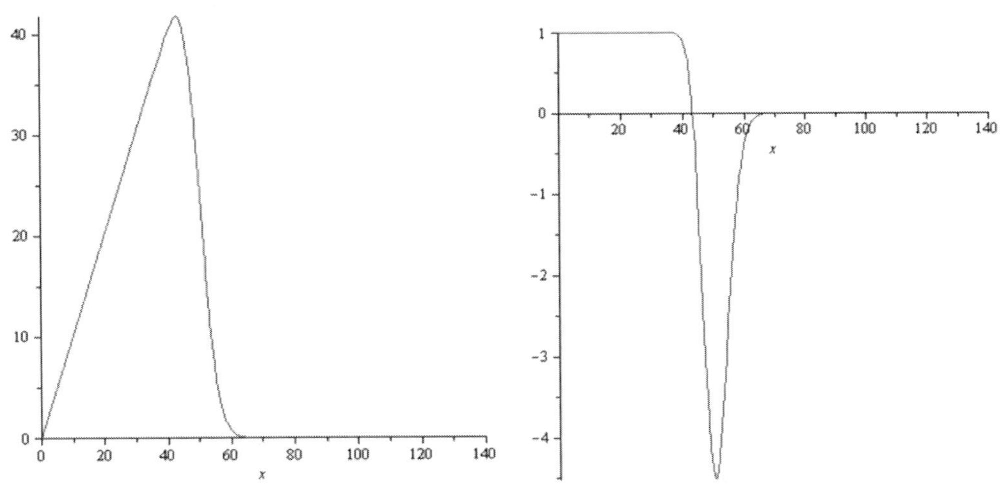

Figure 3.2.7. The inspector's payoff function and its derivative for the lognormal distribution.

Moreover, numerical experiments have yielded the optimal value of b_0 from the inspector's view: $b_0^* = 38.69$. But the expected payoff is smaller than the exacted bribe: $E[f(b_0^*)] = 29.97$. The lognormal distribution with same mean and variance has increased the optimal bribe amount from the inspector's view and the expected payoff (43.26 and 41.75, respectively, see Figure 3.2.7).

Within the framework of this two-level corruption model, Principal does not interfere into the inspector's activity. Any corruption interactions go unpunished. Therefore, the inspector's optimal strategy consists in maximum violation of the homeostasis conditions in exchange for the maximum bribe agent is willing to pay.

Principal is not at all happy with such a situation. First, the matter concerns considerable breach of the homeostasis conditions, causing environmental damage, health hazard for clients and quality standards discredit. Second, Principal does not know real quality indices to-be-reported by inspector. And third, Principal suffers from appreciable losses associated with elimination of homeostasis breach consequences. Furthermore, enterprises do not pay penalties, as the facts of homeostasis violation are not formally fixed. All these factors make anti-corruption measures vital. An obvious measure is establishing penalties for corruption actions, applied to agent and/or inspector. Consider different approaches to anti-corruption struggle, formalized by the following hierarchical system of models.

The inspector penalization model under agent's refusal of bribery bases on the model (3.2.10). Now, agent may inform Principal about the fact of extortion by inspector. Then the latter pays a penalty defined by Principal (a certain function of exacted bribe and new admittance limit). We begin with the case when the penalty depends on exacted bribe only. Here the admittance limit does not affect the Leader's payoff, the penalty strategy and the domain D_2 remain invariable, and the optimal strategy is same. But b_0 is evaluated taking into account the penalty. The inspector's payoff takes the form

$$f(b_0) = \begin{cases} b_0, b^* > b_0, \\ -x(b_0), \ \textit{otherwise}. \end{cases}$$

Inspector aims at expected payoff maximization; this payoff is independent from the agent's choice of b predetermined by the inspector's strategy and b^*:

$$E[f(b_0)] = b_0 P(b^* > b_0) - x(b_0)(1 - P(b^* > b_0)) \to \max_{b_0} .$$

Here $x(b_0)$ denotes a penalty function established by Principal and known to inspector. Actually, this function is statutory and defined in advance. An elementary example lies in a constant penalty function (a fixed penalty independent from bribe amount). More complicated variants include penalties proportional to bribe amounts or piecewise continuous penalty functions. In the latter case, penalties are calculated by certain formulas on dedicated intervals. According to Remark 1 to Article 290 in the Criminal Code of the Russian Federation (CC RF), a considerable bribe is a bribe in an amount exceeding \$500, a grand bribe is a bribe in an amount exceeding $3000, and a serious bribe is a bribe in an amount exceeding $20000. Table 3.2.1 illustrates the existing statutory sanctions for bribery in the Russian Federation.

Table 3.2.1. Sanctions for bribery according to Articles 290, 291 of CC RF

Body of a crime	Sanctions for taking a bribe (Article 290 of CC RF)	Sanctions for giving a bribe (Article 291 of CC RF)
Common bribe	Penalty in the size of 25–50 bribe amounts with ban of holding certain positions or performing certain activity for up to 3 years, **or** imprisonment for up to 3 years with penalty in the size of 20 bribe amounts	Penalty in the size of 15–30 bribe amounts, **or** imprisonment for up to 2 years with penalty in the size of 10 bribe amounts
Considerable bribe	Penalty in the size of 30–60 bribe amounts with ban of holding certain positions or performing certain activity for up to 3 years, **or** imprisonment for up to 6 years with penalty in the size of 30 bribe amounts	Penalty in the size of 20–40 bribe amounts, **or** imprisonment for up to 3 years with penalty in the size of 15 bribe amounts
Grand bribe	Penalty in the size of 70–90 bribe amounts, **or** imprisonment for 7-12 years with ban of holding certain positions or performing certain activity for up to 3 years penalty and penalty in the size of 60 bribe amounts	Penalty in the size of 60–80 bribe amounts with ban of holding certain positions or performing certain activity for up to 3 years, **or** imprisonment for 5-10 years with penalty in the size of 60 bribe amounts
Serious bribe	Penalty in the size of 80–100 bribe amounts with ban of holding certain positions or performing certain activity for up to 3 years, **or** imprisonment for 8-15 years with penalty in the size of 70 bribe amounts	Penalty in the size of 70–90 bribe amounts, **or** imprisonment for 7-12 years with penalty in the size of 70 bribe amounts

In the general case, the Principal's problem consists choosing a penalty function so that the agent's expected payoff is negative (for any b_0 or values within some domain only). Then inspector benefits nothing from suggesting weaker tolerance limits in exchange for a bribe offered by agent.

Designate by $F_{b*}(b_0) = P(b^* \leq b_0)$ the probability distribution function of b^*. For given b_0, Principal strives for satisfying the inequality

$$x(b_0) \geq \frac{b_0(1 - F_{b*}(b_0))}{F_{b*}(b_0)}.$$

As a matter of fact, it is not easy to choose an appropriate penalty function: it applies to all enterprises on the market and, possibly, to all quality indices. Moreover, Principal faces obvious difficulties in assessing b^*, as (in contrast to inspector) Principal does not know the current value of the quality index q_T.

The described model suffers from an essential drawback, since agent displays small interest in exposure of the inspector's illegal activity under petty corruption. A way out of the situation is to introduce an impulsion mechanism for the agent's cooperation with Principal (e.g., in the form of costs reduction in passing to a new production strategy). However, such an approach possesses disadvantages, too. First, agent can provoke inspector's bribery and report about the latter's illegal activity. Second, agent benefits even more from initial homeostasis breach: during audit, agent pays off using an acceptable bribe or receives privileges for cooperation with Principal. The major shortcoming of the model is that the inspector's payoff directly depends on its awareness about the real value of b^*. The penalty increases even if the variance of the corresponding random variable tends to zero (i.e., inspector defines the agent's losses due to elimination of homeostasis breach with high accuracy). In the limit case when inspector knows the exact value of b^*, even the maximum possible penalty becomes inefficient, since agent benefits more via bribery with probability 1.

Now, consider the case when *the penalty function depends on the admittance limit.* Such a setting brings to the following optimization problem:

$$K_1 = \sup_{(a,b)\in D_2} (bP(b^* > b) - x(a,b)(1 - P(b^* > b))).$$

Its solution is less trivial and directly depends on the form of $x(a,b)$. It may happen that inspector reduces the tolerance limits to some intermediate value (instead of the current value of the quality index). Still, the general tendency and the major shortcoming remain same: the exact value of b^* being known, any penalty sanctions fail in corruption elimination.

And finally, take the three-level hierarchical system (Figure 3.2.8) representing a generalization of the system in Figure 3.2.3.

Define the objective functions of all system participants including the Principal's objective function g_0:

$$g_0(a,b,c) = c + z(a) - l_1^*(a,b,c) - l_2^*(a,b,c) \to \min_{c,l_i};$$

$$g_1(a,b,c) = b - l_1^*(a,b,c) \to \max_{a(b)};$$

$$g_2(a,b,c) = u(a) - b - l_2^*(a,b,c) \to \max_{b}, \tag{3.2.11}$$

where c indicates the costs of anti-corruption measures applied by Principal; $z(a)$ is the Principal's losses due to homeostasis breach, $z(a_0)=0$; $l_1(a,b,c)$ specifies the penalty imposed on inspector; $l_2(a,b,c)$ means the penalty imposed on agent; l_1^*, l_2^* are functions describing the shares of the Principal's utility in the penalties. These functions are introduced, since statutory sections have different forms (money, ban of holding certain positions within definite periods, imprisonment). For such measures, one can calculate losses of law breaker; but they have no benefit for Principal. The penalty functions vanish in the absence of corruption or the Principal's costs: $l_i(a_0,0,c)=l_i(a,b,0)=0,\ i=1,2$.

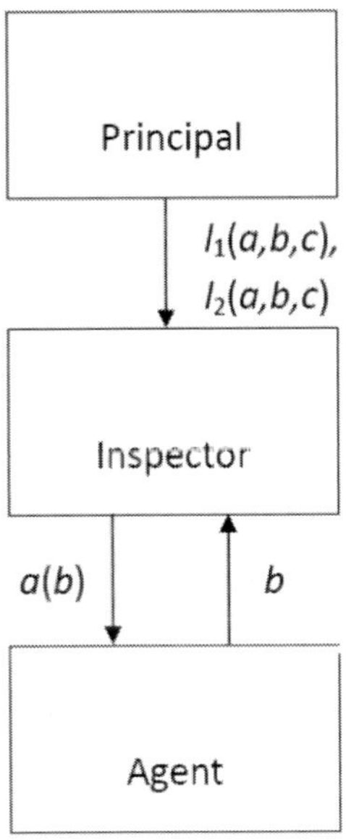

Figure 3.2.8. The three-level "Principal – inspector – agent" hierarchical system.

In the general case, the Principal's control parameters are the penalty functions, the shares of the Principal's utility in the penalties and the costs of anti-corruption measures c. However, in real situations sanctions for corruption can be statutory and municipal or federal authorities (Principal) appear unable to control these parameters except c. We will adhere to this case. Consider the penalty functions

$$l_i(a,b,c)=p(a,c)s_i(a,b), \quad i=1,2 .$$

Here $p(a,c)$ is the probability of corruption detection, which increases for higher costs c of anti-corruption measures and smaller tolerance limits a. The last property means that, the more agent breaks the homeostasis conditions, the easier Principal detects this breach, *ergo* inspector's dishonesty. However, this dependence is not a common rule. In contrast to penalty size, Principal can adjust the intensity of anti-corruption measures and, as a result, the probability of corruption detection for each enterprise independently (e.g., by scheduling of future audits). Next, the function $s_i(a,b)$ specifies the penalty size, $s_i(a,0)=0$, $p(a,0)=0$. The model (3.2.11) takes the form

$$
\begin{aligned}
&g_0(a,b,c) = c + z(a) - l_1^*(a,b,c) - l_2^*(a,b,c) \to \min_c; \\
&g_1(a,b,c) = b - p(a,c)s_1(a,b) \to \max_{a(b)}; \\
&g_2(a,b,c) = u(a) - b - p(a,c)s_2(a,b) \to \max_b,
\end{aligned}
\tag{3.2.12}
$$

Under the above assumptions, the general solution algorithm of the problem (3.2.12) can be described in the following way:

1. For a fixed parameter c, agent and inspector finds a solution of the hierarchical game Γ_2, i.e., the penalty size and the admittance limit. This solution depends on the parameter c.
2. Principal chooses an appropriate value of the parameter c in order to minimize its objective function.

As an example, imagine that the penalty function is defined according to Table 3.2.1. Consider the case of monetary penalty only (no ban of holding certain positions or performing certain activity and no imprisonment). Let the penalty sizes coincide with the upper boundaries of the corresponding intervals. Then the penalty functions acquire the form

$$
s_1(b) = \begin{cases} 50b, & b \in [0,500], \\ 60b, & b \in (500,3000], \\ 90b, & b \in (3000,20000], \\ 100b, & b \in (20000,\infty); \end{cases}
\qquad
\widetilde{s}_2(b) = \begin{cases} 30b, & b \in [0,500], \\ 40b, & b \in (500,3000], \\ 80b, & b \in (3000,20000], \\ 90b, & b \in (20000,\infty); \end{cases}
$$

$$
s_2(a,b) = \widetilde{s}_2(b) - u(a) + u(a_0).
$$

Additional terms in the function s_2 mean that, in the case of corruption detection, agent still has to satisfy the initial homeostasis condition. These terms are not included in the Principal's payoff function: $l_1^*(a,b) = p(a,c)s_1(b)$; $l_2^*(a,b) = p(a,c)\widetilde{s}_2(b)$. Set

$$
s^*(b) = \begin{cases} 80b, b \in [0,500], \\ 100b, b \in (500,3000], \\ 170b, b \in (3000,20000], \\ 190b, b \in (20000,\infty). \end{cases}
$$

Consequently, the problem (3.1.12) acquires the form

$$g_0(a,b,c) = c + z(a) - p(a,c)s^*(b) \rightarrow \min_c;$$
$$g_1(a,b,c) = b - p(a,c)s_1(b) \rightarrow \max_{a(b)};$$
$$g_2(a,b,c) = u(a) - b - p(a,c)s_2(a,b) \rightarrow \max_b,$$

Apply the suggested algorithm to this problem. Consider the case $p(a,c) = p(c)$, as this appreciably simplifies solution of the game Γ_2. Solve the inspector-agent game with the parameter c. The Leader's penalty strategy is still refusal of granting privileges in exchange for bribe: $a^P(b) = a_0$. In comparison with the model (3.2.8) analyzed before, changes affect definition of the domain D_2:

$D_2 = \{(a,b) : g_2(a,b,c) > u(a_0)\}$, whence it follows that
$(1 - p(c))(u(a) - u(a_0)) - b - p(c)\tilde{s}_2(b) > 0$.

The domain corresponding to the last inequality is similar to the domain D_2 constructed for the model (3.2.8), see Figure 3.2.5. Find the maximum value of *b* within this domain:

$$b_i^* = \min\{\frac{(1 - p(c))(u(a) - u(a))}{1 + p(c)k_i}, e_i\}, \tag{3.2.13}$$

where k_i is the coefficient held by b in row *i* of the inspector's penalty function, e_i means the right boundary of the interval in row *i*. And finally, we obtain that

$$b^* = \max_{1 \le i \le 4} b_i^*. \tag{3.2.14}$$

Due to the above assumptions, the inspector's optimal strategy still lies in granting the minimum admissible tolerance limit in exchange for bribe: its objective function does not incorporate it. Actually, Leader solves the problem

$g_1(b,c) = b - p(c)s_1(b) \rightarrow \max,\ 0 \le b \le b^* - \varepsilon$, whence it follows that
$b_0 = \arg \max\limits_{0 \le b \le b^* - \varepsilon} (b - p(c)s_1(b))$.

So long as $s_1(0) = 0$, then $g_1 \ge 0$ and equality here corresponds to zero bribe. Suppose that in this case inspector establishes the tolerance limit a_0, as it has no economic incentives to vary the homeostasis conditions. Therefore, the inspector's optimal strategy is the function

$$a_0^{\varepsilon}(b) = \begin{cases} q_T, b = b_0 \neq 0, \\ a_0, \ otherwise. \end{cases}$$

Economically rational agent has a unique response to this strategy: $b = b_0$.

Now, switch to stage 2 of the algorithm. Find c minimizing the Principal's objective function:

$$g(a,b,c)=c+z(a)-s^*(b)\to\min_c.$$

Optimal a and b in the inspector-agent game are expressed through c:

$$g_0(a(c),b(c),c) = \begin{cases} c + z(q_T) - p(c)s^*(b_0(c)), \ b_0(c) > 0, \\ c, \ b_0(c) = 0. \end{cases}$$

We have in mind that $b_0(0) > 0$, i.e., $g_0(0) = z(q_T)$, $p(c)$ is a nondecreasing function. Suppose that there exists a nondecreasing function $c(p)$ such that $c(p) = \min\{c : p(c) > p\}$. According to (3.2.13)-(3.2.14), for higher values of c the quantity b^* goes down. The parameter b_0 also decreases, as far as (1) penalties grow and (2) the maximization interval gets narrower. Readers can easily receive evidence that

$$b_0 = 0 \Leftrightarrow \forall b > 0 \ b - p(c)s_1(b) \le 0 \Leftrightarrow \forall b > 0 \ p(c) \ge \frac{b}{s_1(b)}.$$

The last inequality holds true under the condition

$$p(c) \ge \frac{b}{b \min\limits_{1 \prec i \le 4}\{\tilde{k}_i\}} = \frac{1}{50},$$

where $\tilde{k}_i$ is the coefficient held by b in row *i* of the inspector's penalty function.

For large c inspector refuses of bribery. But the Principal's objective function also grows; therefore, if is its optimal strategy, then $0 \le c^* \le c(1/50)$. In this case, whenever the Principal's highest priority belongs to anti-corruption struggle, its optimal strategy is $c^* = c(1/50)$.

We have to answer the last question: does Principal benefit from maintaining a certain level of corruption in order to minimize its own costs? In other words, does an internal maximum point exist? The Principal's payoff function has a discontinuity at the point $c(1/50)$. And so, first estimate $g_0(a(c),b(c),c)$ as $c \to c(1/50) - 0$; then $a(c) = q_T$.

For simplicity of calculations, denote $U = u(a) - u(q_T)$ It appears that, if $z(q_T) < \frac{8}{5}\min\{e_1, 49U/80\}$, Principal really benefits from maintaining a nonzero level of corruption. Common bribes become nonbeneficial for Principal under $z > 40000$. For $p(c) \in (0, 0.001)$, one can demonstrate the following result. If $U > 1.92$ and $z(q_T) < 0.99U$, Principal benefits more from maintaining the maximum possible level of corruption than from eliminating it completely.

Once again, take notice that agent's additional penalization after bribery detection facilitates corruption growth. For instance, let the function U also include a compensation of the Principal's losses (or environmental damage) in the form $z(q_T)$. Then Principal prefers dissembling corruption with an appreciably higher probability. Moreover, only very large companies with huge profits afford such bribes. And a possible anti-corruption measure consists in small business development.

In the described model Principal does not participate in corruption directly. It even allocates financial resources on anti-corruption measures and imposes penalties of bribers (ideally, these penalties cover damage due to homeostasis breach). Nevertheless, under definite parameter values Principal has no economic incentives for complete victory over corruption, as it requires higher costs of breach detection and leads to the absence of penalties. At the legislative level, monetary penalties for corruption can be replaced by other sanctions, e.g., criminal responsibility in the form of imprisonment. On the one part, this makes Principal unmotivated: monetary penalties disappear. On the other part, such a policy promotes corruption in the Principal-inspector pair.

Summarizing the outcomes, we have described corruption in quality management of production systems using a sequence of gradually complicated mathematical models. First, we have stated a production system model and the agent's optimization problem (production income maximization). Next, we have added subject 2 (inspector) and considered an associated model based on hierarchical game Γ_2. Several modifications of this model have been discussed, with transition from the deterministic setting to the probabilistic objective functions. And finally, we have incorporated subject 3 (Principal) as the upper level of the hierarchical system. Initially, its objective function has been homeostasis maintenance, i.e., anti-corruption struggle. Then we have performed transition to a new (complicated) model, where Principal joins the game and possesses its own payoff function. The solution of this problem has been constructed by solving a parametric hierarchical game at the lower level and performing subsequent optimization of parameter values from the Principal's position.

In addition to gradual model complication, we have employed the principle of transition from generalized models to concrete ones. For instance, arbitrary-form penalty functions defined by Principal have been concretized according to current legislature. An important result is the description of situations when complete victory over corruption becomes nonbeneficial for Principal. The suggested models and algorithms have been tested on a series of examples using the software complex and proved their applicability. The process approach to production system description and the user's input of almost any-complexity functions appreciably extends the class of admissible input data (Kornienko, 2011).

Let us describe a model of corruption relations arising in electricity consumption accounting (Antonenko and Ougolnitsky, 2014). During read-outs, inspectors acting in collusion with clients introduce illegal modifications into electricity meters (mount jumpers, add extra winding) in order to underestimate appreciably the amount of consumed electricity. Consider the hierarchical systems "Principal (electricity supplier) – supervisor (inspector) – agent (consumer enterprise)." The economic relations in the electricity stealing prevention problem (i.e., the problem of underestimated electricity consumption) have the following form:

The Principal's payoff = its income from electricity supply – the supervisor's bonus – the costs of stealing control.

The supervisor's payoff = its bonus + kickback – penalty in case of detected underestimation.

The agent's payoff = its income from underpayment – kickback.

Introduce the following notation: p is the share of the electricity supplier's income allocated to the supervisor's bonus; q means the share of detected facts of underestimation; b specifies the share of kickback; s gives the electricity consumption reported by inspector (kWh); r represents the actual electricity consumption (KWh); c indicates the price of 1 kWh ($/kWh) $(c = 3.45)$; a designates the costs of detecting all facts of underestimation (RUB); and finally, is a penalty applied in case of detected underestimation ($/kWh).

Therefore, cs gives the supplier's income, pcs yields the inspector's bonus, $c(r - s)$ is the price of hidden electricity consumption (income from underpayment), makes up the kickback, aq corresponds to the costs of stealing control, and $Mq(r - s)$ is the penalty applied in case of detected underestimation of $r - s$. The model can be rewritten as

$$g_P(p,q,s) = (1-p)cs - aq \to \max, \quad 0 \le p \le 1, \quad 0 \le q \le 1; \tag{3.2.15}$$

$$g_S(p,q,s,b) = pcs + (bc - Mq)(r - s) \to \max, \quad 0 \le s \le r; \tag{3.2.16}$$

$$g_A(s,b) = c(1-b)(r-s) \to \max, \quad 0 \le b \le 1. \tag{3.2.17}$$

First, consider the model from the agent's position, see the payoff function (3.2.17). Suppose that the "informational corruption" function $s = s(b)$ is known. In the elementary case, we have a linear function of bribe amount:

$$s(b) = r(1 - b). \tag{3.2.18}$$

In the absence of corruption $(b = 0)$, inspector reports the actual consumption to Principal ($s = r$). And no consumption $(s = 0)$. is reported under the maximum possible kickback $b = 1$. The agent's optimization problem acquires the form

$g_A(b) = crb(1-b) \to \max, \quad 0 \le b \le 1$, and the obvious solution is $b^* = 1/2$, bringing to

$s^* = r/2,\ g_A(b^*) = cr/4,\ cb^*(r - s^*) = cr/4,\ g_P(p,q,s^*) = (1-p)cr/2 - aq$.

Under 50% kickback, the half of the maximum possible income of the supplier is equally shared by corrupt supervisor and agent! Accordingly, the real income of the supplier constitutes less than 50% of its maximum possible counterpart due to the supervisor's bonus and the costs of stealing control.

Here the major problem consists in proper identification of the function $s = s(b)$ so that it gives an adequate description of real corruption: formula (3.2.18) provides merely a rough approximation. For instance, power functions of the form $s(b) = r(1-b)^k$ yield $b^* = 1 - \frac{1}{(k+1)^{1/k}}, s^* = \frac{r}{k+1}$; the only admissible case is $k \geq 1$, as otherwise inspector prefers electricity consumption overestimation. Nevertheless, even these trivial assumptions show serious economic grounds for corruption.

Analysis of the supervisor's optimization problem (3.2.16) leads to the following strategy-proofness condition for the consumption report mechanism:

$$\mathrm{Mq} \geq \mathrm{c(b - p)}. \tag{3.2.19}$$

In this case, $s^* = r$, i.e., supervisor benefits from truth-telling (reporting the actual consumption). On the contrary, supervisor would dissemble electricity consumption $(s^* = 0)$. whenever the condition (3.2.19) fails.

Now, consider the hierarchical game Γ_2 (3.2.16)-(3.2.17) between supervisor and agent, with the Principal's control actions p, q as parameters. Then

$$s^P(b) \equiv r; \quad s^D(b) = \begin{cases} r, & Mq \geq c(b-p); \\ 0, & \text{otherwise}; \end{cases}$$

$$L_A = 0; \quad E_A = [0,1] = X_A; \quad D_A = \{(s,b) : (1-b)(r-s) > 0\} = [0,r) \times [0,1);$$
$$K_2 = \min_{0 \leq b \leq 1} \max_{0 \leq s \leq r} g_S(s,b) = \max_{0 \leq s \leq r}(pc + Mq)s = (pc + Mq)r$$

To evaluate K_1, we have to solve the problem

$$\begin{array}{l} (pc + Mq - bc)s \rightarrow \max \\ (1-b)(r-s) > 0, \quad 0 \leq b \leq 1, \quad 0 \leq s \leq r; \end{array} \quad \text{or} \quad \begin{array}{l} (pc + Mq - bc)s \rightarrow \max \\ 0 \leq b < 1, \quad 0 \leq s < r \end{array}.$$

The solution is $K_1 = (pc + Mq)(r - \varepsilon) < K_2$, and the supervisor's optimal guaranteeing strategy (i.e., the control mechanism supervisor reports to agent as its behavioral rule) takes the form

$$\tilde{s}^*(b) = \begin{cases} r, & Mq > c(b-r), \\ 0, & \text{otherwise}. \end{cases}$$

Owing to this rule, agent chooses its kickback from the condition $b > r + Mq / c$ for avoiding the penalty strategy $s^P(b) = r$ applied by supervisor.

Thus, for any kickback (a) supervisor benefits from truth-telling under the strategy-proofness condition (3.2.19) and (b) supervisor benefits from dissembling the consumption (maximum underestimation) if the condition (3.2.19) is violated. For electricity stealing prevention, Principal must ensure the condition (3.2.19) via hierarchical control methods (compulsion or impulsion) (Ougolnitsky, 2010).

Compulsion $(p = const)$.

$$\begin{array}{l} -aq \to \max \\ 0 \le q \le 1 \\ q \ge \dfrac{c(b-p)}{M} \end{array} \quad \text{or} \quad \begin{array}{l} aq \to \min \\ \dfrac{c(b-p)}{M} \le q \le 1 \end{array}.$$

This problem has the obvious solution

$$q^* = \begin{cases} 1, \dfrac{c(b-p)}{M} > 1, \\ \dfrac{c(b-p)}{M}, \quad 0 \le \dfrac{c(b-p)}{M} \le 1, \\ 0, \quad \text{otherwise.} \end{cases}$$

Impulsion (q = const) .

$$\begin{array}{l} cs(1-p) \to \max \\ 0 \le p \le 1 \\ p \ge b - \dfrac{Mq}{c} \end{array} \quad \text{or} \quad \begin{array}{l} cs(1-p) \to \max \\ b - \dfrac{Mq}{c} \le p \le 1 \end{array}.$$

Again, the obvious solution is

$$p^* = \begin{cases} 1, b - \dfrac{Mq}{c} > 1, \\ b - \dfrac{Mq}{c}, 0 \le b - \dfrac{Mq}{c} \le 1, \\ 0, \quad \text{otherwise.} \end{cases}$$

The higher is the share of kickback, the greater Principal's efforts are required to struggle against corruption using administrative or economic methods. Under some parameter values, the optimal solution becomes economically inefficient, as Principal has to allocate all income to bonus and stealing control (Antonenko and Ougolnitsky, 2014).

3.3. Models of Resource Allocation

This section considers a river water quality control model, *viz.*, a resource allocation problem in a hierarchical control system and a quality control problem for river water

(Gorbaneva, 2010; Gorbaneva and Ougolnitsky, 2013, 2014). First, we solve the resource allocation problem in the absence of corruption, in the cases of capture and extortion during resource allocation, as well as under a corruption mechanism in resource use control. Then we solve the quality control problem for river water in a two-level control system and the resource allocation problems in a three-level system, where the upper level monitors the development of the whole system and affects corruption in it.

Imagine a certain tree-type control system, e.g., an enterprise headed by a general manager and composed of several departments or a network of enterprises (a holding) guided by a management company. This superior subject (the general manager or the management company, respectively) monitors the economic activity of subordinate departments or enterprises and exerts an impact if necessary.

The superior subject has a certain amount of resources to-be-allocated among enterprises. The latter use resources for producing goods and gaining profits from sales. Obviously, each department seeks to obtain as much resources from the superior subject as possible.

During their activity, departments create waste products affecting adversely environmental conditions. These products are released in the form of waste water into some water body (a river system) or in the form of atmospheric emissions. The higher is the scale of production, the more pollutants are discharged into environment.

There is a certain supervising authority responsible for the environmental conditions of a corresponding district (particularly, an object waste water is released into). The supervising authority can influence enterprises by compelling their waste water treatment or imposing penalties for object pollution. If enterprises have insufficient treatment rates, the supervising authority purifies waste water independently out of penalties paid by enterprises.

Thus and so, we consider a hierarchically controlled system (see Figure 3.3.1) with the following elements:

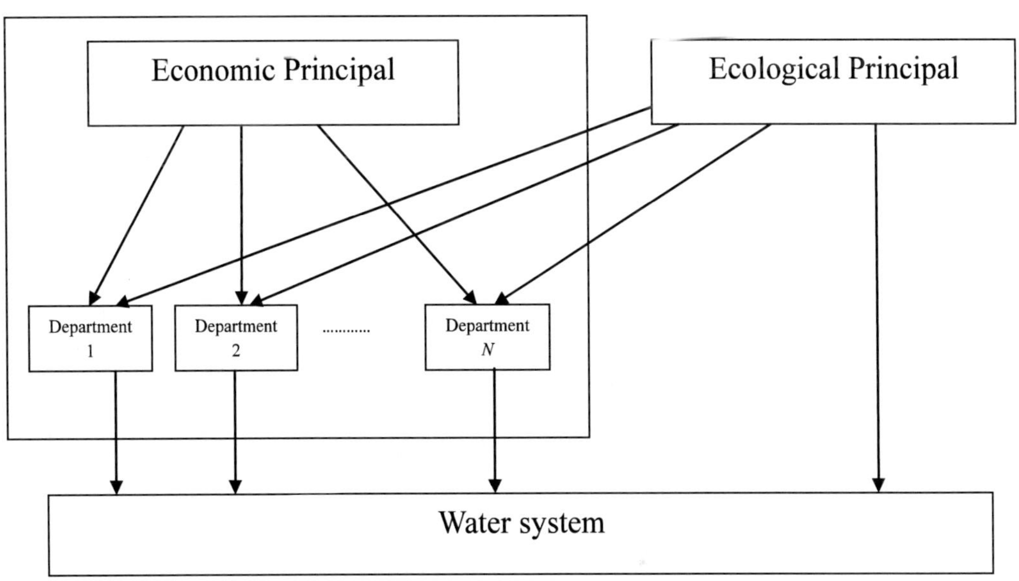

Figure 3.3.1. The diagram of the hierarchically controlled system.

- two upper-level control subjects:
  - Economic Principal;
  - Ecological Principal;
- N lower-level control subjects (the departments of Economic Principal); we will call them Subordinates;
- the controlled system (the river system).

Principals exert their impacts on Agents and Agents exert their impacts on the river system. Economic Principal has no influence on the river system, Ecological Principal can influence it only if Subordinates treat waste water insufficiently: the state of the river system goes beyond the admissible levels.

Consider each of the elements in detail (Gorbaneva, 2010):

1) Agent uses resources allocated by Principal to produce goods. Principal has a limited amount of resources and other Agents also pretend to them. In order to receive as much resources as possible, Agent can offer a bribe to Economic Principal (a share of the amount of resources allocated by Principal). A problem solved by Agent is to distribute a received amount of resources between:

a) the production process;

b) the bribe offered to Economic Principal

so that to maximize the profits from its activity.

Exerting an impact on the river body, Agent strives for its profits maximization, which contradicts the goal of Ecological Principal. For higher profits, Agent must receive more resources from Economic Principal; the more resources Agent obtains, the greater is its production output and the greater amount of waste water Agent releases into the river system; the greater is the amount of waste water released, the worse are the environmental conditions of the river system; and finally, the worse are the environmental conditions of the river system, the higher penalties Agent pays to Ecological Principal. A possible solution of this problem lies in waste water purification by its own means with a given treatment rate. In other words, the second problem of Agent is to choose an appropriate treatment rate of waste water so that to minimize the costs of water treatment and the penalties for water pollution.

2) Economic Principal manages some economic system. It disposes of a limited amount of resources (for convenience, 1) to-be-allocated among Agents so that their production yields the maximum profits to Economic Principal. The matter can be complicated by the following circumstances:

a) Knowing that Agent possibly spends obtained resources not only on production (system objectives) but also on partial interests, Economic Principal can assign a minimum share of resources intended for the system objectives.

b) If Agent tries to bribe Economic Principal for obtaining a higher amount of resources, the latter has to find out which quantity is greater: payoff from bribery or losses from resource nonallocation to more profitable Agents.

3) Ecological Principal. Its primary goal consists in ensuring some objective requirements to the state of the river system. For this, Ecological Principal establishes the following types of penalties for Agent: penalties for admissible pollution (within admissible environmental levels), penalties for inadmissible pollution (beyond admissible but within critical

environmental levels), and penalties for excessive pollution (beyond critical environmental levels).

If Agents do not purify their waste water appropriately (getting away with payments), Ecological Principal does this job independently. In other words, the Ecological Principal's problem is to design a penalty system by maximizing the difference between the penalties collected from Agents and its water purification costs.

4) The river system undergoes waste water release by Agents and water treatment by Agents and Ecological Principal.

Consider the goals and capabilities of each system participant:

1) Economic Principal. This Principal has to allocate resources among Agents in order to maximize profits from the production process of all Subordinates, i.e., to maximize the objective function $\sum_{i=1}^{n} g_i(u_i r_i)$, where $g_i(u_i r_i)$ is the system payoff from production of Agent i, r_i means the share of resource allocated to Agent i (from the total amount $R = 1$), and u_i specifies the share of resources used by Agent i to achieve the system objectives.

The following factors should be taken into account:

a) Economic Principal can establish a minimum share q_i of resources Agent i must spend on the system objectives: explore resource allocation under corruption

$$0 \le q_i \le 1.$$

In other words, q_i gives the lower bound of u_i supervised by Economic Principal;

b) A bribe b_i offered by Agent i to Economic Principal can influence the amount of allocated resources ($r_i = r_i(b_i)$) or the minimum share ($q_i = q_i(b_i)$). The additional profits of Economic Principal in the form of potential bribes must be included in its objective function.

The objective function of Economic Principal comprises two terms, *viz.*, the total income from production of all Agents and the income from misused resources (the income from bribery):

$$J_0 = \sum_{i=1}^{n} g_i(u_i r_i) + \sum_{i=1}^{n} b_i r_i(b_i) \to \max. \tag{3.3.1}$$

Economic Principal defines a minimum share q_i of resources Agent i must spend on the system objectives:

$$0 \le q_i \le 1. \tag{3.3.2}$$

The amount of resources allocated by Economic Principal to Agent i will be measured in percentage or as a share of all resources available to this Principal:

$$0 \le r_i(b_i) \le 1 \tag{3.3.3}$$

Economic Principal disposes of a limited amount of resources (100% or 1); hence,

$$\sum_{i=1}^{n} r_i(b_i) \le 1. \tag{3.3.4}$$

The Economic Principal's problem consists in maximization of the objective function (3.3.1) subject to the constraints (3.3.2)–(3.3.4).

The choice of this Principal affects the following quantities: the shares r_i allocated to different Subordinates and the minimum shares q_i supervised by it.

The quantities r_i and q_i will be measured as shares (not absolute values), since the total amount of resources available to Economic Principal makes up 1 and the bribe b_i represents a share of resources allocated by Economic Principal to Agent *i* (a share of r_i).

2) Ecological Principal. To maintain the necessary environmental state of the river system, Ecological Principal applies the following types of penalties to Agents:

A) penalties K_{ch} for inadmissible pollution (beyond admissible but within critical environmental levels),

B) penalties K_{ca} for excessive pollution (beyond critical environmental levels).

There exist certain thresholds K_{chmax}, K_{camax} of the penalties, i.e.,

$$0 \le K_{ch} \le K_{ch\max}; \; 0 \le K_{ca} \le K_{ca\max}.$$

Whenever the amount of released pollutants by Agent is within the admissible level, the Agent pays nothing for waste water. If the amount of released pollutants by Agent exceeds an admissible level $\tilde{w}_1$, but does not exceed a critical level $\tilde{w}_2$, Ecological Principal imposes the penalty K_{ch} for unit amount of released pollutants above the admissible level $\tilde{w}_1$. In other words, Agent *i* pays the penalty for $(w_i(1-p_i)-\tilde{w}_1)$ units of pollutants, where s_i denotes a penalty function for water pollution (established outside this ecological system, e.g., by government); w_i indicates the amount of released pollutants prior to their treatment by Agent *i*; p_i specifies the waste water treatment rate applied by Subordinate *i* and $w_i(1\text{-}p_i)$ describes the amount of pollutants released after their treatment by Agent *i*.

Waste water not properly treated by Agents is purified by Ecological Principal. Denote by $c_a(y)$ the Ecological Principal's cost function of river water purification, where y is the amount of pollutants of all Agents after water treatment, i.e.,

$$y = \sum_{i=1}^{n} w_i(1-p_i).$$

The objective function of Ecological Principal represents the penalties collected from all Agents minus its costs of river water purification:

$$G_0 = -c_a(y) + \sum_{j=1}^{n} K_{ch} s_i\left(w_i(1-p_i)-\tilde{w}_1\right) \to \max_{Kch}. \tag{3.3.5}$$

The Ecological Principal's problem lies in maximization of the objective function (3.3.5) subject to the constraint

$$0 \le K_{ch} \le K_{ch\max}. \tag{3.3.6}$$

If the amount of pollutants released by Agent after waste water treatment exceeds the critical level $\widetilde{w}_2$, Ecological Principal imposes the penalty K_{ch} for unit amount of released pollutants above the admissible level $\widetilde{w}_1$ and the penalty K_{ca} for unit amount of released pollutants above the critical level $\widetilde{w}_2$. In other words, Agent i pays the first penalty for $(\widetilde{w}_2 - \widetilde{w}_1)$ units of pollutants and the second penalty for $(w_i(1-p_i) - \widetilde{w}_2)$ units of pollutants.

The pollutants after waste water treatment by Agents in the amount of $y = \sum_{i=1}^{n} w_i(1-p_i)$ are purified by Ecological Principal with the cost function $c_a(y)$.

The objective function of Ecological Principal represents the penalties collected from Subordinates minus its costs of river water purification:

$$G_0 = -c_a(y) + \sum_{j=1}^{n} K_{ch} s_i (\widetilde{w}_2 - \widetilde{w}_1) + \sum_{j=1}^{n} K_{ca} s_i (w_i(1-p_i) - \widetilde{w}_2) \to \max_{K_{ch}, K_{ca}} \tag{3.3.7}$$

subject to the constraints (3.3.6) and

$$0 \le K_{ca} \le K_{ca\max}. \tag{3.3.8}$$

Agents. Each Agent i uses resources allocated by Economic Principal for production (the system objectives) and the corresponding income is expressed by a production function $g_i(x)$. For obtaining as much resources as possible, Agent i can offer a bribe to Economic Principal, i.e., a certain share b_i of the amount r_i of resources allocated by this Principal. The obtained amount r_i is spent by Agent i on the system objectives (the amount $u_i r_i$) and bribery (the amount $b_i r_i$), which means that $b_i + u_i \le 1$.

Agent i must spend on the system objectives at least the minimum share q_i defined by Economic Principal, i.e., $q_i(b_i) \le u_i \le 1$.

A bribe represents a share of resources allocated by Economic Principal to Agent i, and hence $0 \le b_i \le 1$.

Producing goods, Agent i pollutes the river system by waste water and accordingly pays a statutory penalty s_i per unit amount of released pollutants; whenever the amount of released pollutants exceeds the admissible or critical level, Agent i either pays extra penalties established by Ecological Principal for excess pollution or purifies its waste water with a chosen treatment rate p_i (measured as a share or percentage of the amount w_i of released substances) incurring the costs $c_p(p_i)$. The water treatment level p_i belongs to the range

$$0 \le p_i \le 1-\varepsilon,$$

where ε specifies the minimum share of pollutants in waste water, i.e., perfect purification (100%) is impossible. The gap ε depends on water treatment equipment applied by Agent.

If after waste water purification the amount of pollutants still exceeds the admissible or critical level, Agent pays an appropriate penalty.

The Agent's objective function represents the income from its production activity minus the payments to government or Ecological Principal and the costs of waste water purification.

If the amount of released pollutants after purification is smaller than the admissible level ($0 \le w_i(1-p_i) \le \widetilde{w}_1$), the Agent's objective function takes the form

$$y_i^{(0)} = g_i(u_i r_i) - w_i C_p(p_i) - s_i w_i (1-p_i) \to \max_{u_i, b_i, p_i}. \tag{3.3.9}$$

If the amount of released pollutants after purification is greater than the admissible level but smaller than the critical level ($\widetilde{w}_1 \le w_i(1-p_i) \le \widetilde{w}_2$), the Agent's objective function takes the form

$$y_i^{(1)} = g_i(u_i r_i) - w_i C_p(p_i) - s_i \widetilde{w}_1 - K_{ch} s_i (w_i(1-p_i) - \widetilde{w}_1) \to \max_{u_i, b_i, p_i}. \tag{3.3.10}$$

If the amount of released pollutants after purification is greater than the critical level ($w_i(1-p_i) \ge \widetilde{w}_2$), the Agent's objective function takes the form

$$y_i^{(2)} = g_i(u_i r_i) - w_i C_p(p_i) - s_i \widetilde{w}_1 - K_{ch} s_i (\widetilde{w}_2 - \widetilde{w}_1) - K_{ca} s_i (w_i(1-p_i) - \widetilde{w}_2) \to \max_{u_i, b_i, p_i}. \tag{3.3.11}$$

The Agent's problem includes the objective function (3.3.9), (3.3.10) or (3.3.11) subject to the constraints

$$q_i(b_i) \le u_i \le 1, \tag{3.3.12}$$

$$0 \le b_i \le 1, \tag{3.3.13}$$

$$b_i + u_i \le 1 \quad , \tag{3.3.14}$$

$$0 \le p_i \le 1-\varepsilon. \tag{3.3.15}$$

The choice of Agent affects the following quantities: u_i (the share of allocated resources spent by Agent i on the system objectives); b_i (the share of allocated resources returned by Agent i to Economic Principal as a bribe) and p_i (the treatment rate of waste water).

4) The river system is a passive object without objective functions and controlled variables.

The expressions (3.3.1)–(3.3.15) form the resource allocation model in tree-shaped systems of water quality control, which is a hierarchical game of (n+2) players: Economic Principal, Ecological Principal and n Agents.

Note that two Principals (Ecological and Economic ones) are mutually independent. The Agent's objective function includes two components:

"the economic component" represented by the first term $g_i(u_i r_i)$. This component of the objective function depends on the Subordinate's strategy u_i (yet, does not affect or depend on the actions of Ecological Principal) and on the strategies r_i and q_i of Economic Principal. Moreover, "the economic component" of the Agent's objective function is independent on the actions of Ecological Principal and, by-turn, does not affect its actions.

"the ecological component" represented by the rest terms of the function (3.3.9), (3.3.10) or (3.3.11). This component depends only on the strategies K_{ch} and K_{ca} of Ecological Principal and on the Agent's strategy p_i, which does not affect and depend on the actions and objective function of Economic Principal.

Having in mind that the mutual independence of the both Principals and the described structure of the Agent's objective function, we decompose the resource allocation model in tree-shaped systems of water quality control into two models, namely, the resource allocation model and the water quality control model.

The resource allocation model in tree-shaped control systems is a game of (n+1) players: Economic Principal and n Agents. The Economic Principal's problem has the form (3.3.1)–(3.3.4), whereas the Agent's problem is defined by

$$J_i = g_i(u_i r_i(b_i)) \to \max \tag{3.3.16}$$

subject to the constraints (3.3.12)–(3.3.14). In this game, as its strategies Economic Principal chooses the amounts of resources r_i allocated to Subordinates and the minimum shares q_i to-be-spent on the system objectives.

The water quality control model is a game of (n+1) players: Ecological Principal and n Agents.

If the amount of released pollutants after purification is smaller than the admissible level ($0 \le w_i(1-p_i) \le \tilde{w}_1$), then the Agent's problem acquires the form

$$G_i = -w_i C_p(p_i) - s_i w_i (1-p_i) \to \max_{p_i}, \tag{3.3.17}$$

subject to the constraints (3.3.15) , and the Ecological Principal's payoff makes up

$$G_0 = -c_a(y). \tag{3.3.18}$$

Here Ecological Principal does not solve its optimization problem: Agent observes the admissible level of waste water release and penalization takes no place.

If the amount of released pollutants after purification is greater than the admissible level but smaller than the critical level ($\tilde{w}_1 \le w_i(1-p_i) \le \tilde{w}_2$), then Agent i solves the optimization problem

$$G_i = -w_i C_p(p_i) - s_i \tilde{w}_1 - K_{ch} s_i \left(w_i (1-p_i) - \tilde{w}_1\right) \to \max_{p_i}, \tag{3.3.19}$$

subject to (3.3.15). The Ecological Principal's problem is defined by

$$G_0 = -c_a(y) + \sum_{j=1}^{n} K_{ch} s_i \left(w_i (1-p_i) - \tilde{w}_1\right) \to \max_{Kch}; \tag{3.3.20}$$

subject to the constraints (3.3.6).

If the amount of released pollutants after purification is greater than the critical level ($w_i(1-p_i) \ge \tilde{w}_2$), then Agent i solves the problem

$$G_i = -w_i C_p(p_i) - s_i \tilde{w}_1 - K_{ch} s_i \left(\tilde{w}_2 - \tilde{w}_1\right) - K_{ca} s_i \left(w_i (1-p_i) - \tilde{w}_2\right) \to \max_{p_i} \tag{3.3.21}$$

subject to the constraints (3.3.15).

In this case, the Ecological Principal's problem acquires the form

$$G_0 = -c_a(y) + \sum_{j=1}^{n} K_{ch} s_i \left(\tilde{w}_2 - \tilde{w}_1\right) + \sum_{j=1}^{n} K_{ca} s_i \left(w_i (1-p_i) - \tilde{w}_2\right) \to \max_{K_{ch}, K_{ca}} \tag{3.3.22}$$

subject to the constraints(3.3.6), (3.3.8).

As their strategies, Ecological Principal and Agent i choose the penalties K_{ch}, K_{ca} and the waste water treatment rate p_i, respectively.

We begin with the resource allocation problem (3.3.1)–(3.3.4), (3.3.12)–(3.3.14), (3.3.16). This model forms a two-player normal-form game. Here Economic Principal establishes the amounts of resources r_i for all Agents and the minimum shares q_i to-be-spent on the system objectives. The following quantities act as the strategies of Agents: the shares of resources u_i spent on the system objectives and the shares of resources b_i given back to Economic Principal as bribes. The first move belongs to Economic Principal. Let us find a Stackelberg equilibrium in this game.

First, consider the behavior of all system participants in the absence of corruption ($r_i(b_i) \equiv r_{i0}$), see (Ougolnitsky and Gorbaneva, 2007). Construct a Stackelberg equilibrium in the case when $g_i(x)$ are production functions. Then the Economic Principal's problem is defined by

$$J_0 = \sum_{i=1}^{n} g_i(u_i r_i) \to \max, \tag{3.3.23}$$

$$0 \le q_i \le 1, \tag{3.3.24}$$

$$0 \le r_i \le 1, \tag{3.3.25}$$

$$\sum_{i=1}^{n} r_i \le 1, \tag{3.3.26}$$

whereas the Agent's problem takes the form

$$J_i = g_i(u_i r_i) \to \max, \tag{3.3.27}$$

$$q_i \le u_i \le 1, \; i = 1,\dots,n. \tag{3.3.28}$$

Theorem 3.3.1. *Let $g_i(x)$ be production functions and β specify the coefficient of return to scale. The following set of strategies of system participants is the Stackelberg equilibrium in the game* (3.3.23)–(3.3.28): if $\beta = 1$, then $u_i = 1$, $b_i = 0$, $q_i = 1$, $r_i = \begin{cases} 1, & i = im, \\ 0, & i \ne im, \end{cases}$

where $g_{im}(1) \ge g_i(1)$, $i = 1,\dots,n$, (i.e., $\max\limits_{i=1,\dots,n} g_i(1)$) is achieved at *im*); if $\beta \ne 1$, then $u_i = 1$,

$b_i = 0$, $q_i = 1$, $r_i^* = \dfrac{\sqrt[1-\beta]{g_i(1)}}{\sum\limits_{i=1}^{n} \sqrt[1-\beta]{g_i(1)}}$.

Proof. Consider the Agent's objective function $J_i = g_i(u_i r_i)$. This function increases in u_i, and so $u_i = 1$. Now, analyze the Economic Principal's problem:

$$J_0 = \sum_{i=1}^{n} g_i(r_i) \to \max,$$

$$\sum_{i=1}^{n} r_i = 1, \; r_i \ge 0. \tag{3.3.29}$$

Here we have two possible cases. 1. Elasticity of production function β = 1. Then $J_0 = \sum\limits_{i=1}^{n} g_i(r_i) = \sum\limits_{i=1}^{n} r_i g_i(1)$.

This is a linear programming problem. Its solution takes the form

$$r_i = \begin{cases} 1, & i = im, \\ 0, & i \ne im. \end{cases}$$

All resources are allocated to Agent with highest production capacity. If β = 1, the most beneficial way lies in giving all resources to one Agent.

2. β ≠ 1. In this case, we arrive at the nonlinear programming problem

$$J_0 = \sum_{i=1}^{n} g_i(r_i) \to \max, \sum_{i=1}^{n} r_i = 1, r_i \geq 0 .$$

Let us construct solution using Lagrange's method of multipliers. The corresponding Lagrange function has the form

$$\Phi(r_i, \lambda) = \sum_{i=1}^{n} g_i(r_i) - \lambda\left(\sum_{i=1}^{n} r_i - 1\right) = \sum_{i=1}^{n} r_i^{\beta} g_i(1) - \lambda\left(\sum_{i=1}^{n} r_i - 1\right).$$

The first-order necessary optimality conditions with respect to the variables r_i and λ yield

$$r_i = \sqrt[\beta-1]{\frac{\lambda}{\beta g_i(1)}}, \; i=1,\ldots,n. \tag{3.3.30}$$

Since $\lambda>0$, it follows that

$$\lambda^* = \frac{\beta}{\left(\dfrac{1}{\sum\limits_{i=1}^{n} g_i(1)^{\frac{1}{1-\beta}}}\right)^{1-\beta}}. \tag{3.3.31}$$

And

$$r_i^* = \sqrt[1-\beta]{\frac{\beta g_i(1)}{\lambda}} = \frac{\sqrt[1-\beta]{g_i(1)}}{\sum\limits_{i=1}^{n} \sqrt[1-\beta]{g_i(1)}}. \tag{3.3.32}$$

Therefore, the point (3.3.31)–(3.3.32) is stationary. Demonstrate that it makes the maximum point. Compile the Hessian matrix:

$$\begin{pmatrix} \beta(\beta-1)r_1^{\beta-2} g_1(1) & \cdots & 0 \\ \vdots & \ddots & \vdots \\ 0 & \cdots & \beta(\beta-1)r_n^{\beta-2} g_n(1) \end{pmatrix} =$$

$$
= \begin{pmatrix} \dfrac{\beta(\beta-1)\sum_{i=1}^{n}\sqrt[1-\beta]{g_i(1)}}{\sqrt[1-\beta]{g_1(1)}} & \cdots & 0 \\ \vdots & \ddots & \vdots \\ 0 & \cdots & \dfrac{\beta(\beta-1)\sum_{i=1}^{n}\sqrt[1-\beta]{g_i(1)}}{\sqrt[1-\beta]{g_n(1)}} \end{pmatrix}.
$$

Obviously, it is negative definite and the point in question gives the maximum. The proof of Theorem 3.3.1 is completed.

Assertion 3.3.1. *The function is constant.*

Proof. Take two arbitrary nonzero points x_1, x_2 and set $\delta = x_1/x_2$. Then

$$
\varphi(x_1) = \varphi(\delta x_2) = \frac{\sqrt[1-\beta]{g_i(\delta x_2)}}{\sum_{i=0}^{n}\sqrt[1-\beta]{g_i(\delta x_2)}} = \frac{\sqrt[1-\beta]{\partial^{\beta} g_i(x_2)}}{\sum_{i=0}^{n}\sqrt[1-\beta]{\partial^{\beta} g_i(x_2)}} = \frac{\sqrt[1-\beta]{\partial^{\beta}}\,\sqrt[1-\beta]{g_i(x_2)}}{\sqrt[1-\beta]{\partial^{\beta}}\sum_{i=0}^{n}\sqrt[1-\beta]{g_i(x_2)}} =
$$

$$
= \frac{\sqrt[1-\beta]{g_i(x_2)}}{\sum_{i=0}^{n}\sqrt[1-\beta]{g_i(x_2)}} = \varphi(x_2)\,.
$$

Due to arbitrariness of the above points, the function is constant.

Corollary 3.3.1. The optimal strategies of Agent i and Economic Principal can be expressed in the following way:if β=1, then $r_i = \begin{cases} 1, & i = im, \\ 0, & i \neq im. \end{cases}$, $q_i = 1$, $u_i = 1$; if $\beta \neq 1$,

then $r_i^* = \dfrac{\sqrt[1-\beta]{g_i(x)}}{\sum_{i=1}^{n}\sqrt[1-\beta]{g_i(x)}}$, $q_i = 1$, $u_i = 1$, where x is any point from (0; 1].

Corollary 3.3.2. The payoff agent I makes up $J_i(r_i^*) = \dfrac{g_i^{\frac{1}{1-\beta}}(1)}{\left(\sum_{i=1}^{n} g_i^{\frac{1}{1-\beta}}(1)\right)^{\beta}}$. The total payoff

of Economic Principal is defined by $J_0(r^*) = \left(\sum_{i=1}^{n} g_i^{\frac{1}{1-\beta}}(1)\right)^{1-\beta}$.

Now, we explore resource allocation under corruption. Further analysis considers the following mechanisms of corruption (Rybasov and Ougolnitsky, 2004):

4. 1) $r_i = r_i(b_i)$ (corruption in resource allocation);
5. 2) $q_i = q_i(b_i)$ (corruption in supervision of the system objectives).

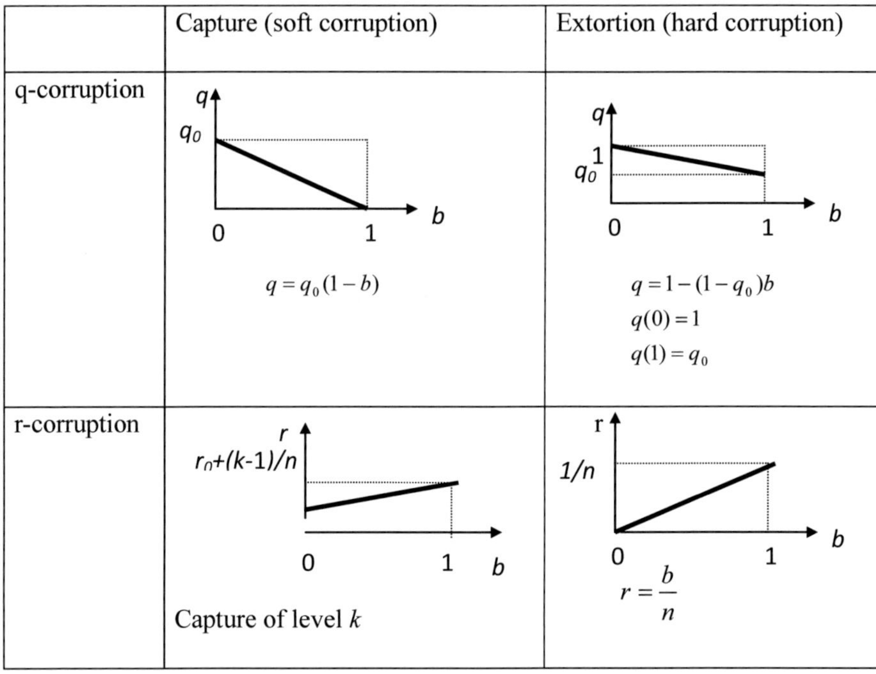

Figure 3.3.2. Corruption types.

Both q-corruption and r-corruption are considered in two cases: soft corruption (capture) and hard corruption (extortion) (Figure 3.3.2). Under soft r-corruption, zero bribe guarantees an initial share of resources r_0 to Subordinate, which can be increased by Economic Principal in exchange for a higher bribe. Under hard r-corruption, zero bribe yields nothing at all to Agent. Under soft q-corruption, zero bribe compels Agent to spend at least the share q_0 on the system objectives, which can be decreased by Economic Principal to zero in exchange for 100% bribe. Under hard q-corruption, zero bribe compels Subordinate to spend 100% of its resources on the system objectives. The share allocated to the system objectives can be reduced to a certain level q_0 in exchange for 100% bribe.

Consider extortion in q-corruption, i.e., the condition $0 \le 1-(1-q_{i0})b_i \le 1$. It is equivalent to the inequality $0 \le (1-q_{i0})b_i \le 1$. The right-hand side implies that $b_i \le \frac{1}{1-q_{i0}}$, i.e., $0 \le 1-(1-q_{i0})b_i \le 1$ can be replaced by $q_{i0} \le 1$. Now, analyze the condition $1-(1-q_{i0})b_i \le u_i \le 1$. It follows from $b_i + u_i \le 1$ that, and so, $-q_{i0}b_i \ge 0$. The nonnegativity of all terms in this inequality dictates that either $q_{i0} = 0$, or $b_i = 0$. If b_i=0, the problem is reduced to its analog without corruption. If $q_{i0} = 0$, then $q_i = 1 - b_i$. The additional conditions $q_i \le u_i$ and $b_i + u_i \le 1$ lead to the following pair of inequalities: $b_i + u_i \ge 1$ and $b_i + u_i \le 1$, and hence $b_i + u_i = 1$. In this case, Economic Principal takes away all resources not spent by Agent on the system objectives: Agent becomes disable to implement its partial interests.

First, we solve the resource allocation problem under extortion in resource allocation $\left(r_i(b_i) = \frac{b_i}{n} \right)$. Construct a Stackelberg equilibrium in the game

$$J_0 = \sum_{i=1}^{n} g_i\left(\frac{u_i b_i}{n}\right) + \sum_{i=1}^{n} \frac{b_i^2}{n} \to \max \tag{3.3.33}$$

$$0 \le \frac{b_i}{n} \le 1, \tag{3.3.34}$$

$$\sum_{i=1}^{n} \frac{b_i}{n} \le 1, \tag{3.3.35}$$

$$J_i = g_i\left(\frac{u_i b_i}{n}\right) \to \max, \tag{3.3.36}$$

subject to the conditions (3.3.14), (3.3.24) and (3.3.29).

Theorem 3.3.2. *Let $g_i(x)$ be production functions and $0<\beta<1$ specify the output coefficient of production expansion. Then the Agent's optimal strategy in the game* (3.3.14), (3.3.24), (3.3.28), (3.3.33)–(3.3.36) *is defined by*

$$u_i = \max\left\{\frac{1}{2}, q_i\right\}, \quad b_i = \begin{cases} \frac{1}{2}, & u_i \ne q_i \\ 1\text{-}q_i, & u_i = q_i \end{cases}.$$

Actually, this theorem claims the following. Whenever Economic Principal creates no barriers for Subordinate in its objective function maximization (i.e., compels Subordinate to spend on the system objectives no more than it is beneficial for Agent), the latter returns 50% of resources to the former as a bribe.

Proof. Since Economic Principal forecasts the Agent's response, first solve the Agent's problem (3.3.24), (3.3.28), (3.3.36):

$$J_i = g_i\left(\frac{u_i b_i}{n}\right) = u_i^{\beta} b_i^{\beta} g_i\left(\frac{1}{n}\right).$$

Application of Lagrange's method of multipliers (under $\beta \neq 1$) yields the critical point $b_i = \frac{1}{2}$, $u_i = \frac{1}{2}$. Consequently, $u_i = \max\left\{\frac{1}{2}, q_i\right\}$. In the first case, we have $b_i = \frac{1}{2}$. And the second case brings to the optimization problem

$$J_i = g_i\left(\frac{q_i b_i}{n}\right) \to \max,\ 0 \le b_i \le 1 - q_i.$$

The objective function increases in b_i, and the obvious solution is $b_i = 1 - q_i$. This concludes the proof.

Set $I = \left\{i \middle| q_i < \frac{1}{2}\right\}$, i.e., $I = \{i | q_i \neq u_i\}$. Then the Economic Principal's problem takes the form

$$J_0 = \sum_{i \in I}\left[\alpha_i\left(\frac{1}{4n}\right)^{\beta} + \frac{1}{4n}\right] + \sum_{i \notin I}\left[\alpha_i\left(\frac{q_i(1-q_i)}{n}\right)^{\beta} + \frac{(1-q_i)^2}{n}\right] \to \max,\ 0 \le q_i \le 1,$$

which is solved by numerical methods. The following result demonstrates the applicability of successive approximation.

Assertion 3.3.2. In the case of $\beta \neq 1$, the optimal strategy q_i of Economic Principal in the problem (3.3.14), (3.3.24), (3.3.28), (3.3.33)–(3.3.36) can be constructed by successive approximation.

Proof. According to Theorem 3.3.2, the Agent's optimal strategy is defined by

$$u_i = \max\left\{\frac{1}{2}, q_i\right\},\ b_i = \min\left\{\frac{1}{2},\ 1 - q_i\right\}.$$

In this case, the Economic Principal's problem is reduced to

$$J_0 = \sum_{i=1}^{n} g_i\left(\frac{u_i b_i}{n}\right) + \sum_{i=1}^{n}\frac{b_i^2}{n} = \sum_{i \in I}\left[\left(\frac{1}{4n}\right)^{\beta} g_i(1) + \frac{1}{4n}\right] + \sum_{i \notin I}\left[\left(\frac{q_i(1-q_i)}{n}\right)^{\beta} g_i(1) + \frac{(1-q_i)^2}{n}\right] \to \max \tag{3.3.37}$$

$$0 \le q_i \le 1.$$

Here it remains to find the minimum shares of resources to-be-spent on the system objectives. Resource allocation proper is not the strategy of Economic Principal, as it now depends on the bribe offered by Subordinate. The first-order optimality condition has the form

$$\frac{\partial J_0}{\partial q_i} = g_i(1)\beta\left(\frac{q_i(1-q_i)}{n}\right)^{\beta-1} * \frac{(1-2q_i)}{n} - \frac{2\cdot(1-q_i)}{n} = 0. \tag{3.3.38}$$

This is a nonlinear programming problem without analytical solution. However, the quantity q_i admits estimation. The first term of the objective function does not affect maximum search, as being independent from q_i.

To solve equation (3.3.38) in q_i, we apply successive approximation. For this, rewrite the equation as $q_i = f(q_i)$:

$$q_i = \frac{1}{2} - \frac{1}{2\alpha_i\beta\left(\frac{q_i(1-q_i)}{n}\right)^{\beta-1} - 2} = \frac{1}{2}\left(2 - \frac{\alpha_i\beta n^{1-\beta}}{\alpha_i\beta n^{1-\beta} - q_i^{1-\beta}(1-q_i)^{1-\beta}}\right). \tag{3.3.39}$$

Establish the convergence condition of the iterative process to the root of (3.3.39). Recall that the iterative process (3.3.39) is convergent if $|f'(q_i)| < 1$ and divergent if $|f'(q_i)| > 1$. Consider the inequality $|f'(q_i)| < 1$ on the segment [0; 1]:

$$|f'(q_i)| = \frac{1}{2}\frac{\alpha_i\beta n^{1-\beta}}{\left(\alpha_i\beta n^{1-\beta} - q_i^{1-\beta}(1-q_i)^{1-\beta}\right)^2} < 1. \tag{3.3.40}$$

Under the condition (3.3.40), the initial estimate of q_i is set equal to 0 or 1 (the software complex uses 0) and further estimation runs according to formula (3.3.39) until a given accuracy is achieved. The proof is finished.

Let us analyze the corruption mechanism $q_i(b_i) = q_{i0}(1-b_i)$ in supervision of the system objectives. In this case, the Economic Principal's problem takes the form (3.3.33)–(3.3.35), while Agent faces the problem (3.3.36), $q_{i0}(1-b_i) \le u_i \le 1$, (3.3.28). Interestingly, the condition $0 \le q_{i0}(1-b_i) \le 1$ holds true if $0 \le q_{i0} \le 1$. Then the Agent's strategy $u_i = \frac{1}{2}$, $b_i = 1/2$ meets the condition $q_{i0}(1-b_i) = \frac{q_{i0}}{2} \le u_i \le 1$. Hence, $u_i = \frac{1}{2}$. All $q_{i0} = 1$,

$$r_i = \frac{1}{2n},\ J_i = \frac{\alpha_i}{(4n)^\beta},\ J_0 = \sum_{i=1}^{n}\left[\alpha_i\left(\frac{1}{4n}\right)^\beta + \frac{1}{4n}\right].$$

Note that Agent becomes disable to implement its partial interests, as Economic Principal takes away all resources not spent by Agent on the system objectives as the bribe.

Therefore, we have considered two resource allocation models: 1) without corruption; 2) with extortion in resource allocation. Now, study the resource allocation model under the capture mechanism $r_i(b_i) = r_{i0} + \frac{(k-1)b_i}{n}$.

Actually, this model generalizes of the two models considered above: if the Agent's optimal strategy is the bribe $b_i = 0$ then the model is reduced to the problem without corruption; if the optimal strategy of Economic Principal is the initial resource allocation $r_{i0} = 0$ for $k = 2$ then the model is reduced to the resource allocation problem with extortion. Thus, capture in resource allocation is reduced to extortion under $r_{i0} = 0$.

Here the major intricacy lies in complete analytical insolvability of the generalized problem. However, we have succeeded to construct the Agent's optimal strategy. In the case of capture in resource allocation, the Economic Principal's problem takes the form:

$$J_0 = \sum_{i=1}^{n} g_i\left(u_i\left[r_{i0} + \frac{(k-1)b_i}{n}\right]\right) + \sum_{i=1}^{n} b_i\left[r_{i0} + \frac{(k-1)b_i}{n}\right] \to \max, \tag{3.3.41}$$

$$0 \le r_{i0} + \frac{(k-1)b_i}{n} \le 1, \tag{3.3.42}$$

$$\sum_{i=1}^{n}\left(r_{i0} + \frac{(k-1)b_i}{n}\right) \le 1, \tag{3.3.43}$$

subject to the constraint (3.3.24). On the other hand, the Agent's problem is described by

$$J_i = g_i\left(u_i\left[r_{i0} + \frac{(k-1)b_i}{n}\right]\right) \to \max, \tag{3.3.44}$$

subject to the constraints (3.3.14), (3.3.28).

Theorem 3.3.3. *Let $g_i(x)$ be power-type production functions and $0<\beta<1$ specify the output coefficient of production expansion. Then the Agent's optimal strategy in the game* (3.3.14), (3.3.24), (3.3.28), (3.3.41)–(3.3.44) *is defined by*

$$u_i = \max\left\{\frac{1}{2} + \frac{nr_{i0}}{2(k-1)}, q_i\right\},\quad b_i = \begin{cases} \dfrac{1}{2} - \dfrac{nr_{i0}}{2(k-1)}, & u_i \ne q_i \\ 1-q_i, & u_i = q_i \end{cases},$$

and, taking into account the constraint (3.3.28),

$$u_i = \begin{cases} q_i, & \dfrac{1}{2} + \dfrac{nr_{i0}}{2(k-1)} \le q_i, \\ \dfrac{1}{2} + \dfrac{nr_{i0}}{2(k-1)}, & q_i < \dfrac{1}{2} + \dfrac{nr_{i0}}{2(k-1)} \le 1, \\ 1, & \dfrac{nr_{i0}}{k-1} > 1 \end{cases}.$$

Hence,
$$b_i = \begin{cases} 1-q_i, & \frac{1}{2}+\frac{nr_{i0}}{2(k-1)} \le q_i, \\ \frac{1}{2}-\frac{nr_{i0}}{2(k-1)}, & q_i < \frac{1}{2}+\frac{nr_{i0}}{2(k-1)} \le 1, \\ 0, & \frac{nr_{i0}}{k-1} > 1 \end{cases}$$

This theorem has the following practical interpretation. Whenever Economic Principal creates no barriers for Agent in its objective function maximization (i.e., compels Agent to spend on the system objectives no more than it is beneficial for Agent), the latter returns less than 50% of resources to the former as a bribe (this amount is smaller than in the case of extortion in resource allocation).

Proof. Since Economic Principal forecasts the Agent's response, first solve the Agent's problem

$$J_i = g_i\left(u_i\left[r_{i0}+\frac{(k-1)b_i}{n}\right]\right) = u_i^{\beta}\left[r_{i0}+\frac{(k-1)b_i}{n}\right]^{\beta} g_i(1).$$

Application of Lagrange's method of multipliers (under $\beta \neq 1$) yields the critical point $b_i = \frac{1}{2}-\frac{nr_{i0}}{2(k-1)}$, $u_i = \frac{1}{2}+\frac{nr_{i0}}{2(k-1)}$. Consequently, $u_i = \max\left\{\frac{1}{2}+\frac{nr_{i0}}{2(k-1)}, q_i\right\}$.

In the first case, we have $b_i = \frac{1}{2}-\frac{nr_{i0}}{2(k-1)}$. And the second case brings to the optimization problem

$$J_i = g_i\left(q_i\left[r_{i0}+\frac{(k-1)b_i}{n}\right]\right) \to \max, \; 0 \le b_i \le 1-q_i .$$

The objective function increases in b_i, and the obvious solution is $b_i = 1-q_i$. The proof is finished.

Theorem 3.3.3 shows that $u_i \ge \frac{1}{2}$, whereas $b_i \le \frac{1}{2}$. In other words, more than 50% of resources are spent on the system objectives, and the residual share (less than 50%) goes to Economic Principal.

Now, solve the Economic Principal's problem using the obtained information about the best responses of Agents on its strategy. Here the minimum share to-be-spent on the system objectives affects the quantity u_i, *ergo* the Economic Principal's payoff. Set $I_1 = \left\{ i \middle| u_i = \frac{1}{2}+\frac{nr_{i0}}{2(k-1)} \right\}$, $I_2 = \{i | u_i = q_i\}$, $I_3 = \{i | u_i = 1\}$. Then the Economic Principal's problem takes the form

$$J_0 = \sum_{i\in I_1}\left[\alpha_i\left(\left(\frac{1}{2}+\frac{nr_{i0}}{2(k-1)}\right)\left(r_{i0}+\frac{k-1}{n}\left[\frac{1}{2}-\frac{nr_{i0}}{2(k-1)}\right]\right)\right)^{\beta}+\right.$$

$$\left.+\left(\frac{1}{2}-\frac{nr_{i0}}{2(k-1)}\right)\left(r_{i0}+\frac{k-1}{n}\left[\frac{1}{2}-\frac{nr_{i0}}{2(k-1)}\right]\right)\right]+$$

$$+\sum_{i\notin I_2}\left[\alpha_i\left(q_i\left(r_{i0}+\frac{k-1}{n}(1-q_i)\right)\right)^{\beta}+(1-q_i)\left(r_{i0}+\frac{k-1}{n}(1-q_i)\right)\right]+\sum_{i\notin I_3}\alpha_i(r_{i0})^{\beta}\to\max$$

$$0\le q_i\le 1,\ 0\le r_{i0}+\frac{(k-1)b_i}{n}\le 1,\ \sum_{i=1}^{n}\left(r_{i0}+\frac{(k-1)b_i}{n}\right)=1\,.$$

This problem admits no analytical solution. However, successive approximation is also applicable to construct its numerical solution. The proof of this result is similar to the case of extortion studied above (see Assertion 3.3.2).

Now, consider the corruption mechanism $q_i(b_i)=q_{i0}(1-b_i)$ in supervision of the system objectives. The Economic Principal's problem is reduced to (3.3.41)–(3.3.43) subject to the constraint $0\le q_{i0}(1-b_i)\le 1$, while the Agent's problem is reduced to (3.3.44) subject to the constraints $q_{i0}(1-b_i)\le u_i\le 1$, (3.3.28). The condition $0\le q_{i0}(1-b_i)\le 1$ holds true under $0\le q_{i0}\le 1$. In this case, the Agent's strategy $u_i=\frac{1}{2}+\frac{nr_{i0}}{2(k-1)}$, $b_i=\frac{1}{2}-\frac{nr_{i0}}{2(k-1)}$ satisfies the inequality $q_{i0}(1-b_i)=\frac{q_{i0}}{2}(k-1+nr_{i0})\le\frac{k-1+nr_{i0}}{2}=u_i\le 1$ regardless of q_{i0}. Hence, $r_i=\frac{nr_{i0}+(k-1)}{2n}$.

Our analysis switches to the river water quality control problem.

Theorem 3.3.4. The problem (3.3.15), (3.3.17)–(3.3.18) is solved by the following Agent's strategy:

$$p_i=\begin{cases}\max\left\{1-\frac{\widetilde{w}_1}{w_i},0\right\}, & s_i<\frac{D}{(1-\nu)}*\max^2\left\{\frac{w_i}{\widetilde{w}_1},1\right\},\\ 1-\sqrt{\frac{D}{(1-\nu)s_i}}, & \frac{D}{(1-\nu)}*\max^2\left\{\frac{w_i}{\widetilde{w}_1},1\right\}\le s_i\le\frac{D}{(1-\nu)\varepsilon^2},\\ 1-\varepsilon, & s_i>\frac{D}{(1-\nu)\varepsilon^2}.\end{cases}\qquad(3.3.45)$$

Proof. Let us solve the problem

$$y_i^{(0)} = -w_i \frac{Dp_i}{1-p_i} - (1-\nu)s_i w_i (1-p_i) \to \max_{p_i},$$

$$0 \le w_i(1-p_i) \le \widetilde{w}_1,\ 0 \le p_i \le 1-\varepsilon.$$

Consider the condition $0 \le w_i(1-p_i) \le \widetilde{w}_1$. Expanding it with respect to the variable p_i gives

$$1 - \frac{\widetilde{w}_1}{w_i} \le p_i \le 1. \qquad (3.3.46)$$

In the case of $w_i \le \widetilde{w}_1$, the inequality takes place for any p_i: whatever strategy (waste water treatment rate) Agent chooses, the amount of pollutants released into river water meets the condition of the first subproblem. Combining (3.3.45) with (3.3.15), we obtain the admissible values of waste water treatment rates $0 \le p_i \le 1-\varepsilon$ (if $w_i \le \widetilde{w}_1$) and $1-\frac{\widetilde{w}_1}{w_i} \le p_i \le 1-\varepsilon$ (if $w_i > \widetilde{w}_1$). Interestingly, if $\varepsilon > \frac{\widetilde{w}_1}{w_i}$, the problem (3.3.15), (3.3.17)–(3.3.18) does not arise regardless of the Agent's strategy. Here only Agent solves its optimization problem.

Apply the first-order optimality conditions to the objective function to find the critical point

$$p_i = 1 - \sqrt{\frac{D}{(1-\nu)s_i}}.$$

In fact, this is a maximum point and the associated value of the function makes up $y_i^{(0)} = w_i D - 2w_i\sqrt{D(1-\nu)s_i}$. However, the above value possibly lies beyond the segment $0 \le p_i \le 1-\varepsilon$. In the case of $w_i \le \widetilde{w}_1$, the inequality $0 \le 1-\sqrt{\frac{D}{(1-\nu)s_i}} \le 1-\varepsilon$ holds true if

$$\frac{D}{(1-\nu)} \le s_i \le \frac{D}{(1-\nu)\varepsilon^2}. \qquad (3.3.47)$$

Otherwise ($w_i > \widetilde{w}_1$), the inequality $1-\frac{\widetilde{w}_1}{w_i} \le p_i \le 1-\varepsilon$ is valid provided that

$$\frac{Dw_i^2}{(1-\nu)\widetilde{w}_1^2} \le s_i \le \frac{D}{(1-\nu)\varepsilon^2}. \qquad (3.3.48)$$

By combining (3.3.47) and (3.3.48), we arrive at (3.3.45). The proof is complete.

Theorem 3.3.5. The optimal Agent's strategy in the problem (3.3.6), (3.3.15), (3.3.19)–(3.3.20) possesses the form

$$p_i = \begin{cases} \max\left\{1-\frac{\tilde{w}_2}{w_i},0\right\}, & K_{ch} < \frac{D}{s_i} * \max^2\left\{\frac{w_i}{\tilde{w}_2},1\right\}, \\ 1-\sqrt{\frac{D}{K_{ch}s_i}}, & \frac{D}{s_i} * \max^2\left\{\frac{w_i}{\tilde{w}_2},1\right\} \le K_{ch} \le \frac{D}{s_i\varepsilon^2}, \\ 1-\varepsilon, & K_{ch} > \frac{D}{s_i\varepsilon^2}. \end{cases} \tag{3.3.49}$$

Proof. Consider the problem

$$J_0 = -c_1\sum_{i=1}^{n} w_i(1-p_i) + \sum_{j=1}^{n} K_{ch}s_i\left(w_i(1-p_i) - \tilde{w}_1\right) \to \max_{Kch},$$

$$y_i^{(0)} = -w_i\frac{Dp_i}{1-p_i} - (1-\nu)s_i w_i - K_{ch}s_i\left(w_i(1-p_i)-\tilde{w}_1\right) \to \max_{p_i},$$

$$0 \le p_i \le 1-\varepsilon, \; 0 \le K_{ch} \le K_{ch\max},$$

$$\tilde{w}_1 \le w_i(1-p_i) \le \tilde{w}_2.$$

Recall that in this case optimization problems are solved both by Ecological Principal and Agent, since the latter's choice K_{ch} affects the payoffs of Ecological Principal and Agent.

Consider the condition $\tilde{w}_1 \le w_i(1-p_i) \le \tilde{w}_2$. Expanding it with respect to the variable p_i yields

$$1-\frac{\tilde{w}_2}{w_i} \le p_i \le 1-\frac{\tilde{w}_1}{w_i}. \tag{3.3.50}$$

If $w_i \le \tilde{w}_2$, the inequality holds true for any p_i: regardless of the water treatment rate selected by Agent, the amount of pollutants released into river water always meets the condition of the second subproblem. Combine formulas (3.3.50) and (3.3.15) to get the following admissible water treatment rates:

$$0 \le p_i \le 1-\max\left\{\frac{\tilde{w}_1}{w_i},\varepsilon\right\}, \text{ for } w_i \le \tilde{w}_2;$$

$$1-\frac{\widetilde{w}_2}{w_i} \le p_i \le 1-\max\left\{\frac{\widetilde{w}_1}{w_i}, \varepsilon\right\}, \text{ for } w_i > \widetilde{w}_2 .$$

Interestingly, if $\varepsilon > \frac{\widetilde{w}_2}{w_i}$, the problem (3.3.6), (3.3.15), (3.3.19)–(3.3.20) does not arise whichever strategies Agent prefers.

Let us evaluate a Stackelberg equilibrium. For this, first construct the Agent's optimal response to a fixed strategy K_{ch}, $0 \le K_{ch} \le K_{ch\max}$, of Ecological Principal. Apply the first-order optimality conditions to the Agent's objective function and find the critical point:

$$y_i' = -\frac{w_i D}{(1-p_i)^2} + K_{ch} s_i w_i = 0; \quad p_i = 1-\sqrt{\frac{D}{K_{ch} s_i}} .$$

In fact, this is the maximum point. Naturally, greater values of K_{ch} lead to higher water treatment rates. However, the maximum point possibly lies beyond the segment $0 \le p_i \le 1-\varepsilon$. In the case of $w_i \le \widetilde{w}_2$, the inequality $0 \le 1-\sqrt{\frac{D}{K_{ch} s_i}} \le 1-\max\left\{\frac{\widetilde{w}_1}{w_i}, \varepsilon\right\}$ holds true provided that

$$\frac{D}{s_i} \le K_{ca} \le \frac{D}{s_i \varepsilon^2} . \tag{3.3.51}$$

If $W_i > \widetilde{W}_1$, the inequality $1-\frac{\widetilde{w}_1}{w_i} \le p_i \le 1-\varepsilon$ takes place whenever

$$\frac{D w_i^2}{s_i \widetilde{w}_2^2} \le K_{ca} \le \frac{D}{s_i * \max^2\left\{\frac{\widetilde{w}_1}{w_i}, \varepsilon\right\}} . \tag{3.3.52}$$

By combining (3.3.51) and (3.3.52), we arrive at (3.3.49). The proof is finished.

Corollary 3.3.3. The Agent's payoff is defined by

$$y_i^{(1)} = w_i D - 2 w_i \sqrt{D K_{ch} s_i} - (1-\nu) s_i \widetilde{w}_1 + K_{ch} s_i \widetilde{w}_1 .$$

Having in mind the Agent's response, find the optimal strategy of Ecological Principal. Substitute the Agent's optimal strategy into the objective function of Ecological Principal. This brings to the problem

$$J_0 = -c_1 \sum_{i=1}^{n} w_i \left(\sqrt{\frac{D}{K_{ch} s_i}} \right) + \sum_{j=1}^{n} K_{ch} s_i \left(w_i \sqrt{\frac{D}{K_{ch} s_i}} - \widetilde{w}_1 \right) \to \max_{K_{ch}},$$

or

$$J_0 = -c_1 \sqrt{\frac{D}{K_{ch}}} \sum_{i=1}^{n} \frac{w_i}{\sqrt{s_i}} + \sqrt{DK_{ch}} \sum_{i=1}^{n} w_i \sqrt{s_i} - \widetilde{w}_1 K_{ch} \sum_{i=1}^{n} s_i \to \max_{K_{ch}}. \quad (3.3.53)$$

Again, to calculate the critical point, apply the first-order optimality conditions to the objective function of Ecological Principal with respect to the variable K_{ch}:

$$\frac{c_1}{2} \sqrt{\frac{D}{K_{ch}^3}} \sum_{i=1}^{n} \frac{w_i}{\sqrt{s_i}} + \frac{1}{2} \sqrt{\frac{D}{K_{ch}}} \sum_{i=1}^{n} w_i \sqrt{s_i} - \widetilde{w}_1 \sum_{i=1}^{n} s_i = 0, \quad (3.3.54)$$

which yields $c_1 \sqrt{D} \sum_{i=1}^{n} \frac{w_i}{\sqrt{s_i}} + K_{ch} \sqrt{D} \sum_{i=1}^{n} w_i \sqrt{s_i} - 2\widetilde{w}_1 \sqrt{K_{ch}^3} \sum_{i=1}^{n} s_i = 0$.

Unfortunately, this problem has no analytic solution in the general case.

Theorem 3.3.6. The optimal strategies of the participants in the problem (3.3.6) (3.3.8), (3.3.15), (3.3.21)–(3.3.22) have the form

$$p_i = \begin{cases} 0, & K_{ca} < \dfrac{D}{s_i}, \\ 1 - \sqrt{\dfrac{D}{K_{ca} s_i}}, & \dfrac{D}{s_i} \le K_{ca} \le \dfrac{D}{s_i \max^2 \left\{ \dfrac{\widetilde{w}_2}{w_i}, \varepsilon \right\}}, \\ 1 - \varepsilon, & K_{ca} > \dfrac{D}{s_i \max^2 \left\{ \dfrac{\widetilde{w}_2}{w_i}, \varepsilon \right\}}. \end{cases} \quad (3.3.55)$$

$K_{ch} = K_{ch\max}$.

Proof. Solve the problem (3.3.6) (3.3.8), (3.3.15), (3.3.21)–(3.3.22):

$$J_0 = -c_1 \sum_{i=1}^{n} w_i (1 - p_i) + \sum_{j=1}^{n} K_{ch} s_i (\widetilde{w}_2 - \widetilde{w}_1) + \sum_{j=1}^{n} K_{ca} s_i (w_i (1 - p_i) - \widetilde{w}_2) \to \max_{Kch, Kca};$$

$$y_i^{(2)} = -w_i \frac{Dp_i}{1-p_i} - (1-\nu)s_i\widetilde{w}_1 - K_{ch}s_i(\widetilde{w}_2 - \widetilde{w}_1) - K_{ca}s_i(w_i(1-p_i) - \widetilde{w}_2) \to \max_{p_i};$$

$$0 \le p_i \le 1-\varepsilon,\ w_i(1-p_i) \ge \widetilde{w}_2,\ 0 \le K_{ch} \le K_{ch\max},\ 0 \le K_{ca} \le K_{ca\max}.$$

Consider the condition $w_i(1-p_i) > \widetilde{w}_2$. Expanding it with respect to the variable p_i yields

$$1 - \frac{\widetilde{w}_2}{w_i} > p_i. \tag{3.3.56}$$

If $w_i \le \widetilde{w}_2$, this inequality fails for any p_i. By combining (3.3.56) with (3.3.15), we obtain the following admissible water treatment rates in the case of $w_i \le \widetilde{w}_2$:

$$1 - \frac{\widetilde{w}_2}{w_i} > p_i.$$

Using (3.3.56) together with (3.3.15), we finally get the admissible water treatment rates

$$0 \le p_i \le 1 - \max\left\{\frac{\widetilde{w}_2}{w_i}, \varepsilon\right\}.$$

Construct a Stackelberg equilibrium, i.e., first evaluate the Agent's optimal response to the strategy K_{ch}, $0 \le K_{ch} \le K_{ch\max}$, chosen by Ecological Principal. The first-order optimality conditions applied to the Agent's objective function bring to the critical point

$$y_i' = -\frac{w_i D}{(1-p_i)^2} + K_{ca}s_i w_i = 0;\ p_i = 1 - \sqrt{\frac{D}{K_{ca}s_i}},$$

which is actually the maximum point. Naturally, greater values of K_{ca} lead to higher water treatment rates. If $w_i \le \widetilde{w}_2$, the inequality $0 \le 1 - \sqrt{\frac{D}{K_{ca}s_i}} \le 1 - \max\left\{\frac{\widetilde{w}_2}{w_i}, \varepsilon\right\}$ holds true provided that

$$\frac{D}{s_i} \le K_{ca} \le \frac{D}{s_i * \max^2\left\{\frac{\widetilde{w}_2}{w_i}, \varepsilon\right\}}. \tag{3.3.57}$$

The Agent's payoff is defined by

$$y_i^{(2)} = w_i D - 2w_i\sqrt{DK_{ca}s_i} - (1-\nu)s_i\widetilde{w}_1 + K_{ca}s_i\widetilde{w}_2 - K_{ch}(\widetilde{w}_2 - \widetilde{w}_1).$$

Taking into account the Agent's response, find the optimal strategy of Ecological Principal. For this, substitute the Agent's optimal strategy into the objective function of Ecological Principal. Then we arrive at the problem

$$J_0 = -c_1\sum_{i=1}^{n} w_i\left(\sqrt{\frac{D}{K_{ch}s_i}}\right) + \sum_{j=1}^{n} K_{ch}s_i(\widetilde{w}_2 - \widetilde{w}_1) + \sum_{j=1}^{n} K_{ca}s_i\left(w_i\sqrt{\frac{D}{K_{ch}s_i}} - \widetilde{w}_2\right) \to \max_{K_{ch},K_{ca}},$$

or

$$J_0 = -c_1\sqrt{\frac{D}{K_{ch}}}\sum_{i=1}^{n}\frac{w_i}{\sqrt{s_i}} + +K_{ch}(\widetilde{w}_2 - \widetilde{w}_1)\sum_{j=1}^{n} s_i + \sqrt{DK_{ca}}\sum_{i=1}^{n} w_i\sqrt{s_i} - \widetilde{w}_2 K_{ca}\sum_{i=1}^{n} s_i \to \max_{K_{ch},K_{ca}}$$

Clearly, the objective function increases in the variable K_{ch}. Hence, $K_{ch} = K_{ch\max}$. The proof of Theorem 3.3.6 is complete.

The fact that $K_{ch} = K_{ch\max}$ can be explained by the assumption that the Agent's water treatment rate p_i satisfies the condition $w_i(1-p_i) \geq \widetilde{w}_2$: it has to pay any penalty for the first breach, while Ecological Principal benefits from assigning the maximum penalty.

To find the critical point K_{ca}, we apply the first-order optimality conditions to the objective function of Ecological Principal with respect to the variable K_{ca}:

$$\frac{c_1}{2}\sqrt{\frac{D}{K_{ca}^{\ 3}}}\sum_{i=1}^{n}\frac{w_i}{\sqrt{s_i}} + \frac{1}{2}\sqrt{\frac{D}{K_{ca}}}\sum_{i=1}^{n} w_i\sqrt{s_i} - \widetilde{w}_2\sum_{i=1}^{n} s_i = 0, \qquad (3.3.58)$$

or $c_1\sqrt{D}\sum_{i=1}^{n}\frac{w_i}{\sqrt{s_i}} + K_{ca}\sqrt{D}\sum_{i=1}^{n} w_i\sqrt{s_i} - 2\widetilde{w}_2\sqrt{K_{ca}^{\ 3}}\sum_{i=1}^{n} s_i = 0$.

In the general case, the above problem admits no analytical solution.

Assertion 3.3.2. The problem (3.3.54), (3.3.58) can be solved by the Newton method.

Proof. Let us demonstrate that the left-hand side of equation (3.3.54) possesses same-sign derivatives of first and second order:

$$f' = \left(\frac{c_1}{2}\sqrt{\frac{D}{K_{ch}^{3}}}\sum_{i=1}^{n}\frac{w_i}{\sqrt{s_i}} + \frac{1}{2}\sqrt{\frac{D}{K_{ch}}}\sum_{i=1}^{n} w_i\sqrt{s_i} - \tilde{w}_2\sum_{i=1}^{n} s_i \right)' = ,$$

$$= -\frac{3c_1}{4}\sqrt{\frac{D}{K_{ch}^{5}}}\sum_{i=1}^{n}\frac{w_i}{\sqrt{s_i}} - \frac{1}{4}\sqrt{\frac{D}{K_{ch}^{3}}}\sum_{i=1}^{n} w_i\sqrt{s_i} < 0$$

$$f'' = \left(-\frac{3c_1}{4}\sqrt{\frac{D}{K_{ch}^{5}}}\sum_{i=1}^{n}\frac{w_i}{\sqrt{s_i}} - \frac{1}{4}\sqrt{\frac{D}{K_{ch}^{3}}}\sum_{i=1}^{n} w_i\sqrt{s_i} \right)' =$$

$$= \frac{15c_1}{8}\sqrt{\frac{D}{K_{ch}^{7}}}\sum_{i=1}^{n}\frac{w_i}{\sqrt{s_i}} + \frac{3}{8}\sqrt{\frac{D}{K_{ch}^{5}}}\sum_{i=1}^{n} w_i\sqrt{s_i} > 0 .$$

Hence, Newton's method is applicable to equation (3.3.54). Its applicability to equation (3.3.58) can be established by analogy. This completes the proof.

In this case, one should choose $K_{ch}^{0} = 0$ (the minimum penalty) as the initial estimate and construct the next estimate via the successive approximation procedure

$$K_{ch}^{k+1} = K_{ch}^{k} - \frac{f(K_{ch}^{k})}{f'(K_{ch}^{k})} = K_{ch}^{k} - \frac{\frac{c_1}{2}\sqrt{\frac{D}{K^{k}{}_{ch}^{3}}}\sum_{i=1}^{n}\frac{w_i}{\sqrt{s_i}} + \frac{1}{2}\sqrt{\frac{D}{K^{k}{}_{ch}}}\sum_{i=1}^{n} w_i\sqrt{s_i} - \tilde{w}_1\sum_{i=1}^{n} s_i}{-\frac{3c_1}{4}\sqrt{\frac{D}{K^{k}{}_{ch}^{5}}}\sum_{i=1}^{n}\frac{w_i}{\sqrt{s_i}} - \frac{1}{4}\sqrt{\frac{D}{K^{k}{}_{ch}^{3}}}\sum_{i=1}^{n} w_i\sqrt{s_i}}$$

for (3.3.54) and the successive approximation procedure

$$K_{ca}^{k+1} = K_{ca}^{k} - \frac{f(K_{ca}^{k})}{f'(K_{ca}^{k})} = K_{ca}^{k} - \frac{\frac{c_1}{2}\sqrt{\frac{D}{K^{k}{}_{ca}^{3}}}\sum_{i=1}^{n}\frac{w_i}{\sqrt{s_i}} + \frac{1}{2}\sqrt{\frac{D}{K^{k}{}_{ca}}}\sum_{i=1}^{n} w_i\sqrt{s_i} - \tilde{w}_2\sum_{i=1}^{n} s_i}{-\frac{3c_1}{4}\sqrt{\frac{D}{K^{k}{}_{ca}^{5}}}\sum_{i=1}^{n}\frac{w_i}{\sqrt{s_i}} - \frac{1}{4}\sqrt{\frac{D}{K^{k}{}_{ca}^{3}}}\sum_{i=1}^{n} w_i\sqrt{s_i}}$$

for (3.3.58).

Now, consider the static resource allocation problem in the three-level control system (Gorbaneva and Ougolnitsky, 2013). We endeavor to study the impact of the corruption mechanism in resource allocation on the behavior of all participants and assess anti-corruption measures in the case of compulsion and impulsion mechanisms. In the case of compulsion, upper-level subject exerts an impact on the strategy set of lower-level subject. In the case of impulsion, upper-level subject affects the objective function of lower-level subject (see Section 1.2). For this, construct the corresponding model as a game Γ_2 and explore it using the Germeier theorem (Gorelik and Kononenko, 1982).

Imagine a three-level control system (see Figure 3.3.3), e.g., the one comprising the owner of an industrial enterprise, its financial director and departments. Lower-level subjects ("departments") manufacture some products and exert an impact on a controlled system (production output, profits). The middle-level subject ("financial director") influences lower-level ones via impulsion (resource allocation among lower-level subjects) or compulsion (resource usage supervision). Actually, the middle-level subject is not concerned with the controlled system state. The upper-level subject ("enterprise owner") monitors the controlled system state, i.e., maintains profits or production output above a given threshold by an appropriate impact on the middle-level subject via compulsion (constraints on strategies) and impulsion (bonuses, incentives).

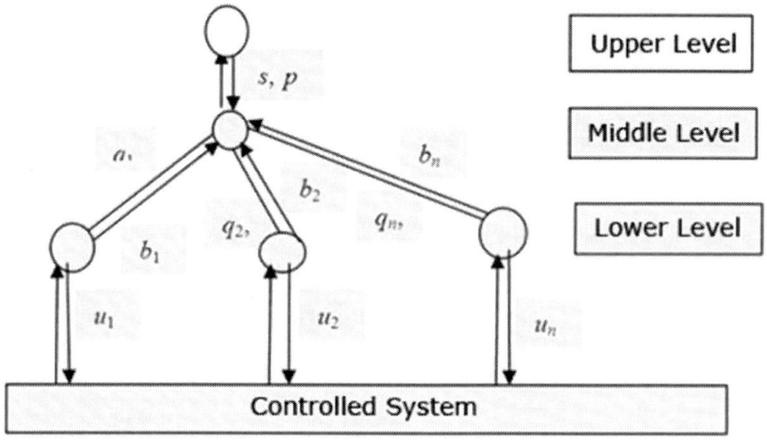

Figure 3.3.3. A three-level hierarchical system.

The middle-level subject disposes of a certain amount R of resources (generally, financial resources) to-be-allocated among lower-level subjects in order to maximize resource usage gains. A lower-level subject spends resources on the system objectives (production). Being aware of this, the middle-level subject establishes a lower bound q_i for the amount of resources necessarily spent on the system objectives. Yet, a lower-level subject can affect the middle-level one through a corruption mechanism b_i to obtain more resources r_i or to reduce the bound q_i.

The upper-level subject monitors the controlled system state and influences the middle-level subject in the following way. It establishes (a) the minimum admissible value s for the bounds q_i and (b) the quantity p as the share of the total payoff of all lower-level subjects returned to the middle-level subject as a bonus for meeting the sustainable development requirements (the total income from the activity of all lower-level subjects must be not smaller than a threshold a).

Introduce the following notation: M, J_0, J_i, $i = 1, \ldots, n$ designate the objective functions of the upper-, middle- and lower-level subjects, respectively; g_i is the production function of the system activity of a lower-level subject with the elasticity factor β; r_i specifies the share of resources allocated by the middle-level subject to lower-level subject i (the control variable of the middle-level subject); u_i gives the share of resources in r_i spent by lower-level subject i on the system objectives (the control variable of lower-level subject i); b_i means the share of resources in r_i returned by lower-level subject i to the middle-level subject as a bribe (the control variable of lower-level subject i); q_i represents the lower bound of u_i established by the middle-level subject for lower-level subject i to spend on the system objectives (the control variable of the middle-level subject); a is the sustainable development threshold of the system; s indicates the minimum admissible value of q_i which can be used by the middle-level subject (the control variable of the upper-level subject); p denotes the share of the total income from the system activity of all lower-level subjects, which is returned to the middle-level subject as its bonus (the control variable of the upper-level subject); s_0 corresponds to the minimum value of s meeting the sustainable development requirement ($\sum_{i=1}^{n} g_i(s_0 r_i) = a$ under $r_i = const$); and finally, r_0 is the minimum value of r_i meeting the sustainable development requirement.

The objective function of the upper-level subject depends on satisfaction of the sustainable development requirement, i.e.,

$$M\left(\sum_{i=1}^{n} g_i(u_i r_i) - a\right) \to \max, \tag{3.3.59}$$

where M is defined in two possible ways:

1. The piecewise constant function $M\left(\sum_{i=1}^{n} g_i(u_i r_i) - a\right) = \begin{cases} const, & \sum_{i=1}^{n} g_i(u_i r_i) \geq a, \\ -\infty, & \sum_{i=1}^{n} g_i(u_i r_i) < a. \end{cases}$

Such an upper-level subject does not care about the existing deviation of $\sum_{i=1}^{n} g_i(u_i r_i)$ from the threshold a. Its goals do not include increasing the income $\sum_{i=1}^{n} g_i(u_i r_i)$ from the system activity of all lower-level subjects. This subject is only concerned with sustainable development satisfaction, at least as equality. In the sequel, we will call it "disinterested."

2. The linear function $M \cdot \left(\sum_{i=1}^{n} g_i(u_i r_i) - a\right)$, where M is a positive constant. If the sustainable development requirement is met, the upper-level subject gains a positive payoff (bonus, wage); otherwise, it pays a penalty for sustainable development breach. In contrast to case 1, here the upper-level subject seeks to maximize the quantity $\sum_{i=1}^{n} g_i(u_i r_i)$, *ergo* its deviation from the threshold a ("interested" upper-level subject).

The upper-level subject controls the variables s and p with the constraints

$$0 \leq s \leq 1, \tag{3.3.60}$$

$$0 \leq p \leq 1. \tag{3.3.61}$$

The objective function of the middle-level subject comprises the income from the total system activity of all lower-level subjects and its bribe offered by the latter subjects:

$$J_0 = p\sum_{i=1}^{n} g_i(u_i r_i) + \sum_{i=1}^{n} b_i r_i \to \max. \tag{3.3.62}$$

The middle-level subject controls the variables q_i and r_i with the constraints

$$s \le q_i \le 1, \tag{3.3.63}$$

$$0 \le r_i \le 1, \tag{3.3.64}$$

$$0 \le \sum_{i=1}^{n} r_i \le 1. \tag{3.3.65}$$

The objective function of lower-level subject i consists of its income from the system activity after deduction of the share paid to the middle-level subject as a bonus for sustainable development satisfaction:

$$J_i = (1-p) g_i(u_i r_i) \to \max. \tag{3.3.66}$$

Lower-level subject i controls the variables u_i and b_i with the constraints

$$q_i \le u_i \le 1, \tag{3.3.67}$$

$$0 \le u_i + b_i \le 1. \tag{3.3.68}$$

The sustainable development requirement is defined by

$$\sum_{i=1}^{n} g_i(u_i r_i) \ge a. \tag{3.3.69}$$

We underline that the model incorporates one upper-level subject, one middle-level subject and arbitrary many lower-level subjects. It is possible to consider n $\ge$ 2 middle-level subjects, but in the noncooperative setting neither the objective functions nor the strategies of middle-level subjects depend on each other. Hence, such a generalized model would be naturally decomposed into n models with one middle-level subject. However, this does not apply to lower-level subjects. The amount of resources allocated to lower-level subject i depends on the amounts of resources allocated to other lower-level subjects (available resources are limited: $0 \le \sum_{i=1}^{n} r_i \le 1$). In other words, the problem is not additive with respect to lower-level subjects and admits no decomposition into n subproblems each having one lower-level subject.

The middle- and lower-level problems (3.3.59)-(3.3.69) form a game Γ_2 which has been explored using the Germeier theorem in the cases of compulsion and impulsion at each level. Actually, we have found two equilibria:

– when the upper-level subject applies compulsion, the middle-level subject chooses impulsion (the compulsion-impulsion model);

– when the upper-level subject applies impulsion, the middle-level subject chooses impulsion (the impulsion-impulsion model).

In the case of compulsion, the upper-level subject's problem is reduced to (3.3.59)–(3.3.60) under $p = const$. Here the upper-level subject controls only the variable s, while p is fixed. The middle-level problem takes the form (3.3.62)–(3.3.63) under $r_i = const$. By analogy to the upper-level subject, here the middle-level subject affects lower-level subject i using the variable q_i, while r_i is fixed. The lower-level problem and the sustainable development require remain same, see formulas (3.3.66)–(3.3.69).

Consequently, the compulsion-compulsion model is described by the expressions (3.3.59)–(3.3.60), (3.3.62)–(3.3.63), (3.3.66)-(3.3.69). It has been demonstrated that, in this game, compulsion becomes pointless: lower-level subjects benefit from spending all available resources on the system objectives and paying zero bribe. Reformulating this statement, the middle-level subject is unable to establish q so that lower-level subjects would prefer bribery.

In the case of compulsion-impulsion, the upper-level problem is reduced to (3.3.59)–(3.3.60) under $p = const$. The middle-level problem takes the form (3.3.62), (3.3.64)–(3.3.65) subject to the constraint $s_i \le r_i \le 1$. Here the middle-level subject exerts an impact on lower-level subject i via the variable r_i, while q_i disappears from the model. The lower-level problem is reduced to (3.3.66), (3.3.68). And so, the compulsion-impulsion model is defined by (3.3.59)–(3.3.60), (3.3.62), (3.3.64)–(3.3.65), (3.3.66), (3.3.68)–(3.3.69).

Equilibrium design in this game has shown that the middle-level subject benefits most from the following strategy of lower-level subject i ($Arg\ K_1$):

$$u_i = \frac{s+\varepsilon}{r_i},\ b_i = 1 - \frac{s}{r_i} - \frac{\varepsilon}{r_i}.$$

Equivalently, exactly $u_i r_i = s + \varepsilon$ resource units are spent on the system objectives (regardless of how many resources a concrete lower-level subject obtains, the amount spent on the system objectives is constant).

Therefore, the following relationship between the amounts of resources and bribe guarantees the maximum payoff to the bribetaker:

$$r_i = \frac{s+\varepsilon}{u_i} = \frac{1}{u_i}(s+\varepsilon) = \frac{1}{1-b_i}(s+\varepsilon).$$

The optimal strategy of the middle-level subject is any set of values r_i such that $\sum_{i=1}^{n} r_i = 1$ (a constant quantity, too). In other words, all resources are arbitrarily allocated among lower-level subjects.

In the case of the "disinterested" upper-level subject, its optimal strategy follows from maximization of its objective function:

$$s = \begin{cases} r_{0,} & u_i r_i > r_0, \\ \dfrac{1-\beta\sqrt[\beta]{g_i(1)u_i}}{\sum_{i=1}^{n} 1-\beta\sqrt[\beta]{g_i(1)u_i}}, & u_i r_i \le r_0, \end{cases}$$

But here the upper-level subject can affect the middle-level subject if

$$r_0 < \frac{1-\beta\sqrt[\beta]{g_i(1)u_i}}{\sum_{i=1}^{n} 1-\beta\sqrt[\beta]{g_i(1)u_i}}.$$

In this case, anti-corruption struggle takes no place, but the sustainable development requirements are satisfied.

For the "interested" upper-level subject, we obtain that

$$s = \frac{1-\beta\sqrt[\beta]{g_i(1)u_i}}{\sum_{i=1}^{n} 1-\beta\sqrt[\beta]{g_i(1)u_i}}.$$

As far as

$$\sum_{i=1}^{n} \frac{1-\beta\sqrt[\beta]{g_i(1)u_i}}{\sum_{i=1}^{n} 1-\beta\sqrt[\beta]{g_i(1)u_i}} = 1,$$

the upper-level subject compels the middle-level one to allocate all resources among lower-level subjects, thereby disabling its bribery. Hence, compulsion is efficient against corruption under the "interested" upper-level subject.

The impulsion–impulsion model acquires the following form. The upper-level problem is reduced to (3.3.59), (3.3.61). Here the upper-level subject controls only the variable p (compulsion is not applied and the variable s disappears from the model). The middle-level problem is reduced to (3.3.62), (3.3.64)–(3.3.65). Similarly to the upper-level subject, the middle-level one affects lower-level subject i via the variable r_i; the quantity q_i is absent in the model. The lower-level problem takes the form (3.3.66)–(3.3.68).

Therefore, the impulsion-impulsion model is described by the expressions (3.3.59), (3.3.61)–(3.3.62), (3.3.64)–(3.3.69).

Equilibrium design in this game has demonstrated that the middle-level subject benefits most from the following strategy of lower-level subject i:

$$u_i = \frac{\sqrt[1-\beta]{g_i(1)(1-p)}}{r_i}, \quad b_i = 1 - u_i = 1 - \frac{\sqrt[1-\beta]{g_i(1)(1-p)}}{r_i}. \tag{3.3.70}$$

Equivalently, the amount of resources $u_i r_i = \sqrt[1-\beta]{g_i(1)(1-p)}$ must be spent on the system objectives (regardless of how much resources a concrete lower-level subject obtains, the amount spent on the system objectives is constant).

Thus, the optimal relationship between the amounts of resources and bribe is defined by $r_i = \frac{\sqrt[1-\beta]{g_i(1)(1-p)}}{u_i} = \frac{\sqrt[1-\beta]{g_i(1)(1-p)}}{1-b_i}$. Clearly, the amount of resources represents a decreasing function of a quantity inversely proportional to bribe amount. This agrees with the results derived for the compulsion–impulsion model. The optimal strategy of the middle-level subject is any set of values r_i, i.e.,

$$r_i = \begin{cases} \forall r_i \mid \sum_{i=1}^{n} r_i = 1, & u_i = \dfrac{\sqrt[1-\beta]{g_i(1)(1-p)}}{r_i}, \\ & b_i = 1 - \dfrac{\sqrt[1-\beta]{g_i(1)(1-p)}}{r_i}; \\ 0, & \text{otherwise.} \end{cases}$$

The strategy of the "disinterested" upper-level subject has the form

$$p = \begin{cases} \dfrac{\sum_{i=1}^{n} b_i r_i}{\sum_{i=1}^{n} g_i(r_0)} - \varepsilon_1, & \forall i u_i r_i \ge r_0, \\ 0, & \exists i u_i r_i < r_0. \end{cases}$$

where b_i^* obeys formula (3.3.70). However, the upper-level subject can affect the middle-level one only if $\frac{\sum_{i=1}^{n} b_i r_i}{\sum_{i=1}^{n} g_i(r_0)} - \varepsilon_1 \le 1$.

For the "interested" upper-level subject, we obtain that

$$p = \begin{cases} \frac{\sum_{i=1}^{n} b_i r_i}{\sum_{i=1}^{n} g_i(r_i)} - \varepsilon_1, & \forall i: r_i \ge r_{i0}, \sum_{i=1}^{n} r_i = 1, \\ 0, & \exists i: r_i < r_{i0} \text{ or } \sum_{i=1}^{n} r_i < 1. \end{cases}$$

where b_i* is defined by (3.3.70). In this case, the upper-level subject benefits from complete allocation of all resources among lower-level subjects. And the middle-level subject cannot reserve some amount of resources for itself. Yet, the upper-level subject affects the middle-level one provided that $\frac{\sum_{i=1}^{n} b_i r_i}{\sum_{i=1}^{n} g_i(r_i)} - \varepsilon_1 \le 1$.

The above model possesses least efficiency in the sense of anti-corruption struggle, but it is possible to guarantee that the middle- and lower-level subjects use resources according to intended purpose.

Therefore, we have constructed and studied the static three-level model of resource allocation with corruption mechanisms. It has appeared that the game of the middle- and lower-level subjects admits no compulsion equilibrium. In the case of the "interested" upper-level subject, anti-corruption struggle is possible in the compulsion–impulsion model. The rest cases (including all cases with the "disinterested" upper-level subject) merely allow corruption restriction.

In addition, we have designed and analyzed the resource allocation model in the river water quality control system. Particularly, Stackelberg equilibria have been evaluated in the two- and three-level games of resource allocation and river water quality control.

3.4. Quality Control Models of Water Resources

This section models corruption based on game-theoretic approach and the hierarchical control concept of ecological-economic systems development for their homeostasis maintenance (Ougolnitsky, 1999, 2010; Ougolnitsky and Usov, 2010-2014). Our consideration focuses on the three-level quality control model of water resources (a model of the "Principal–supervisor–agent-object" type) (Ougolnitsky and Usov, 2012).

Mathematical Model of River Water Quality Control

First, let us construct a mathematical model of river water quality control without corruption in the stationary case (Ougolnitsky and Usov, 2012). Modeling employs the example of a three-level fan-type control system which includes upper-, middle- and lower-level control subjects (federal Principal (FP), local authority (LA) and industrial enterprises (IE), respectively), as well as a controlled system (CS). The mutual relations of these elements are organized as follows: FP exerts an impact on LA and IE, LA on IE, and IE on CS.

By assumption, the behavior and awareness of different control subjects satisfy the following set of rules:

1) FP chooses its strategy first (makes the first move) and reports the choice to all other control subjects; FP maximizes its objective function on the set of strategies maintaining CS in the homeostasis condition. FP knows the objective functions of all other control subjects;
2) LA chooses its strategy being aware of the choice of FP; LA seeks to achieve its own goals under known objectives functions of all IE;
3) IE make their move under known strategies of all other control subjects and maximize their objective functions ignoring the state of CS.

LA establishes payments for pollution by IE (impulsion control) or minimum admissible treatment rates of waste water by IE (compulsion control). FP has to maintain CS in the homeostasis condition: pollutants in the river system must not exceed maximum permissible concentrations (MPC). This control subject defines penalties for pollutants release into river water, which are paid by IE to LA. Impulsion and compulsion are studied as control methods in the system, see Section 1.2.

Consider the case of a single pollutant (e.g., nitrogen-containing substances) and a single IE. The system is said to be at homeostasis under fulfilled quality standards

$$0 \le B \le B_{max} \tag{3.4.1}$$

(river water) and

$$\frac{W[1-P]}{Q^0} \le Q_{max} \tag{3.4.2}$$

(waste water released into the system by IE). Here B denotes the concentration of pollutants in river water; Q^0 specifies water discharge by IE; W is the amount of pollutants released into the system prior to waste water treatment; P represents the share of pollutants eliminated by IE via waste water treatment; the quantities B_{max} and Q_{max} are given.

Suppose that the concentration of pollutants in the river system is defined by

$$B = B_0 + kW(1-P); \quad B_0, k = const. \tag{3.4.3}$$

The primary goal of FP lies in homeostasis maintenance in the system. In addition, this control subject strives for maximizing the objective function

$$J_0 = (1-P)W\,F(T)(1-H) - C_F(y) \to \max_H \tag{3.4.4}$$

The quantity $y = W(1-P)$ makes up the total amount of pollutants released into the river system; $F(T)$ is a known function, T indicates payment for unit pollution amount in the absence of corruption; H means the share of payments for pollution, which is transferred to LA; $C_F(y)$ is a certain function characterizing material losses of society due to water pollution; the functions $F(T)$ and $C_F(y)$ strictly increase in their arguments and $F(T) = C_F(y) = 0$.

LA is interested in its income maximization. The objective function of this control subject has the form

$$J_y = (1-P)W\,F(T)H - C_0(y) \to \max_{T(q)} \tag{3.4.5}$$

Here q specifies the minimum admissible treatment rates of waste water by IE; $C_0(y)$ describes the LA costs function of river water quality improvement, which depends on the total amount of pollutants y released into the river system; this function is increasing in y and $C_0(0) = 0$.

LA chooses payments for river system pollution or minimum admissible treatment rates of waste water by IE. Maximization in (3.4.5) runs with respect to one variable only: q (compulsion) or T (impulsion). By-turn, IE seeks to maximize its profits:

$$J_{IE} = zR(\Phi) - (1-P)W\,F(T) - W\,C_{IE}(P) \to \max_P \tag{3.4.6}$$

where $C_{IE}(P)$ is the IE cost function associated with purification of the unit amount of released pollutants; Φ describes its production assets; $R(\Phi)$ represents the production function of IE; and finally, z gives its profits from selling the unit amount of products. The function $C_{IE}(P)$ increases in P on the segment [0,1] and, moreover, $C_{IE}(0) = 0$ and

$$\lim_{P\to 1} C_{IE}(P) = \infty.$$

Suppose that the total amount of released pollutants (before treatment) linearly depends on the production output of IE with a coefficient β, i.e.,

$$W = \beta R(\Phi) \quad . \tag{3.4.7}$$

Consider the production function

$$R(\Phi) = \theta\Phi^{\eta}; \quad \eta, \theta = const; \quad 0 < \eta < 1 \tag{3.4.8}$$

The problems (3.4.1)-(3.4.8) are solved under the following constraints:

$$q \le P \le 1 - \varepsilon; \tag{3.4.9}$$

$$\gamma \le H \le 1; \tag{3.4.10}$$

$$0 \le q \le 1 - \varepsilon; \; 0 \le T \le T_{\max}, \tag{3.4.11}$$

where $T_{\max}$, ε, and γ stand for given constants; the quantity ε depends on the waste water treatment technology applied by IE; γ defines the minimum share of financial resources received from IE and transferred to LA; $0 < \varepsilon, \gamma < 1$.

It follows from (3.4.1)-(3.4.3) that CS is in homeostasis under the sufficient condition

$$p_{+} \le P \le 1 - \varepsilon \;, \tag{3.4.12}$$

where

$$p_{+} = \max\left(1 - \frac{Q_{\max}Q^{0}}{W}; 1 - \frac{B_{\max} - B_{0}}{kW}\right).$$

Further exposition proceeds from the assumption that $p_{+} \ge 0$.

In the absence of corruption, we have the problem (3.4.4)–(3.4.12), actually representing a nonlinear stationary optimization problem subject to the phase constraints under the existing hierarchy of relations among all control subjects.

Analysis of the model (3.4.4)–(3.4.12) can be performed for different information rules (Germeier games Γ_1 and Γ_2) and different hierarchical control methods (compulsion and impulsion) (Gorelik and Kononenko, 1982; Kononenko, 1977; Ougolnitsky, 1999, 2010, 2011). The definitions of equilibria and their design algorithms in different cases have been described in the previous section.

Corruption Modeling in River Water Quality Control Systems

Let us model corruption within the framework of Germeier game Γ_1 (Stackelberg equilibria) under a known corruption function (Kononenko, 1977; Ougolnitsky and Usov, 2010).

The interests of FP and LA in the model (3.4.4)–(3.4.12) do not coincide, and LA can benefit via bribery. There exist two types of corruption: administrative and economic ones. In the case of economic corruption, LA underestimates the amount of payments for river system pollution exchange for a bribe. In the case of administrative corruption, it underestimates the minimum admissible treatment rates of waste water by IE in exchange for a bribe. In other words, for LA bribes serve as an additional factor in the total balance of its interests (along with payments for pollution). FP has to create conditions so that homeostasis maintenance becomes economically sound for LA even in the presence of corruption. Unfortunately, this is not always possible.

FP supervises the activity of LA and IE, imposing penalties for their bribery. The amounts of penalties depend on "scale" factors established by FP. If scale factors are great (i.e., the probability of corruption detection and associated penalty are high), giving and taking bribes appears economically unreasonable. Scale factors are defined during audits and control of LA and IE. Higher scale factors increase the FP control costs.

Economic Corruption

Economic corruption takes place when LA applies impulsion to IE as its hierarchical control.

The objective functions of control subjects accordingly acquire the form:

- FP

$$J_0=(1-P)W[F(T^0)(1-H)-h(L)+L\delta(\alpha_1(b)+\alpha_2(b))]-C_F(y)\to\max_{H,L}, \tag{3.4.13}$$

- LA

$$J_y=(1-P)W[F(T^0)H-L\delta\alpha_2(b)+\delta b]-C_O(y)\to\max_{T,\delta}; \tag{3.4.14}$$

- IE

$$J_{IE}=zR(\Phi)-(1-P)W[F(T^0)+L\delta\alpha_1(b)+\delta b]-WC_{IE}(P)\to\max_{P,b}. \tag{3.4.15}$$

Here $F(T^0)$ is the penalty function for the unit amount of pollutants released into river water under corruption;

$$T^0=\begin{cases}T+S-\delta a(b) & \text{if} \quad T+S-\delta a(b)\geq 0;\\ 0, & \text{if} \quad T+S-\delta a(b)<0;\end{cases}$$

δ is a coefficient equaling 0 (bribe rejected) or 1 (otherwise); b denotes bribe amount; $a(z)$ designates the bribe "efficiency" function characterizing the actual decrease in the payments for pollution; $\alpha_1(z)$ and $\alpha_2(z)$ are the penalty functions of LA and IE for bribery; L means a "scale" factor for bribe penalty adjustment; $h(L)$ is the FP cost function associated with "scale" factor evaluation per unit amount of pollutants; $S\geq 0$ represents a constant (if $S=0$, we have capture; otherwise, extortion). In the case of capture, a basic set of services is guaranteed, while additional relaxations are provided via bribery. In the case of extortion, a bribe is required even for a basic set of services.

Maximization of the objective functions (3.4.13), (3.4.14) and (3.4.15) runs with respect to two variables, H and L, T and δ, and P and b, respectively. The problems (3.4.13)-(3.4.15) are solved under the following control constraints:

$$0 \le P \le 1 - \varepsilon;\ 0 \le b \le b_{\max}; \tag{3.4.16}$$

$$\gamma \le H \le 1;\ 0 \le L \le L_{\max}; \tag{3.4.17}$$

$$\delta = \begin{cases} 0; & 0 \le T \le T_{\max} \\ 1 \end{cases}, \tag{3.4.18}$$

where $b_{\max}$, $L_{\max}$ are given constants.

Under economic corruption, one faces the problem (3.4.7), (3.4.8), (3.4.12)–(3.4.18). Its solution is constructed according to the following algorithm:

1) Minimize the function (3.4.15) simultaneously with respect to the two variables P and b subject to the constraints (3.4.16) and evaluate the optimal strategies of IE depending on the control actions of LA: $P^*(q,T,\delta)$; $b^*(q,T,\delta)$.

2) Substitute the optimal strategies of IE (see Step 1 of the algorithm) into (3.4.14). Then maximize the function (3.4.14) with respect to $\{T,\delta\}$ taking into account (3.4.18) under a fixed value of q. This yields the optimal strategies of LA depending on the control actions of FP: $T^*(H,L)$; $\delta^*(H,L)$.

3) Maximize the function (3.4.13) under

$$P = P^*(q,T^*,\delta^*);\quad b = b^*(q,T^*,\delta^*);\quad T = T^*(H,L);\quad \delta = \delta^*(H,L)$$

taking into account the constraints (3.4.17) and the homeostasis condition (3.4.12). For FP, the optimal values H^*, L^* yield the maximum income to this control subject under the satisfied conditions (3.4.12).

2) In the case of economic corruption, the system equilibrium is a set $\{H^*, L^*, T_*, \delta_*, P_*, b_*\}$, where

$$P_* = P^*(q,T_*,\delta_*);\quad b_* = b^*(q,T_*,\delta_*).$$

Generally, equilibrium design employs simulation modeling based on direct ordered enumeration of admissible control domains (Ougolnitsky and Usov, 2010).

Administrative Corruption

Administrative corruption takes place when LA prefers compulsion as its hierarchical control method for IE.

The objective functions of the control subjects have the form:

- FP

$$J_0 = (1-P)W[F(T)(1-H) - h(L) + L\delta(\alpha_1(b)+\alpha_2(b))] - C_F(y) \to \max_{H,L} \quad ; \tag{3.4.19}$$

- LA

$$J_y = (1-P)W[F(T)H - L\delta\alpha_2(b) + \delta b] - C_O(y) \to \max_{q,\delta}; \tag{3.4.20}$$

- IE

$$J_{IE} = zR(\Phi) - (1-P)W[F(T) + L\delta\alpha_1(b) + \delta b] - W C_{IE}(P) \to \max_{P,b} \quad . \tag{3.4.21}$$

In this case, the objective function of LA is optimized with respect to q and δ.
The control constraints (3.4.16), (3.4.18) become

$$q^0(q,b) \le P \le 1 - \varepsilon; \quad 0 \le b \le b_{\max}; \tag{3.4.22}$$

$$\delta = \begin{cases} 0; & 0 \le q \le 1 - \varepsilon \, . \\ 1 & \end{cases} \tag{3.4.23}$$

Actually, the constraint (3.4.17) remains invariable.

The function $q^0(q,b)$ describes bribery. It characterizes how far a bribe reduces the minimum admissible treatment rates of waste water by IE. This function enjoys the following properties: non-decrease in q on the segment $[0, 1-\varepsilon]$ and non-increase in b on the segment $[0, b_{\max}]$. Under compulsion, in exchange for a bribe LA underestimates q (the minimum admissible treatment rate of waste water). Such corruption possibly damages environment whenever LA breaks system homeostasis.

We speak about capture if $q^0(q,0) = q$ and extortion if $q^0(q,0) > q$ (Antonenko et al., 2013). The case of $q^0(q,0) < q$ (no statutory regulation) is not considered. Under capture without homeostasis breach, the function q^0 can be taken in the following form:

$$q^0(q,b) = q(1 - \frac{b}{b_{\max}}) + p_+ \frac{b}{b_{\max}} \quad , \tag{3.4.24}$$

where the quantity p_+ guarantees homeostasis maintenance in the system.

In this case,

If LA is ready to break homeostasis in exchange for a bribe, then

$$q^0(q,b) = q(1 - \frac{b}{b_{\max}}); \tag{3.4.25}$$

Under extortion,

$$q^0(q,b) = q\frac{b}{b_{\max}} + (b_{\max} - b)\frac{1-\varepsilon}{b_{\max}};\quad q^0(q,0)=1-\varepsilon;\ q^0(q,b_{\max})=q, \tag{3.4.26}$$

and such corruption does not interfere with system homeostasis.

In the case of administrative corruption, the system is described by the expressions (3.4.7), (3.4.8), (3.4.12), (3.4.17), (3.4.19)–(3.4.26). Below we study the function (3.4.24), which admits the following interpretation. LA is sure that, in the case of homeostasis breach, FP would toughen control and the probability of a considerable penalty for bribery is really high. Therefore, LA takes a bribe trying to maintain system homeostasis. The equilibrium design algorithm under administrative corruption is similar to the one in the case of economic corruption.

Examples

Perform transition from constraints in the form of inequalities to equalities in the optimization problems. Subsequently, the model can be explored using Lagrange's method of multipliers (Ougolnitsky and Usov, 2012).

Example 3.4.1. Consider the model (3.4.7), (3.4.8), (3.4.12)–(3.4.18) with economic corruption and the input functions

$$\begin{aligned} &a(b)=A_1 b;\ \alpha_1(x)=\vartheta_1 x;\alpha_2(x)=\vartheta_2 x;\ h(L)=kL;\\ &C_O(y)=C_O y;\ C_F(y)=C_F y;\\ &C_{IE}(P)=D\frac{P}{1-P};\quad C_o, C_F, A_1, \vartheta_1, \vartheta_2, k, D - const \end{aligned} \tag{3.4.27}$$

and, in addition, $F(T)=T$. The optimal strategies of different control subjects will be denoted by $\delta^*, T^*, b^*, P^*, L^*, H^*$.

If $A_1 - 1 - \vartheta_1 L^* > 0$, the bribe is "efficient" from the position of IE, so long as $b^* = b_{\max}$. Otherwise, bribery disappears: $b^* = 0$. Under any input functions, for LA we have that $T^* = T_{\max}$. Set

$$p^0(b,L) = 1 - \sqrt{\frac{D}{T_{\max} + S - b(A_1 - 1 - \vartheta_1 L)}}.$$

Then

$$P^*(b,L)=\begin{cases} 0, & if \quad p^0(b,L)<0 \\ p^0(b,L), & if \quad 0\le p^0(b,L)\le 1-\varepsilon \\ 1-\varepsilon, & if \quad p^0(b,L)>1-\varepsilon. \end{cases}$$

The last formula shows that economic corruption reduces the optimal treatment rate of waste water from the position of IE.

For simplicity, further consideration focuses on the case of

$$\gamma A_1<1;\ \varepsilon^2(T_{\max}+S-b_{\max}(A_1-1-\vartheta_1 L_{\max}))<D<T_{\max}+S-b_{\max}(A_1-1) \quad . (3.4.28)$$

The first inequality in (3.4.28) makes bribe taking beneficial to LA in the absence of control ($L = 0$), while the second inequality implies that $P^*=p^0(b,L)$.

Then, if $p^0(0,0)<p_+$, homeostasis maintenance becomes impossible even in the absence of corruption. FP and LA have insufficient economic capabilities to influence LA and IE, respectively, and impulsion fails. Imagine that bribery is not penalized, i.e., $k=\vartheta_1=\vartheta_2=0$; LA takes bribe ($\delta^*=1$) under $H^*<\frac{1}{A_1}$, and rejects it ($\delta^*=0$) otherwise.

Therefore, even without administrative control of LA and IE, FP can uproot system corruption by economic methods: create conditions so that LA benefits nothing from bribery. If $p^0(b_{\max},0)\ge p_+$; $A_1 > 1$ and

$$((1-\gamma)(T_{\max}+S-A_1 b_{\max})-C_F)\sqrt{\frac{D}{T_{\max}+S-A_1 b_{\max}+b_{\max}}}>$$
$$\sqrt{\frac{D}{T_{\max}+S}}((T_{\max}+S)(1-\frac{1}{A_1})-C_F) \quad (3.4.29)$$

then corruption appears economically sound for FP and

$$H^*=\gamma;\ T^*=T_{\max};\ \delta^*=1;\ b^*=b_{\max};\ P^*=p^0(b_{\max},0)\,. \quad (3.4.30)$$

In the case of $p^0(b_{\max},0)\ge p_+$; $A_1 > 1$ and non-fulfillment of (3.4.29), FP has no economic motives for system corruption. And it transfers a certain share of financial resources obtained from IE to LA, making bribery non-beneficial for the latter. Consequently,

$$H^*=1-\frac{1}{A_1};\ T^*=T_{\max};\ \delta^*=0;\ b^*=0;\ P^*=p^0(0,0)\,. \quad (3.4.31)$$

Under $A_1 > 1$ and $p^0(b_{max}, 0) < p_+ \le p^0(0,0)$, the system is in homeostasis only without bribery: corruption decreases the optimal treatment rate of waste water from the position of IE. FP prevents system corruption and the corresponding solution is defined by formulas (3.4.31).

If $A_1 < 1$ and $p_+ \le p^0(0,0)$, the system has no corruption and stays in homeostasis so that

$$H^* = \gamma; T^* = T_{max}; \delta^* = 0; b^* = 0; \ p^* = p^0(0,0) . \qquad (3.4.32)$$

In the case of (3.4.30)–(3.4.32), compulsion is efficient in the presence of corruption, the homeostasis requirements hold true.

We will analyze penalization for bribery

$$(k > 0; \ \vartheta_1 > 0; \ \vartheta_2 > 0 \ )$$

under the condition $A_1 > 1$ (otherwise, the solution is described by (3.4.32)).

If $(\vartheta_1 + \vartheta_2)b_{max} < k$, then $L^* = 0$.

Controlling LA and IE is nonbeneficial for FP, and further consideration gets reduced to the case of no penalization for bribery. Otherwise, the framework of the suggested model makes corruption economically sound for FP. Actually, FP spends its own resources to control LA and IE and can recover them only through penalization of LA and IE for bribery. Thus and so, whenever corruption does not interfere with homeostasis maintenance in the system, FP does not struggle against it. If $p^0(b_{max}, L_{max}) < p_+ \le p^0(0,0)$, the system stays in homeostasis only in the absence of corruption. In this case, if $1 - A_1 - \vartheta_2 L_{max} \ge 0$, corruption is not eliminated, impulsion fails and the homeostasis requirements are violated.

Otherwise, i.e., when $p^0(b_{max}, L_{max}) < p_+ \le p^0(0,0)$, corruption disappears and

$$L^* = L_{max}; H^* = \max(\gamma, \frac{1 - \vartheta_2 L_{max}}{A_1}); \ T^* = T_{max}; \delta^* = 0; b^* = 0; \ p^* = p^0(0,0) .$$

If (FP benefits from control) and $p^0(b_{max}, L_1) > p_+$,

where L_1 is a certain value such that $0 \le L_1 \le L_{max}$ (homeostasis maintenance is possible in the presence of corruption), then

$$L^* = \max\left(0, \min\left(\frac{A_1-1}{\vartheta_1}; \frac{1-\gamma A_1}{\vartheta_2}; \frac{(A_1-1)b_{\max} + \dfrac{D}{(1-p_+)^2} - T_{\max} - S}{\vartheta_1 b_{\max}}\right)\right);$$

$$H^* = \gamma; T^* = T_{\max}; \delta^* = 1; b^* = b_{\max}; P^* = p^0(b_{\max}, L^*).$$

In this case, FP seeks for the maximum possible degree of control of LA and IE meeting the homeostasis requirement, while LA and IE still benefit from bribery (despite control by FP).

The condition $L^* \le \frac{A_1-1}{\vartheta_1}$ makes giving bribe beneficial for IE. Next, the condition $L^* \le \frac{1-\gamma A_1}{\vartheta_2}$ makes bribe taking beneficial for LA. And finally, the condition

$$L^* \le \frac{(A_1-1)b_{\max} + \dfrac{D}{(1-p_+)^2} - T_{\max} - S}{\vartheta_1 b_{\max}}$$

guarantees homeostasis maintenance in the system.

Consequently, FP supervising LA and IE benefits from controlled corruption in the system only when it does not break homeostasis maintenance.

Example 3.4.2. Here we study administrative corruption (the model (3.4.7), (3.4.8), (3.4.12), (3.4.17), (3.4.19)–(3.4.23)) in the case of (3.4.24) or (3.4.26) with the input functions (3.4.27).

Suppose that $\varepsilon \ll 1$, which leads to satisfaction of the inequalities

$$\varepsilon^2(T+b_{\max}) < D < T + b_{\max}; \tag{3.4.33}$$

$$-\varepsilon F(T) - \frac{D}{1-\varepsilon} + 2\sqrt{D}\sqrt{F(T)+b_{\max}} + \sqrt{\frac{D}{F(T)+b_{\max}}}\vartheta_1 L_{\max} b_{\max} < 0.$$

For IE, the conditions (3.4.33) make the strategy $\left(b^* = b_{\max}; p^* = 1 - \sqrt{\frac{D}{F(T)+b_{\max}+\vartheta_1 L_{\max} b_{\max}}}\right)$ preferable to the strategy ($b^* = 0; p^* = 1-\varepsilon$), whenever the both belong to the admissible control set. In addition, let

$$F(T)\gamma - C_0 > 0; \quad F(T)(1-\gamma) - C_F > 0. \tag{3.4.34}$$

Inequalities (3.4.34) show that FP and LA allocate financial resources (obtained from IE as penalties for pollution) on waste water treatment. If $k>(\vartheta_1+\vartheta_2)b$, control of LA and IE becomes economically unreasonable for FP, and therefore $L^*=0$. Otherwise, FP needs controlled corruption in the system and $L^*=\frac{1}{\vartheta_2}$. Then LA benefits by taking bribes offered by IE, and the system stays in homeostasis owing to the choice of the function (3.4.24).

Under $L^*=\frac{1}{\vartheta_2}$, LA compels (!) IE to offer a bribe by choosing $q^*=1-\varepsilon$. In the majority of cases, LA benefits from the maximum admissible treatment rate of waste water by IE, which maintains system homeostasis; in other words, this control subject benefits from the IE strategy $p=p_+$. But LA takes full advantage of its position in the hierarchy of all control subjects in the system. Being aware of the objective function of IE and inequality (3.4.33), LA observes that IE would try to bribe it. The whole point is bribe amount and hence $q^*=1-\varepsilon$. This q can be nonoptimal for LA without corruption, but it chooses such q due to the guaranteed bribe.

As a result, if $k<(\vartheta_1+\vartheta_2)h$, then $H^*=\gamma; L^*=\frac{1}{\vartheta_2};\ q^*=1-\varepsilon;\ \delta^*=1.$

In the case of $k>(\vartheta_1+\vartheta_2)b$, we obtain similar strategies:

$$H^*=\gamma; L^*=0;\ q^*=1-\varepsilon;\ \delta^*=1.$$

For IE, both under capture and extortion, the optimal strategy is defined by

$$p_1=\begin{cases} p_+ & \text{if} \quad 1-\sqrt{\dfrac{D}{F(T)+b_{\max}+\vartheta_1 L^* b_{\max}}}<p_+ \\ 1-\sqrt{\dfrac{D}{F(T)+b_{\max}+\vartheta_1 L^* b_{\max}}} & \text{if} \quad 1-\sqrt{\dfrac{D}{F(T)+b_{\max}+\vartheta_1 L^* b_{\max}}}>p_+ \end{cases} \tag{3.4.35}$$

or $p_2=p_+\dfrac{b_2}{b_{\max}}+(b_{\max}-b_2)\dfrac{1-\varepsilon}{b_{\max}}$,

in the case of $0\le b_2\le b_{\max}$, where b_2 gives the root of the equation

$$-(1-(p_+\frac{b_2}{b_{\max}}+(b_{\max}-b_2)\frac{1-\varepsilon}{b_{\max}}))+(F(T)+b_2)(\frac{p_+}{b_{\max}}-\frac{1-\varepsilon}{b_{\max}})-$$

$$D(\frac{p_+}{b_{\max}}-\frac{1-\varepsilon}{b_{\max}})\frac{1}{(1-(p_+\frac{b_2}{b_{\max}}+(b_{\max}-b_2)\frac{1-\varepsilon}{b_{\max}}))^2}=0\cdot \qquad (3.4.36)$$

If $b_2 \notin [0, b_{\max})$, the optimal strategy takes the form (3.4.35). Equation (3.4.36) can be solved, e.g., by the Newton method.

The Differential Model of the River Water Quality Control System

First, construct a mathematical two-level dynamical model of the river water quality control system without corruption.

Consider an industrial enterprise (IE) located on a riverbank. It releases pollutants into the river in the form of waste water. For simplicity, we again analyze the case of a single pollutant, e.g., nitrogen-containing substances. Suppose that impulsion control is applied. The activity of IE (Follower) is controlled by a governmental authority, i.e., a Principal (Leader). IE strives for maximizing its profits and, hence, releasing waste water without extra utilization costs. Leader (Principal) regulates the quality of both river and waste water and charges extra payments for pollution from IE.

The Leader's primary aim lies in homeostasis maintenance for the whole system. In fact, this aim can be achieved in different ways and, hence, Leader also seeks to maximize its residual resources after all environmental measures on waste water treatment. In the finite-horizon setting without discounting, the Leader's objective function has the form

$$J_0=\int_0^{\Delta}\left(-C_A(y(t))+F(T(t))(1-P(t))W(t)\right)dt \to \max_{T(t)}, \qquad (3.4.37)$$

$$y(t)=(1-P(t))W(t).$$

Here t denotes time; $T(t), F(T(t))$ are the amount and function of payments for unit pollution by IE; $W(t)$ $((1-P(t))W(t))$ specifies the amount of pollutants released into the river by IE before (after) waste water treatment at time moment t; $P(t)$ indicates the share of pollutants eliminated by IE during waste water treatment; $C_A(y)$ is the Principal's cost function of river water quality improvement, which depends on the total amount of pollutants released into the river; and finally, Δ is the horizon.

IE seeks to maximize its profits from production activity (income minus waste water treatment costs and payments for pollution). The objective function of IE has the form

$$J_1 = \int_0^{\Delta} \left\{ zR(\Phi(t)) - C_p(P(t))W(t) - F(T(t))[1 - P(t)]W(t) \right\} dt \to \max_{P(t)}, \quad (3.4.38)$$

where $C_P(P)$ is the cost function of unit pollution treatment; indicates production assets; $R(\Phi)$ represents the production function of IE; and finally, z specifies a constant unit price.

The production assets dynamics of IE obeys the ordinary differential equation

$$\frac{d\Phi}{dt} = -k\Phi + Y, \quad \Phi(0) = \Phi_0, \quad (3.4.39)$$

where k is the amortization coefficient of production assets; Y designates investments in production (a constant quantity); the initial value Φ_0 is given.

Suppose that the total amount of released pollutants (before waste water treatment) linearly depends on the production output and the production functions have the form

$$W(t) = \beta R(\Phi), \quad R(\Phi) = \gamma \Phi^{0,5}(t), \quad \gamma, \beta = \text{const}. \quad (3.4.40)$$

We will characterize river water quality using the pollutants concentration $B(t)$. Its dynamics is described by the ordinary differential equation

$$\frac{dB}{dt} = F(B(t), P(t), t), \quad (3.4.41)$$

where $F(B(t), P(t), t)$ is a given function. The optimization problems (3.4.37), (3.4.38) are solved subject to the control constraints

$$0 \le P(t) \le 1 - \varepsilon; \qquad 0 \le t \le \Delta, \quad (3.4.42)$$

$$0 \le T(t) \le T_{\max}, \quad 0 \le t \le \Delta, \quad (3.4.43)$$

where the quantity ε gets predetermined by the waste water treatment technology applied by IE; $T_{\max}$ is a certain threshold.

There exist governmental standards for pollutants concentration in the river system:

$$0 \le B(t) \le B_{\max}, \quad 0 \le t \le \Delta, \quad (3.4.44)$$

and for the quality of waste water released into the river system $(0 \le t \le \Delta)$:

$$\frac{W(t)[1-P(t)]}{Q^0(t)} \le Q_{\max}, \tag{3.4.45}$$

where $Q^0(t)$ is the water flow in IE at the moment t; the quantities $B_{\max}, Q_{\max}$ are given.

The dynamic model (3.4.37)–(3.4.45) can be studied for different informational rules (Germeier games Γ_1 and Γ_2) and different hierarchical control methods (compulsion and impulsion) (Gorelik and Kononenko, 1982; Kononenko, 1977; Ougolnitsky and Usov, 2013, 2014). The definitions and design algorithms of corresponding equilibria have been described earlier. In what follows, we consider the impulsion equilibrium design algorithm in Germeier game Γ_{1t} considering the sustainable development conditions.

We pass to the discrete analog of the model (3.4.37)–(3.4.45) (Ougolnitsky and Usov, 2013) by setting

$$P(t)=\begin{cases} P_1, & \text{if} \quad 0 \le t < t_1, \\ P_2, & \text{if} \quad t_1 \le t < t_2, \\ & \dots \\ P_N, & \text{if} \quad t_{N-1} \le t < \Delta, \end{cases} \qquad T(t)=\begin{cases} T_1, & \text{if} \quad 0 \le t < t_1, \\ T_2, & \text{if} \quad t_1 \le t < t_2, \\ & \dots \\ T_N, & \text{if} \quad t_{N-1} \le t < \Delta, \end{cases}$$

where $P_i, T_i = \text{const}, t_i = i\Delta t; \Delta t = \Delta / N;$ N is the number of constant control intervals. The discrete analogs of the objective functions of different control subjects and the associated control constraints acquire the following form:

— the objective functionals:

of Leader, see (3.4.37)

$$J_0 = \sum_{i=1}^{N} (F(T_i)(1-P_i) \int_{t_{i-1}}^{t_i} W(t)dt - \int_{t_{i-1}}^{t_i} C_A(W(1-P_i))\, dt) \to \max_{\{\{T_i\}_{i=1}^N} ; \tag{3.4.46}$$

of Follower, see (3.4.38)

$$J_1 = \sum_{i=1}^{N} z \int_{t_{i-1}}^{t_i} R(\Phi)dt - (C_p(P_i) + F(T_i)[1-P_i]) \int_{t_{i-1}}^{t_i} W(t)dt \to \max_{P_i}, \; i=1,\dots,N \; ;(3.4.47)$$

— the control constraints:

of Leader, see (3.4.43)

$$0 \le T_i \le T_{\max}, \qquad i = 1,2,\dots,N; \tag{3.4.48}$$

of Follower, see (3.4.44)

$$0 \le P_i \le 1-\varepsilon, \qquad i = 1,2,...,N. \tag{3.4.49}$$

Under fixed production investments ($Y = \text{const}$), we obtain from (3.4.39) that

$$\Phi(t) = \Phi(0)e^{-kt} + \frac{Y}{k}\left(1 - e^{-kt}\right) \tag{3.4.50}$$

In the case of (3.4.40), the N-dimensional optimization problem (3.4.37), (3.4.49) is decomposed into N independent one-dimensional optimization problems. Indeed, denote

$$(J_1)_i = z\int_{t_{i-1}}^{t_i} R(\Phi)dt - (C_p(P_i) + F(T_i)[1-P_i])\int_{t_{i-1}}^{t_i} W(t)dt = \tag{3.4.51}$$

$$= \left(z - \beta(C_p(P_i) + F(T_i)[1-P_i])\right)\gamma\sqrt{\Phi_0}\,\frac{2}{k}\left(e^{-\frac{k}{2}t_{i-1}} - e^{-\frac{k}{2}t_i}\right) \to \max_{P_i}.$$

Subsequently,

Subsequently,

$$J_1 = \sum_{i=1}^{N} (J_1)_i. \tag{3.4.52}$$

The problem (3.4.37), (3.4.49) is equivalent to N optimization problems of the form (3.4.51), (3.4.49) ($i = 1,2,..., N$), while the objective function (3.4.37) is reduced to (3.4.52). Suppose that

$$F(B(t), P(t), t) = -\lambda B(t) + CW(t)(1 - P(t))\ ; \qquad \lambda, C = \text{const}\ . \tag{3.4.53}$$

Then equation (3.4.41) admits analytical solution by arbitrary constant variation method. As a result,

$$B(t) = B(0) + e^{-\lambda t}\int_0^t e^{\lambda\tau} W(\tau)(1 - P(\tau))d\tau\,\cdot$$

Having in mind the constant control intervals, for $t_{i-1} \le t < t_i$ we obtain that

$$B(t) = B(0) + \frac{C_1\beta\gamma\sqrt{\Phi_0}e^{-\lambda t}}{\lambda - 0.5k}\left\{\sum_{j=0}^{i-1}(1-P_j)\left(e^{(\lambda-0.5k)t_{j+1}} - e^{(\lambda-0.5k)t_j}\right) + (1-P_i)\left(e^{(\lambda-0.5k)t} - e^{(\lambda-0,k)t_i}\right)\right\}$$

$$. \tag{3.4.54}$$

Find stationary points of the function $B(t)$ on each segment $[t_{i-1}, t_i]\ (i=1,2,\ldots,N)$, *ergo* the points t_k to verify the condition (3.4.44).

The equation $\frac{dB}{dt}=0$ yields

$$t_i^0 = \frac{\ln\left[\dfrac{\lambda e^{(\lambda-0.5k)t_i} - \lambda\sum_{j=1}^{i-1}(1-P_j)\left(e^{(\lambda-0.5k)t_{i-1}} - e^{(\lambda-0.5k)t_i}\right)}{(1-P_i)\,0.5k}\right]}{\lambda-0.5k} \quad (3.4.55)$$

Hence, it is necessary to verify the condition (3.4.44) for N points $t_i = i\Delta t\ (i=1,2,\ldots,N)$ and all points t_i^0 from (3.4.54) meeting the inequality $t_{i-1} \le t_i^0 < t_i,\ i=1,2,\ldots,N,$ (i.e., no more than for $2N$ points). Rewrite the condition (3.4.45) as

$$P(t) \ge 1 - \frac{Q_{\max} Q^0(t)}{W(t)}. \quad (3.4.56)$$

Suppose that the function $Q^0(t)e^{\frac{k}{2}t}$ enjoys monotonicity on each segment $[t_{i-1}, t_i]\ (i=1,2,\ldots,N)$. Then it suffices to verify the condition (3.4.45) merely for N points $t_i = i\Delta t\ (i=1,2,\ldots,N)$.

The solution algorithm of the problem (3.4.46)—(3.4.56), (3.4.40) in the case of (3.4.50), (3.4.53) includes the following steps.

1. Solve N independent optimization problems (3.4.51), (3.4.49). Evaluate the optimal strategies of IE depending on the control actions of Principal, i.e., the grid function

2. Substitute the function $\left\{P_i^* = P_i^*(T_i)\right\}_{i=1}^N$ (see above) into (3.4.46) and into (3.4.54)—(3.4.56). For Principal, the optimal strategy is the grid function $\left\{T_i^*\right\}_{i=1}^N$ maximizing the objective function (3.4.56) under the satisfied conditions (3.4.54), (3.4.56) for the points (3.4.55) and $t_i = i\Delta t\ (i=1,2,\ldots,N)$.

3. The equilibrium considering the sustainable development conditions is the pair of grid functions $\left(\left\{T_i^*\right\}_{i=1}^N, \left\{P_i^*(T_i^*)\right\}_{i=1}^N\right)$.

The simulation modeling algorithm for the problem (3.4.46)—(3.4.56), (3.4.40) in the case of (3.4.50), (3.4.53) consists in the following.

1. Choose the shape and values of all input functions and parameters of the model.

2. Define the Principal's current strategy, i.e., the grid function $\left\{T_i\right\}_{i=1}^N$.

3. Solve N independent simulation modeling problems. For each $i = 1, 2, ..., N$, use direct ordered constant-step enumeration for the admissible responses of IE to find its best response to the Principal's strategy. Construct N grid functions $P_i^*(T_i)\ (i=1,2,...,N)$ maximizing the objective functional (3.4.46).

4. Verify the condition (3.4.44) for the points $t_i = i\Delta t\ (i=1,2,...,N)$ and for points t_i^0 from (3.4.55) such that $t_{i-1} \le t_i^0 < t_i$. Verify the condition (3.4.56) for N points $t_i = i\Delta t\ (i=1,2,...,N)$. If the conditions (3.4.44) or (3.4.56) are violated at least for a single time moment, proceed to Step 5 of the algorithm. Otherwise, compare the Principal's current strategy with the best among the considered ones in order to estimate its objective function (3.4.46).

5. If the maximum number of iterations is not achieved, choose a new strategy of Principal by considering a new scenario or perturbing its current strategy and then revert to Step 3 of the algorithm.

Therefore, within a finite number of iterations it is possible to construct the suboptimal strategies of control subjects under the existence of an equilibrium considering the sustainable development conditions.

Now, study elementary examples of the dynamic hierarchic systems of river water quality control with exact solution. Set

$$C_p(Y) = D\frac{Y}{1-Y}, \quad C_A(y) = C_1 y, \quad D, C_1 = \text{const}.$$

Example 3.4.3. In the case of $F(T) = AT$, the optimization problems (3.4.46), (3.4.48), (3.4.51), (3.4.49) are solved by the Lagrange method of multipliers. As a result,

$$T^*(t) = T_{\max}, \quad P^*(t) = 1 - \sqrt{\frac{D}{AT_{\max}}}, \quad 0 \le t < \Delta \cdot$$

Impulsion control is efficient if the conditions (3.4.44), (3.4.45) hold true for

$$P(t) = 1 - \sqrt{\frac{D}{AT_{\max}}}, \quad 0 \le t < \Delta \cdot$$

Example 3.4.4. In the case of $F(T) = A\sqrt[4]{T}$, for any $i = 1, 2, ..., N$ Principal has two stationary strategies:

$$(T_i^0)_1 = T_{\max} \text{ and } (T_i^0)_2 = \sqrt[4]{\frac{2C_1}{A}}. \qquad (3.4.57)$$

Then

$$P_i^* = 1 - \sqrt{\frac{D}{AT_i^*}}, \ i = 1,2,...,N. \tag{3.4.58}$$

If the sustainable development conditions are satisfied for $P_i^*((T_i^0)_2)$, $i = 1,2,...,N$, then $T_i^* = \sqrt[4]{\frac{2C_1}{A}}$, $i = 1,2,...,N$. Otherwise, the Principal's optimal strategy results from enumerating the two stationary points (3.4.57), and the optimal strategy of IE is defined by formula (3.4.58).

Game-Theoretic Models of Economic Corruption in Dynamic Systems of River Water Quality Control

We explore anti-corruption struggle in the dynamic three-level system of river water quality control, which includes upper-, middle- and lower-level control subjects (federal Principal (FP), local authority (LA) and industrial enterprises (IE), respectively), as well as a controlled dynamic system (CDS), see (Ougolnitsky and Usov, 2013, 2014).

IE seeks to maximize its production profits. During production, pollutants are released into the river system (CDS). LA establishes payments for pollution by IE as a function of bribe amount and strives to maximize its income from IE. FP is responsible for homeostasis maintenance in CDS. Under impulsion, FP defines the share of financial resources (obtained from IE as payments for pollution) to-be-allocated to LA. Under compulsion, FP defines the minimum admissible treatment rate of waste water by IE (compulsion applied by LA to IE) or the minimum possible payment for pollution (impulsion applied by LA to IE).

LA pursues its own goals only, possibly taking bribes from IE. In exchange for bribes, LA underestimates payments for pollution. For LA officials, bribery represents an important factor in the overall balance of their interests, in addition to payments for pollution. Actually, LA often acts as a commercial structure despite the declared protection of governmental interests. The well-being of LA depends on FP only, irrespective of the environmental conditions. Thus and so, the quality standards of river water and waste water can be violated due to economic corruption. FP has to create appropriate conditions so that homeostasis maintenance is beneficial for LA even under corruption. Such conditions can be ensured in different ways, and FP also seeks to maximize its objective functional. In the finite-horizon setting without discounting, the objective function of FP has the form

$$J_{UPP}(p(\cdot),q_1(\cdot),q_2(\cdot),r(\cdot),u(\cdot),b(\cdot)) = \int_0^T \{-C_{UPP}(a(t)) + (1-p(t))r(b(t))a(t)\}\,dt \to \max; \tag{3.4.59}$$

where t denotes time; $u(t)$ is the share of pollutants removed by IE during waste water treatment; $W(t)(a(t) = W(t)(1-u(t)))$ specifies the amount of pollutants released by IE before (after) waste water treatment at time moment t; $C_{UPP}(a(t))$ - represents the Principal's cost function of river water quality improvement, which depends on the total amount of pollutants ($a(t)$); indicates the planning horizon; $r(b(t))$ is the payment function for unit pollution by IE (in the conditions of corruption, it depends on the bribe amount $b(t)$); $p(t)$ means the share of financial resources from IE transferred to LA; $q_1(t), q_2(t)$ are the control actions applied by FP under compulsion in the cases of compulsion and impulsion, respectively, chosen by LA.

The term $C_{UPP}(a(t))$ in (3.4.59) reflects the river water treatment costs of FP, while the term $a(t)(1-p(t)r(b(t))$ answers for the payments of IE for river system pollution. The objective function (3.4.59) is maximized in $p(t)$ (impulsion control) and $q_1(t)$ or $q_2(t)$ (compulsion control). Thus, the objective functional of FP incorporates the costs of centralized river water treatment and the income from IE in the form of payments for river water pollution.

LA seeks to maximize the incoming financial resources from IE (bribes and payments for pollution taking into account corruption) after deduction of river water treatment costs. The objective functional of LA is defined by

$$J_{MID}(p(\cdot),r(\cdot),s(\cdot),u(\cdot),b(\cdot))=\int_0^T\{-C_{MID}(a(t))+a(t)r(b(t))p(t)+b(t)a(t)\}dt\to\max \tag{3.4.60}$$

Here $C_{MID}(a(t))$ stands for the LA cost function of river water quality improvement; LA controls the payments $r(b(t))$ for pollution (impulsion) and the minimum admissible treatment rate $s(b(t))$ of waste water by IE (compulsion).

In the objective function (3.4.60), the term $C_{MID}(a(t))$ describes the river water treatment costs of LA, the term $a(t)\,p(t)\,r(b(t))$ corresponds to the payments of IE for river system pollution, and the term $a(t)\ b(t)$ is the bribe paid for river water pollution in the amount of $a(t)$.

IE is interested in its profits maximization under corruption, i.e.,

$$J_{LOW}(r(\cdot),u(\cdot),b(\cdot))=\int_0^T\{zR(\Phi(t))-C_{LOW}(u(t))W(t)-r(b(t))a(t)-b(t)a(t)\}dt\to\max. \tag{3.4.61}$$

Here $C_{LOW}(u(t))$ designates the cost functions of unit pollution treatment by IE; indicates production assets; $R(\Phi)$ represents the production function of IE; and finally, z specifies a constant unit price. The objective function (3.4.61) is maximized in two functions, $u(t)$ and $b(t)$.

The term $zR(\Phi(t))$ expresses the IE income from selling $R(\Phi(t))$ units of its products, while the term $a(t)r(b(t))$ reflects the payments for river water pollution. In addition, the term $C_{LOW}(u(t))W(t)$ characterizes the costs of waste water treatment by IE and the term $a(t)\ b(t)$ answers for the bribe paid for river water pollution in the amount of $a(t)$. We will consider the case when $C(u(t)) = D\dfrac{u(t)}{1-u(t)}$; $D = const.$

The optimization problems (3.4.59)-(3.4.61) are solved subject to the following control constraints:

- FP

$$\gamma_1 \le p(t) \le \gamma_2;\ 0 \le q_1(t) \le 1-\varepsilon;\ 0 \le q_2(t) \le r_{\max};\ \forall t : t \in [0,T]; \tag{3.4.62}$$

- LA

$$q_1(t) \le s(t) \le 1-\varepsilon;\ q_2(t) \le r(b(t)) \le r_{\max};\ \forall t : t \in [0,T]; \tag{3.4.63}$$

- IE

$$s(t) \le u(t) \le 1-\varepsilon;\ 0 \le b(t) \le b_{\max};\ \forall t : t \in [0,T]; \tag{3.4.64}$$

The quantity ε depends on the waste water treatment technology applied by IE; $b_{\max}$ specifies the maximum admissible bribe per unit pollution; $r_{\max}$ is the maximum admissible payment for pollution without corruption; γ_1, γ_2 mean the minimum admissible shares of financial resources coming from IE to FP and LA; the parameters $r_{\max}, b_{\max}, \gamma_1, \gamma_2$ are given. The production assets dynamics of IE obeys the ordinary differential equation

$$\frac{d\Phi}{dt} = -k\Phi + Y,\quad \Phi(0) = \Phi_0, \tag{3.4.65}$$

where k is the amortization coefficient of production assets; Y designates investments in production (a constant quantity); the initial value Φ_0 is given. Suppose that the total amount of released pollutants (before waste water treatment) linearly depends on the production output and the production functions have the form

$$W(t) = \beta R(\Phi),\quad R(\Phi) = \chi \Phi^{0.5}(t),\quad \chi, \beta = \text{const} \tag{3.4.66}$$

As a measure of river water quality, choose the pollutants concentration $x(t)$ obeying the ordinary differential equation

$$\frac{dx}{dt} = F(x(t), u(t), t);\ x(0) = x_0, \tag{3.4.67}$$

where $F(x(t),u(t),t)$ is a certain known function. There exist maximum permissible concentrations x_{max} of pollutants in the river system:

$$0 \le x(t) \le x_{max}, \quad \forall t : t \in [0,T] \tag{3.4.68}$$

as well as governmental constraints on waste water quality:

$$\frac{W(t)[1-u(t)]}{Q^0(t)} \le Q_{max}, \quad \forall t : t \in [0,T], \tag{3.4.69}$$

where $Q^0(t)$ specifies the water flow in IE at the moment t; the quantities x_{max}, Q_{max} are given.

The hierarchical three-player game has four modifications of informational rules (C–compulsion, I–impulsion), see (Ougolnitsky, 1999; Ougolnitsky and Usov, 2013):

1) FP and LA both apply compulsion (CC);
2) FP chooses compulsion, whereas LA prefers impulsion (CI);
3) FP chooses impulsion, whereas LA prefers compulsion (IC);
4) FP and LA both apply impulsion (II).

Let us analyze the last modification in detail. The both control subjects apply impulsion, and compulsion takes no place. LA stimulates IE to choose strategies ensuring satisfaction of its own interests. In addition, FP stimulates LA to choose strategies guaranteeing sustainable development with proper consideration of its own interests.

There exist the following possible combinations of equilibria in dynamic games Γ_{1t} and Γ_{2t} (Gorelik and Kononenko, 1982; Kononenko, 1977) among different-level control subjects in the model (3.4.59)-(3.4.69):

- an equilibrium in Stackelberg game Γ_{1t} between FP and LA, an equilibrium in Germeier game Γ_{2t} between LA and IE;
- an equilibrium in Germeier game Γ_{2t} between FP and LA, an equilibrium in Stackelberg game Γ_{1t} between LA and IE;
- equilibrium in Germeier games Γ_{2t} for the both pairs of control subjects;
- equilibrium in Stackelberg games Γ_{1t} for the both pairs of control subjects;

In the case of impulsion, we believe that $q_1(t) \equiv q_2(t) \equiv s(t) \equiv 0$, the control variables are the functions $p(t), r(t), u(t), b(t)$. Introduce the projections $\pi(\tilde{r}) = r(p(r),u,b)$; $\pi(\tilde{\tilde{u}}) = u(r(p(r),u,b))$. Assume that $\varepsilon^2 r_{max} \le D \le r_{max}$ and design equilibria in the case when the both pairs of control subjects play Germeier games Γ_{2t} (Ougolnitsky and Usov, 2013, 2014).

The information rules have the form

$$\tilde{p} \in \tilde{P} = \{\tilde{p} : R \to P\}; \tilde{\tilde{r}} \in \tilde{\tilde{R}} = \{\tilde{\tilde{r}} : \tilde{P} \times U \to R\}; u \in U;$$

FP chooses a strategy $\tilde{p} \in \tilde{P}$ and reports it to LA. Next, LA chooses a strategy $\tilde{\tilde{r}} \in \tilde{\tilde{R}}$ such that $r = \tilde{\tilde{r}}(p(u), u)$ belongs to the optimal response set

$$R^{II}_{MID}(\tilde{p}, u) = Arg \max_{r \in R} J_{MID}(p(u), r, u, x)$$

and reports it to IE. And finally, IE chooses the best response

$$u \in R^{II}_{LOW}(\tilde{\tilde{r}}) = Arg \max_{u \in U} J_{LOW}(p(u), r, u, x)$$

The guaranteed result of FP makes up

$$\gamma^{II}_{UPP} = \sup_{\tilde{p} \in \tilde{P}} \inf_{r \in R^{II}_{MID}(\tilde{p}, u)} \inf_{u \in R^{II}_{LOW}(\tilde{\tilde{r}})} J_{UPP}(\pi(\tilde{p}, \tilde{\tilde{r}}, u, x)$$

The impulsion-impulsion equilibrium in Germeier game Γ_{2t} has the form

$$(\tilde{p}^*, \tilde{\tilde{r}}^*, u^*) \in BR^{II} : J_{UPP}(\pi(\tilde{p}^*, \tilde{\tilde{r}}^*, u^*, x^*)) = \gamma^{II}_{UPP}$$

$$BR^{II} = \{(\tilde{p}, \tilde{\tilde{r}}, u) \in \tilde{P} \times \tilde{\tilde{R}} \times U : r(p(u), u) \in R^{II}_{MID}(\tilde{p}, u), u \in R^{II}_{LOW}(\tilde{\tilde{r}})\},$$

where the trajectory x^* is induced by the control action u^*.

The solution of the problem (3.4.59)–(3.4.69) is constructed using the following algorithm:

1. Evaluate the quantity

$$L^{II}_{LOW} = T(D - 2\sqrt{Dr_{\max}})\int_0^T W(t)dt + \int_0^T zR(\Phi)dt$$
,

the penalty strategies are described by

$$\tilde{p}^P = \tilde{p}(r_{\max}) = 0; \tilde{\tilde{r}}^P = \tilde{\tilde{r}}(\tilde{p}(r_{\max}), u^P, b^P) = r_{\max}; u^P = 1 - \sqrt{\frac{D}{r_{\max}}}; b^P = 0.$$

2. Define the set

$$D^{II}_{LOW} = \{(\tilde{\tilde{r}}, \tilde{\tilde{\tilde{u}}}, b) : -\int_0^T W(t)\left\{D\frac{\pi(\tilde{\tilde{\tilde{u}}})}{1-\pi(\tilde{\tilde{\tilde{u}}})} + (1-\pi(\tilde{\tilde{\tilde{u}}})(\pi(\tilde{\tilde{r}}) + b(t))\right\}dt$$

$$\le T(D - 2\sqrt{Dr_{\max}})\int_0^T W(t)dt\}.$$

3. Evaluate the quantity

$$L^{II}_{MID} = \sup_{(\tilde{\tilde{r}}, \tilde{\tilde{\tilde{u}}}, b)\in D^{II}_{H}} \int_0^T \left\{-C_C(W(t)(1-\pi(\tilde{\tilde{\tilde{u}}})) + (1-\pi(\tilde{\tilde{\tilde{u}}}))W(t)b(t))\right\}dt.$$

4. Introduce the set

$$D^{*}_{MID} = \{(\tilde{p}, \tilde{\tilde{r}}, \tilde{\tilde{\tilde{u}}}, b) : \int_0^T \left\{-C_C((1-\pi(\tilde{\tilde{\tilde{u}}}))W(t)) + (1-\pi(\tilde{\tilde{\tilde{u}}}))W(t)(\pi(\tilde{\tilde{r}})p(r(t)) + b(t))\right\}dt$$

$$\ge L^{II}_{C},\ -\int_0^T W(t)\left\{D\frac{\pi(\tilde{\tilde{\tilde{u}}})}{1-\pi(\tilde{\tilde{\tilde{u}}})} + (1-\pi(\tilde{\tilde{\tilde{u}}}))(\pi(\tilde{\tilde{r}}) + b(t))\right\}dt \le T(D - 2\sqrt{Dr_{\max}})\int_0^T W(t)dt,$$

$$\left.\forall t\ \ 0 \le x(t) \le x_{\max},\ \frac{W(t)[1-u(t)]}{Q^0(t)} \le Q_{\max}\right\}$$

5. Evaluate the quantity

$$\gamma^{II}_{UPP} = \sup_{(\tilde{p}, \tilde{\tilde{r}}, \tilde{\tilde{\tilde{u}}}, b)\in D^{*}_{C}} \int_0^T \left\{-C_B(W(t)(1-\pi(\tilde{\tilde{\tilde{u}}})) + (1-p(r(t)))W(t)\pi(\tilde{\tilde{r}})(1-\pi(\tilde{\tilde{\tilde{u}}}))\right\}dt.$$

and find the impulsion-impulsion equilibrium.

Consider a series of equilibrium design examples. In all of them, impulsion-impulsion equilibria are calculated by direct ordered enumeration under the hypothesis of constant control actions on some time intervals (Ougolnitsky and Usov, 2013).

In particular, assume that the control subjects vary their control actions n times at known instants, i.e.,

$$m(t) = \begin{cases} m_1, & \text{if} \quad 0 \le t < t_1 \\ m_2, & \text{if} \quad t_1 \le t < t_2 \\ & \dots \\ m_N, & \text{if} \quad t_{n-1} \le t < T, \end{cases}$$

where $m_i = \text{const}; t_i = i\Delta t; \Delta t = \dfrac{T}{n}; m(t)$ is the control action of a control subject (one of the functions $p(t), r(t), u(t), b(t)$).

Example 3.4.5. Set $F(x(t),u(t),t) = -\omega x + C_1 W(t)(1-u(t))$; $C_B(a(t)) = C_2 a(t); C_C(a(t)) = C_3 a(t)$;

$C_1, C_2, C_3 = \text{const}$; $C_2 = \$20; C_3 = \$30$; $C_1 = 0.015(l \cdot day^{-1})$; $z = 25\,\text{day}^{-1}; r_{\max} = \$200; b_{\max} = \$70; T = 540\,\text{day}$; $n = 3$; $x_{\max} = 10\text{mg/l}$; $Q_{\max} = 100$; $\Phi_0 = \$10^{16}$; $D = 18$; $x_0 = 6\,\text{mg/l}$; $\chi = 2; \gamma_1 = 0.3; \gamma_2 = 0.8$; $\varepsilon = 0.1$; $\beta = 0.3\,\text{mg/(\$}\cdot\text{day)}; Q^0(t) = 0.6W(t)/Q_{\max}$; $Y = 0$; $k = 0.001\,\text{day}^{-1}$; $C_1 = 0.015(1 \cdot \text{day}^{-1})$;

$z = 25\,\text{day}^{-1}; r_{\max} = \$200; b_{\max} = \$70; T = 540\,\text{day}$; $n = 3$; $x_{\max} = 10\text{mg/l}$; $Q_{\max} = 100$; $\Phi_0 = \$10^{16}$; $D = 18$; $x_0 = 6\,\text{mg/l}$; $\chi = 2; \gamma_1 = 0.3; \gamma_2 = 0.8$; $\varepsilon = 0.1$; $\beta = 0.3\,\text{mg/(\$}\cdot\text{day)}; Q^0(t) = 0.6W(t)/Q_{\max}$;

(day–24 hours; m–meter; mg–milligram; l-liter). Corruption exists in this system and $L^{II}_{UPP} =$ –`\$132507; $L^{II}_{MID} = \$285317; \gamma^{II}_{UPP} = \$105764; J^{II}_{MID} = \$285882$; $J^{II}_{LOW} = -\$132483$.

where $J^{II}_{MID}, J^{II}_{LOW}$ are the profits of LA and IE, respectively, in the impulsion-impulsion equilibrium.

Example 3.4.6. In the case of the input data of Example 3.4.5 and smaller costs of waste water treatment by IE ($D = 1$), corruption exists in the system, the profits of IE and other subjects increase and decrease, respectively. Really, IE benefits from higher waste water treatment rates:

$$L^{II}_{LOW} = \$397870; L^{II}_{MID} = \$93911; \gamma^{II}_{UPP} = \$2166;$$

$$J^{II}_{MID} = \$94262; J^{II}_{LOW} = \$398121.$$

Example 3.4.7. In the case of the input data of Example 3.4.5 and higher costs of river water treatment by LA ($C_3 = \$200$), the latter subject has losses and corruption exists in the system:

$$L^{II}_{LOW} = -\$132507.; L^{II}_{C} = -\$269677;$$

$$\gamma^{II}_{UPP} = \$175732; J^{II}_{MID} = -\$269156; J^{II}_{LOW} = -\$132452.$$

Example 3.4.8. Equilibrium II considering the sustainable development conditions exists far from always. For instance, it disappears under the input data of Example 3.4.5 and higher costs of waste water treatment by IE ($D = 100$), greater maximum possible bribe amount ($b_{\max} = \$500$), smaller maximum admissible payments for pollution ($r_{\max} = \$10$) or worse environmental conditions of the system ($x_0 = 9\,\text{mg/l}$).

Example 3.4.9. In the case of the input data of Example 3.4.5 and smaller maximum possible bribe $b_{\max} = \$10$, corruption vanishes in the system, the profits of FP and IE increase, whereas the profits of LA decrease:

$$L^{II}_{LOW} = -\$132507; L^{II}_{MID} = -\$47712; \gamma^{II}_{UPP} = \$301948; J^{II}_{MID} = \$68267;\ J^{II}_{LOW} = -\$111052.$$

Now, analyze the informational rules of compulsion-compulsion (CC). Here we believe that $q_2(t) \equiv 0$, the functions $p(t), r(t)$ are given and fixed, the control variables represent the functions $q_1(t), s(t), u(t), b(t)$. Suppose that $\forall t : t \in [0,T] \rightarrow D \geq \varepsilon^2 r(t)$.

The solution of the problem (3.4.59)–(3.4.69) is constructed according to the algorithm described above:

If $1 - \sqrt{D/(r(t)+b_{\max})} \leq s(t) \leq 1 - \varepsilon$, then $b^*(t) = 0; u^*(t) = s(t)$;

if $1 - \sqrt{D/r(t)} \leq s(t) < 1 - \sqrt{D/(r(t)+b_{\max})}$, then

$(b^*(t) = b_{\max}; u^*(t) = 1 - \sqrt{D/(r(t)+b_{\max})})$

or $(b^*(t) = 0; u^*(t) = s(t))$ depending on the input data of the model.

If $s(t) < 1 - \sqrt{D/r(t)}$, then $(b^*(t) = b_{\max}; u^*(t) = 1 - \sqrt{D/(r(t)+b_{\max})})$

or $(b^*(t) = 0; u^*(t) = 1 - \sqrt{D/r(t)})$.

2) Solve the parametric maximization problem of the functional (3.4.60), (3.4.63) subject to the constraints (3.4.65), (3.4.66) under $b(t) = b^*(t), u(t) = u^*(t)$. Its solution is the operator $s^*(t) = s^*(q_1(t), b(t))$.

3. For FP, solve the optimal control problem (3.4.59), (3.4.62), (3.4.65)–(3.4.69) under

$$s(t) = s^*(q_1(t), b^*(t)), u(t) = u^*(s^*(q_1(t), b^*(t))), b(t) = b^*(t).$$

Find the compulsion-compulsion equilibrium.

The compulsion-compulsion equilibrium is evaluated by direct ordered enumeration under the hypothesis of constant control actions on some time intervals in the case of $p(t) = 0.4; r(t) = r_{\max}/2$. Note that the results appreciably depend on the given functions $p(t),\ r(t)$.

Example 3.4.10. Under the input data of Example 3.4.5, the incomes of FP and IE increase, while the income of LA goes down (in comparison with Example 3.4.5):

$$J_{UPP}^{CC} = \$142658; J_{MID}^{CC} = \$35664; J_{LOW}^{CC} = \$109371,$$

where $J_{UPP}^{CC}, J_{MID}^{CC}, J_{LOW}^{CC}$ are the profits of FP, LA and IE, respectively, in the compulsion-compulsion equilibrium.

Example 3.4.11. Under the input data of Example 3.4.6, the incomes of FP and IE again increase, while the income of LA goes down (in comparison with Example 3.4.6):

$$J_{UPP}^{CC} = \$28531; J_{MID}^{CC} = \$7132; J_{LOW}^{CC} = \$4588851.$$

Example 3.4.12. Under the input data of Example 3.4.7, the incomes of FP and IE decrease, while the income of LA grows (in comparison with Example 3.4.7):

$$J_{UPP}^{CC} = \$28531; J_{MID}^{CC} = -\$114127; J_{LOW}^{CC} = -\$632454.$$

Example 3.4.13. Under the input data of Example 3.4.8, the CC equilibrium considering the sustainable development requirements exists in all mentioned cases. The sustainable development conditions are ensured via compulsion.

For the information rules of compulsion-impulsion (CI), we believe that $q_1(t) \equiv 0; s(t) \equiv 0$, the function $p(t)$ is given and the control variables represent the functions $q_2(t), r(t), u(t), b(t)$. Introduce the projections

$$\pi(\tilde{\tilde{r}}) = r(q,u,b);\ \pi(\tilde{\tilde{\tilde{u}}}) = u(r(q,u,b)).$$

The solution of the problem (3.4.59)–(3.4.69) is constructed according to the above algorithm (see the informational rules of CI) under economic corruption:

1. Evaluate the quantity

$$L_{LOW}^{CI} = -\frac{1-\varepsilon}{\varepsilon}\int_0^T W(t)dt - \varepsilon\int_0^T r(t)W(t)dt + \int_0^T zR(\Phi)dt \quad ;$$

$$q_2^p = 1-\varepsilon;\ \tilde{\tilde{r}}^p = \tilde{\tilde{r}}(q_2^p, u^p, b^p) = r_{\max};\ u^p = 1-\varepsilon;\ b^p = 0.$$

2. Define the set

$$D_{LOW}^{CI} = \{(\tilde{\tilde{r}}, \tilde{\tilde{\tilde{u}}}, b) : -\int_0^T W(t)\left\{D\frac{\pi(\tilde{\tilde{\tilde{u}}})}{1-\pi(\tilde{\tilde{\tilde{u}}})} + (1-\pi(\tilde{\tilde{\tilde{u}}})(\pi(\tilde{\tilde{r}}) + b(t))\right\}dt \le$$

$$\left.\frac{1-\varepsilon}{\varepsilon}\int_0^T W(t)dt + \varepsilon\int_0^T r(t)W(t)dt\right\}.$$

3. Evaluate the quantity

$$\gamma_{MID}^{CI}(q_2)=\sup_{(\tilde{\tilde{r}},\tilde{\tilde{u}},b)\in D_{LOW}^{CI}}\int_0^T\left\{-C_C(W(t)(1-\pi(\tilde{\tilde{u}}))+p(t)W(t)\pi(\tilde{\tilde{r}})(1-\pi(\tilde{\tilde{u}}))\right\}dt.$$

Denote by $\tilde{\tilde{r}}^*,(\tilde{\tilde{u}}^*,b^*)$ the strategies of LA and IE implementing the quantity $\gamma_{MID}^{CI}(q_2)$.

4. For FP, solve the optimal control problem (3.4.59), (3.4.62), (3.4.63)-(3.4.69) under $\tilde{\tilde{r}}=\tilde{\tilde{r}}^*,(\tilde{\tilde{u}},b)=(\tilde{\tilde{u}}^*,b^*)$ and find the compulsion-impulsion equilibrium considering the sustainable development requirements under economic corruption.

Similarly to the previous cases, the CI equilibrium is calculated by direct ordered enumeration and appreciably depends on the choice of the function $p(t)$. In what follows, we set $p(t)\equiv 0.4$.

Example 3.4.14. Under the input data of Examples 3.4.5, 3.4.8, and 3.4.9, the compulsion-impulsion equilibrium considering the sustainable development conditions does not exist. LA and IE benefit from breaking the sustainable development conditions, whereas FP has insufficient capabilities to affect them.

Example 3.4.15. Under the input data of Example 3.4.6, the incomes of LA and IE increase, while the income of FP goes down (in comparison with Example 3.4.6). The system has corruption and

$$L_{LOW}^{CI}=\$387556;J_{UPP}^{CI}=\$62665;\ L_{MID}^{CI}=\$42002;\ J_{LOW}^{CI}=\$389882,$$

where $J_{UPP}^{CI},J_{MID}^{CI},J_{LOW}^{CI}$ are the profits of FP, LA and IE, respectively, in the compulsion-impulsion equilibrium.

Example 3.4.16. Under the input data of Example 3.4.7, the income of IE decreases, while the income of FP and LA goes up (in comparison with Example 3.4.6). The system has corruption and

$$L_{LOW}^{CI}=-\$703783;\ J_{UPP}^{CI}=\$136309;J_{MID}^{CI}=-\$68154;\ J_{LOW}^{CI}=-\$636750.$$

Therefore, within the information rules of II and CI, it is not always possible to construct an equilibrium considering the sustainable development conditions of a system. In other words, FP fails to guarantee sustainable development due to corruption. Compulsion-compulsion equilibria exist for a wider class of input functions. The equilibrium profits of different control subjects appreciably depend on the accepted informational rules.

Summarizing the outcomes, we have analyzed compulsion and impulsion equilibria considering the sustainable development conditions under corruption in three-level control systems. Compulsion and impulsion in hierarchical control are formalized as the informational extensions of two-player games mostly answering the rules Γ_{1t} and Γ_{2t} (Gorelik et al., 1991).

The sustainable development conditions are taken into account as phase constraints in a differential game. Administrative and economic corruption are interpreted as feedback by bribe amount in compulsion and impulsion control actions.

In the aspect of control methods, three-player games admit four modifications of information rules: either control subjects apply a same method (compulsion or impulsion) or they choose different methods. In all cases, control actions of the middle-level player incorporate administrative or economic corruption (Ougolnitsky and Usov, 2012, 2013, 2014). The compulsion-compulsion equilibrium considering the sustainable development conditions under administrative corruption is designed by solving a sequence of interconnected parametric optimal control problems subject to appropriate phase constraints. To evaluate the impulsion-impulsion equilibrium considering the sustainable development conditions under economic corruption, we have proposed an original procedure based on constructing interconnected programs beneficial for players. The compulsion-impulsion and impulsion-compulsion equilibria considering the sustainable development conditions under corruption are calculated using the combination of these approaches.

Analysis of the above models of economic and administrative corruption yields the following conclusions:

1. In all the cases considered, FP is indifferent to existing corruption whenever the latter does not affect its economic interests and does not break system homeostasis.
2. Corruption exerts an ambiguous impact on the controlled system. Economic corruption possibly prevents from homeostasis maintenance, as it decreases the optimal waste water treatment rate applied by IE. If corruption breaks homeostasis, FP struggles against corruption regardless of its economic interests. On the contrary, administrative corruption even promotes sustainable development when LA seeks to avoid penalization for its bribery and maintains system homeostasis.
3. In the case of supervision of LA and IE, FP always benefits from controlled corruption which does not break system homeostasis. For FP, the optimal strategy is the maximum supervision degree under which IE and LA benefit from bribery.
4. Under administrative corruption, IE has to give bribes to LA if the latter takes them.
5. In the case of sufficient capabilities, FP can struggle against corruption using administrative tools (supervision) and economic tools (increasing the share of financial resources transferred from IE to LA, increasing the supervision degree of IE and LA).
6. Under administrative corruption, there is no fundamental difference between extortion and capture.

CONCLUSION

Eastern wisdom claims that only bedbugs are incorruptible. This statement does not represent a mathematical theorem, but the topicality of the current monograph seems undisputed, especially in Russian conditions. Corruption is a vulnerable spot of modern Russia. As far back as 1999, Deputy Attorney General Yury Chaika acknowledged that Russia is in the top ten of most corrupt countries in the world and corruption makes its most destructive factor. In 2006, First Deputy Attorney General Alexander Buksman declared that, by some expert judgements, the market of corruption services in Russia constitutes 240-320 billions USD annually. And this index appreciably increased by 2010. In his November message to the Federal Assembly, Russian President of that time Dmitry Medvedev noted that in 2010 200 billions USD was spent on saw cuts and kickbacks in the segment of public procurement (from 840 billions USD allocated by the government). Unfortunately, corruption is widespread in other spheres of life including politics, legislature, law enforcement, education and medical care. According to the annual rating of corruption compiled by Transparency International, in 2010 Russia ranked 154 among 180 countries with CPI 2.1 (CPI 0 corresponds to maximum corruption, whereas CPI 10 means the absence of corruption), see Figure C.1. For several years, Russia fails to improve its positions in the rating. This fact testifies that governmental measures are insufficient to solve the problem. Not only Russian experts, but many high-level officials have a clear view of the situation, pointing to the absence of a real improvement in the field. The described tendency remains in force in recent years, despite numerous attempts of high-level authorities to struggle against corruption.

Obviously, an efficient anti-corruption campaign requires a thorough study, deep comprehension and rigorous description for the existing regularities of corruption behavior. The monograph has endeavored to do it using systems analysis, mathematical modeling and information technology. The main results obtained are the following.

1. An original concept of corruption modeling for hierarchical organizational systems based on theory of sustainable management has been developed and verified in terms of its key postulates using specific models.
2. The theoretical static models of administrative and economic corruption in one-, two- and three-level control systems have been designed and studied (a gradually complicated sequence of models of the form "optimization problem–hierarchical

two-player game–hierarchical three-player game”). The differences between the above types of corruption, as well as between extortion and capture have been substantiated via mathematical formalization. The quantitative indexes of briber’s compliancy and greediness have been proposed. The relationships between the briber’s behavioral strategies and model parameters have been established and appropriate recommendations on corruption restriction have been given.

3. The theoretical dynamic models of administrative and economic corruption in one-, two- and three-level control systems have been designed and studied (a gradually complicated sequence of models of the form “optimal control problem–dynamic hierarchical two-player game–dynamic hierarchical three-player game”). Compulsion and impulsion equilibria considering the sustainable development conditions under corruption have been defined and their calculation algorithms have been proposed. These algorithms are important as a general analysis tool of hierarchical differential games with different information rules.
4. Static optimization and game-theoretic control models and investment and construction projects with corruption have been developed and studied. A corresponding software complex has been created and recommendations on anti-corruption measures have been given using simulation experiments.
5. Quality control models of different-structure production systems with corruption have been developed and studied.
6. Dynamic sequences of quality control models for water resources and bioresources under corruption have been developed and studied. They illustrate application of the suggested concepts and general solution procedures of hierarchical differential games.
7. Resource allocation models in hierarchical control systems with corruption have been developed and studied.

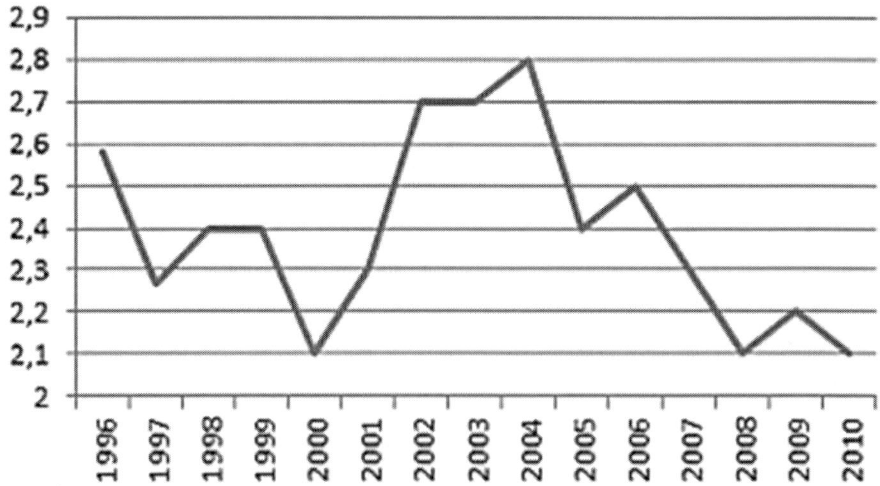

Figure C.1. CPI (Corruption Perceptions Index) of Russia.

The authors believe that the performed fundamental research is mostly valuable for the resulting logically consistent and noncontradictory system of universal theoretical models of corruption in hierarchical control systems, which proceeds from reasonable assumptions regarding the nature of corrupt relations (some of them can be refined to become axioms). The axiomatic ideology predetermines the principal advantages of the suggested concept (clarity, consistency, and universalism) and its inherent drawbacks (intentionality, artificiality). One of the chapters is dedicated to different applications of the theoretical models and, to the authors' view, convincingly demonstrates the potential utility of these and other applications. However, by now the application-oriented component of our research seems rather general and even illustrative. This is not surprising, as the main content of the suggested concept has been developed in the three recent years according to ascending-order design imported from structured programming. This technology dictates to begin with the general idea of a designed system and then to construct its "stub" and "core." The latter is gradually supplemented, augmented and deployed into an arbitrarily complex system.

Exactly such system design gives a positive answer to the question: "Are mathematical models able to provide an adequate description to socioeconomic phenomena?" (Druzhinin and Ougolnitsky, 2010). In the limit case, a sequence of gradually complicated models describes a real object with any accuracy required, but higher adequacy is costly as follows. First, the number of parameters increases, imposing tougher requirements to data acquisition for modeling. This is especially the case for corruption as a nontrivial and delicate phenomenon. And second, the complexity of problem solution (its analytical or numerical study) also grows dramatically.

This principle of complementarity is immanent to mathematical modeling and causes seeking for a compromise. An infinite sequence of gradually complicated models considering new and new regularities of the object's behavior describes the latter with any accuracy required. But the complexity of model analysis and the requirements to its information support increase infinitely, too. Therefore, a concrete problem of applied research (choosing the number of approximations) must be posed and solved by considering real goals and existing resources. In mathematical modeling of corruption in hierarchical control systems, we are at the beginning of the line. Here is a (by far incomplete) list of problems for future investigations:

- study the optimization problem (2.1.3) for different classes of the functions $g(b)$ (combinations of $s(b)$ and g_0), derive general results;
- consider the game (2.1.5) for more general classes of the functions g_1, g_2, find the ε-optimal guaranteeing strategies of supervisor;
- study the optimization problem (2.1.9) for different classes of the functions $r(b)$, derive general results;
- analyze the model (2.1.12) for different classes of the functions $g(u,b)$, solve the optimization problem, generalize the results;
- consider the game (2.1.13) for different classes of the functions $r(b)$, find the ε-optimal guaranteeing strategies of supervisor, generalize the results;
- similarly for the model (2.1.15);
- derive more general results for the model (2.1.19);

- evaluate and analyze the indexes of compliancy and greediness in the above models;
- give a practical interpretation to the parameters of corruption models and formulate recommendations on anti-corruption struggle in its terms;
- continue research of applied problems, suggest models describing concrete schemes of corruption, misuse of resources, and evasion of taxation.

The scope of a paper appreciably complicates detailed description of the systems concept and draws well-founded criticism. The authors hope that the monographic style of exposition eliminates a series of such issues and provides a rather complete picture of the suggested concept. Moreover, the authors expect that the presented material and the above list of problems would attract the interest of experts in operations research, mathematical economics and organizational control and yield fruitful feedback and remarks. Of crucial importance is to continue investigations on practical interpretation of the established results in order to involve professional strugglers against corruption.

REFERENCES

[1] Acemoglu D., Verdier T. (2000). The Choice between Market Failures and Corruption//*The American Economic Review,* 90(1), 194-211.

[2] Acemoglu D., Robinson J., Verdier T. (2004). Kleptocracy and Divide-and-Rule//*J. of the European Economic Association,* 2(2-3).

[3] Ades A., Di Tella R. (1999). Rents Competition and Corruption//*The American Economic Review,* 89(4), 982-994.

[4] Aidt T.S. (2003). Economic Analysis of Corruption: A Survey//*Economic Journal,* 113(491), 632-652.

[5] Andvig J.C., Moene K.O. (1990). How Corruption May Corrupt//*J. of Economic and Organization Behavior,* 13(1), 63-76.

[6] Antonenko A.V. (2012). *Models and Software Complex for Control of Investment and Construction Projects with Corruption.* Candidate of Science Dissertation (Engineering), Rostov-on-Don. (in Russian).

[7] Antonenko A.V., Ougolnitsky G.A. (2013). Static Models of Corruption in Hierarchical Systems//*Advances in Systems Science and Application,* 13(1), 37-52.

[8] Antonenko A.V., Ugol'nitskii G.A., Usov A.B. (2013). Static Models of Struggle with Corruption in Hierarchical Management Systems//*Journal of Computer and Systems Science International,* 52(4), 664-675.

[9] Antonenko A.V., Ugol'nitskii G.A. (2014). Incentive Management Models in Electric Power Industry and Problems of Their Identification//*Large-scale Systems Control,* 47, 92-124. (in Russian).

[10] Auriol E. (2006). Corruption in Procurement and Public Purchase//*International Journal of Industrial Organization,* 24, 867-885.

[11] Bac M. (1996a). Corruption and Supervision Cost in Hierarchies//*J. of Comparative Economics,* 22(2), 99-118.

[12] Bac M. (1996b). Corruption, Supervision and the Structure of Hierarchies//*J. of Law, Economics and Organization,* 12(2), 277-298.

[13] Bac M. (2001). Corruption, Connections and Transparency: Does a Better Screen Imply a Better Scene?//*Public Choice,* 107(1/2), 87-96.

[14] Bac M., Bag P.K. (2006). Beneficial Collusion in Corruption Control: The Case of Nonmonetary Penalties//*J. of Development Economics,* 81, 478-499.

[15] Bag P.K. (1997). Controlling Corruption in Hierarchies//*J. of Comparative Economics,* 22(3), 322-344.

[16] Balafoutas L. (2011). Public Beliefs and Corruption in a Repeated Psychological Game//*J. of Economic Behavior and Organization,* 78, 51-59.
[17] Banerjee A. (1997). A Theory of Misgovernance//*Quaterly Journal of Economics,* 112(4), 1289-1232.
[18] Banfield E. (1975). Corruption as a Feature of Government Organizations//J. *of Law and Economics,* 18(3), 587-605.
[19] Bardhan P. (1997). Corruption and Development: A Review of Issues//*J. of Economic Literature,* 35(3), 1320-1346.
[20] Bardhan P., Mookherjee D. (2000*). Corruption and Decentralization of Infrastructure Delivery in Developing Countries.* - Mimeo, Boston University.
[21] Basar T., Olsder G.Y. *Dynamic Noncooperative Game Theory.* – SIAM, 1999.
[22] Basu K., Bhattacharya S., Mishra A. (1992). Notes on Bribery and Control of Corruption//*J. of Public Economics,* 48(3), 349-359.
[23] Becker G. (1968). Crime and Punishment: An Economic Approach//*J. of Political Economy,* 76, 169-218.
[24] Bhattacharyya S., Hodler R. (2010). Natural Resources, Democracy and Corruption//*European Economic Review,* 54, 608-621.
[25] Bicchieri C., Rovelli C. (1995). Evolution and Revolution: The Dynamic of Corruption//*Rationality and Society,* 7(2), 201-224.
[26] Blackburn K., Bose N., Hague M.E. (2006). The Incidence and Persistence of Corruption in Economic Development//*J. of Economic Dynamic and Control,* 30, 2447-2467.
[27] Blackburn K., Forgues-Puccio G.F. (2010). Financial Liberalization, Bureaucratic Corruption and Economic Development//*J. of International Money and Finance,* 29, 1321-1339.
[28] Blackburn K., Powell J. (2011). Corruption, Inflation and Growth//*Economic Letters,* 113, 225-227.
[29] Bliss C., Di Tella R. (1997). Does Competition Kill Corruption?//*J. of Politica*l *Economy,* 105 (5), 1001-1023.
[30] Bure V.M., Kumacheva S.Sh. (2010). A Game-theoretic Model of Tax Auditing Using Statistical Information about Taxpayers//*Vestnik Sankt-Peterburg. Gos. Univ.,* 10(4), 16-24. (in Russian).
[31] Calvo G.A., Wellisz S. (1978). Supervision, Loss of Control and the Optimal Firm Size//*J. of Political Economy,* 86(5), 943-952.
[32] Carrillo J.D. (2000). Corruption in Hierarchies//*Annales d'Economie et de Statistique,* 59, 37-61.
[33] Caulkins J.P., Feichtinger G., Grass D. et al. (2013). Leading Bureaucracies to the Tipping Point: An Alternative Model of Multiple Stable Equilibrium Levels of Corruption//*European Journal of Operational Research,* 225, 541-546.
[34] Cerqueti R., Coppier R. (2009). Tax Revenues, Fiscal Corruption and "Shame Costs"//Economic Modelling, 26(6), 1239-1244.
[35] Cerqueti R., Coppier R. (2011). Economic Growth, Corruption and Tax Evasion//*Economic Modelling,* 28, 489-500.
[36] Chakrabarti R. (2001). *Corruption: A General Equilibrium Approach*//Indian School of Business WP, July.

[37] Chander P., Wilde L. (1992). Corruption in Tax Administration//*J. of Publ. Econ.,* 49(3), 333-349.

[38] Chaudhuri S., Gupta M.R. (1996). Delayed Formal Credit, Bribing and the Informal Credit Market in Agriculture: A Theoretical Analysis//*J. of Development Economics,* 51, 433-449.

[39] Chaudhuri S., Dastidar K.G. (2011). Corruption in a Model of Vertical Linkage between Formal and Informal Credit Sources and Credit Subsidy Policy//*Economic Modelling,* 28, 2596-2599.

[40] Choi J.P., Thum M. (2005). Corruption and the Shadow Economy//*International Economic Review,* 46(3), 817-836.

[41] Cule M., Fulton M. (2005). Some Implications of the Unofficial Economy – Bureaucratic Corruption Relationship in Transition Countries//*Economic Letters,* 89, 207-211.

[42] Cule M., Fulton M. (2009). Business Culture and Tax Evasion: Why Corruption and the Unofficial Economy Can Persist//*J. of Economic Behavior and Organization,* 72, 811-822.

[43] Deming E.W. (2000). *Out of the Crisis.* – Massachusetts: The MIT Press, 2 ed.

[44] Denin K.I., Ugol'nitskii G.A. (2010). Game Theoretic Model of Corruption in Hierarchical Control Systems//*Journal of Computer and Systems Science International,* 49(1), 152-157.

[45] *Differential Games in Economics and Management Science* (2000)./Dockner E., Jorgensen S., Van Long N., Sorger G. – Cambridge University Press.

[46] Dougherty C. (2011). *Introduction to Econometrics.* – Oxford: Oxford University Press, 4 ed.

[47] Drugov M. (2010). Competition in Bureaucracy and Corruption//*J. of Development Economics,* 92, 107-114.

[48] Druzhinin A.G., Ougolnitsky G.A. (2011). Problems and Prospects of Applying Mathematical Modeling Tools in Socioeconomic Geography//*South-Russian Forum: Sociology, Politology, Socioeconomic Geography,* 2(3), 102-112. (in Russian)

[49] D'Souza P., Klein A. (1999). *Ex Ante and Ex Post Collusion in Hierarchies.* Mimeo, University of Munich.

[50] Eliseeva I.I., Shchirina A.N. (2009). *Possible Approaches to Evaluation of Corruption Market*//Voprosy Statistiki, 6, 23-31. (in Russian).

[51] Evrenk H. (2011). Why a Clean Politician Supports Dirty Politics: A Game-theoretical Explanation for the Persistence of Political Corruption//*J. of Economic Behavior and Organization.* DOI: 10.1016/j.jebo.2011.05.004.

[52] Feichtinger G., Wirl F. (1994). On the Stability and Potential Cyclicity of Corruption in Governments Subject to Popularity Constraints//*Mathematical Social Sciences,* 28, 215-236.

[53] Gangopadhyay S., Goswami O., Sanyal A. (1991). Tax Enforcement with a Hierarchy of Corrupt Auditors. - Mimeo, Indian Statistical Institute, Delhi.

[54] Germeier Yu.B. (1985). Non-Antagonistic Games (Theory and Decision Library). – Springer.

[55] Gorbaneva O.I. (2010). Resource Allocation Game Models in the Hierarchical Systems of River Water Quality Control//Mathematical Game Theory and Applications, 2(1), 27-46.

[56] Gorbaneva O.I., Ougolnitsky G.A. (2013). Purpose and Non-purpose Resource Use Models in Two-level Control Systems//*Advances in Systems Science and Application,* 13(4), 378-390.

[57] Gorbaneva O.I., Ougolnitsky G.A. (2013). Static Models of Corruption in Resource Allocation Mechanisms for Three-Level Control Systems//*Large-scale Systems Control,* 42, 195-216. (in Russian).

[58] Gorbaneva O.I., Ougolnitsky G.A. (2014). Resource Allocation Game-Theoretical Models of River Water Quality Control with Corruption. Part I//*Heuristic Algorithms and Distributed Computing*, 1(1), 16-24. (in Russian).

[59] Gorbaneva O.I., Ougolnitsky G.A. (2014). Resource Allocation Game-Theoretical Models of River Water Quality Control with Corruption. Part II//*Heuristic Algorithms and Distributed Computing,* 1(2), 21-29. (in Russian).

[60] Gorelik V.A., Kononenko A.F. (1982). *Game-Theoretic Models of Decision-Making in Ecological-Economic Systems.* - Moscow: Radio i Svyaz.' (in Russian).

[61] Gorelik V.A., Gorelov M.A., Kononenko A.F. (1991). *Analysis of Conflicts in Control Systems.* - Moscow: Radio i Svyaz.' (in Russian).

[62] GOST R ISO 9000-2008 (2008). *Quality Management Systems. Basic Statements and Glossary.* - Moscow: Izd. Standartov.

[63] Gupta M.R., Chaudhuri S. (1997). Formal Credit, Corruption and the Informal Credit Market in Agriculture: A Theoretical Analysis//*Economica,* 64(254), 331-343.

[64] Guriev S. (2004). Red Tape and Corruption//*J. of Development Economics, 73*(2), 489-504.

[65] Hindriks J., Keen M., Muthoo A. (1999). Corruption, Extortion and Evasion//*J. of Public Econ.,* 74(3), 395-430.

[66] *International Handbook on the Economics of Corruption* (2006). Ed. by S. Rose-Ackerman. – Cheltenham, UK; Northampton, USA: Edward Elgar.

[67] Jain A. (2001). Corruption: A Review//*J. of Economic Surveys,* 15(1), 71-121.

[68] Kahana N., Qijun L. (2010). Endemic Corruption//*European Journal of Political Economy,* 26, 82-88.

[69] Kessing S.G., Konrad K.A., Kotsogiannis Ch. (2006). Federal Tax Autonomy and the Limits of Cooperation//*J. of Urban Economics,* 59, 317-329.

[70] Kingston Ch. (2008). Social Structure and Cultures of Corruption//*J. of Economic Behavior and Organization,* 67, 90-102.

[71] Klitgaard R. (1998). *Controlling Corruption.* - Berkeley, CA: University of California Press.

[72] Klyamkin I.M., Timofeev L.M. (2000). *Shadow Russia. An Economic and Sociological Study.* – Moscow: Russian State University for the Humanities. (in Russian).

[73] Kofman F., Lawarree J. (1993). Collusion in Hierarchical Agency//*Econometrica,* 61(3), 629-656.

[74] Kofman F., Lawarree J. (1996). A Prisoner's Dilemma Model of Collusion Deterrence//*J. of Public Economics,* 59(1), 117-136.

[75] Kononenko A.F. (1977). On Multistep Conflicts with Information Exchange//*Zhurnal Vychislitel'noi Matematiki i Matematicheskoi Fiziki,* 4, 922-931. (in Russian).

[76] Kornienko S.A. (2011) *A Quality Assessment Model in Production Systems with Corruption. Master* of Science Dissertation, Rostov-on-Don. (in Russian).

[77] Kornienko S.A., Ougolnitsky G.A. (2010). Quality Evaluation in Production Systems of Different Structure//*Large-scale Systems Control,* 30.1, 319-336. (in Russian).

[78] Kumacheva S.Sh. (2011). *Mathematical Models of Tax Audits.* Candidate of Science Dissertation (Physical-Mathematical Sciences), St. Petersburg. (in Russian).

[79] Lambert-Mogiliansky A., Majumdar M., Radner R. (2007). Strategic Analysis of Petty Corruption: Entrepreneurs and Bureaucrats//*J. of Development Economics,* 83, 351-367.

[80] Lambsdorff J.G. (2007). *The Institutional Economics of Corruption and Reform.* – Cambridge University Press.

[81] Lazarev E.A. (2011). Corruption and Political Stability: An Institutional Perspective//*Politeia,* 1(60), 50-68. (in Russian).

[82] Levin M.I., Tsirik M.L. (1998). Corruption as an Object of Mathematical Modeling//*Economics and Mathematical Methods,* 34(3), 40-62. (in Russian).

[83] Levin M.I., Tsirik M.L. (1998). Mathematical Models of Corruption//*Economics and Mathematical Methods,* 34(4), 34-55. (in Russian).

[84] Levin M.I., Levina E.A. (2001). Modeling of Lobbying//*Economics and Mathematical Methods*, 37(3), 76-96. (in Russian).

[85] Levin M.I., Levina E.A., Pokatovich E.V. (2011). *Lectures on Corruption Economics.* – Moscow: Higher School of Economics. (in Russian).

[86] Levin M. I., Satarov G. A. (2011). *A Study of Corruption during the Russian Transition: Measurement and Influences*//China and Russia: Development in Transition. Beijing: Economic Science Publisher. P. 93-108.

[87] Levin M., Satarov G. (2012). *Corruption in Russia: A Classification and Dynamics*//Voprosy Ekonomiki, 10, 4-29. (in Russian).

[88] Levin M. I., Satarov G. A. (2013). *Russian Corruption//The Oxford Handbook of Russian Economy*/Ed. by M. V. Alexeev, S. Weber. – N.Y. : Oxford University Press. P. 286-309.

[89] Ljung L. (1999). *System Identification: Theory for the User.* – New York: Prentice Hall, 2 ed.

[90] Lui F.T. (1996). A *Dynamic Model of Corruption Deterrence*//J. of Public Economics, 31(2), 215-236.

[91] Luneev V. (2000). *Corruption: Political, Economic, Organizational and Legal Problems*//Gosudarstvo i Pravo, 4, 99-111. (in Russian).

[92] Marjit S., Shi H. (1998). On Controlling Crime with Corrupt Officials//*J. of Economic Behavior and Organization*, 34(1), 163-172.

[93] Maskin E., Tirole J. (2004). The Politician and the Judge: Accountability in Government//*American Economic Review,* 94(4), 1034-1054.

[94] Mauro P. (2004). The Persistence of Corruption and Slow Economic Growth//*IMF Stuff Papers,* 51(1).

[95] Mikhailov A.P. (1999). A Model of Corrupt Power Hierarchies//*Matematicheskoe Modelirovanie,* 11(1), 3-16. (in Russian).

[96] Mikhailov A.P., Lankin D.F. (2006). Modeling of Optimal Strategies of Corruption Restriction//*Matematicheskoe Modelirovanie,* 18(12), 115-124. (in Russian).

[97] Mishra A. (2002). Hierarchies, Incentives and Collusion//*J. of Economic Behavior and Organization,* 47(2), 165-178.

[98] Mishra A. (2006a). Persistence of Corruption: Some Theoretical Perspectives//*World Development,* 34(2), 349-359.

[99] Mishra A. (2006b). Corruption, Hierarchies and Bureaucratic Structure//*International Handbook on the Economics of Corruption*/Ed. by S. Rose- Ackerman. Edward Elgar. - P. 189-215.

[100] Mookherjee D. (2003). *Delegation and Contracting Hierarchies: An Overview.* Mimeo, Boston University.

[101] Mookherjee D., Png I. (1995). Corruptible Law Enforcers: How Should They Be Compensated?//*Economic Journal,* 105(428), 145-159.

[102] Myerson R. (1993). Effectiveness of Electoral Systems for Reducing Government Corruption: A Game-theoretic Analysis//*Game and Economic Behavior,* 5, 118-132.

[103] Myslovskii E.N. (2007). *Corruption in Russia: Crime or Lifestyle.* – Moscow: Ekon-Inform. (in Russian).

[104] Novikov D.A. (2013). *Theory of Control in Organizations.* – New York: Nova Science Publishers.

[105] *Optimal Control of Nonlinear Processes: With Applications in Drugs, Corruption, and Terror* (2008). Grass D., Caulkins J., Feichtinger G. et al. – Springer-Verlag: Berlin-Heidelberg.

[106] Ougolnitsky G.A. (1999). *Control of Ecological-Economic Systems.* – Moscow: Vuzovskaya Kniga. (in Russian).

[107] Ougolnitsky G.A. (2009). Optimization and Game Theoretic Models in Real Estate Development//*Mathematical Game Theory and Applications,* 1(2), 82-97. (in Russian).

[108] Ougolnitsky G.A. (2010). Hierarchical Control of Sustainable Development. – Moscow: Fizmatlit. (in Russian).

[109] Ougolnitsky G.A. (2011). *Sustainable Development of Organizations.* – Moscow: Fizmatlit. (in Russian).

[110] Ougolnitsky G.A., Gorbaneva O.I. (2007). A Resource Allocation Problem in an Organizational System with Corruption and Its Ecological Applications//Izvestiya Vuzov. Severo-Kavkazskii Region. *Natural Sciences,* 1, 43-47. (in Russian).

[111] Ougolnitsky G., Denin K. (2011). *Mathematical Models of Corruption: Theory and Applications.* – LAP Lambert Academic Publishing. (in Russian).

[112] Ougolnitsky G.A., Usov A.B. (2010). Control of Sustainable Development of Hierarchical Systems in Conditions of Corruption//*Control Sciences,* 6, 19-26. (in Russian).

[113] Ougolnitsky G.A., Usov A.B. (2010). The Sustainable Development of Control Systems in the Conditions of Corruption//*Mathematical Game Theory and Applications,* 2(4), 106-119. (in Russian).

[114] Ougolnitsky G.A., Usov A.B. (2012). The Static Corruption Models in the Water Resources Quality Control Systems//*Control Sciences,* 4, 38-44. (in Russian).

[115] Ougolnitsky G.A., Usov A.B. (2013). Dynamic Hierarchical Two-Player Games in Open-loop Strategies and Their Applications//*Mathematical Game Theory and Applications,* 5(2), 82-104. (in Russian).

[116] Ougolnitsky G.A., Usov A.B. (2014). *Modeling of Corruption in Three-Level Control Systems*//Control Sciences, 1, 53-62. (in Russian).

[117] Polinsky A.M., Shavell S. (2001). *Corruption and Optimal Law Enforcement*//J. of Public Economics, 81(1), 1-24.

[118] Polterovich V.M. (1998). *Factors of Corruption*//Economics and Mathematical Methods, 34(3), 30–39. (in Russian).

[119] Qian Y. (1994). *Incentives and Loss of Control in an Optimal Hierarchy*//Review of Economic Studies, 61(3), 527-544.

[120] Radner R. (1992). Hierarchy: The Economics of Managing//*J. of Economic Literature,* 30(3), 1382-1415.

[121] Rauch J. (2001). Leadership Selection, Internal Promotion, and Bureaucratic Corruption in Less Developed Policies//*Canadian Journal of Economics*, 34(1), 240-258.

[122] Rose-Ackerman S. (1975). The Economics of Corruption//*J. of Public Economics*, 4, 187-203.

[123] Rose-Ackerman S. (1978). *Corruption: A Study in Political Economy.* – N.Y., Academic Press.

[124] Rose-Ackerman S. (1999). *Corruption and Government: Causes, Consequences and Reform.* – Cambridge University Press.

[125] Rose-Ackerman S. (2010). The Law and Economics of Bribery and Extortion//*Annual Review of Law and Social Sciences*, 6, 217-238.

[126] Rozin M.D., Sushchii S.Ya., Ougolnitsky G.A., Antonenko A.V. (2011). A Descriptive Approach to Corruption Modeling as a Factor of Social//*Engineering Journal of Don,* 3 [Electronic journal]. http://ivdon.ru/magazine/archive/n3y2011/561. (in Russian).

[127] Rozin M.D., Sushchii S.Ya., Ougolnitsky G.A. (2011). Methodological Modeling Aspects of Struggle Against Corruption as a Factor of Social Conflict and Terrorism//*Scientific Thought of Caucasus,* 2(18), 32-51. (in Russian).

[128] Rybasov E.A., Ougolnitsky G.A. (2004). Mathematical Modeling of Hierarchical Control of Ecological-Economic Systems with Corruption//*Computer Modeling.* Ecology, 2, 46-65. – Moscow: Vuzovskaya Kniga. (in Russian).

[129] Sah R., Stiglitz J. (1986). The Architecture of Economic Systems: Hierarchies and Polyarchies//*American Economic Review,* 76(4), 716-727.

[130] Sanyal A. (2000). Audit Hierarchy in a Corrupt Tax Administration//*J. of Comparative Economics,* 28(2), 364-378.

[131] Satarov G. (2007) How to Measure and Control Corruption//*Voprosy Ekonomiki,* 1, 4-10. (in Russian).

[132] Satarov G.A. (2013). *Russian Corruption: Level, Structure, Dynamics: An Experience of Sociological Study*/Ed. by G.A. Satarov. – Moscow: Liberal Mission Fund. (in Russian).

[133] Savvateyev A.V. (2003). Optimal Strategies of Suppressing Corruption//*Economics and Mathematical Methods,* 39(1), 62-75. (in Russian).

[134] Schelling T.C. (1978). *Micromotives and Macrobehavior.* – Norton, New York.

[135] Schumacher I. (2013). Political Stability, Corruption and Trust in Politicians//*Economic Modelling,* 31, 359-369.

[136] Shleifer A., Vishny R. (1993). Corruption//*Quarterly Journal of Economics,* 108(3), 599-617.

[137] Skiba A.K. (1978). Optimal Growth with a Convex-Concave Production Function//*Econometrica,* 46(3), 527-539.

[138] Soskice D., Bates R., Epstein D. (1992). Ambition and Constraint: The Stabilizing Role of Institutions//*J. of Law, Economics and Organization,* 8(3), 547-560.

[139] Timofeev L.M. (2000). *Institutional Corruption: Theoretical Sketches.* – Moscow: Russian State University for the Humanities. (in Russian).

[140] Tirole J. (1986). Hierarchies and Bureaucracies: On the Role of Collusion in Organizations//*J. of Law, Economics and Organization,* 2(2), 181-214.

[141] Tirole J. (1992). Collusion and the Theory of Organizations//*Advances in Economic Theory.* Ed. J.J. Laffont, Cambridge University Press, 151-206.

[142] *Toward a Theory of the Rent-Seeking Society* (1980). Eds. J. Buchanan, R. Tollison, G. Tullock. – College Station: Texas A&M University Press.

[143] Tullock G. (1967). *The Welfare Costs of Tariffs, Monopolies, and Theft*//Western Economic Journal, 5, 224-232.

[144] Ugol'nitskii G.A. (2002). Game-theoretical Study of Some Hierarchical Control Methods//*Journal of Computer and Systems Science International,* 41(1), 93-97.

[145] Ugol'nitskii G.A. (2005). Game-theoretic Optimality Principles of Hierarchical Control of Sustainable Development//*Journal of Computer and Systems Science International,* 44(4), 570-576.

[146] Ugol'nitskii G.A., Usov A.B. (2013). A Study of Differential Models for Hierarchical Control Systems via Their Discretization//*Automation and Remote Control,* 74(2), 252-263.

[147] Ugol'nitskii G.A., Usov A.B. (2014). Equilibria in Models of Hierarchically Organized Dynamic Systems with Regard to Sustainable Development Conditions//*Automation and Remote Control,* 75(6), 1055-1068.

[148] Vasin A., Panova E. *The Collectability of Taxes and Corruption in Taxation Authorities.* – Moscow: Regional Financial and Economic Institute, 1999. (in Russian).

[149] Vasin A.A., Kartunova P.A., Urazov A.S. (2010). Models for the Organization of State Inspections and the Struggle against Corruption//*Mathematical Models and Computer Simulations,* 22(4), 67–89.

[150] Vasin A.A., Nikolaev P.V., Urazov A.S. (2011). Mechanisms for Suppressing Corruption//*Journal of the New Economic Association,* 10, 10–30. (in Russian).

[151] Vybornov R.A. (2006). *Models and Methods of Control for Organizational Systems with Corruption Behavior of Participants.* – Moscow: Trapeznikov Institute of Control Sciences RAS. (in Russian).

[152] Waller C.J., Verdier T., Gardner R. (2002). Corruption: Top Down or Bottom Up?//*Economic Inquiry*, 40(4), 688-703.

[153] Williamson O.E. (1967). Hierarchical Control and Optimal Firm Size//*J. of Political Economy,* 75(2), 123-138.

[154] Williamson O.E. (1983). *Markets and Hierarchies: Analysis and Antitrust Implications.* –Freepress.

[155] Wilson J.K., Damanya R. (2005). Corruption, Political Competition and Environmental Policy//*J. of Environmental Economics and Management,* 49, 516-535.

[156] Yang D.D. (2005). Corruption by Monopoly: Bribery in Chinese Enterprise Licensing as a Repeated Bargaining Game//*China Economic Review,* 16, 171-188.

[157] Yudkevich M.M., Podkolzina E.A., Ryabinina A.Yu. (2002). *Fundamentals of Contract Theory: Models and Problems.* – Moscow: Higher School of Economics. (in Russian).

[158] Zarenkov V.A. (2006). *Project Management.* – Moscow: ASV; St. Petersburg: St. Petersburg State University of Architecture and Civil Engineering. (in Russian).

[159] Zenkevich N.A., Petrosjan L.A., Yeung D.W.K. (2009). *Dynamic Games and Applications in Management.* – St. Petersburg: Graduate School of Management Press. (in Russian).

About the Authors

Olga I. Gorbaneva
Associate Professor
Guennady A. Ougolnitsky
Professor and Head
Anatoly B. Usov
Professor
Department of Applied Mathematics and Computer Science
Southern Federal University, Russian Federation

Olga I. Gorbaneva graduated from the Kalmyk State University in 2002, finished postgraduate studies in the Southern Federal University (2006) and received her PhD in the Stavropol State University (2009). She is currently an Associate Professor in the Department of Applied Mathematics and Computer Science, Southern Federal University, and is a specialist in the modeling of organizational systems.

Guennady A. Ougolnitsky graduated from the Southern Federal University in 1984 and has been heading the Department of Applied Mathematics and Computer Science since 1997. A known specialist in mathematical modeling of the social-economic systems, a member of the editorial boards of the Russian journals Control Sciences, Control in Big Systems, Mathematical Game Theory and its Applications, Heuristic Algorithms and Distributed Calculations. Described his research concept in the book Sustainable Management (2011).

Anatoly B. Usov graduated from the Southern Federal University in 1990. He is currently a Professor in the Department of Applied Mathematics and Computer Science, Southern Federal University, and a specialist in numerical methods of solution of the complex dynamic problems.

INDEX

A

B

C

D

E

F

G

H

I

J

L

M

N

O

P

Q

R

W

Y